W9-AEH-058

Contemporary Field Research

Contemporary Field Research

A Collection of Readings

Robert M. Emerson
University of California, Los Angeles

HM
24
.C6537
1988

WAVELAND
PRESS, INC.
Prospect Heights, Illinois

Credits and Acknowledgments

From Leon Festinger, Henry W. Riecken, and Stanley Schachter, *When Prophecy Fails: A Social and Psychological Study of a Modern Group that Predicted the Destruction of the World.* Copyright © 1957 by the University of Minnesota. Reprinted by permission of The University of Minnesota Press.

From *Tally's Corner* by Elliot Liebow. Copyright © 1967 by Little, Brown and Company (Inc.). Reprinted by permission of the publisher.

From Jennifer Platt, "The Origin Myth of 'Participant Observation' ". Paper presented to the American Sociological Association Meetings, San Francisco, 1982. Used by permission.

From Jonathan Rubinstein, *City Police* (New York: Farrar, Straus & Giroux, 1973). Reprinted by permission.

From Alfred Schutz, *Collected Papers, Volume I: The Problem of Social Reality* (The Hague: Martinus Nijoff, 1962). Reprinted by permission.

From John Van Maanen, "Notes on the Production of Ethnographic Data in an American Police Agency" in Robin Luckham, ed., *Law and Social Enquiry.* Copyright © 1981 by the authors, the Scandinavian Institute of African Studies, and the International Center for Law in Development. Reprinted by permission.

For information about this book, write or call:

Waveland Press, Inc.
P.O. Box 400
Prospect Heights, Illinois 60070
(708) 634-0081

INDIANA-
PURDUE
WITHDRAWN
JUN 5 1995
FORT WAYNE

Copyright © 1983 by Robert M. Emerson
1988 reissued by Waveland Press, Inc.

ISBN 0-88133-342-5

All rights reserved. No part of this book may be reproduced, stored in a retrieval system, or transmitted in any form or by any means without permission in writing from the publisher.

Printed in the United States of America

FTW
AFV 3687

12 11 10 9 8

To Everett C. Hughes,
whose teaching and sensitivities
link generations of fieldworkers

Preface

The past decade and a half have seen a fundamental refocusing in the theory and methods employed in field research. Perhaps the most critical change involves the emergence of a more fully articulated and less defensive conception of the nature of fieldwork itself. Within this emerging conception two specific themes stand out: first, fieldworkers increasingly understand and carry out their craft as an *interpretive* enterprise; second, fieldworkers have come to devote close attention to the actual *practice* of doing fieldwork. I have assembled the materials in this book with an eye toward furthering and consolidating these developments. To do so I have put together a number of divergent strands within contemporary field research. What is common to these strands is an impulse to honor, and occasionally to revel in, the distinctive character of fieldwork as an enterprise deeply tied to matters of interpretation and practice.

Over the past several decades, field researchers have come to recognize more clearly the inappropriateness for qualitative research of methodological procedures narrowly modeled on those of the natural sciences. As an alternative, fieldworkers have increasingly articulated an "interpretive paradigm" (Wilson 1970) in which "facts" and "data" are understood not as "objective entities," but rather as social meanings attributed by social actors — including the fieldworker — in interaction with others. As a result, field researchers have felt growing ease in discarding much of the classic apparatus of the natural sciences — for example, hypothesis testing, formulation of specifically defined variables, and strict concern with reliability and replicability. As field research has become more explicit about and more committed to such an interpretive paradigm, it has not only become less apologetic about field methods and findings, but has also begun the difficult task of tracing through the full implications of such an approach.

This effort is tied to a second major theme in reflections on fieldwork methodology — growing sensitivity to the actual practice of fieldwork. Rather than focusing exclusively on the end-products or findings of fieldwork, many recent discussions show a concern with the process of "doing" fieldwork. Consider, for example, the titles of two of the major monographs of fieldwork methods to appear in the 1970s — *Doing Fieldwork* by Rosalie

H. Wax and *Doing Field Research* by John M. Johnson. These and other studies insist that in evaluating field data it is essential to describe such matters as what the fieldworker said and did in the field, how those "hosting" the research defined and responded to the fieldworker's words and deeds, and how all these doings influenced the fieldworker's on-the-spot interpretations and more polished analyses of events.

To focus on processes of interpretation and practice is to move toward a more reflective, self-conscious stance toward the fieldwork enterprise. In a 1972 paper Nash and Wintrob signaled movement toward such a stance in anthropology by noting "the emergence of self-consciousness in ethnography." Similar reflective examinations of the fieldwork process itself have also been provided by sociological field researchers. Such self-consciousness emerges with the recognition that fieldwork itself is a social phenomenon, inescapably part of the very social worlds it seeks to discover, describe, and analyze. This recognition dispels any last vestiges of the belief that the fieldworker can somehow avoid or transcend the sorts of practical concerns and personal involvements that pervade everyday social life. For not only is the subject matter of fieldwork the social worlds of others, but its methods for apprehending these worlds are social as well. Stressing the social character of fieldwork, we are in a position to see more clearly the variety of personal, interactional, moral, and political processes that lie at its core.

One major goal of this book is to bring these issues of self-consciousness and the social character of fieldwork itself to the forefront of thinking about fieldwork methods. Furthermore, I am convinced that these matters are not only critical to practicing field researchers, but also provide an essential element in the training of novice fieldworkers. The following considerations indicate why I think this is so, and hence how this book might be used in teaching field research.

It is clear, in the first place, that we only learn fieldwork by doing it, a truth expressed unnecessarily harshly in the traditional anthropological sink-or-swim method of teaching fieldwork. This is true for several reasons. Fieldwork is wrongly conceived as learning a set of techniques and specific methods that can be applied in the right situation. Rather, fieldwork is better understood as a resocialization process that involves and affects the whole person. As experience, as resocialization, fieldwork is much more than narrow technical or even intellectual training. Furthermore, fieldwork is highly situational and contextual in character, which makes it difficult to provide general principles for proceeding that hold across projects and settings. At best, we talk as if some of the practices we employ in the setting we have worked in may hold in other settings.

If people are to be trained in fieldwork they have to begin to do it, and one relevant sort of material they can read is that offering advice and commentary on "how to do it." A number of such how-to-do-it manuals exist and undoubtedly prove useful to students, although probably not so much as cookbooks as reassurance that other fieldworkers exist and are involved in some sort of common enterprise that regularly runs up against problems similar to theirs.

The materials included in this book are intended not primarily as a "how-to-do-it" manual, either in providing a set of reflections or recipes on how to proceed in the field, nor as a set of substantive illustrations of what the final products of field research might look like. Rather, the materials seek to alert fieldworkers, both novices and experienced hands, to the basic nature and implications of their methods and analytic procedures. They address the issue, then, not of how to do it, but of just what it is that is being done. That is, the focus is on fieldwork as methodology, not as method or substance.

For even if fieldwork is learned in and through its doing, it involves a doing that benefits from, and perhaps even requires, thought and reflection on what is going on. If fieldwork is not technically systematic in the sense of being able to specify in advance its exact methods, it does gain a different sort of systematic quality from the careful, self-conscious reflection on its doings. These sorts of reflections, either as one is actively engaged in carrying out a fieldwork project or as one is subsequently analyzing and thinking about a study already completed, need to be encouraged. Too much fieldwork is carried out naively, borne ahead solely by the enthusiasm of the fieldworker and lacking sustained, considered reflection on just what the "data" and "findings" mean and how they have come to be discovered.

In urging self-conscious reflection, then, I am not urging that we forsake our demands for empirically rich and theoretically insightful substantive field studies, as obviously such products provide the ultimate justification for our efforts. Nor am I advocating self-consciousness as license to parade before a reading audience any and all emotional ups and downs, moral agonizings, and "intimacy trophies" (Erving Goffman's term from a lecture on field methods at Brandeis University in 1967) collected in the field. Rather, I think that self-consciousness about what we are doing and how we are doing it produces fieldwork that is stronger on both scientific and humanistic grounds.

A final note on readers into whose hands I would like this book to fall: It is striking how uninformed contemporary writings on fieldwork in sociology are by parallel research in anthropology. And vice versa. Yet the division between the two fields is primarily a matter of disciplinary politics. As anthropologists increasingly make their field trips to nether regions of Western societies, and as sociologists go abroad in pursuit of foreign comparisons, most meaningful distinctions between the two disappear. We are left, of course, with differences in the traditions and current insignia, but I hope this collection will help bridge some of these barriers. As a sociologist, I have probably overrepresented the sociological tradition of fieldwork with which I am most familiar, and I may have misrepresented the anthropological tradition, particularly its more contemporary expressions. But I have made an effort to include materials from anthropologists which I think should have a wider audience among sociologists, and I hope that the sociological materials will prove similarly suggestive to anthropological fieldworkers.

Finally, I would like to acknowledge my debt both to those who have influenced my understanding and practice of fieldwork and to those who have provided more immediate help in preparing this volume. I received my initial training in fieldwork in the 1960s at Brandeis University under the guidance of Everett C. Hughes, Robert S. Weiss, and Irving K. Zola. Their teachings are reflected in many of the concerns and issues addressed in the following pages. Over the past decade I have managed increasingly to involve my friend and colleague, Melvin Pollner, in the practice and theory of fieldwork; his thinking and distinctive sociological concerns inform much of the material that follows. Barrie Thorne and John Van Maanen have provided careful and incisive readings of and comments on the various proposals and drafts of the chapters sent to them, often on very short notice. Madelyn Leopold, former sociology editor at Little, Brown, encouraged this project from its inception, and without her support it might never have moved beyond that stage. Susan Bowers, Bradford Gray, and Victoria Keirnan at Little, Brown have been immensely helpful in seeing the project through the various stages of publication. Linda L. Shaw, James A. Holstein, Judith R. Saxon, and Marlies Dietrich all contributed invaluably in the hectic scramble to meet the various deadlines. And finally, this whole project would not have been possible without the encouragement of my wife, Ginger, and the forbearance of our children, Kenny, Nat, Kristin, and Eva.

Contents

Contemporary Field Research

Introduction

In its most inclusive sense, field research is the study of people acting in the natural courses of their daily lives. The fieldworker ventures into the worlds of others in order to learn firsthand about how they live, how they talk and behave, and what captivates and distresses them. Whether it is the classic anthropologist trekking across the world to live with some remote tribe, the urban anthropologist moving into some hidden segment of the modern city, the participant-observer sharing in and observing the life-ways of a local community or joining the rush-hour commute to study the life-worlds of some modern bureaucracy, the fieldworker's first commitment is to enter the ongoing worlds of other people to observe them firsthand.

Contemporary fieldwork, however, often connotes something more than simply research conducted in natural settings. It is also seen as a method of study whose practitioners try to understand the meanings that activities observed in these settings have for those engaged in them. In this view, intense immersion in others' social worlds is critical not primarily because it provides access to those worlds, but because it introduces fieldworkers to the subjective meanings and concerns of those they study. Immersion is sought primarily for the distinctive modes of understanding that it brings. Indeed, some contemporary fieldworkers identify such understanding as the essential characteristic of the method. Murray Wax, for example, has argued that: "The task of the fieldworker is to enter into the matrix of meanings of the researched, to participate in their system of organized activities, and to feel subject to their code of moral regulation" (1980:272–273).

The current practice of fieldwork reflects a certain tension between these two views of the essence of field research. On the one hand, some characterize fieldwork as any (and all) research actually conducted "in the field"; fieldwork is thus defined by *where it takes place*. Emphasis is placed on "observation *in situ*" (Hughes 1971:496), on what can be learned by going to some natural setting and observing behaviors and other goings-on as they naturally occur. Fieldwork is distinguished by its *naturalism* (see, for example, Denzin 1971; Schatzman and Strauss 1973). The observer who views events naturalistically avoids creating artificial interaction and encapsulated social worlds of the sort characteristic of much experimental research.

On the other hand, some fieldworkers derive the essence of the method less from *the place* in which research occurs than from *the way it is conducted*. In this view fieldwork is understood as a way of knowing that results from procedures variously characterized as "immersion," acquiring "intimate familiarity," or, more simply, active, empathetic participation in the rounds and structures of life and meaning of those being studied. What distinguishes the field method in this view is not "the observer's physical presence at the location where interaction occurs" but his or her "ability to grasp the symbolic nexus between thought and action in a particular social milieu" (Schwartz and Merton 1971:280–281).

These two views — fieldwork as what is done in the field and fieldwork as a distinctive way of knowing — are not mutually exclusive approaches but rather differ in emphasis. Particular fieldworkers may place more or less emphasis on one or the other view, but typically they try to incorporate and balance both. Furthermore, the concepts of place and way of knowing provide central themes in the historical development of the fieldwork tradition in both anthropology and sociology. In the remainder of this introduction I will address the historical background and current analysis of these issues, which now stand at the forefront of contemporary field research.

Fieldwork as Research in the Field: Boas and Malinowski

Somewhat surprisingly, nineteenth-century anthropologists did not consider it important to go into the field to collect their own data. Working within the prevalent social evolutionary framework, they were usually content to use the field accounts provided by explorers, traders, missionaries, and colonial officials. M. Wax suggests that the ideology and politics of this era discouraged fieldwork:

> These exotic peoples were "savages," "Stone Age men," who bore the remnants of primitive antiquity. They merited study, not in their own right as human beings, but because such study might illuminate the origins of civilized, European Society and might help explain such puzzling, less civilized features of that society as its religious institutions. (1972:2)

Some anthropologists, however, distrustful of traveler and missionary accounts, began urging that anthropologists go out into the field to assemble more accurate and unbiased descriptions of the lives and artifacts of "primitive" peoples. Yet the model of the field expedition was typically that of the naturalist going out to collect as many specimens as possible during the brief period he or she stayed in the native locale. In the case of anthropology, specimens included native artifacts, texts, skull and other bodily measurements, and sometimes the natives themselves — Boas' first contact with the Northwest Coast Indians came in 1885 in Berlin "while several Bella Coola Indians were being exhibited in the Museum of Ethnology there" (Rohner 1966:158). Until the 1920s fieldwork in general continued to be disparaged: "Comparing, analyzing, and interpreting sources was considered scholarship; working in the field was *merely* collecting" (Rohner 1966:211).

Franz Boas, a German-trained scholar who dominated the anthropology department at Columbia from 1896 until his death nearly half a century later, played a major role in making fieldwork a central part of the anthropological enterprise. Beginning in 1886 Boas made regular field trips to the Northwest Coast and spent time among the Indians there. In subsequent years Boas directed his field efforts toward collecting native language texts, a procedure he saw as the most effective way of acquiring data that reflected the natives' own points of view. His insistence on the importance of going to the field and of working in the language of the people studied had a strong impact on American anthropology.

Boas retained much of the prevailing practices in his fieldwork. He sought to collect and hence preserve texts and artifacts from dying cultures. His visits to the field took on many of the aspects of a collecting expedition, marked by stays of relatively brief duration and frequent movement between settlements and language groups.[1] Boas's deep interest lay in texts and the past, not in current social life and organization among the Indians. As R. Wax observed, "In what was actually going on before their eyes, Boas, and many of the fieldworkers trained by him, evinced relatively little interest" (1971:33). While Boas urged ethnographers to become fluent in the native language "because much information can be gained by listening to conversations of the natives and by taking part in their daily lives" (1911:60), he practiced little of his own advice. Instead, Boas relied heavily on finding a native informant "who was fluent in English and the native language, knew the old stories and customs, and was willing to dictate and translate texts by the hour, day, week, or month" (R. Wax 1971:32). In these ways Boas remained physically distant from — outside of — the daily lives of "his people." In particular,

> Boas rarely lived in an Indian household or community unless circumstances required that he do so. He usually stayed in a hotel or some other public accommodation within walking distance from the village where he wanted to work. (Rohner 1966:210)

It is clear from these descriptions that the origins of contemporary fieldwork are traced more directly to Malinowski than to Boas. For it was Malinowski who established the practice that characterizes modern field re-

---

[1] Between 1886 and 1930 Boas made thirteen field trips to the Northwest Coast, spending a total period of just less than two and a half years in the field (Rohner 1966:152).

search: "the personal field trip intensively focused on a single people" (M. Wax 1972:1).

Malinowski, a Polish emigré, conducted fieldwork in several New Guinea islands during World War I: the Mailu Islands from 1914–1915 and the Trobriands in 1915–1916 and 1917–1918. In the first chapter of *Argonauts of the Western Pacific* (1961/1922) Malinowski emphasized the major research breakthrough that occurred when he gave up the usual practice of taking up "abode in the compound of some neighbouring white man, trader or missionary" and instead went to live "right among the natives" (1961: 4,6). Indeed, Malinowski came to emphasize that the "proper conditions for ethnographic work . . . consist mainly in cutting oneself off from the company of other white men, and remaining in as close contact with the natives as possible, which really can only be achieved by camping right in their villages" (1961:6).

As Murray Wax pointed out, to forsake European society to live among the natives was a highly significant social and personal act: "Between the world of the Melanesian natives and of the British colonial administration was a steep barrier of status, wealth, and power" (1972:5). Later published writings and Malinowski's diary from the period (1967) reveal a deep antipathy to the colonial structure and to its representatives. Malinowski frequently felt out of place in their company and put off by "the manner in which my white informants spoke about the natives and put their views" (1961:5). Entries in his diary reveal that he was often unhappy and depressed during his first field trip, when he lived within the colonial world, walking daily to native villages to do his work and returning at night. Gradually he began to spend more time alone with the natives, and he reported occasional stays in native villages from early 1915, both activities appearing to have lifted his spirits. By the end of his first field trip Malinowski apparently came to recognize that "living among the natives (was) personally more pleasant and scientifically more productive" (M. Wax 1972: 7). He actually settled in the village of Omarkana on his second field trip, there developing the principle of "living intimately and for a prolonged period of time within a single native community whose language he had mastered" (M. Wax 1972:7).

With this change of habits, the fieldworker's daily life approximates that of those studied, and exposure and mutual influence increase. Malinowski noted, for example, his natural tendency to spend time with other Europeans when he was bored or depressed by contacts with the natives:

> But if you are alone in a village beyond reach of this [white society], you go for a solitary walk for an hour or so, return again and then quite naturally seek out the natives' society, this time as a relief from loneliness, just as you would any other companionship. And by means of this natural intercourse, you learn to know him, and you become

familiar with his customs and beliefs far better than when he is a paid, and often bored, informant. (1961:7)

Malinowski emphasized his deeper appreciation of "the imponderabilia of actual life" afforded by living in the midst of native society:

> Here belongs such things as the routine of a man's working day, the details of his care of the body, of the manner of taking food and preparing it; the tone of conversational and social life around the village fires, the existence of strong friendships or hostilities, and of passing sympathies and dislikes between people; the subtle yet unmistakable manner in which personal vanities and ambitions are reflected in the behavior of the individual and in the emotional reactions of those who surround him. (Malinowski 1961:18–19)

Yet while Malinowski lived in the midst of native life, and recurrently described "the Trobriand natives, and by implication all natives, as rational moral human beings in whose society a civilized man would be content to live" (M. Wax 1972:11), he did not participate deeply or intimately or fully share in that life. He spent most of his time interrogating native informants much in the older style, but now done in the midst of the village. Rather than living on a level of parity with the villagers, "Malinowski established himself in the heart of native villages in the style of a petty lord attended by a large retinue of personal servants" (M. Wax 1972:10). On some level, the natives remained "savages" (or worse; see M. Wax 1972:9) to him all his life; he came to share very little of the perspective of even those Trobrianders he had frequent contact with.[2]

Through both the example of their own fieldwork and their programmatic urgings of the adoption of field methods, Boas and Malinowski influenced later anthropologists to go to the field and study other cultures firsthand. During the 1920s and 1930s, students of Boas, including Ruth Benedict, Margaret Mead, Robert Lowie, and Alfred Kroeber, and British social anthropologists trained and strongly influenced by Malinowski, including Evans-Pritchard, Raymond Firth and Hortense Powdermaker, carried out long-term field research in a number of African, Pacific, and native American cultures. But before considering the further development of anthropo-

---

[2] Malinowski's failure to share the natives' perspective is strikingly revealed in a series of passages from his diary, quoted by M. Wax (1972:11), in which he expresses irritation with two aristocratic natives for taking too much of his supply of betel-nut. As Wax suggests: "To help themselves to his supply was impudence from the European perspective. Yet to withhold his supply was for the natives failure to acknowledge native norms of generosity. The native view is evident in Malinowski's comment (1935/1965:40–41) on the Paramount Chief: were his stores of tobacco or betel-nut 'exposed to the public gaze, he would, on the principles of *noblesse oblige,* have to distribute them among the surrounding people.'" Clearly Malinowski failed to connect the "native" patterns he analyzed so closely with his own situation and experience in the field.

logical fieldwork, it is necessary to turn to the separate yet not unrelated emergence of fieldwork within sociology.

Fieldwork as Real-Life Research: Social Surveys and the Chicago School

The roots of sociological fieldwork extend back to turn-of-the-century social reform movements in which observers sought to describe the life and conditions of the urban poor systematically in order to change and better them. Particularly significant for later sociological fieldwork was the late nineteenth-century social survey movement. Charles Booth's *Life and Labour of the People in London* remains the best known of these massive surveys, one more systematic form of the "social exploration" (Keating 1976: 11ff) characteristic of this period in England. The surveys of Booth and others aimed at penetrating and understanding the unknown worlds of the poor. As Booth wrote in *Life and Labour* (cited in Keating 1976:137):

> East London lay hidden from view behind a curtain on which were painted terrible pictures: starving children, suffering women, over-worked men, horrors of drunkenness and vice; monsters and demons of inhumanity; giants of disease and despair.

Booth's efforts lay in "showing how things are" behind this curtain, appreciating forms of life fundamentally misconstrued from the outside. Rather than seeing all the poor as one homogeneous class, for example, Booth distinguished four separate classes of the "poor" and "very poor," and carefully separated Class A, "the lowest class of occasional laborers, loafers, and semi-criminals," from "the criminal class" (Keating 1976:113ff). He also described in detail and with appreciation such key institutions of the East End as the pubs, noting their central place in the life of the community.

In his studies, Booth combined statistical data, widespread interviewing, and direct observation to amass an extremely detailed and systematic description of the lives of the poor in London. In their use of direct observation Booth and his colleagues at times entered directly into the world of the poor. In reporting on his initial work in the East End, for example, Booth noted (Keating 1976:125):

> For three separate periods I have taken up quarters, each time for seven weeks, where I was not known, and as a lodger have shared the lives of people who would figure in my schedules as belonging to classes C, D, and E. Being more or less boarded, as well as lodged, I became intimately acquainted with some of those I met, and the lives and habits of many others came naturally under observation.

Similarly, Beatrice Potter, a coworker of Booth's and later married to social reformer Sidney Webb, regularly ventured into the day-to-day life of the poor, working as a seamstress in order to experience sweatshop conditions firsthand.[3]

This reforming impulse and methods of direct observation were first introduced within a university setting in the classic Chicago school of sociology that dominated the discipline during the first decades of the twentieth century. As Hughes (1971:543) has noted, "Sociology was a social movement before it was part of the academic establishment" and it was in the early years of the Chicago School at the turn of the century that this joining of movement and establishment first took place. Most of the early sociologists at Chicago were continuously and often intensely involved in social reform movements centered outside the university. The reform efforts of Albion Small are well known, as are Robert Park's pre-University of Chicago participation in the Congo Reform Association and his long-term connection with Booker T. Washington and the Tuskegee Institute. Less well known is the extensive and continuing involvement of both W. I. Thomas and George Herbert Mead in the reform activities centered around Hull House, the leading social settlement house in the country and a source of great intellectual and social ferment (see Deegan and Burger 1978, 1981).[4]

These close ties with vibrant social reform efforts in Chicago are evident in the concerns of many early Chicago school sociologists with the city. Much like the nineteenth-century social explorers and surveyors, leading figures at the University of Chicago, notably Robert Park, were drawn to and fascinated by the varied "moral regions" and distinctive social worlds found within the sprawling metropolis. For Park the city provided a critical arena for sociological study: he urged exploration of its various "natural areas," its tightly-knit ethnic settlements and neighborhoods of anonymous roominghouse dwellers, its distinctive occupational and institutional forms, and its underlying patterns of development and change (see Hannerz 1980:23–26).

Such investigations required "firsthand observations" of life in these enclaves and locales. As Park urged students in the 1920s:

> Go and sit in the lounges of the luxury hotels and on the doorsteps of the flophouses; sit on the Gold Coast settees and on the slum shakedowns; sit in Orchestra Hall and in the Star and Garter Burlesk. In

---

[3] The substantive and methodological writings of the Webbs were made a central part of the training of sociology students; Rosalie Wax (1971:39) reported that Robert E. Park assigned the text by the Webbs, *Methods of Social Study* (1932) to his students at the University of Chicago.

[4] Thomas, for example, was a personal friend of Hull House founder and leader, Jane Addams, and was closely connected with a variety of reform movements radiating from Hull House, including the juvenile court movement, child protection, and a variety of reform efforts concerned with prostitution, immigration, and race relations (Deegan and Burger 1981).

short, gentlemen, go get the seat of your pants dirty in *real* research. (McKinney 1966:71)

As models for how to proceed in the field, Park and others proposed using methods from anthropology and the social survey. In his influential 1916 article "The City," for example, Park offered the anthropological methods of Boas and Lowie as one example of how to carry out the sociological exploration of the city (1915/1952:15).[5] Indeed, until 1929, sociology and anthropology were a combined department at the University of Chicago, and after formal separation Park worked closely with a number of students who became well-known anthropologists, notably Robert Redfield. Park's emphasis on using a variety of methods to collect data on life in the city reflects the eclecticism of the social survey, using not only census materials, but also direct observation, interviewing, and the more general collection of personal documents. Before 1940 the survey actually described an extensive study using a variety of methods and was often aimed at social reform.

To complement the survey — and in partial contrast to it — Chicago school sociologists came to refer to intensive "case study." The case study, personal document, or life-history method, exemplified by Thomas and Znaniecki's *The Polish Peasant in Europe and America* (Vols. I and II published in 1917), sought to capture the "subjective aspect" of culture as represented in a variety of "personal documents." The intent of the life-history method to convey the subjective experience of those studied was highlighted by E. W. Burgess in his preface to Shaw's *The Natural History of a Delinquent Career* (1931:ix).

> No one will question the value of the life-history as a human document when written freely and frankly. It admits the reader into the inner experience of other men, men apparently widely different from himself: criminals, hobos, and other adventurers.

Methodologically, the case study relied on data collected in interviews, autobiographical life-histories written by the informant, letters and diaries, newspaper stories, and official records from courts, social agencies, and other institutional sources. Indeed, Thomas valued letters, diaries and life-history accounts more highly than interview data, feeling that the latter "manipulated the respondent excessively" (Janowitz 1966:1).

This framing of field data as "documents" suggests the limited conception of participation in the minds of early Chicago school sociologists. They had little concern with the process of assembling these documents, only with using them to reveal the subject's "point of view," "in his own words." They emphasized neither firsthand exposure to and observation of events,

[5] W. I. Thomas was similarly familiar with the work of Boas and remained deeply interested in comparative studies, ethnography, and evolutionary issues right up to his death in 1941 (Janowitz 1966:xx).

naturally unfolding participation in the lives of those studied, nor the insights gained from such participation. The life-history, for example, is not a procedure that encompasses the researcher's experiences; rather it assumes that those studied can directly convey their own meanings and experiences. Moreover, as Platt (1982:9) has noted, during this period the term "participant observer" referred to "a natural insider recruited by the investigator as an informant, not the investigator himself." Platt quotes the following comment by A. E. Holt from a 1926 article:

> The minister can be a "participant observer" in religious experience, and if he reports faithfully what he observes we can build up a body of material on the basis of which theological education can be remade.

As Platt concludes, "There is a concern with access to personal experience and its meanings, but this is certainly not seen as achieved by sympathetic participation of the investigator in a role" (1982:11).

The Emergence of Self-Consciousness in Fieldwork

By the end of the 1930s, fieldwork had emerged as the major method of inquiry within anthropology, and, closely tied with the general approach of the Chicago school, as an established method within sociology. During the following two decades fieldwork in both disciplines came to assume increasingly self-conscious forms. The researcher went to the field, but more and more to participate in the daily lives of those studied in order to share their subjective perspectives and meanings.

Signs of this movement toward self-consciousness appeared throughout the 1940s and even in the late 1930s. Nash and Wintrob (1972) located initial anthropological statements of such concerns in works whose authors urged that the personal biases of the fieldworker be brought into the open (e.g., Mead 1949, Redfield 1953, and Lewis 1953) and in a series of studies exploring ways in which the researcher's field role determined what information he or she could collect (especially Paul 1953). In the 1960s there were further accounts of the personal processes and problems arising in fieldwork (e.g., R. Wax 1960, Maybury-Lewis 1965, Powdermaker 1966, and Briggs 1970), and in general a growing sensitivity toward and willingness to explore in print "the existential situation of the fieldworker" (Maquet 1964). The image of the fieldworker as "a self-effacing creature without any reactions other than those of a recording machine" gave way to that of "a *human* scientist whose own self and relationships with subjects have become important factors in evaluating his observations" (Nash and Wintrob 1972:527, 528).

Similar developments can be traced within sociological fieldwork in greater sensitivity to field processes and relations, and more emphasis on participation in the groups and events studied. Reflecting these trends, the term "participant observation" came to refer to a method providing access to actors' meanings. Platt (1982) located the first clear use of the term in this sense in Lohman's 1937 article, "The Participant Observer in Community Studies." Lohman argued that "the sympathies and identities established through a close familiarity will reveal meanings and insights denied the formal investigator" (891). In sociology, as in anthropology, there are often disjunctures between abstract accounts of fieldwork methods and actual methodological practice. Whyte's classic work, *Street Corner Society,* for example, which was originally published in 1943, clearly used the method of participant observation, even though that term is not used in the original edition, and even though Whyte provided almost no accounts of his method.[6]

How do we account for this increasing self-consciousness in fieldwork? Nash and Wintrob (1972:529) argued that within anthropology these changes reflected the "increasing personal involvement of ethnographers with their subjects." [7] Such involvement was in turn facilitated by the decline of colonialism and more assertive claims to independence by native peoples. The colonial regimes had supported and made possible the conditions for conducting field research (Maquet 1964). The pervasive and yet often unspoken power of the colonial presence could be relied on to facilitate many of the nitty-gritty tasks of fieldwork, such as securing access and cooperation. Yet under most conditions, the fieldworker tended to remain oblivious to this power.[8] Indeed, Barnes argued that the colonial system provided a structure that had allowed anthropological fieldworkers to view the field and those in it with complete detachment, as if it were a natural science laboratory: "The field of inquiry was perceived as exterior to themselves, something which could be observed by an outsider without significant distortion" (1967:194).

With the decline of colonialism, conditions that had been taken for granted became uncertain and problematic. Researchers had to obtain the approval of the people to be studied more directly, without the implicit or explicit inducement of being able to represent their interests to the colonial

---

[6] Whyte added the famous methodological appendix, "On the Evolution of 'Street Corner Society' " only to the second edition in 1955. The first edition discussion of method is largely limited to the comment that the only way to gain "intimate knowledge of local life" is to "live in Cornerville and participate in the activities of its people" (xv–xvi).

[7] Nash and Wintrob suggest that the generation of anthropological fieldworkers who followed Boas and Malinowski became much more closely and intensely immersed in the lives of the peoples they studied. But since they adhered to prevailing notions of scientific objectivity, they were unwilling or unable to publish accounts of these personal experiences.

[8] Such obliviousness characterized Malinowski's fieldwork in the Trobriands (Wax 1972). Malinowski accepted as totally natural the fact that he could pitch his tent in the middle of Omarkana and that the local authorities would be cooperative with his efforts. Wax suggests that this cooperation was forthcoming from the paramount chief on the assumption that Malinowski would reciprocate in some way by influencing the British colonial administration favorably toward him, an obligation which Malinowski never recognized or acknowledged.

powers. As access and the day-to-day process of fieldwork became more problematic, more dependent on actively establishing working relations with particular people, personal and relational self-consciousness inevitably increased. As Nash and Wintrob suggested, given native independence, the fieldworker "had to take the native point of view into account before, during, and after his field research. It became more important than ever before to be aware of what the natives were thinking" (1972:531).

Under these conditions it is difficult for the fieldworker to avoid confronting his or her own activities and uses of power, or to maintain an image of the field as essentially independent of such activities. The notion of the field as scientific laboratory, a notion that maximizes distance between studier and studied by positing (and creating!) essential differences between them, collapses. Moreover, as literacy spread among the peoples studied, and as field reports began to hold greater relevance for governmental administrators, fieldworkers could no longer maintain that their studies would have no significant impact on those they studied. In these areas too, the decline of colonialism brought an end to the unexamined assumption that anthropological research was *in* but not necessarily *part of* the field. As Barnes (1967:197) concluded, "the division between those under the microscope and those looking scientifically down the eyepiece has broken down."

In sociological fieldwork as well, growing self-consciousness resulted from changes that made fieldworkers' access to and movement in the settings under study problematic and locally negotiable. "Research bargains" and "entree" had rarely been matters of explicit concern to early Chicago fieldworkers; many had access to settings of interest before beginning their research. Through his connections at Hull House, for example, W. I. Thomas had established contacts with settlement house workers and others working with "unadjusted girls." Nels Anderson had been a hobo and he relied on his established knowledge and contacts in the hobo world when he went back to do research in it. In either case, the fieldworker had an established place in the world to be studied, a place that existed independently of his or her research concerns and that could be used in order to do research, rather than having to be created for purposes of research.

These preestablished ties (and the social relations they involved) cloaked implicit power relations much as the colonial regimes had. For in many instances the contacts of earlier field researchers with those studied were not direct but filtered through distinctive social institutions, particularly settlement houses and other social agencies. In many early Chicago field studies, for example, researchers used reports of settlement house and other charity workers to describe the community and personal life of specific segments of the poor, deprived, foreign, or delinquent. And even where "documents" were obtained directly from such people, it is apparent that the contacts were made through the settlement house structure (and sometimes even the accounts were collected by these people). In these instances, Chicago fieldworkers relied on the settlement house and the social worker for access to groups that the latter worked with; they remained relatively oblivious to the special place of social agencies and reform groups in urban ethnic communities.

In this context *Street Corner Society* is significant in that Whyte left the settlement house through which he initially made contact with his main informant, Doc (1955:290ff), and ventured out directly onto the streets to become immersed in the everyday world of the cornerboys. Indeed, it was only with the perspective gained from the streets that Whyte came to recognize the distinctive meaning and place of the settlement house in the ethnic enclave. Whyte concluded that the settlement house, staffed by middle-class people, had a primary function "to stimulate social mobility, to hold out middle-class standards and middle-class rewards to lower-class people" (1955:104).

To leave the settlement house was also to leave the preestablished set of relations which it could provide and to enter into the highly problematic and uncertain task of developing working personal relations on the street. Clearly Whyte was able to cross a significant class barrier more fully than many of the earlier Chicago fieldworkers, entering *as an outsider* and becoming immersed in a world strange and unknown to him. This process, in fact, reversed what seems to have been the more usual pattern in early Chicago fieldwork. Hughes has noted, for example, that Park, the most forceful teacher in the department during the 1920s, frequently took established "insiders" and converted them to sociology (1971:547):

> The first world war had broken the careers of many young Americans of religious and reforming bent. For a number of them who turned up in the department of sociology at Chicago, Park made an object of study and a new career out of what had been a personal problem or a crusade. Two, Frederic Thrasher and Clifford Shaw, probation officers, wrote *The Gang* and *The Natural History of a Delinquent Career,* ground-breaking monographs. Wirth, a social worker, became a sociologist and wrote *The Ghetto.*

The career of Nels Anderson perhaps best exemplifies this practice of field research by established insiders. Anderson had been raised in and on the edges of the hobo world, and he had been a hobo for a number of years before attending college and then beginning graduate study in sociology at the University of Chicago (1923/1961:v–xiii). As he remarked retrospectively on his field research for the classic, *The Hobo* (xiii):

> I did not descend into the pit, assume a role there, and later ascend to brush off the dust. I was in the process of moving out of the hobo world. To use a hobo expression, preparing the book was a way of "getting by," earning a living while the exit was under way. The role was familiar before the research began.

Where people are already intensely involved in activities and groups that they then come to study, the typical problems seem to involve creating sufficient distance and detachment to begin to look at these matters sociologically. Park, in particular, emphasized this sort of detachment and "objectivity" in his teachings. As the fieldworker increasingly began as an outsider to the groups and settings under study, directly crossing major ethnic, class, and status barriers, the processes of establishing trust and rapport, of sustaining ongoing personal relations under difficult circumstances, became more problematic. Under these conditions one would indeed expect increasing sensitivity to problems of field relations, to the salience of personal ties and reactions, and to the difficulties of grasping the meanings and understandings of new and strange peoples. Here, where closeness becomes problematic and sought after, intimate participation and sympathetic understanding, not detachment, come to be emphasized as the key processes in fieldwork.

Several additional factors can be linked to the increasing emphasis on self-reflection and self-consciousness in fieldwork. First, the emergence of symbolic interaction approaches, which emphasize the creation of meaning in and through interaction, calls attention to the fieldworker's own interactional and role problems. Second, belief in what has been termed "naive empiricism" — the notion that "the world 'out there' is isomorphic in every respect with the image the detached observer will form of it" — has declined (Nash and Wintrob 1972:529). With this change fieldwork no longer appeared to involve only mechanical observing and reporting of objects with preestablished, "objective" meanings. Finally, Wax (1971) and Platt (1982) have suggested that self-conscious use of the term "participant observation" and its explicit elaboration as a distinctive method were closely linked with the success within sociology of the new survey research methods associated with Lazarsfeld and Merton at Columbia in the 1940s. Proponents of survey research claimed strict scientific rigor in the use of statistical techniques, experimental design, etc. As Wax suggested (1971:40): "Faced with this challenge, a cluster of Chicagoans came to scrutinize their methodology more closely and to reconceptualize it around the term 'participant observation.' " The methodological writings on fieldwork and participant observation by Hughes, Becker, Geer, and Strauss in the 1950s stand as the primary illustrations of this tendency.

Interpretation and Practice in Contemporary Fieldwork

Emphases on self-consciousness and on knowing through acquiring access to meanings have become established principles for many fieldworkers during the past two decades. These changes have led to a far-reaching reconceptualization of the nature of the fieldwork enterprise.

One starting point in this change lies in the fundamental differences field-workers identify between physical reality as described by the natural scientist, and social reality as described and analyzed by the social scientist. It is worthwhile to quote at length Alfred Schutz's discussion of this issue (1962:58–59):

> ... there is an essential difference in the structure of the thought objects or mental constructs formed by the social sciences and those formed by the natural sciences. It is up to the natural scientist and to him alone to define, in accordance with the procedural rules of his science, his observational field, and to determine the facts, data, and events within it which are relevant for his problem or scientific purpose at hand. Neither are those facts and events pre-selected, nor is the observational field pre-interpreted. The world of nature, as explored by the natural scientist, does not "mean" anything to molecules, atoms, and electrons. But the observational field of the social scientist — social reality — has a specific meaning and relevance structure for the human beings living, acting, and thinking within it. By a series of common-sense constructs they have pre-selected and pre-interpreted this world which they experience as the reality of their daily lives. It is these thought objects of theirs which determine their behavior by motivating it. The thought objects constructed by the social scientist, in order to grasp this social reality, have to be founded upon the thought objects constructed by the common-sense thinking of men, living their daily life within their social world.

In studying the social world, therefore, the researcher's core problem is to grasp or understand the *meanings* that actions and events have for those studied. Such understanding is itself a "second-order" interpretation of what has already been "pre-interpreted" by members of the social group.

To grasp members' meanings demands *appreciation* of their distinctive concerns, forms of life, and ways of behaving found in their particular social world. Appreciation in this sense compels the fieldworker "to comprehend and to illuminate the subject's view and to interpret the world *as it appears to him*" (Matza 1969:25). Goffman provides a forceful statement of this goal in his preface to *Asylums*:

> My immediate object in doing fieldwork at St. Elizabeths was to try to learn about the social world of the hospital inmate, as this world is subjectively experienced by him ... It was then and still is my belief that any group of persons — prisoners, primitives, pilots, or patients — develop a life of their own that becomes meaningful, reasonable, and normal once you get close to it, and that a good way to learn about any of these worlds is to submit oneself in the company of the members to the daily round of petty contingencies to which they are subject. (1961a:ix–x)

Appreciation of the worlds and concerns of others involves the process of *verstehen,* or interpretive understanding, rather than the use of positivist procedures of the natural sciences. Murray Wax (1967:332) has suggested that verstehen is a mode of inquiry leading to "the perception of action as meaningful." Such understanding requires grasping "the vast background of shared meanings" through which the social world is organized into socially recognized categories in the first place (M. Wax 1967:326). These meanings become most clearly visible when a person has not been initially socialized into them, but has to acquire them de novo. Field research, particularly in another culture but also in one's own, involves just such a process of acquiring a sense of the meanings attributed to objects and events in a given society (Wax 1967:325):

> ... the student begins "outside" the interaction, confronting behaviors he finds bewildering and inexplicable: the actors are oriented to a world of meanings that the observer does not grasp .... the fieldworker finds initially that he does not understand the meanings of the actions of this strange people, and then gradually he comes to be able to categorize peoples (or relationships) and events: e.g., this man who is visiting as a brother-in-law to my host; last week his wife gave mine a gift; today he is expecting some reciprocity.

Implicit in the notion of verstehen is the claim that grasping others' meanings is not simply an intellectual process but a deeper form of experiential learning. At the core of fieldwork is not the collection of "facts" or the controlled observation of "objective" events, but rather a deeper holistic experience of learning about the lives, behaviors, and thoughts of others. Much fieldwork is at least potentially a deeply personal and transformative experience, as the fieldworker's self, providing the major research instrument, is often fundamentally affected by and perhaps changed in the process. As Whyte maintains in the appendix to *Street Corner Society,* ideas in field research "grow up in part out of our immersion in the data and out of the whole process of living. . . . (M)uch of this process of analysis proceeds on the unconscious level" (1955:280). Furthermore, interpretive understanding is acquired through regular and intimate involvement, maintained over time and under a variety of diverse circumstances, in the worlds of others. For such understanding is cultural, and as such "is something borne and maintained and created by joint activity" (Wax 1967:327). Participation in this sense is a form of practice in which the fieldworker's actions serve as tests of the meanings of others, and hence as ways of coming to understand those meanings.

Finally, Wax and others insist that interpretive understanding based on participation produces not merely intuitive insight or personal "hunches" that at best can serve as hypotheses to be verified by more systematic, quantitative methods. Rather, it produces a rigorous knowledge of the social world that is held in common by members of a particular society or social group; in sum, rigorous knowledge founded upon "the perspectives of the actors themselves and upon the categories of distinctions which the actors recognize and respond to" (Wax 1967:329).

Plan of the Book

In the first two parts of the book I will examine the issues and problems that such an interpretive view of social science knowledge creates for field research. Part I, "Ethnography and Understanding Members' Worlds," examines the process of trying to grasp and describe the social worlds of actors in ways that remain faithful to their meanings. Part II, "Theory and Evidence in Field Research," addresses two major issues: First, how do we generate theory of general scope and applicability from data that seek to capture the distinctive meanings of events and objects in a particular social world? And second, what kinds of criteria are appropriate for "appraising" the adequacy of the findings and theoretical claims that we ultimately arrive at through field research?

The view of fieldwork as an essentially interpretive procedure is closely linked with deepening attention to actual fieldwork practice. In fieldwork, "the observer is part of the field of action" (Cicourel 1964); *what* is known can never be grasped independently of *how* it is known. Parts III and IV address the nature of fieldwork practice. Part III, "Relational and Personal Processes in Fieldwork," considers the relevance of field relations for "findings," and the implications of the emerging, more humanistic conception of fieldwork practice. In this view, practice involves not only what a fieldworker does "as a researcher," but also as a "person"; indeed, the very distinction between what is done as a researcher and as a person becomes extremely artificial. Part IV, "Ethical and Political Issues in Field Research," examines the ethical and political issues that fieldwork inevitably generates.

I

Ethnography and Understanding Members' Worlds

Introduction

Clifford Geertz
Thick Description: Toward an Interpretive Theory of Culture

Charles O. Frake
Ethnography

Michael Agar
Ethnography and Cognition

D. Lawrence Wieder
Telling the Convict Code

Introduction

As noted in the introduction, fieldwork is a mode of inquiry that involves participant observation in the daily lives of some bounded group of people. While a central goal of such an inquiry is to contribute to general theoretical statements about cultural and social life, the initial and in some senses foundational task of fieldwork is to provide rich, empirically based *descriptions* of the distinctive social life and activities of those studied. Fieldwork thus seeks to produce an *ethnography* of the people or setting studied, that is, "a description of the way of life, or culture, of a society" that identifies "the behaviors and the beliefs, understandings, attitudes, and values they imply" found in that social world (Berreman 1968:337).

In early anthropological fieldwork researchers typically went about the task of describing another culture by collecting and listing various traits — ranging from material culture to social organization — of the group being studied. But description focused on such traits and isolated features came to be seen as but one aspect of a comprehensive understanding. In contemporary ethnographic studies in both sociology and anthropology fieldworkers now typically understand their essential task to be identifying and communicating the distinctive interpretations of reality that are made by members of the group under study. As Agar has recently characterized this central concern of ethnography (1980:194): "whatever the interests of the ethnographer, he must understand the way that group members interpret the flow of events in their lives." Ethnography, in sum, is fieldwork committed to describing the social and cultural worlds of a particular group. Such descriptions are sensitive to the interpretations recognized and acted on by members of that group.

While ethnography is essentially descriptive in intent, the process of describing the activities and realities of other people is not as straightforward a task as we often assume. First, there are problems inherent in the description of even the most commonplace or "obvious" of events and activities. Second are the perhaps more vexing problems which derive from the ethnographer's interest not simply in "events" and "activities" themselves — if there be such — but in the ways in which they are engaged in, guided, described, and generally assigned significance by group members.

In the following pages I will first explore the problems that confront efforts to describe these two aspects of the worlds of others. Then I will discuss the major strategies which fieldworkers have developed in attempting to meet these problems.

The Process of "Simple" Description

The first task of ethnographic fieldwork is to assemble richly textured and accurate descriptions of events and activities in the lives of those studied. Producing such descriptions, however, is not a simple and direct task. Ethnographers in particular have come to realize that describing even seemingly obvious events is extremely complex and problematic.

These problems remain hidden when we conceptualize description as the mere discovery and recording of "the facts," a notion that underlies what has been termed "simple" or "literal" description. Consider the fundamental assumptions that underlie such a model of description. First, description is depicted as the straightforward observation and reporting of "real objects" that are fixed, stable, and possess inherent meanings. On looking, the observer sees "things" — "brute data" — which can be more or less faithfully reported to others. Second, since objects have fixed and invariant meaning, these objects can be apprehended by anyone who cares to look at or for them. Thus, if two observers look at the same "thing," they will come up with essentially the same descriptions of it.

Fieldworkers concerned with ethnographic description have found the notion of literal description to be unsatisfactory, and they have increasingly questioned its assumptions regarding inherent meaning and observer-independent means of discovery. Many researchers argue, in the first place, that where and what to look at, and how to report what has been observed as a result of this looking, are not the almost mechanical processes that the model of literal description implies. For example, it is impossible to observe everything that takes place in a particular scene, as there is simply too much happening on too many different levels. Perceptual matters aside, it is impossible — or more relevantly, without purpose — to describe everything that has been seen. These features mean that any and all description is inevitably *partial* and *selective;* descriptions include some traits, features, or aspects, and exclude others.

What is included or excluded, however, is not determined randomly; rather, processes of looking and reporting are guided by the observer's implicit or explicit concepts that make some details more important and relevant than others. Thus, what is selected for observation and recording reflects the working theories or conceptual assumptions employed, however implicitly, by the ethnographer. To insist on a sharp polarity between description and analysis is thus misleading: description is necessarily analytic. As Berreman has argued, theory is always "inherent in ethnography":

> The underlying assumptions by which [the researcher] selects what he
> will observe from the mass of stimuli with which he is confronted in
> his research, what he will record from the innumerable observations
> he has made, and what he will report from the multitudinous records
> he has kept, comprise his theory or theories. If he regards it as more
> important to record a ceremony than a bull session, a song than an
> epithet, how and where people eat than how and where they defecate,
> the rules by which they marry rather than the infractions of these
> rules, the circumstances in which they take grievances to court than
> the circumstances in which they become embarrassed, what they do
> when someone dies than when someone belches (or vice versa), it is
> because he has a set of understandings or assumptions about the nature
> of human society, how it works and what is important in it. A theory
> is nothing more than a coherent set of assumptions. (1968:339)

The inevitable analytic component of descriptions in general has crucial
implications for ethnographic descriptions in particular. First, an ethnographic description can never be an exact, literal picture of some "thing"
such as an event or social action. It is always a theory-informed *re-presen-
tation* of that thing, a rendering of the event that transforms it in particular
ways (e.g., by presenting "what happened" in partial and selective ways).
A description of shooting heroin or fixing in the street world of the junkie,
for example, is inevitably partial and selective (compare the different descriptive accounts provided by Agar 1973:52–55 and Gould et al. 1974:
26–30). Such a description "re-presents" some set of activities that has
taken place in ways that inevitably differ from the actual experience of
shooting up or even from the direct experience of observing such shooting up.

Second, descriptions of the same social scene will vary depending on the
constructs that observers bring to and use in their witnessings and repre-
sentations. Bennett (1946) observed, for example, that studies of Pueblo
Indian culture by different ethnographers did not produce replications but
rather strikingly different interpretations of that society. Depending on
whether particular ethnographers were committed to an organic theory
highlighting social integration and harmonious sets of values, or a repression
theory alive to "*covert* tension, suspicion, anxiety, hostility, fear, and ambi-
tion" (363), they would describe and analyze the "same events" in very
different ways. Viewed with the first concept, work among the Hopi represents "an example of 'harmonious' and spontaneous cooperative attitudes
toward fulfillment of the universal plan of Nature" (Bennett 1946:366).
In the light of the second concept, work is not a product of voluntary cooperation, but of a pervasive, harsh socialization necessitated by the demands
of irrigation.[1]

In using concepts or theories, whether explicit or implicit ones, the eth-

---

[1] In turn, these different theories, Bennett emphasized, reflect distinctive value commitments: the organic theory values "solidified, homogeneous group life"; the repression theory values "equalitarian democracy and non-neurotic, 'free' behavior" (1946:
366).

nographer organizes what might otherwise be irrelevant and unconnected events and features into some pattern or order. This interpretive process of ordering begins immediately with perception; we perceive not the "things in themselves" but something made meaningful by being seen in relation to some known category, generally coded into language:

> Almost immediately what is perceived is interpreted by the addition of concepts, the conceptualization assimilating sensory stimuli to ideas derived from the anthropologist's own cultural experience or from the society being studied. An investigator noting that "the officiant shaves some hair from the girl's temples and the back of her neck," by applying concepts (the officiant, hair, the act of shaving, etc.) to parts of a total event, in effect conceptualizes the whole event by organizing the parts into a single activity. (Honigmann 1976:245)

Several different issues are involved here. First, the observer uses categories to identify and interpret certain things as meaningful: e.g., "shaves." Second, the observer links these features together, organizing them as parts of a single activity, thereby making a higher level interpretation of meaning.

The partial and selective character of descriptions is not only a product of the general theory and language-based categories used to observe, order, and describe events. It is, more generally, a product of how an observer *attends* to what is to be observed and described. Attending includes but is not limited to the use of concepts and categories to order and interpret. It also ranges from the basic ways in which the describer engages with the world as a condition for describing it to the fieldworker's actual practice of inquiry. Such decisions as exactly where and when to go to observe, and how to present yourself and your observings to those being watched can critically shape descriptions. In this respect, no description is independent of the describer and his or her actual methods for making and reporting observations. I can, of course, only raise the issue of practice here; it will be explored in depth in Parts II and III.

Describing Meanings

The ethnographer's problems are rendered qualitatively more complex by the recognition that he or she is not interested in the commonplace or extraordinary in and of themselves, but in the ways in which the commonplace and the extraordinary — all of the actions and events comprising the life of the people — are oriented and responded to, comprehended and guided by, the interpretations of group members. The central focus of the ethnographer is not the "things in themselves" — if indeed there are such things — but things as they are grasped and shaped through the meaning-conferring response of members. For some, the fact that groups impose structures of meaning on "things" comprises the mandate of ethnography and indeed the social sciences.

The ethnographic mandate leads, in the first place, to the description of socially meaningful behavior, rather than of human behavior viewed as a physiological process. As Geertz shows (this volume, pages 39*ff*), description of the social world is not concerned with contractions of the eyelids, but with the interpreted significance of winks, parodied winks, and the like. Similarly, ethnographic description seeks to identify the subjective meanings people attribute to events rather than the "objective" characteristics of such events. Consider the problem of describing drug use in these terms. Pharmacologists generally describe methadone and heroin as essentially similar drugs and contend that street addicts cannot tell the difference between them under double-blind conditions. Yet as Gould et al. (1974:xix) have insisted, in describing the world of the heroin user, "the only reality we need concern ourselves with is the reality that is experienced by the research subjects." And addicts recognize fundamental differences between the two drugs: for addicts methadone is a fallback drug, used to prevent sickness or cut down on a habit, while heroin is used to get high. On the level of meaning, pharmacological reality is irrelevant to understanding and describing street drug worlds, since it is the addicts' beliefs about the drugs, rather than existing scientific knowledge of their effects, that is critical for addicts' behaviors.

But again, just as descriptions of events and activities are not those things in themselves, so descriptions of meanings are not those meanings in themselves, but rather the ethnographer's representation of them. Schutz's analysis of the general relationship between members' common-sense theories and those of the social scientist is helpful in specifying this difference:

> [The social scientist's] observational field, the social world, is not essentially structureless. It has a particular meaning and relevance structure for the human beings living, thinking, and acting therein. They have preselected and preinterpreted this world by a series of common-sense constructs of the reality of daily life, and it is these thought objects which determine their behavior, define the goal of their action, the means available for attaining them — in brief, which help them to find their bearings within their natural and sociocultural environment and to come to terms with it. The thought objects constructed by the social scientists refer to and are founded upon the thought objects constructed by the common-sense thought of man living his everyday life among his fellow-men. Thus, the constructs used by the social scientist are, so to speak, constructs of the second degree, namely constructs of the constructs made by the actors on the social scene, whose behavior the scientist observes and tries to explain in accordance with the procedural rules of his science. (1962:5–6)

Similarly, the ethnographer's descriptions are second-order interpretations — interpretations of members' interpretations; or, in Geertz's (this volume, page 42) phrase, "our own constructions of other people's constructions of what they and their compatriots are up to."

To frame the problem of describing meanings in terms of the relation between members' constructs and the ethnographer's constructs of those constructs may prove more useful than maintaining the standard distinction made within anthropology between descriptions based on *emic* and those based on *etic* constructs. These terms derive from the work of the linguist Kenneth Pike (1954:8–28), who pointed out a contrast between the procedures and presuppositions of phon*etics,* the classification of sound bits according to their acoustic properties, and phon*emics,* the classification of sounds on the basis of their internal function in the language in question. In a parallel way, anthropologists have come to term "etic" those descriptions that use categories from outside the culture studied, and "emic" those accounts based on concepts that come from within the culture that would be used or recognized by its members. In general, those who stress etics insist that descriptions should be based on concepts that allow cross-cultural comparisons. The ethnographer may well derive such concepts not from the native culture, but "from his own mind, from ethnological theory, or from other particular cultures, including his own" (Naroll 1967:511). Advocates of emic approaches, in contrast, see the goal as description of a particular culture in its own terms; native categories should not be ignored even if they do not lend themselves to comparison with other cultures.

Viewed in light of Schutz's argument, the sharp dichotomy between emic and etic descriptions collapses. For that dichotomy rests on the assumption that the constructs underlying emic accounts are literally members' constructs rather than second-order renderings of those constructs produced in one fashion or another by the ethnographer. Every emic descriptive account will therefore have an etic component deriving from the ethnographer's reconstructions of members' meanings. This fact makes the contrast itself of limited usefulness. The more critical issues in describing meanings surround the ethnographer's procedures for discovering and interpreting members' meanings.

There have been a range of proposals as to how ethnographers might confront the fact that they interpretively (i.e., partially, selectively, perspectually) seek to comprehend indigenous or naturally occurring interpretations. Although most ethnographers agree on the nature of meaningful worlds, they recommend various procedures for apprehending and representing these worlds. In the remainder of this introduction I will examine three proposals concerned with how ethnography should proceed in these matters.

"Thick Description"

In his influential chapter beginning *The Interpretation of Cultures* (this volume, pages 37–59), Geertz argues that ethnography should provide "thick description" of cultural and social activities. Thick descriptions present in close detail the context and meanings of events and scenes that are relevant to those involved in them. This task requires the ethnographer to identify and communicate the connections between actions and events, especially those salient to the variety of local actors themselves. In this sort of descriptive enterprise, actions are not stripped of locally relevant context and interconnectedness, but are tied together in textured and holistic accounts of social life. Ethnographic thick description proceeds on the assumption that context is not an obstacle to understanding but a resource for it.

In directing attention toward context, thick description relies heavily on what Geertz has elsewhere (1976:223) termed "experience-near" rather than "experience-distant" concepts. The former are emic-like concepts that a member of a society would "naturally and effortlessly use to define what he or his fellows see, feel, think, imagine, and so on, and which he would readily understand when similarly applied by others." The latter are etic-like concepts employed by specialists "to forward their scientific, philosophical, or practical aims" (1976:223). Specifically, " 'Love' is an experience-near concept, 'object cathexis' is an experience-distant one." Thick description starts with — but does not restrict itself to — experience-near concepts (see pages 54–58).

This sensitivity to, and even preoccupation with, locally meaningful context in ethnographic, thick descriptions contrasts sharply with most standard social science procedures, in which observers typically try either to ignore or to reduce contextual meanings in the interests of standardization and comparability.[2] Consider the differences between description in this thick vein and observational methods that employ fixed, predetermined categories for coding behavior. In a number of studies of police decision making (Black and Reiss 1970; Reiss 1971; Lundman 1974), observers were sent into the field, riding along with patrolmen, armed with code sheets for recording all interactions between officers and civilians. Such code sheets are essentially predetermined questions which the observer/coder will ask of each and every observed incident qualifying for observation. The questions are in fact variables, and since each is asked of every incident observed, data relevant to each variable are systematically collected for all observations. One variable sometimes examined in this way, for example, is the use of physical force by each police officer (see Reiss 1968). Based on a prespecified definition of force (here, one that excluded instances of "simple restraint"), all observed cases are classified on the basis of specific criteria into either "necessary" or "unnecessary" uses of force (Reiss 1968:12).

These procedures produce data that are extremely useful for many purposes, for example, the researchers can specify the frequency with which

---

[2] Mishler (1979) argues that methodological procedures that seek to discover invariant relations between discrete variables lead to "the stripping away of contexts." While experimental procedures represent one extreme in these terms, all methods that seek "pure variables," i.e., those that are "independent, free-standing, orthogonal — that is, unrelated to measures of other variables" (3), simplify and remove contextual factors and seek to reduce social life to separate, measurable variables.

such events occur, then see if these different variables correlate.[3] Yet, such emphasis on standardization necessarily restricts the appreciation of meaning and context. The complexity of social life is inevitably neglected when events are classified into predetermined categories rather than thickly described. Such matters as the emergent interactional processes leading up to the use of force (see the suggestive description and analysis in Van Maanen 1978a), or the subjective concerns and experiences of those involved in such encounters are ignored, or reduced to correlations. Instead, the goal of these procedures is to reduce such exchanges to one global classification. In so doing the observer orients to any particular incident primarily to decide how its features fit within the predetermined categories.

The purpose of ethnographic description is not to determine the frequencies and correlations of predetermined variables, but to present or represent the local meanings and contexts of complex human actions. These contrasting purposes and procedures are illustrated by the following extract from Rubinstein's ethnographic study of police patrolmen (1973:304–305):

> A young white officer noticed a man standing near a street corner turn away as the patrol car approached. He stopped his car and rolled down the window to look at the elderly Negro man. Instead of getting out of the car, he yelled across the deserted street to him, "Take your hand out of your coat." The man had turned back toward the car when it stopped, and he had his right hand jammed inside. He did not react to the command. They were frozen for several seconds; then the patrolman repeated his demand. When the man remained silent, the officer drew his pistol, continuing to remain seated in his car. He placed his gun in plain view and again ordered the man to show his hand. The man was very agitated but he remained silent. Slowly he began to extract his hand, but he gave the appearance of concealing some intention which threatened the patrolman, who cocked his gun and pointed it directly at the man. Suddenly the old man drew out his hand and threw a pistol to the ground. He stood trembling. The patrolman uncocked his gun with a shaking hand and approached. He was on the verge of tears, and in a moment of confusion, fear, and anxiety, he struck the man with the butt of his pistol. "Why didn't you take your hand out when I told you? I almost shot you, you dumb bastard." The man protested the treatment he had received, complaining that there was no reason to hit him. He said he had had no intention of using the gun but was carrying it for self-protection. The patrolman recovered from his fright, but despite his regret for striking the man in anger, he refused to acknowledge any responsibility. "Are

---

[3] Summarizing the results of this procedure, Reiss notes: "In the seven-week period [of observation], we found thirty-seven cases in which force was used improperly. In all, forty-four citizens had been assaulted. In fifteen of these cases, no one was arrested. Of these, eight had offered no verbal or physical resistance whatsoever, while seven had" (1968:12). Elsewhere (1971:142) he reports that the rate of excessive police force was on the order of three instances per every 1,000 citizen encounters.

you wearing a sign? How the fuck am I supposed to know what you're gonna do?"

Rubinstein uses this incident to make a number of different analytic points about the nature of police work. He introduces it as an illustration of the danger "hidden hands" signal to the patrolman, and of the pressure the patrolman is under to decide "in a few seconds what course of action to take" when confronting someone whose hands stay concealed. Rubinstein also suggests that this incident represents what most police would see as "bad" patrol work, less because of the use of force than because of the officer's actions that escalated the possibilities of shooting:

> From a purely technical point of view, the patrolman had initially made an error by failing to close the distance between himself and the suspect, allowing himself no alternative but to leave or to use his gun. If he had charged the man immediately upon suspecting him of some misdeed, any passer-by might have "seen" an elderly black man being "assaulted" by a policeman, but the patrolman would have avoided the chance of a much more serious incident. (1973:305)

This sort of account does not seek to reduce observed happenings to a specific set of variables (although it does reduce these happenings to a finite encounter and hence to data). Rather, it tries to convey the nature of police work as the police themselves understand, talk about, and evaluate it. As a description it is "thick" to the extent that it offers or sustains multiple interpretations, and it allows the reader to search for and identify such interpretations even while it has been constructed to advance specific interpretations of its own.[4]

While contextual and experience-near, thick descriptions are neither totally devoid of theoretical significance, nor totally emic in character. Purely emic descriptions, even if possible, would seem useless and uninteresting for social science. The task, rather, is to "grasp concepts which, for another people, are experience-near, and to do so well enough to place them in illuminating connection with experience-distant concepts theorists have fashioned to capture the general features of social life" (Geertz 1976:224). The critical question here, Geertz suggests, is

> ... how, in each case, ought one to deploy them so as to produce an interpretation of the way a people lives which is neither imprisoned within their mental horizons, an ethnography of witchcraft as written by a witch, nor systematically deaf to the distinctive tonalities of their existence, an ethnography of witchcraft as written by a geometer. (1976:223)

Geertz's notion of thick description has struck a responsive chord with fieldworkers, providing a general model of and justification for pursuing

---

[4] In this piece of field data it is apparent that Rubinstein "builds in" his interpretation of patrolman-recognized "technical error" by noting *the course of action not taken*: "Instead of getting out of the car, ..." But his account of the incident is still sufficiently textured to allow readers to ask other questions of it.

meaning-rich, context-sensitive, and holistic descriptions of social activities. In so doing the skill of ethnography is transformed from that of an arduous collection of facts to the subtle interpretation and communication of symbolic meanings. As Leach (1976:1) has depicted this change: "Ethnography has ceased to be an inventory of custom, it has become the art of thick description; the intricate interweaving of plot and counterplot as in the work of a major novelist."

Description and Cognitive Anthropology

While most ethnographers seek to discover members' meanings, such a process is the central task of a variety of systematic approaches to description commonly identified as cognitive anthropology or ethnoscience. In these views ethnography should provide descriptions of the cultural knowledge used by members to interpret and classify events and objects in a particular society. Culture is understood as a cognitive code for attributing meaning, "a system of standards for perceiving, believing, evaluating, and acting" (Goodenough 1971:41). In this sense culture in any specific social setting consists of whatever it is one has to know in order to operate in a manner acceptable to its members. Specifying such cultural codes or rules represents the major goal of ethnographic description (see the Frake and Agar readings which follow).

Cultural codes in this view are inextricably tied to and expressed through language, and cognitive anthropologists view "the focus on language as the prime inroad to understanding group life" (Agar 1982:85). Moreover, cognitive anthropologists advocate adapting formal linguistic models and procedures to the task of describing cultural knowledge: Just as the systematic writing out of linguistic rules makes it possible to produce utterances that make sense and are acceptable to native speakers of a particular language, so writing out systematic cultural rules, "formulating ethnographic algorithms" (Sanday 1979:534), makes it possible to produce actions acceptable to a local culture. Through the use of formal questioning or "elicitation" procedures, cognitive anthropologists seek to "generate a valid, reliable, and systematic picture of an informant's 'domain' of knowledge" (Manning and Fabrega 1976:39).

As Sanday has emphasized, this approach to ethnographic description differs from Geertz's thick description "not in aim but in method, focus, and mode of reporting" (1979:534). As she elaborates this difference (535):

> Videotapes, tape recorders, and ethnoscience elicitation procedures are used to gauge the underlying rules for behavior and the implicit categorizations by which people order their world. These rules and categorizations are framed by the ethnographer in a kind of grammar of culture. The mode of reporting is also highly technical, more like

the lexicon and grammar published by the linguist than like "thick description."

Two features in particular differentiate the approach of cognitive anthropology from thick description. First, cognitive anthropologists emphasize the use of standardized, systematic procedures for eliciting cultural categories. As a result, they argue that their findings can be replicated by other researchers. Second, cognitive anthropologists produce descriptions that are highly formal, even abstract, in character. While members' meanings (at least in the sense of cognitive categories or classifications) are central to these descriptions, the categories are presented without local context and without concrete situational, biographical, or historical detail. In his description of the socially meaningful world of drug addicts, for example, Agar (this volume pages 74–77) is not concerned with the meanings particular junkies attached to particular events or scenes, but with the general categories that lie behind such specific occurrences. The description involves specifying the *formal* relations between such general but locally indigenous categories as "hustling," "copping," and "getting off" rather than in conveying the more concrete, situationally specific meanings implicit in a particular incident in the street addict world.

In an early paper Frake (1962a) suggested that this process of discovering codes was much more complex than most ethnographers realized. For example, much ethnographic research had involved simply compiling a list of member (native) terms for objects presumed to be equivalent to objects with the same name in the ethnographer's culture. Description thus became "the name-getting task ... of simply matching verbal labels for "things" in two languages" (Frake 1962a:73). Ideally, the ethnographer would point to an object and elicit the native's name for it, then match this name with his or her own word for that object (Frake 1962a:73): "The logic of the operation is: if the informant calls object X a *mbubu* and I call object X a *rock,* then *mbubu* means *rock.*" Not only is such an approach methodologically uncertain (the ethnographer assumes, among other things, that the native understands that his finger points to "rock" as opposed to its color, size, texture, etc.), but it also provides only limited understanding of the native culture. To learn that the Eskimo have many words for snow while English-speaking people have only one not only tells us very little about their world and how it is meaningful, but also essentially describes that world only by contrast with our own society and its concepts. Rather than "finding the 'things' that go with the words," Frake argues that the task of ethnographic description is better seen as "finding out what are in fact the 'things' in the environment of the people being studied" (1962a:74). That is, Frake insists that no object "has been described *ethnographically* until one has stated the rules for its identification in the culture being studied" (1962b:55). To return to the illustration of Eskimos and snow: An ethnographic description involves explaining how the Eskimo themselves go about making the distinctions between these different kinds of snow (and perhaps indeed whether it is "snow" that is being distinguished).

When cognitive anthropologists move from the description of the culturally based classification of more finite objects (plants, firewood, colors, and even kinship) to the description of more complex social activities, additional difficulties arise. Here the strategy of the ethnographer is to identify the background cultural knowledge needed to perform particular actions in another culture in ways that would be recognized as appropriate by members of that culture. In describing the kinds of cultural knowledge someone must have to properly enter a Yakan house, for example, Frake (1975) traces out a variety of Yakan understandings of the different social spaces within a house, and of their proper uses on different social occasions.[5]

Underlying this approach is an effort to ground descriptions on distinctions consistently drawn from within the culture being described rather than from an outside culture. Moerman (1969:464) illustrates the logic of this procedure by examining the seemingly innocuous descriptive claim that "the Thai are noisy in temple." If what is meant by this statement is "the Thai I saw in temple were noisier than Methodists are supposed to be in church," it frames Thai behavior in temples against an external criterion, thereby caricaturing rather than describing that behavior on its own terms. To establish the claim that the Thai are noisy in temple requires the development of *intracultural contrasts;* that is, comparison of the noise (and other aspects of social behavior) in this setting with the noise in other locally comparable situations (among the Thai, for example, dispute hearings, village meetings, and casual conversations). Thus, the observer is led to a comparison of public behaviors in different settings in Thai society, and to contrasting organizational and interactional patterns found within them.[6]

The goals, assumptions, and procedures of cognitive anthropology have generated a number of questions and criticisms. Some anthropologists (e.g., Berreman 1966) hold that the pursuit of rigor has led to relatively sterile

[5] The catch here, of course, is to identify what is relevantly "different" to the Yakan in each instance. In Frake's (1964b:133) view this provides the goal of ethnography: "the model of an ethnographic statement is not: 'if a person is confronted with stimulus X, he will do Y,' but: 'if a person is in situation X, performance Y will be judged appropriate by native actors.'"

[6] Once again, for Moerman's concerns, "objective" noise levels are irrelevant. One could compare the decibel levels in a Thai temple to those in a Methodist church, but such a comparison does not describe behaviors in locally meaningful terms. As Moerman insists (1969:464): "If I am correct in asserting that the Thai are quieter in temple than they are in other locally delimited situations, then however loud they sound to Methodists and however quiet to [Jamaican] Pocamanians, the Thai whether ethnographically or for purposes of comparative ethnology . . . are quiet in temple."

descriptions of more "trivial" areas of cultural knowledge. Others complain that cognitive anthropologists tend to use their formal eliciting procedures in rather mechanical, nonreflective ways, ignoring the social properties of elicitation interviews as "formal interchanges between an expert who asks and a respondent who fills the role of information-provider" (Manning and Fabrega 1976:44). This neglect leaves unaddressed the possibility that the informant's responses were produced specifically for the eliciting anthropologist and have little natural currency in ordinary social life (Moerman 1969). Finally, many anthropologists suggest that cognitive anthropology produces an overly rational and artificially systematic description of culture. Culture knowledge as actually used in specific situations may not be coherently and inclusively ordered. Moreover, such knowledge may vary widely across groups and individuals within any particular society, as Worsley (1968:xxiv) found regarding religious and ritual knowledge among Australian aboriginals. The roots of this over-ordered view of culture are traced by some to a model of language itself as "a universal, structurally uniform, rule-governed code which is shared by all members of a culture" (Manning and Fabrega 1976:42). The result of using this model is an idealized account of members' knowledge, ignoring both context and the emergent qualities of naturally occurring interactions (Coulter 1971).

Several recent articles by cognitive anthropologists have been responsive to such criticisms. While a strong commitment to methodological explicitness continues to mark cognitive anthropology, concern with rigid elicitation procedures and with presenting cultural knowledge in formal taxonomies has declined (Agar 1982:85). Greater attention has been directed toward the interactional and social contexts of questioning informants (Frake 1977), and toward exploring the relations between knowledge structures and people's actual purposes and intentions (Agar 1982:85). Finally, proposals for a more dynamic and variable notion of culture have been advanced. Frake, for example, has suggested the following alternative to the model of culture as a fixed, static "cognitive map":

> People are not just map-readers; they are map-makers. People are cast out into the imperfectly charted, continually shifting seas of everyday life. Mapping them out is a constant process resulting not in an individual cognitive map, but in a whole chart case of rough, improvised, continually revised sketch maps. Culture does not provide a cognitive map, but rather a set of principles for map-making and navigation. Different cultures are like different schools of navigation designed to cope with different terrains and seas. (1977:6–7)

Ethnomethodology and the Reflexivity of Descriptions

Many of the concerns of cognitive anthropology, as well as some of the questions asked by its critics, are echoed within sociology in the writings of ethnomethodologists. Central to ethnomethodological stances is the study of the ways in which members of a particular society actually use their "folk knowledge," including ways in which members produce descriptions of their social worlds.

Following Schutz (1962), ethnomethodology holds that the social world is preinterpreted, or, to fit our concerns here, "predescribed." People live in social worlds in which particular meanings are attributed to events. Member descriptions, therefore, are of central concern to the ethnomethodologists. In a major statement of this approach, Harold Garfinkel (1967) argues that members' descriptions of their social worlds create or constitute those social worlds as meaningful phenomena. For members' descriptions are not "mere words," but are *ways of doing things with words*. A description characterizes members' circumstances in particular ways for particular purposes; in this way it identifies specific meanings and thereby excludes other meaning possibilities.

A concrete example may help at this point. When Melvin Pollner and I began fieldwork on psychiatric emergency teams (PET teams) operating out of community mental health clinics, a number of PET workers described their job as "shit work" (Emerson and Pollner 1976). The term provided a description — albeit a capsulated and negative one — of what PET was doing. But on reflection we came to realize that this "dirty work" description is misunderstood if it is treated as a neutral, detached, "factual" characterization of what PET was up to. Rather, we came to see PET talk of dirty work as providing a set of instructions to us and to others, instructions on how to "see" the "real meaning" of PET activities, particularly in circumstances that might well have been read otherwise. For example, despite a strong commitment to crisis intervention modes of therapy and to "community treatment," "day after day PET hospitalized people who did not want to be hospitalized, used coercion in effecting hospitalization, and so forth" (252). Yet in describing such actions as dirty work, PET workers provided a narrative instructing observers to attribute certain meanings and not others to them. Thus (252):

> Talk of shit work, for example, formulates involuntary hospitalization and the use of coercion as exceptions to the "real" purpose of PET. Through such talk PET personnel made themselves and others aware that the actual treatment accorded cases ought not to be taken as representative of what they would prefer to do or what PET, at heart, was designed to do.

Moreover, these descriptions were *consequential* in and for the organizational context within which PET workers operated. To invoke the notion of dirty work as a resistant patient was physically restrained and taken off to the hospital, for example, communicated that the worker knew that this was not "helping" yet he or she remained committed to the value of providing therapy. Thus, these descriptions provided *accounts* (Garfinkel 1967) that both instructed others in a setting in how to appreciate its situationally specific meanings and order, and simultaneously, invoked and created those very meanings and order.

Descriptions, then, are not simply *about* some social world, but are also *part* of that world. In this sense descriptions are *reflexive* in character: "descriptions about some aspect of the social world are simultaneously within (part of) the very world that they described" (Schwartz and Jacobs 1979:51). Since descriptions are reflexive in this way, fieldworkers cannot treat members' descriptive talk as "objective reporting" of "factual data." To do so would involve treating such talk as independent of the social world that produced it, as somehow transcending the specific social situation within which it was generated.

The selection from D. Lawrence Wieder which ends this section, "Telling the Convict Code," develops this view of description as a reflexive, socially consequential process of providing meaning-creating accounts. Wieder found that residents of a halfway house for ex-drug addicts often referred to the "convict code" in describing events in the house. When a resident invoked the code and its specific tenets, he was not offering a neutral, transcendent description; rather, reference to the code was a way of taking action in the social organization of the house, an organization made relevant to this particular occasion by these very statements. Thus, when a resident drew upon the code to justify his refusal to talk to staff (or a fieldworker) about personal matters, this action (a sort of description) made a statement about his relations with others in the house. It indicated, for example, that he stood with residents against staff, or that within the house the fieldworker was to be treated as staff.

Wieder's specific analysis of the telling of the code, and ethnomethodological concerns with description in general, have a number of important implications for ethnography. To begin, the relationship between members' descriptions and the accounts that the fieldworker comes to offer must be explicitly examined. In fact, ethnomethodologists suggest that many fieldworkers take over members' accounts and descriptions as their own, using these accounts to describe and explain events in that particular social world. To cite an example from Wieder's study: the classic sociological literature on prisons (e.g., Sykes 1958) used the prisoners' own description of the convict code as a resource for explaining how prison life was organized; for example, to suggest that rehabilitative efforts were bound to fail because they ran counter to the requirements of the code. In this way, the code is turned from a member's description into the sociologist's explanation; just as members explain behavior by reference to the code and its provisions, so too does the sociologist.

This happens, of course, because the sociologist treats the member's description as fact, as a report about "real" events standing outside the social order described. Ethnomethodologists suggest an alternative view: that members' descriptions are inevitably embedded in and part of the

order they describe. They then recommend the investigation of these descriptions as phenomena in their own right. Cicourel's (1968) analysis of
how probation officers write up reports of contacts with delinquent youth
provides a case in point. These reports provided not "pure descriptions"
of delinquent behavior, but rather a heavily selected recounting of such
behavior intended to further certain practical organizational concerns of
the probation officer. In looking at how probation officers assembled such
reports, the ethnographer treats descriptive partiality, selectivity, and perspective as topics as well as problems.

Furthermore, since descriptions are integral parts of the social worlds
they describe, descriptions will vary with the describer's particular "practical or theoretical problem at hand" (Schutz 1964:235). As these problems of purposes vary, so will the nature of the descriptions provided.
Members with different responsibilities in the same organization, for example, will provide descriptions of the organization that reflect their distinctive
problems. For example, attendants in mental hospitals, whose work centers
on ordering the flow of daily life on the wards, describe patients in terms
that reflect these practical demands; as "tidy" or "untidy," "mobile" or
"feeble," "cooperative" or "bad," and "working" or "idle" (Bucher and
Schatzman 1962:340–343). Psychiatrists in these settings would tend to
describe the same patients in terms of their psychodynamics or their degree
of "insight," descriptions reflecting their diagnostic and therapeutic responsibilities.

Since members' descriptions are formulated for particular purposes,
ethnomethodologists suggest that close attention be paid to these purposes.
As a result, ethnographic accounts should not be limited to describing members' general concepts, categories, or perspectives. Rather, ethnographers
should seek to describe the *actual use* of such concepts and categories in
specific social interactions. Merely describing these concepts is of limited
utility, since knowing only these categories abstractly and in principle we
still do not know exactly how members apply them in real social situations.[7] By way of illustration: as Wieder suggests, the ethnographer cannot
assume in advance exactly how the convict code will be applied or invoked
in particular situations in the halfway house. The code, for example, contains no specific provisions about how to treat fieldworkers; its provisions
will have to be expanded, changed, modified, or extended in one way or
another to cover this situation. Similarly, even if we know that PET workers
describe much of what they do as "shit work," we cannot predict exactly
what situations they would so characterize until they actually do so. De-

---

[7] Ethnomethodological researchers suggest that many ethnographers treat members'
perspectives or categories as a set of "rules" with which to explain member behavior.
Ethnomethodology holds that such categories or rules do not "cause" behavior so
much as make it meaningful, and that like all rules their application to particular
situations is problematic and not specified or specifiable by these rules themselves.

scriptions that are limited to member categories without reference to actual use thus remain incomplete and empty.

Finally, ethnomethodologists are inclined to turn ethnographic description back on itself by insisting that the ethnographer's accounts are in no fundamental way different from those members provide. Both reflect the describer's purposes at hand; that the ethnographer's purposes are perhaps more "theoretical" does not make his or her descriptions any less partial, selective, or perspectival than members' descriptions — only different. Similarly, both ethnographic and folk descriptions make frequent use of specific interpretive procedures to find and convey meaning and regularity. As Garfinkel explains one such procedure, the "documentary method of interpretation":

> The method consists of treating an actual appearance as "the document of," as "pointing to," as "standing on behalf of" a presupposed underlying pattern. Not only is the underlying pattern derived from its individual documentary evidences, but the individual documentary evidences, in their turn, are interpreted on the basis of "what is known" about the underlying pattern. Each is used to elaborate the other. (1967:78)

The convict code provides an instance of such a pattern, used by member and fieldworker alike to interpret a variety of specific actions in the halfway house. All descriptions employ such procedures; hence, for ethnomethodologists, ethnographic as well as member methods for assembling descriptions should be examined in terms of their use of such procedures.

Thick Description: Toward an Interpretive Theory of Culture

Clifford Geertz

I

In her book, *Philosophy in a New Key,* Susanne Langer remarks that certain ideas burst upon the intellectual landscape with a tremendous force. They resolve so many fundamental problems at once that they seem also to promise that they will resolve all fundamental problems, clarify all obscure issues. Everyone snaps them up as the open sesame of some new positive science, the conceptual center-point around which a comprehensive system of analysis can be built. The sudden vogue of such a *grande idée,* crowding out almost everything else for a while, is due, she says, "to the fact that all sensitive and active minds turn at once to exploiting it. We try it in every connection, for every purpose, experiment with possible stretches of its strict meaning, with generalizations and derivatives."

After we have become familiar with the new idea, however, after it has become part of our general stock of theoretical concepts, our expectations are brought more into balance with its actual uses, and its excessive popularity is ended. A few zealots persist in the old key-to-the-universe view of it; but less driven thinkers settle down after a while to the problems the idea has really generated. They try to apply it and extend it where it applies and where it is capable of extension; and they desist where it does not apply or cannot be extended. It becomes, if it was, in truth, a seminal idea in the first place, a permanent and enduring part of our intellectual armory. But it no longer has the grandiose, all-promising scope, the infinite versatility of apparent application, it once had. The second law of thermodynamics, or the principle of natural selection, or the notion of unconscious motivation, or the organization of the means of production does not explain everything, not even everything human, but it still explains something; and our attention shifts to isolating just what that something is, to disentangling ourselves from a lot of pseudoscience to which, in the first flush of its celebrity, it has also given rise.

Whether or not this is, in fact, the way all centrally important scientific concepts develop, I don't know. But certainly this pattern fits the concept of culture, around which the whole discipline of anthropology arose, and

From *The Interpretation of Cultures: Selected Essays,* by Clifford Geertz, Copyright © 1973 by Basic Books, Inc., New York. Reprinted by permission of the publisher.

whose domination that discipline has been increasingly concerned to limit, specify, focus, and contain. It is to this cutting of the culture concept down to size, therefore actually insuring its continued importance rather than undermining it, that the essays below are all, in their several ways and from their several directions, dedicated. They all argue, sometimes explicitly, more often merely through the particular analysis they develop, for a narrowed, specialized, and, so I imagine, theoretically more powerful concept of culture to replace E. B. Tylor's famous "most complex whole," which, its originative power not denied, seems to me to have reached the point where it obscures a good deal more than it reveals.

The conceptual morass into which the Tylorean kind of *pot-au-feu* theorizing about culture can lead, is evident in what is still one of the better general introductions to anthropology, Clyde Kluckhohn's *Mirror for Man*. In some twenty-seven pages of his chapter on the concept, Kluckhohn managed to define culture in turn as: (1) "the total way of life of a people"; (2) "the social legacy the individual acquires from his group"; (3) "a way of thinking, feeling, and believing"; (4) "an abstraction from behavior"; (5) a theory on the part of the anthropologist about the way in which a group of people in fact behave; (6) a "storehouse of pooled learning"; (7) "a set of standardized orientations to recurrent problems"; (8) "learned behavior"; (9) a mechanism for the normative regulation of behavior; (10) "a set of techniques for adjusting both to the external environment and to other men"; (11) "a precipitate of history"; and turning, perhaps in desperation, to similes, as a map, as a sieve, and as a matrix. In the face of this sort of theoretical diffusion, even a somewhat constricted and not entirely standard concept of culture, which is at least internally coherent and, more important, which has a definable argument to make is (as, to be fair, Kluckhohn himself keenly realized) an improvement. Eclecticism is self-defeating not because there is only one direction in which it is useful to move, but because there are so many: it is necessary to choose.

The concept of culture I espouse, and whose utility the essays below attempt to demonstrate, is essentially a semiotic one. Believing, with Max Weber, that man is an animal suspended in webs of significance he himself has spun, I take culture to be those webs, and the analysis of it to be therefore not an experimental science in search of law but an interpretive one in search of meaning. It is explication I am after, construing social expressions on their surface enigmatical. But this pronouncement, a doctrine in a clause, demands itself some explication.

II

Operationalism as a methodological dogma never made much sense so far as the social sciences are concerned, and except for a few rather too well-swept corners — Skinnerian behaviorism, intelligence testing, and so on — it is largely dead now. But it had, for all that, an important point to make, which, however we may feel about trying to define charisma or alienation in terms of operations, retains a certain force: if you want to understand what a science is, you should look in the first instance not at its theories or its findings, and certainly not at what its apologists say about it; you should look at what the practitioners of it do.

In anthropology, or anyway social anthropology, what the practitioners do is ethnography. And it is in understanding what ethnography is, or more exactly *what doing ethnography is,* that a start can be made toward grasping what anthropological analysis amounts to as a form of knowledge. This, it must immediately be said, is not a matter of methods. From one point of view, that of the textbook, doing ethnography is establishing rapport, selecting informants, transcribing texts, taking genealogies, mapping fields, keeping a diary, and so on. But it is not these things, techniques and received procedures, that define the enterprise. What defines it is the kind of intellectual effort it is: an elaborate venture in, to borrow a notion from Gilbert Ryle, "thick description."

Ryle's discussion of "thick description" appears in two recent essays of his (now reprinted in the second volume of his *Collected Papers*) addressed to the general question of what, as he puts it, *"Le Penseur"* is doing: "Thinking and Reflecting" and "The Thinking of Thoughts." Consider, he says, two boys rapidly contracting the eyelids of their right eyes. In one, this is an involuntary twitch; in the other, a conspiratorial signal to a friend. The two movements are, as movements, identical; from an I-am-a-camera, "phenomenalistic" observation of them alone, one could not tell which was twitch and which was wink, or indeed whether both or either was twitch or wink. Yet the difference, however unphotographable, between a twitch and a wink is vast; as anyone unfortunate enough to have had the first taken for the second knows. The winker is communicating, and indeed communicating in a quite precise and special way: (1) deliberately, (2) to someone in particular, (3) to impart a particular message, (4) according to a socially established code, and (5) without cognizance of the rest of the company. As Ryle points out, the winker has not done two things, contracted his eyelids and winked, while the twitcher has done only one, contracted his eyelids. Contracting your eyelids on purpose when there exists a public code in which so doing counts as a conspiratorial signal *is* winking. That's all there is to it: a speck of behavior, a fleck of culture, and — *voilà!* — a gesture.

That, however, is just the beginning. Suppose, he continues, there is a third boy, who, "to give malicious amusement to his cronies," parodies the first boy's wink, as amateurish, clumsy, obvious, and so on. He, of course, does this in the same way the second boy winked and the first twitched: by contracting his right eyelid. Only this boy is neither winking nor twitching, he is parodying someone else's, as he takes it, laughable, attempt at winking. Here, too, a socially established code exists (he will "wink" laboriously, overobviously, perhaps adding a grimace — the usual artifices of the clown); and so also does a message. Only now it is not conspiracy but ridicule that is in the air. If the others think he is actually winking, his whole project misfires as completely, though with somewhat different results, as if they think he is twitching. One can go further: uncertain of his mimicking abilities, the would-be satirist may practice at home before the mirror, in which case he is not twitching, winking, or parodying, but rehearsing; though so far as what a camera, a radical behaviorist, or a believer in protocol sentences would record he is just rapidly contracting his right eyelids like all the others. Complexities are possible, if not practically without end, at least logically so. The original winker might, for example, actually have been fake-winking, say, to mislead outsiders into imagining there was a conspiracy afoot when there in fact was not, in which case our descriptions of what the parodist is parodying and the rehearser rehearsing of course shift accordingly. But the point is that between what Ryle calls the "thin description" of what the rehearser (parodist, winker, twitcher . . .) is doing ("rapidly contracting his right eyelids") and the "thick description" of what he is doing ("practicing a burlesque of a friend faking a wink to deceive an innocent into thinking a conspiracy is in motion") lies the object of ethnography: a stratified hierarchy of meaningful structures in terms of which twitches, winks, fake-winks, parodies, rehearsals of parodies are produced, perceived, and interpreted, and without which they would not (not even the zero-form twitches, which, *as a cultural category,* are as much nonwinks as winks are nontwitches) in fact exist, no matter what anyone did or didn't do with his eyelids.

Like so many of the little stories Oxford philosophers like to make up for themselves, all this winking, fake-winking, burlesque-fake-winking, rehearsed-burlesque-fake-winking, may seem a bit artificial. In way of adding a more empirical note, let me give, deliberately unpreceded by any prior explanatory comment at all, a not untypical excerpt from my own field journal to demonstrate that, however evened off for didactic purposes, Ryle's example presents an image only too exact of the sort of piled-up structures of inference and implication through which an ethnographer is continually trying to pick his way:

> The French [the informant said] had only just arrived. They set up twenty or so small forts between here, the town, and the Marmusha area up in the middle of the mountains, placing them on promontories so they could survey the countryside. But for all this they couldn't guarantee safety, especially at night, so although the *mezrag,* tradepact, system was supposed to be legally abolished it in fact continued as before.
>
> One night, when Cohen (who speaks fluent Berber), was up there, at Marmusha, two other Jews who were traders to a neighboring tribe

came by to purchase some goods from him. Some Berbers, from yet another neighboring tribe, tried to break into Cohen's place, but he fired his rifle in the air. (Traditionally, Jews were not allowed to carry weapons; but at this period things were so unsettled many did so anyway.) This attracted the attention of the French and the marauders fled.

The next night, however, they came back, one of them disguised as a woman who knocked on the door with some sort of a story. Cohen was suspicious and didn't want to let "her" in, but the other Jews said, "oh, it's all right, it's only a woman." So they opened the door and the whole lot came pouring in. They killed the two visiting Jews, but Cohen managed to barricade himself in an adjoining room. He heard the robbers planning to burn him alive in the shop after they removed his goods, and so he opened the door and, laying about him wildly with a club, managed to escape through a window.

He went up to the fort, then, to have his wounds dressed, and complained to the local commandant, one Captain Dumari, saying he wanted his 'ar — i.e., four or five times the value of the merchandise stolen from him. The robbers were from a tribe which had not yet submitted to French authority and were in open rebellion against it, and he wanted authorization to go with his *mezrag*-holder, the Marmusha tribal *sheikh,* to collect the indemnity that, under traditional rules, he had coming to him. Captain Dumari couldn't officially give him permission to do this, because of the French prohibition of the *mezrag* relationship, but he gave him verbal authorization, saying, "If you get killed, it's your problem."

So the *sheikh,* the Jew, and a small company of armed Marmushans went off ten or fifteen kilometers up into the rebellious area, where there were of course no French, and, sneaking up, captured the thief-tribe's shepherd and stole its herds. The other tribe soon came riding out on horses after them, armed with rifles and ready to attack. But when they saw who the "sheep thieves" were, they thought better of it and said, "all right, we'll talk." They couldn't really deny what had happened — that some of their men had robbed Cohen and killed the two visitors — and they weren't prepared to start the serious feud with the Marmusha a scuffle with the invading party would bring on. So the two groups talked, and talked, and talked, there on the plain amid the thousands of sheep, and decided finally on five-hundred-sheep damages. The two armed Berber groups then lined up on their horses at opposite ends of the plain, with the sheep herded between them, and Cohen, in his black gown, pillbox hat, and flapping slippers, went out alone among the sheep, picking out, one by one and at his own good speed, the best ones for his payment.

So Cohen got his sheep and drove them back to Marmusha. The French, up in their fort, heard them coming from some distance ("Ba, ba, ba" said Cohen, happily, recalling the image) and said, "What the hell is that?" And Cohen said, "That is my 'ar." The French couldn't believe he had actually done what he said he had done, and accused him of being a spy for the rebellious Berbers, put him in prison, and took his sheep. In the town, his family, not having heard from him in so long a time, thought he was dead. But after a while the French released him and he came back home, but without his sheep. He then went to the Colonel in the town, the Frenchman in charge of the whole region, to complain. But the Colonel said, "I can't do anything about the matter. It's not my problem."

Quoted raw, a note in a bottle, this passage conveys, as any similar one similarly presented would do, a fair sense of how much goes into ethnographic description of even the most elemental sort — how extraordinarily "thick" it is. In finished anthropological writings, including those collected here, this fact — that what we call our data are really our own constructions of other people's constructions of what they and their compatriots are up to — is obscured because most of what we need to comprehend a particular event, ritual, custom, idea, or whatever is insinuated as background information before the thing itself is directly examined. (Even to reveal that this little drama took place in the highlands of central Morocco in 1912 — and was recounted there in 1968 — is to determine much of our understanding of it.) There is nothing particularly wrong with this, and it is in any case inevitable. But it does lead to a view of anthropological research as rather more of an observational and rather less of an interpretive activity than it really is. Right down at the factual base, the hard rock, insofar as there is any, of the whole enterprise, we are already explicating: and worse, explicating explications. Winks upon winks upon winks.

Analysis, then, is sorting out the structures of signification — what Ryle called established codes, a somewhat misleading expression, for it makes the enterprise sound too much like that of the cipher clerk when it is much more like that of the literary critic — and determining their social ground and import. Here, in our text, such sorting would begin with distinguishing the three unlike frames of interpretation ingredient in the situation, Jewish, Berber, and French, and would then move on to show how (and why) at that time, in that place, their copresence produced a situation in which systematic misunderstanding reduced traditional form to social farce. What tripped Cohen up, and with him the whole, ancient pattern of social and economic relationships within which he functioned, was a confusion of tongues.

I shall come back to this too-compacted aphorism later, as well as to the details of the text itself. The point for now is only that ethnography is thick description. What the ethnographer is in fact faced with — except when (as, of course, he must do) he is pursuing the more automatized routines of data collection — is a multiplicity of complex conceptual structures, many of them superimposed upon or knotted into one another, which are at once strange, irregular, and inexplicit, and which he must contrive somehow first to grasp and then to render. And this is true at the most down-to-earth, jungle fieldwork levels of his activity: interviewing informants, observing rituals, eliciting kin terms, tracing property lines, censusing households . . . writing his journal. Doing ethnography is like trying to read (in the sense of "construct a reading of") a manuscript — foreign, faded, full of ellipses, incoherencies, suspicious emendations, and tendentious commentaries, but written not in conventionalized graphs of sound but in transient examples of shaped behavior.

III

Culture, this acted document, thus is public, like a burlesqued wink or a mock sheep raid. Though ideational, it does not exist in someone's head; though unphysical, it is not an occult entity. The interminable, because unterminable, debate within anthropology as to whether culture is "subjective" or "objective," together with the mutual exchange of intellectual insults ("idealist!" — "materialist!"; "mentalist!" — "behaviorist!"; "impressionist!" — "positivist!") which accompanies it, is wholly misconceived. Once human behavior is seen as (most of the time; there *are* true twitches) symbolic action — action which, like phonation in speech, pigment in painting, line in writing, or sonance in music, signifies — the question as to whether culture is patterned conduct or a frame of mind, or even the two somehow mixed together, loses sense. The thing to ask about a burlesqued wink or a mock sheep raid is not what their ontological status is. It is the same as that of rocks on the one hand and dreams on the other — they are things of this world. The thing to ask is what their import is: what it is, ridicule or challenge, irony or anger, snobbery or pride, that, in their occurrence and through their agency, is getting said.

This may seem like an obvious truth, but there are a number of ways to obscure it. One is to imagine that culture is a self-contained "superorganic" reality with forces and purposes of its own; that is, to reify it. Another is to claim that it consists in the brute pattern of behavioral events we observe in fact to occur in some identifiable community or other; that is, to reduce it. But though both these confusions still exist, and doubtless will be always with us, the main source of theoretical muddlement in contemporary anthropology is a view which developed in reaction to them and is right now very widely held — namely, that, to quote Ward Goodenough, perhaps its leading proponent, "culture [is located] in the minds and hearts of men."

Variously called ethnoscience, componential analysis, or cognitive anthropology (a terminological wavering which reflects a deeper uncertainty), this school of thought holds that culture is composed of psychological structures by means of which individuals or groups of individuals guide their behavior. "A society's culture," to quote Goodenough again, this time in a passage which has become the *locus classicus* of the whole movement, "consists of whatever it is one has to know or believe in order to operate in a manner acceptable to its members." And from this view of what culture is follows a view, equally assured, of what describing it is — the writing out of systematic rules, an ethnographic algorithm, which, if followed, would make it possible so to operate, to pass (physical appearance aside) for a native. In such a way, extreme subjectivism is married to extreme formalism, with the expected result: an explosion of debate as to whether particular analyses (which come in the form of taxonomies, paradigms, tables, trees, and other ingenuities) reflect what the natives "really" think or are merely clever simulations, logically equivalent but substantively different, of what they think.

As, on first glance, this approach may look close enough to the one being developed here to be mistaken for it, it is useful to be explicit as to what divides them. If, leaving our winks and sheep behind for the moment, we take, say, a Beethoven quartet as an, admittedly rather special but, for these purposes, nicely illustrative, sample of culture, no one would, I think, identify it with its score, with the skills and knowledge needed to play it, with the understanding of it possessed by its performers or auditors, nor, to take care, *en passant,* of the reductionists and reifiers, with a particular performance of it or with some mysterious entity transcending material existence. The "no one" is perhaps too strong here, for there are always incorrigibles. But that a Beethoven quartet is a temporally developed tonal structure, a coherent sequence of modeled sound — in a word, music — and not anybody's knowledge of or belief about anything, including how to play it, is a proposition to which most people are, upon reflection, likely to assent.

To play the violin it is necessary to possess certain habits, skills, knowledge, and talents, to be in the mood to play, and (as the old joke goes) to have a violin. But violin playing is neither the habits, skills, knowledge, and so on, nor the mood, nor (the notion believers in "material culture" apparently embrace) the violin. To make a trade pact in Morocco, you have to do certain things in certain ways (among others, cut, while chanting Quranic Arabic, the throat of a lamb before the assembled, undeformed, adult male members of your tribe) and to be possessed of certain psychological characteristics (among others, a desire for distant things). But a trade pact is neither the throat cutting nor the desire, though it is real enough, as seven kinsmen of our Marmusha sheikh discovered when, on an earlier occasion, they were executed by him following the theft of one mangy, essentially valueless sheepskin from Cohen.

Culture is public because meaning is. You can't wink (or burlesque one) without knowing what counts as winking or how, physically, to contract your eyelids, and you can't conduct a sheep raid (or mimic one) without knowing what it is to steal a sheep and how practically to go about it. But to draw from such truths the conclusion that knowing how to wink is winking and knowing how to steal a sheep is sheep raiding is to betray as deep a confusion as, taking thin descriptions for thick, to identify winking with eyelid contractions or sheep raiding with chasing woolly animals out of pastures. The cognitivist fallacy — that culture consists (to quote another spokesman for the movement, Stephen Tyler) of "mental phenomena which can [he means "should"] be analyzed by formal methods similar to those of mathematics and logic" — is as destructive of an effective use of the concept as are the behaviorist and idealist fallacies to which it is a misdrawn correction. Perhaps, as its errors are more sophisticated and its distortions subtler, it is even more so.

The generalized attack on privacy theories of meaning is, since early Husserl and late Wittgenstein, so much a part of modern thought that it need not be developed once more here. What is necessary is to see to it that the news of it reaches anthropology; and in particular that it is made clear that to say that culture consists of socially established structures of meaning in terms of which people do such things as signal conspiracies and join them or perceive insults and answer them, is no more to say that it is a psychological phenomenon, a characteristic of someone's mind, personality, cognitive structure, or whatever, than to say that Tantrism, genetics, the progressive form of the verb, the classification of wines, the Common Law, or the notion of "a conditional curse" (as Westermarck defined the concept of *'ar* in terms of which Cohen pressed his claim to damages) is. What, in a place like Morocco, most prevents those of us who grew up winking other winks or attending other sheep from grasping what people are up to is not ignorance as to how cognition works (though, especially as, one assumes, it works the same among them as it does among us, it would greatly help to have less of that too) as a lack of familiarity with the imaginative universe within which their acts are signs. As Wittgenstein has been invoked, he may as well be quoted:

> We . . . say of some people that they are transparent to us. It is, however, important as regards this observation that one human being can be a complete enigma to another. We learn this when we come into a strange country with entirely strange traditions; and, what is more, even given a mastery of the country's language. We do not *understand* the people. (And not because of not knowing what they are saying to themselves.) We cannot find our feet with them.

IV

Finding our feet, an unnerving business which never more than distantly succeeds, is what ethnographic research consists of as a personal experience; trying to formulate the basis on which one imagines, always excessively, one has found them is what anthropological writing consists of as a scientific endeavor. We are not, or at least I am not, seeking either to become natives (a compromised word in any case) or to mimic them. Only romantics or spies would seem to find point in that. We are seeking, in the widened sense of the term in which it encompasses very much more than talk, to converse with them, a matter a great deal more difficult, and not only with strangers, than is commonly recognized. "If speaking *for* someone else seems to be a mysterious process," Stanley Cavell has remarked, "that may be because speaking *to* someone does not seem mysterious enough."

Looked at in this way, the aim of anthropology is the enlargement of the universe of human discourse. That is not, of course, its only aim — instruction, amusement, practical counsel, moral advance, and the discovery of natural order in human behavior are others; nor is anthropology the only discipline which pursues it. But it is an aim to which a semiotic concept of culture is peculiarly well adapted. As interworked systems of construable signs (what, ignoring provincial usages, I would call symbols), culture is not a power, something to which social events, behaviors, institutions, or processes can be causally attributed; it is a context, something within which they can be intelligibly — that is, thickly — described.

The famous anthropological absorption with the (to us) exotic — Berber horsemen, Jewish peddlers, French Legionnaires — is, thus, essentially a device for displacing the dulling sense of familiarity with which the mysteriousness of our own ability to relate perceptively to one another is concealed from us. Looking at the ordinary in places where it takes unaccustomed forms brings out not, as has so often been claimed, the arbitrariness of human behavior (there is nothing especially arbitrary about taking sheep theft for insolence in Morocco), but the degree to which its meaning varies according to the pattern of life by which it is informed. Understanding a people's culture exposes their normalness without reducing their particularity. (The more I manage to follow what the Moroccans are up to, the more logical, and the more singular, they seem.) It renders them accessible: setting them in the frame of their own banalities, it dissolves their opacity.

It is this maneuver, usually too casually referred to as "seeing things from the actor's point of view," too bookishly as "the *verstehen* approach," or too technically as "emic analysis," that so often leads to the notion that anthropology is a variety of either long-distance mind reading or cannibalisle fantasizing, and which, for someone anxious to navigate past the wrecks of a dozen sunken philosophies, must therefore be executed with a great deal of care. Nothing is more necessary to comprehending what anthropological interpretation is, and the degree to which it *is* interpretation, than an exact understanding of what it means — and what it does not mean — to say that our formulations of other peoples' symbol systems must be actor-oriented.[1]

What it means is that descriptions of Berber, Jewish, or French culture must be cast in terms of the constructions we imagine Berbers, Jews, or Frenchmen to place upon what they live through, the formulae they use to define what happens to them. What it does not mean is that such descrip-

---

[1] Not only other peoples': anthropology *can* be trained on the culture of which it is itself a part, and it increasingly is; a fact of profound importance, but which, as it raises a few tricky and rather special second order problems, I shall put to the side for the moment.

tions are themselves Berber, Jewish, or French — that is, part of the reality they are ostensibly describing; they are anthropological — that is, part of a developing system of scientific analysis. They must be cast in terms of the interpretations to which persons of a particular denomination subject their experience, because that is what they profess to be descriptions of; they are anthropological because it is, in fact, anthropologists who profess them. Normally, it is not necessary to point out quite so laboriously that the object of study is one thing and the study of it another. It is clear enough that the physical world is not physics and *A Skeleton Key to Finnegans Wake* not *Finnegans Wake*. But, as, in the study of culture, analysis penetrates into the very body of the object — that is, *we begin with our own interpretations of what our informants are up to, or think they are up to, and then systematize those* — the line between (Moroccan) culture as a natural fact and (Moroccan) culture as a theoretical entity tends to get blurred. All the more so, as the latter is presented in the form of an actor's-eye description of (Moroccan) conceptions of everything from violence, honor, divinity, and justice, to tribe, property, patronage, and chiefship.

In short, anthropological writings are themselves interpretations, and second and third order ones to boot. (By definition, only a "native" makes first order ones: it's *his* culture.)[2] They are, thus, fictions; fictions, in the sense that they are "something made," "something fashioned" — the original meaning of *fictiō* — not that they are false, unfactual, or merely "as if" thought experiments. To construct actor-oriented descriptions of the involvements of a Berber chieftain, a Jewish merchant, and a French soldier with one another in 1912 Morocco is clearly an imaginative act, not all that different from constructing similar descriptions of, say, the involvements with one another of a provincial French doctor, his silly, adulterous wife, and her feckless lover in nineteenth-century France. In the latter case, the actors are represented as not having existed and the events as not having happened, while in the former they are represented as actual, or as having been so. This is a difference of no mean importance; indeed, precisely the one Madame Bovary had difficulty grasping. But the importance does not lie in the fact that her story was created while Cohen's was only noted. The conditions of their creation, and the point of it (to say nothing of the manner and the quality) differ. But the one is as much a *fictiō* — "a making" — as the other.

Anthropologists have not always been as aware as they might be of this

[2] The order problem is, again, complex. Anthropological works based on other anthropological works (Lévi-Strauss', for example) may, of course, be fourth order or higher, and informants frequently, even habitually, make second order interpretations — what have come to be known as "native models." In literate cultures, where "native" interpretation can proceed to higher levels — in connection with the Maghreb, one has only to think of Ibn Khaldun; with the United States, Margaret Mead — these matters become intricate indeed.

fact: that although culture exists in the trading post, the hill fort, or the sheep run, anthropology exists in the book, the article, the lecture, the museum display, or, sometimes nowadays, the film. To become aware of it is to realize that the line between mode of representation and substantive content is as undrawable in cultural analysis as it is in painting; and that fact in turn seems to threaten the objective status of anthropological knowledge by suggesting that its source is not social reality but scholarly artifice.

It does threaten it, but the threat is hollow. The claim to attention of an ethnographic account does not rest on its author's ability to capture primitive facts in faraway places and carry them home like a mask or a carving, but on the degree to which he is able to clarify what goes on in such places, to reduce the puzzlement — what manner of men are these? — to which unfamiliar acts emerging out of unknown backgrounds naturally give rise. This raises some serious problems of verification, all right — or, if "verification" is too strong a word for so soft a science (I, myself, would prefer "appraisal"), of how you can tell a better account from a worse one. But that is precisely the virtue of it. If ethnography is thick description and ethnographers those who are doing the describing, then the determining question for any given example of it, whether a field journal squib or a Malinowski-sized monograph, is whether it sorts winks from twitches and real winks from mimicked ones. It is not against a body of uninterpreted data, radically thinned descriptions, that we must measure the cogency of our explications, but against the power of the scientific imagination to bring us into touch with the lives of strangers. It is not worth it, as Thoreau said, to go round the world to count the cats in Zanzibar.

V

Now, this proposition, that it is not in our interest to bleach human behavior of the very properties that interest us before we begin to examine it, has sometimes been escalated into a larger claim: namely, that as it is only those properties that interest us, we need not attend, save cursorily, to behavior at all. Culture is most effectively treated, the argument goes, purely as a symbolic system (the catch phrase is, "in its own terms"), by isolating its elements, specifying the internal relationships among those elements, and then characterizing the whole system in some general way — according to the core symbols around which it is organized, the underlying structures of which it is a surface expression, or the ideological principles upon which it is based. Though a distinct improvement over "learned behavior" and "mental phenomena" notions of what culture is, and the source of some of the most powerful theoretical ideas in contemporary anthropology, this hermetical approach to things seems to me to run the danger (and increasingly to have been overtaken by it) of locking cultural analysis away from its proper object, the informal logic of actual life. There is little profit in extricating a concept from the defects of psychologism only to plunge it immediately into those of schematicism.

Behavior must be attended to, and with some exactness, because it is through the flow of behavior — or, more precisely, social action — that cultural forms find articulation. They find it as well, of course, in various sorts of artifacts, and various states of consciousness; but these draw their meaning from the role they play (Wittgenstein would say their "use") in an ongoing pattern of life, not from any intrinsic relationships they bear to one another. It is what Cohen, the sheikh, and "Captain Dumari" were doing when they tripped over one another's purposes — pursuing trade, defending honor, establishing dominance — that created our pastoral drama, and that is what the drama is, therefore, "about." Whatever, or wherever, symbol systems "in their own terms" may be, we gain empirical access to them by inspecting events, not by arranging abstracted entities into unified patterns.

A further implication of this is that coherence cannot be the major test of validity for a cultural description. Cultural systems must have a minimal degree of coherence, else we would not call them systems; and, by observation, they normally have a great deal more. But there is nothing so coherent as a paranoid's delusion or a swindler's story. The force of our interpretations cannot rest, as they are now so often made to do, on the tightness with which they hold together, or the assurance with which they are argued. Nothing has done more, I think, to discredit cultural analysis than the construction of impeccable depictions of formal order in whose actual existence nobody can quite believe.

If anthropological interpretation is constructing a reading of what happens, then to divorce it from what happens — from what, in this time or that place, specific people say, what they do, what is done to them, from the whole vast business of the world — is to divorce it from its applications and render it vacant. A good interpretation of anything — a poem, a person, a history, a ritual, an institution, a society — takes us into the heart of that of which it is the interpretation. When it does not do that, but leads us instead somewhere else — into an admiration of its own elegance, of its author's cleverness, or of the beauties of Euclidean order — it may have its intrinsic charms; but it is something else than what the task at hand — figuring out what all that rigamarole with the sheep is about — calls for.

The rigamarole with the sheep — the sham theft of them, the reparative transfer of them, the political confiscation of them — is (or was) essentially a social discourse, even if, as I suggested earlier, one conducted in multiple tongues and as much in action as in words.

Claiming his 'ar, Cohen invoked the trade pact; recognizing the claim, the sheikh challenged the offenders' tribe; accepting responsibility, the offenders' tribe paid the indemnity; anxious to make clear to sheikhs and peddlers alike who was now in charge here, the French showed the imperial hand. As in any discourse, code does not determine conduct, and what was actually said need not have been. Cohen might not have, given its illegitimacy in Protectorate eyes, chosen to press his claim. The sheikh might, for similar reasons, have rejected it. The offenders' tribe, still resisting French authority, might have decided to regard the raid as "real" and fight rather than negotiate. The French, were they more *habile* and less *dur* (as, under Mareschal Lyautey's seigniorial tutelage, they later in fact became), might have permitted Cohen to keep his sheep, winking — as we say — at the continuance of the trade pattern and its limitation to their authority. And there are other possibilities: the Marmushans might have regarded the French action as too great an insult to bear and gone into dissidence themselves; the French might have attempted not just to clamp down on Cohen but to bring the sheikh himself more closely to heel; and Cohen might have concluded that between renegade Berbers and Beau Geste soldiers, driving trade in the Atlas highlands was no longer worth the candle and retired to the better-governed confines of the town. This, indeed, is more or less what happened, somewhat further along, as the Protectorate moved toward genuine sovereignty. But the point here is not to describe what did or did not take place in Morocco. (From this simple incident one can widen out into enormous complexities of social experience.) It is to demonstrate what a piece of anthropological interpretation consists in: tracing the curve of a social discourse; fixing it into an inspectable form.

The ethnographer "inscribes" social discourse; *he writes it down.* In so doing, he turns it from a passing event, which exists only in its own moment of occurrence, into an account, which exists in its inscriptions and can be reconsulted. The sheikh is long dead, killed in the process of being, as the French called it, "pacified"; "Captain Dumari," his pacifier, lives, retired to his souvenirs, in the south of France; and Cohen went last year, part refugee, part pilgrim, part dying patriarch, "home" to Israel. But what they, in my extended sense, "said" to one another on an Atlas plateau sixty years ago is — very far from perfectly — preserved for study. "What," Paul Ricoeur, from whom this whole idea of the inscription of action is borrowed and somewhat twisted, asks, "what does writing fix?"

> Not the event of speaking, but the "said" of speaking, where we understand by the "said" of speaking that intentional exteriorization constitutive of the aim of discourse thanks to which the *sagen* — the saying — wants to become *Aus-sage* — the enunciation, the enunciated. In short, what we write is the *noema* ["thought," "content," "gist"] of the speaking. It is the meaning of the speech event, not the event as event.

This is not itself so very "said" — if Oxford philosophers run to little stories, phenomenological ones run to large sentences; but it brings us anyway to a more precise answer to our generative question, "What does the ethnographer do?" — he writes.[3] This, too, may seem a less than startling discovery, and to someone familiar with the current "literature," an implausible one. But as the standard answer to our question has been, "He observes, he records, he analyzes" — a kind of *veni, vidi, vici* conception of the matter — it may have more deep-going consequences than are at first apparent, not the least of which is that distinguishing these three phases of knowledge-seeking may not, as a matter of fact, normally be possible; and, indeed, as autonomous "operations" they may not in fact exist.

The situation is even more delicate, because, as already noted, what we inscribe (or try to) is not raw social discourse, to which, because, save very marginally or very specially, we are not actors, we do not have direct access, but only that small part of it which our informants can lead us into understanding.[4] This is not as fatal as it sounds, for, in fact, not all Cretans are liars, and it is not necessary to know everything in order to understand something. But it does make the view of anthropological analysis as the conceptual manipulation of discovered facts, a logical reconstruction of a mere reality, seem rather lame. To set forth symmetrical crystals of significance, purified of the material complexity in which they were located, and then attribute their existence to autogenous principles of order, universal properties of the human mind, or vast, a priori *weltanschauungen,* is to pretend a science that does not exist and imagine a reality that cannot be found. Cultural analysis is (or should be) guessing at meanings, assessing the guesses, and drawing explanatory conclusions from the better guesses, not discovering the Continent of Meaning and mapping out its bodiless landscape.

VI

So, there are three characteristics of ethnographic description: it is interpretive; what it is interpretive of is the flow of social discourse; and the interpreting involved consists in trying to rescue the "said" of such discourse from its perishing occasions and fix it in perusable terms. The *kula* is gone or altered; but, for better or worse, *The Argonauts of the Western Pacific* remains. But there is, in addition, a fourth characteristic of such description, at least as I practice it: it is microscopic.

[3] Or, again, more exactly, "inscribes." Most ethnography is in fact to be found in books and articles, rather than in films, records, museum displays, or whatever; but even in them there are, of course, photographs, drawings, diagrams, tables, and so on. Self-consciousness about modes of representation (not to speak of experiments with them) has been very lacking in anthropology.

[4] So far as it has reinforced the anthropologist's impulse to engage himself with his informants as persons rather than as objects, the notion of "participant observation" has been a valuable one. But, to the degree it has led the anthropologist to block from his view the very special, culturally bracketed nature of his own role and to imagine himself something more than an interested (in both senses of that word) sojourner, it has been our most powerful source of bad faith.

This is not to say that there are no large-scale anthropological interpretations of whole societies, civilizations, world events, and so on. Indeed, it is such extension of our analyses to wider contexts that, along with their theoretical implications, recommends them to general attention and justifies our constructing them. No one really cares anymore, not even Cohen (well . . . maybe, Cohen), about those sheep as such. History may have its unobtrusive turning points, "great noises in a little room"; but this little go-round was surely not one of them.

It is merely to say that the anthropologist characteristically approaches such broader interpretations and more abstract analyses from the direction of exceedingly extended acquaintances with extremely small matters. He confronts the same grand realities that others — historians, economists, political scientists, sociologists — confront in more fateful settings: Power, Change, Faith, Oppression, Work, Passion, Authority, Beauty, Violence, Love, Prestige; but he confronts them in contexts obscure enough — places like Marmusha and lives like Cohen's — to take the capital letters off them. These all-too-human constancies, "those big words that make us all afraid," take a homely form in such homely contexts. But that is exactly the advantage. There are enough profundities in the world already.

Yet, the problem of how to get from a collection of ethnographic miniatures on the order of our sheep story — an assortment of remarks and anecdotes — to wall-sized culturescapes of the nation, the epoch, the continent, or the civilization is not so easily passed over with vague allusions to the virtues of concreteness and the down-to-earth mind. For a science born in Indian tribes, Pacific islands, and African lineages and subsequently seized with grander ambitions, this has come to be a major methodological problem, and for the most part a badly handled one. The models that anthropologists have themselves worked out to justify their moving from local truths to general visions have been, in fact, as responsible for undermining the effort as anything their critics — sociologists obsessed with sample sizes, psychologists with measures, or economists with aggregates — have been able to devise against them.

Of these, the two main ones have been: the Jonesville-is-the-USA "microcosmic" model; and the Easter-Island-is-a-testing-case "natural experiment" model. Either heaven in a grain of sand, or the farther shores of possibility.

The Jonesville-is-America writ small (or America-is-Jonesville writ large) fallacy is so obviously one that the only thing that needs explanation is how people have managed to believe it and expected others to believe it. The notion that one can find the essence of national societies, civilizations, great religions, or whatever summed up and simplified in so-called typical small towns and villages is palpable nonsense. What one finds in small towns and villages is (alas) small-town or village life. If localized, microscopic studies were really dependent for their greater relevance upon such a premise — that they captured the great world in the little — they wouldn't have any relevance.

But, of course, they are not. The locus of study is not the object of study. Anthropologists don't study villages (tribes, towns, neighborhoods . . .); they study *in* villages. You can study different things in different places, and some things — for example, what colonial domination does to established frames of moral expectation — you can best study in confined localities. But that doesn't make the place what it is you are studying. In the remoter provinces of Morocco and Indonesia I have wrestled with the same questions other social scientists have wrestled with in more central locations — for example, how comes it that men's most importunate claims to humanity are cast in the accents of group pride? — and with about the same conclusiveness. One can add a dimension — one much needed in the present climate of size-up-and-solve social science; but that is all. There is a certain value, if you are going to run on about the exploitation of the masses in having seen a Javanese sharecropper turning earth in a tropical downpour or a Moroccan tailor embroidering kaftans by the light of a twenty-watt bulb. But the notion that this gives you the thing entire (and elevates you to some moral vantage ground from which you can look down upon the ethically less privileged) is an idea which only someone too long in the bush could possibly entertain.

The "natural laboratory" notion has been equally pernicious, not only because the analogy is false — what kind of a laboratory is it where *none* of the parameters are manipulable? — but because it leads to a notion that the data derived from ethnographic studies are purer, or more fundamental, or more solid, or less conditioned (the most favored word is "elementary") than those derived from other sorts of social inquiry. The great natural variation of cultural forms is, of course, not only anthropology's great (and wasting) resource, but the ground of its deepest theoretical dilemma: how is such variation to be squared with the biological unity of the human species? But it is not, even metaphorically, experimental variation, because the context in which it occurs varies along with it, and it is not possible (though there are those who try) to isolate the y's from x's to write a proper function.

The famous studies purporting to show that the Oedipus complex was backwards in the Trobriands, sex roles were upside down in Tchambuli, and the Pueblo Indians lacked aggression (it is characteristic that they were all negative — "but not in the South"), are, whatever their empirical validity may or may not be, not "scientifically tested and approved" hypotheses. They are interpretations, or misinterpretations, like any others, arrived at in the same way as any others, and as inherently inconclusive as any others, and the attempt to invest them with the authority of physical experimentation is but methodological sleight of hand. Ethnographic findings are not privileged, just particular: another country heard from. To regard them as anything more (*or anything less*) than that distorts both them and their implications, which are far profounder than mere primitivity, for social theory.

Another country heard from: the reason that protracted descriptions of distant sheep raids (and a really good ethnographer would have gone into what kind of sheep they were) have general relevance is that they present the sociological mind with bodied stuff on which to feed. The important thing about the anthropologist's findings is their complex specificness, their circumstantiality. It is with the kind of material produced by long-term, mainly (though not exclusively) qualitative, highly participative, and almost obsessively fine-comb field study in confined contexts that the mega-concepts with which contemporary social science is afflicted — legitimacy, modernization, integration, conflict, charisma, structure, . . . meaning — can be given the sort of sensible actuality that makes it possible to think not only realistically and concretely *about* them, but, what is more important, creatively and imaginatively *with* them.

The methodological problem which the microscopic nature of ethnography presents is both real and critical. But it is not to be resolved by regarding a remote locality as the world in a teacup or as the sociological equivalent of a cloud chamber. It is to be resolved — or, anyway, decently kept at bay — by realizing that social actions are comments on more than themselves; that where an interpretation comes from does not determine where it can be impelled to go. Small facts speak to large issues, winks to epistemology, or sheep raids to revolution, because they are made to.

VII

Which brings us, finally, to theory. The besetting sin of interpretive approaches to anything — literature, dreams, symptoms, culture — is that they tend to resist, or to be permitted to resist, conceptual articulation and thus to escape systematic modes of assessment. You either grasp an interpretation or you do not, see the point of it or you do not, accept it or you do not. Imprisoned in the immediacy of its own detail, it is presented as self-validating, or, worse, as validated by the supposedly developed sensitivities of the person who presents it; any attempt to cast what it says in terms other than its own is regarded as a travesty — as, the anthropologist's severest term of moral abuse, ethnocentric.

For a field of study which, however timidly (though I, myself, am not timid about the matter at all), asserts itself to be a science, this just will not do. There is no reason why the conceptual structure of a cultural interpretation should be any less formulable, and thus less susceptible to explicit canons of appraisal, than that of, say, a biological observation or a physical experiment — no reason except that the terms in which such formulations can be cast are, if not wholly nonexistent, very nearly so. We are reduced to insinuating theories because we lack the power to state them.

At the same time, it must be admitted that there are a number of characteristics of cultural interpretation which make the theoretical development of it more than usually difficult. The first is the need for theory to stay rather closer to the ground than tends to be the case in sciences more able to give themselves over to imaginative abstraction. Only short flights of ratiocination tend to be effective in anthropology; longer ones tend to drift off into logical dreams, academic bemusements with formal symmetry. The whole point of a semiotic approach to culture is, as I have said, to aid us in gaining access to the conceptual world in which our subjects live so that we can, in some extended sense of the term, converse with them. The tension between the pull of this need to penetrate an unfamiliar universe of symbolic action and the requirements of technical advance in the theory of culture, between the need to grasp and the need to analyze, is, as a result, both necessarily great and essentially irremovable. Indeed, the further theoretical development goes, the deeper the tension gets. This is the first condition for cultural theory: it is not its own master. As it is unseverable from the immediacies thick description presents, its freedom to shape itself in terms of its internal logic is rather limited. What generality it contrives to achieve grows out of the delicacy of its distinctions, not the sweep of its abstractions.

And from this follows a peculiarity in the way, as a simple matter of empirical fact, our knowledge of culture . . . cultures . . . a culture . . . grows: in spurts. Rather than following a rising curve of cumulative findings, cultural analysis breaks up into a disconnected yet coherent sequence of bolder and bolder sorties. Studies do build on other studies, not in the sense that they take up where the others leave off, but in the sense that, better informed and better conceptualized, they plunge more deeply into the same things. Every serious cultural analysis starts from a sheer beginning and ends where it manages to get before exhausting its intellectual impulse. Previously discovered facts are mobilized, previously developed concepts used, previously formulated hypotheses tried out; but the movement is not from already proven theorems to newly proven ones, it is from an awkward fumbling for the most elementary understanding to a supported claim that one has achieved that and surpassed it. A study is an advance if it is more incisive — whatever that may mean — than those that preceded it; but it less stands on their shoulders than, challenged and challenging, runs by their side.

It is for this reason, among others, that the essay, whether of thirty pages or three hundred, has seemed the natural genre in which to present cultural interpretations and the theories sustaining them, and why, if one looks for systematic treatises in the field, one is so soon disappointed, the more so if one finds any. Even inventory articles are rare here, and anyway of hardly more than bibliographical interest. The major theoretical contributions not only lie in specific studies — that is true in almost any field — but they are very difficult to abstract from such studies and integrate into anything one might call "culture theory" as such. Theoretical formulations hover so low over the interpretations they govern that they don't make much sense or hold much interest apart from them. This is so, not because they are not general (if they are not general, they are not theoretical), but because, stated independently of their applications, they seem either commonplace or vacant. One can, and this in fact is how the field progresses conceptually, take a line of theoretical attack developed in connection with one exercise in ethnographic interpretation and employ it in another, pushing it forward to greater precision and broader relevance; but one cannot write a "General Theory of Cultural Interpretation." Or, rather, one can, but there appears to be little profit in it, because the essential task of theory building here is not to codify abstract regularities but to make thick description possible, not to generalize across cases but to generalize within them.

To generalize within cases is usually called, at least in medicine and depth psychology, clinical inference. Rather than beginning with a set of observations and attempting to subsume them under a governing law, such inference begins with a set of (presumptive) signifiers and attempts to place them within an intelligible frame. Measures are matched to theoretical predictions, but symptoms (even when they are measured) are scanned for theoretical peculiarities — that is, they are diagnosed. In the study of culture the signifiers are not symptoms or clusters of symptoms, but symbolic acts or clusters of symbolic acts, and the aim is not therapy but the analysis of social discourse. But the way in which theory is used — to ferret out the unapparent import of things — is the same.

Thus we are led to the second condition of cultural theory: it is not, at least in the strict meaning of the term, predictive. The diagnostician doesn't predict measles; he decides that someone has them, or at the very most *anticipates* that someone is rather likely shortly to get them. But this limitation, which is real enough, has commonly been both misunderstood and exaggerated, because it has been taken to mean that cultural interpretation is merely post facto: that, like the peasant in the old story, we first shoot the holes in the fence and then paint the bull's-eyes around them. It is hardly to be denied that there is a good deal of that sort of thing around, some of it in prominent places. It is to be denied, however, that it is the inevitable outcome of a clinical approach to the use of theory.

It is true that in the clinical style of theoretical formulation, conceptualization is directed toward the task of generating interpretations of matters already in hand, not toward projecting outcomes of experimental manipulations or deducing future states of a determined system. But that does not mean that theory has only to fit (or, more carefully, to generate cogent interpretations of) realities past; it has also to survive — intellectually survive — realities to come. Although we formulate our interpretation of an outburst of winking or an instance of sheep-raiding after its occurrence, sometimes long after, the theoretical framework in terms of which such an interpretation is made must be capable of continuing to yield defensible interpretations as new social phenomena swim into view. Although one starts any effort at thick description, beyond the obvious and superficial, from a state of general bewilderment as to what the devil is going on — trying to find one's feet — one does not start (or ought not) intellectually empty-handed. Theoretical ideas are not created wholly anew in each study; as I have said, they are adopted from other, related studies, and, refined in the process, applied to new interpretive problems. If they cease being useful with respect to such problems, they tend to stop being used and are more or less abandoned. If they continue being useful, throwing up new understandings, they are further elaborated and go on being used.[5]

Such a view of how theory functions in an interpretive science suggests that the distinction, relative in any case, that appears in the experimental or observational sciences between "description" and "explanation" appears here as one, even more relative, between "inscription" ("thick description") and "specification" ("diagnosis") — between setting down the meaning particular social actions have for the actors whose actions they are, and stating, as explicitly as we can manage, what the knowledge thus attained demonstrates about the society in which it is found and, beyond that, about social life as such. Our double task is to uncover the conceptual structures that inform our subjects' acts, the "said" of social discourse, and to construct a system of analysis in whose terms what is generic to those structures, what belongs to them because they are what they are, will stand out against the other determinants of human behavior. In ethnography, the office of theory is to provide a vocabulary in which what symbolic action has to say about itself — that is, about the role of culture in human life — can be expressed. . . .

It is not only interpretation that goes all the way down to the most immediate observational level: the theory upon which such interpretation conceptually depends does so also. My interest in Cohen's story, like Ryle's in winks, grew out of some very general notions indeed. The "confusion of tongues" model — the view that social conflict is not something that happens when, out of weakness, indefiniteness, obsolescence, or neglect, cul-

---

[5] Admittedly, this is something of an idealization. Because theories are seldom if ever decisively disproved in clinical use but merely grow increasingly awkward, unproductive, strained, or vacuous, they often persist long after all but a handful of people (though *they* are often most passionate) have lost much interest in them. Indeed, so far as anthropology is concerned, it is almost more of a problem to get exhausted ideas out of the literature than it is to get productive ones in, and so a great deal more of theoretical discussion than one would prefer is critical rather than constructive, and whole careers have been devoted to hastening the demise of moribund notions. As the field advances one would hope that this sort of intellectual weed control would become a less prominent part of our activities. But, for the moment, it remains true that old theories tend less to die than to go into second editions.

tural forms cease to operate, but rather something which happens when, like burlesqued winks, such forms are pressed by unusual situations or unusual intentions to operate in unusual ways — is not an idea I got from Cohen's story. It is one, instructed by colleagues, students, and predecessors, I brought to it.

Our innocent-looking "note in a bottle" is more than a portrayal of the frames of meaning of Jewish peddlers, Berber warriors, and French proconsuls, or even of their mutual interference. It is an argument that to rework the pattern of social relationships is to rearrange the coordinates of the experienced world. Society's forms are culture's substance.

VIII

There is an Indian story — at least I heard it as an Indian story — about an Englishman who, having been told that the world rested on a platform which rested on the back of an elephant which rested in turn on the back of a turtle, asked (perhaps he was an ethnographer; it is the way they behave), what did the turtle rest on? Another turtle. And that turtle? "Ah, Sahib, after that it is turtles all the way down."

Such, indeed, is the condition of things. I do not know how long it would be profitable to meditate on the encounter of Cohen, the sheikh, and "Dumari" (the period has perhaps already been exceeded); but I do know that however long I did so I would not get anywhere near to the bottom of it. Nor have I ever gotten anywhere near to the bottom of anything I have ever written about. Cultural analysis is intrinsically incomplete. And, worse than that, the more deeply it goes the less complete it is. It is a strange science whose most telling assertions are its most tremulously based, in which to get somewhere with the matter at hand is to intensify the suspicion, both your own and that of others, that you are not quite getting it right. But that, along with plaguing subtle people with obtuse questions, is what being an ethnographer is like.

There are a number of ways to escape this — turning culture into folklore and collecting it, turning it into traits and counting it, turning it into institutions and classifying it, turning it into structures and toying with it. But they *are* escapes. The fact is that to commit oneself to a semiotic concept of culture and an interpretive approach to the study of it is to commit oneself to a view of ethnographic assertion as, to borrow W. B. Gallie's by now famous phrase, "essentially contestable." Anthropology, or at least interpretive anthropology, is a science whose progress is marked less by a perfection of consensus than by a refinement of debate. What gets better is the precision with which we vex each other. . . .

My own position in the midst of all this has been to try to resist subjectivism on the one hand and cabbalism on the other, to try to keep the analysis of symbolic forms as closely tied as I could to concrete social events and occasions, the public world of common life, and to organize it in such a way that the connections between theoretical formulations and descriptive interpretations were unobscured by appeals to dark sciences. I have never been impressed by the argument that, as complete objectivity is impossible in these matters (as, of course, it is), one might as well let one's sentiments run loose. As Robert Solow has remarked, that is like saying that as a perfectly aseptic environment is impossible, one might as well conduct surgery in a sewer. Nor, on the other hand, have I been impressed with claims that structural linguistics, computer engineering, or some other advanced form of thought is going to enable us to understand men without knowing them. Nothing will discredit a semiotic approach to culture more quickly than allowing it to drift into a combination of intuitionism and alchemy, no matter how elegantly the intuitions are expressed or how modern the alchemy is made to look.

The danger that cultural analysis, in search of all-too-deep-lying turtles, will lose touch with the hard surfaces of life — with the political, economic, stratificatory realities within which men are everywhere contained — and with the biological and physical necessities on which those surfaces rest, is an ever-present one. The only defense against it, and against, thus, turning cultural analysis into a kind of sociological aestheticism, is to train such analysis on such realities and such necessities in the first place. It is thus that I have written about nationalism, about violence, about identity, about human nature, about legitimacy, about revolution, about ethnicity, about urbanization, about status, about death, about time, and most of all about particular attempts by particular peoples to place these things in some sort of comprehensible, meaningful frame.

To look at the symbolic dimensions of social action — art, religion, ideology, science, law, morality, common sense — is not to turn away from the existential dilemmas of life for some empyrean realm of deemotionalized forms; it is to plunge into the midst of them. The essential vocation of interpretive anthropology is not to answer our deepest questions, but to make available to us answers that others, guarding other sheep in other valleys, have given, and thus to include them in the consultable record of what man has said.

Ethnography

Charles O. Frake

Introduction

Deficiencies in the way anthropologists practice ethnography stem not only from the very real difficulties inherent in fieldwork, but also from a failure to appreciate that good ethnography is an exercise in the construction of cultural theory. Ethnography is the science — and art — of cultural description. I believe we should eliminate the condescending "mere" that often occurs before "description" in anthropological discourse. Over the past decade the theoretical payoffs inherent in practicing ethnography and in worrying about ethnographic practice have continued to be demonstrated by many investigators with varied disciplinary affiliations and theoretical orientations. The present volume attests to that claim. Although these ethnographic efforts have not resulted in much noticeable agreement on a single coherent theory of culture, they have displayed some critical issues about the nature of culture and the limits of *a* culture in ways that other approaches to theory construction, dependent on a priori definitions of units and measures, have often obscured.

One who aspires to describe culture cannot avoid the fundamental issue: where to find it. Culture is to be found in the doings (and sayings) of people. The ethnographer goes to "the field" to capture these doings. The finally captured doing is typically enclosed in a phrase of the form: "the so and so's do such and such." The practice of ethnography has shown us that the referents of both terms of the ethnographic phrase, the subject so and so's as well as the predicated doings of such and such, are highly problematic.

How the so and so's get delimited — by the investigator and by themselves — is looming as a critical question for cultural theory, but it is a

Used by permission of the author. Copyright © 1983 by Charles O. Frake.
These remarks on ethnography were originally written in 1972 at the request of a National Institute of Mental Health Committee on Social and Cultural Processes. Although I did not refrain from presenting my own particular view of things, my discussion was directed at the Committee's presumed aim of improving the social science research support programs of NIMH. In this essay, with the interests of a different audience in mind, I have deleted sections of the original report dealing specifically with grant review problems and with the ethics of proposal writing, but, otherwise, the original is mostly intact. I use this introduction to expand somewhat on my theoretical arguments and to assess the 1972 review from the perspective of a decade later.

question which I sidestep here in a manner made familiar by ethnomethodologists. The ethnomethodologists' so and so's are called "members." I call mine "natives." I think they would recognize each other.

The basic issue with the description of doings hinges on whether or not they can be captured *as cultural objects* in categories preconstructed by investigators who, in their scientific sophistication, know better than the natives what the natives are doing. This so-called objective reporting of "what's really there" (in spite of what the natives might think) is seen by some investigators as necessary for the cross-cultural comparability upon which grand theory depends. These are investigators who would, in spite of Geertz's classic treatment of the phenomenon (this volume, pages 37–59) still record and count eye twitches as, say, objective measures of energy expenditure — never mind whether, for the natives, they are winks or blinks. Never mind, in other words, what the natives think.

The opposite point of view is that what the natives think is what in fact constitutes as cultural doings and cultural objects the body movements, vocal noises, and material artifacts produced by humans. Culture, the object of our description, resides within the thinking of natives. But thinking — and we must mean thinking in the broadest sense of what people think about, believe, ponder, and wonder, as well as how they calculate and infer — can only be seen through behavioral displays in social contexts. The human thinking that pervades these displays is never transparent; it always must be glimpsed through an interpretation of what some display might "mean." This opacity is as much a fact for natives as it is for ethnographers. Natives, too, must find out what is happening, what is getting done, around them. Natives must do ethnography in the conduct of their daily lives. It is in their social practice of ethnography, in their negotiated interpretations of their doings, that we find displayed the "thinking" that constitutes culture. And it is the natives, not the investigator, who must be accorded the privileged interpretation of their own cultural texts.

This conclusion addresses what remains the critical issue in ethnographic practice: if the success of an ethnography is a test of the cultural theory it implies, then how do we judge the adequacy of an ethnography? Much of the diversity and conflict in current cultural theory stem from varied attempts to meet or avoid this persistent issue. In spite of a number of perceptive recent discussions, the state of the art is little different today than it was a decade ago. Training in fieldwork techniques is, if anything, even more neglected. It is the elegance of the investigator's prose that still counts. The battle lines are drawn between advocates of the rich, juicy elegance of fine literature thickly packaged between hard covers, and those who push the lean, dry elegance of formal logic thinly sliced by Occam's razor. I see little prospect for abandoning this appeal to the rhetoric of our own discourse until we learn how to take the natives seriously as interpretive ethnographers of their own lives.

Ethnography as a Field

Anthropologists do not generally regard ethnography as a field of specialization comparable to areas such as social organization or political anthropology. To respond to a colleague's question "What's your field?" by saying "ethnography" evokes puzzled smiles. One does not ask of an anthropologist, "Is he an ethnographer?" but, "Is he a good ethnographer?" The professional ideal is that every anthropologist [1] does ethnography periodically. Some have built brilliant professional careers relying largely on other people's ethnography, but they lose points for such practices. Ethnography underlies just about every tradition of investigation within anthropology. Labeling the process through which an investigator confronts his or her primary data as "ethnography" is what best distinguishes an anthropologist from companion social/behavioral scientists.

Most research in anthropology somehow involves ethnography, but few studies focus on ethnography itself as a methodological or theoretical topic of investigation. Although the ideal anthropologist is a "good ethnographer," he or she is also not "just an ethnographer." Most anthropologists still equate ethnography with fieldwork, data gathering, and description. The tradition of the profession tells us that data gathering and description are not enough. We must have theory. Anthropology must be science, not natural history. Proponents of what is sometimes called "the new ethnography" have tried in the last decade to elevate ethnography to a theoretical topic in its own right, comparable to the role of descriptive theory in linguistics. But these efforts have had limited success.

Ethnography as Fieldwork

However they regard the nature of ethnography, anthropologists would all agree that when one does ethnography the first step is to "go to the field." Doing fieldwork has a hallowed place in an anthropologist's career. The science of anthropology is built on data obtained "in the field." Given this revered role of fieldwork, two things are surprising: First, it is not at all clear just what kind of work counts as fieldwork; second, very little attention is paid to training people to do it.

What is fieldwork? A sociologist going from door to door with a questionnaire in an American community doesn't get credit for doing fieldwork, but an anthropologist doing the same thing in highland New Guinea probably would. However much the modern anthropologist tries to deny it, the fieldwork image in fact still strongly entails exotic settings, strange cultures, unfamiliar languages, and a certain amount of suffering by the investigator. The ideal fieldworker lives in the exotic setting, adapts to the

[1] These remarks exclude archaeologists as well as linguists who professionally identify as anthropologists (a dying breed).

culture (bravely overcoming the "culture shock"), learns the awesomely difficult language, and thoroughly enjoys the experience in spite of the suffering. Minimally, I suppose, fieldwork requires reasonably prolonged and continuous face-to-face contact with people in the natural setting of their daily lives. Certainly conducting laboratory experiments, mailing questionnaires, and culling census data from government documents do not count as fieldwork.

Once "in the field," what does an ethnographer actually do? Anyone who has sat on grant review panels knows that what he does is to employ "traditional ethnographic methods." Ask an anthropologist to name one. He will say ". . . uh . . . well, there's the genealogical method, for example." It is true that the genealogical method is one procedure which the anthropologist can call his own and take some pride in. It is extremely useful to almost any kind of investigation; the way to ask questions is clear as is the ultimate objective and format. There is very little else in the way of standard field techniques that has these properties. Yet it is also true that, in the seventy years anthropologists have been employing this relatively straightforward and highly productive procedure, there has emerged no single best way to write down the answers to genealogical questions. Everyone figures it out individually. There has been no accumulated tradition of advances in data recording techniques. Advanced techniques such as genealogical recording for personal genealogies, kinship terminology, and household composition developed by A. K. Romney and his colleagues in the 1960s have been largely ignored beyond his circle of associates and students. The essential features of the Romney kin-type notation have been independently invented at least three times, and I have no doubt that somewhere in the Amazon jungle some ethnographer is inventing them again.

Of course there are a variety of devices, techniques, and methods available to the fieldworker (who takes time to learn them) for accomplishing particular tasks, things like cinemaphotography, projective tests, and ethnosemantic eliciting procedures. But, although they have sometimes been advocated as such (or claimed by critics to have been so advocated) none of these techniques are substitutes for prolonged observation, participation in daily life, flexible and sensitive questioning, and skilled use of a wide range of techniques. There are no shortcuts to good ethnography, but there ought to be some way to insure accumulated improvement in the quality of ethnographic work.

There are a number of reasons, some of them inherent in the nature of fieldwork, for the poor development of ethnographic techniques. The conditions of fieldwork are so varied that what works well in one situation may be impractical or even dangerous in another. Being a good fieldworker depends on qualities of sensitivity, adaptability, and insight that are difficult to train for or to identify in advance. Nevertheless there are many techniques of general utility which can be taught but rarely are: ways of recording and organizing field notes, elementary mapping, procedures for collecting plant and animal specimens, interviewing strategies, sampling techniques, etc. No amount of sensitivity, adaptability, and insight is of much use when the research problem requires knowing the areas of agricultural fields and the fieldworker has no idea how to find this out. Even techniques for recording and learning unfamiliar languages are not routinely taught to all students in most graduate programs. In fact systematic training in field linguistics is much less common now than a decade ago. These deficiencies in the development of ethnographic techniques are widely known, frequently lamented, and unremedied to this day.

Ethnographic Theory and Method

The common attitude that fieldwork is data collecting and analysis and "write up" take place after the fieldworker comes home underlies much of the inadequacy of ethnographic field technique. There is a lack of integration of data recording techniques, methods of analysis, and theory. Although they must be integrated in practice, these three phases of ethnographic work must be kept conceptually distinct (much of the controversy over "ethnoscientific methods" arose through the confounding — both by practitioners and critics — of technique with method). Ethnographic technique comprises the procedures through which the researcher compiles a record of events. Ethnographic method comprises the procedures through which he or she arrives at an ethnographic statement from an ethnographic record. Ethnographic theory is concerned with such questions as criteria for evaluating competing ethnographic statements, motivations for decisions about what to record, units of analysis, and the relation between elicited and observed data. These questions of course entail a theory of culture — a theory of what it is that is being described. Doing ethnography is a way of testing and building cultural theory independent of the particular theoretical concerns that motivated the investigation. There is plenty of bad description in the ethnographic literature, but there is no such thing as good "mere description." A good ethnographic statement is an assertion about the nature of culture.

Unlike American linguistics, which tends at any given period to be dominated by a single paradigm that defines the nature of the phenomenon to be accounted for (e.g. as behavioral or mental), states the basic questions to be asked, specifies procedures of research, and demands common standards of evaluation, American anthropology exhibits little agreement among practitioners on these issues at any one time. A diversity of descriptive theory, and consequently a diversity of methods and techniques, can be expected. The problem for the immediate future is not who has the right theory but, in particular research projects, explicitly integrating method and technique with an ethnographic theory of some sort.

The tradition within anthropology that has given the most explicit attention to these problems is the one commonly called "ethnoscience" or the "new ethnography." The unity of this tradition is mostly in the eyes of its critics. Certainly it is not a coherent paradigm of research. At least three kinds of interests get labeled as ethnoscience: concern with ethnographic method and theory; an interest in cognition and decision models motivated by the notion that culture is a mental phenomenon; and a methodological interest in lexical semantics. Some investigators manifest all three interests, but many do not.

The impetus for the concern with ethnographic theory was expressed in the 1950s by structural linguists, whose field was then in its glory of paradigmatic dominance. Three aspects of the linguistic paradigm most attracted anthropologists. First was its insistence on strict relativism; the units of analysis and their arrangements had to be discovered in the systems being described. Second was its faith in operationalism. Third was the fact that the data on which the analysis was based (a set of texts) could be made public. This meant that a linguistic statement could be evaluated by referring back to the data. Ethnographers, on the other hand, used predefined units of analysis (as exemplified by the categories of the Human Relations Area Files) and nonexplicit and intuitive procedures, which were never based on a public set of data and could only be evaluated in terms of the persuasive power of the ethnographer's rhetoric.

In one respect, however, early ethnoscientists radically revised the structuralist assumptions. Ethnoscientists were avowedly mentalistic both in their interpretation of structural linguistics and in their conception of culture. In what is probably the closest thing to a charter for the ethnoscience tradition, Ward Goodenough (1957) argued that culture was not observable behavior, events, and artifacts but the knowledge of these elements in people's heads. He also stated that linguistics was the best method ever devised for getting inside people's heads. He was talking at that time about behavioristic structural linguistics. This mentalistic reinterpretation of structural linguistics provided the basis of the ethnoscientific argument: culture is knowledge, and the way to get at knowledge is to apply linguistic methods both to cultural behavior and (especially) to meanings of words (structural linguistics eschewed the study of meaning as mentalistic). Theory and method were to be tested by doing ethnographic description. The joker in this package is that there must be some criteria for judging the success of an ethnographic statement. This problem has never been resolved.

This type of ethnographic theory arose in large part as a reaction to the standardization of ethnographic descriptive categories advocated by cross-cultural methodologists using the Human Relations Area Files. The most vocal attacks on the ethnoscience position came, however, from behavioristically oriented theorists. In the polemic and programmatic literature, a contrast was set up between those who believed in using verbal data to make inferences about what is going on inside people's heads and those who believed in the objective recording of "real" events. Fortunately few ethnographers have followed either extreme in practice. No ethnographer with any sense would purposely ignore either what people do or what people say about what they do.

A more serious blow to ethnoscience came from the linguists. In the 1960s a bloody paradigmatic revolution took place in linguistics. The new paradigm of transformational grammar was avowedly mentalistic, a welcome change, but it also renounced discovery procedures, operationalism, empiricism, and relativism. A language, when probed deeply enough, was no longer a cultural phenomenon but part of speakers' innate and universal competence as human beings.

The fact that linguists changed their paradigm doesn't necessarily mean that the old paradigm was wrong for the questions it asked or for the ethnographic applications proposed by anthropologists. Paradigms come and go. But it does mean that ethnographic theorists can no longer justify their paradigm by pointing to linguistics, which is probably a good thing.

Problems and Prospects

The vital, yet seemingly insoluble, problem for the field of ethnography is the absence of reasonable means of evaluating ethnographic descriptions. If we cannot assess the adequacy of a description, how can we judge the cultural theory it entails? Ideally, of course, a description, being a theory about a particular case, should make predictions that can be tested. Apart from the fact that there is little agreement about what should be predicted (behavior or native interpretations of events?), there is rarely, if ever, any realistic possibility of systematically testing ethnographic statements. Short of testing one could hope that ethnographers would endeavor to make as much of their descriptive record public as is possible and be explicit about their methods of deriving an ethnographic statement from that record. But this often-made appeal doesn't really help very much. Good ethnographies don't result from routine application of operational methods to a set of data. Like any exercise in theory construction, ethnography requires insight, intuition, guesswork, and reliance on recollections of events beyond what is set down in field notes. The way anthropologists in fact evaluate ethnographies is in terms of the ethnographer's rhetorical persuasiveness, reputation as a "good" ethnographer, and the relevance of his or her case to theoretical problems of current interest. I see little realistic prospect for improving this situation other than increasing the quality of ethnographic training so that readers can have more confidence that any given ethnographer will be a good ethnographer.

It is now clear that neither the structural nor the transformational linguistic paradigm provides an adequate basis for an ethnographic theory. Both paradigms restrict their domain to sentences isolated from wider linguistic and social contexts; both assume a homogeneous speech community; and both are concerned only with the acceptability, not the frequency, of events. A number of linguists have been giving attention to discourse beyond the sentence, to social context, and to variability and frequency, promising further revisions of the linguistic paradigm, one hopes in ways that will make linguistic and ethnographic theory more relevant to each other. The study of everyday social situations as contexts of behavior is an increasingly popular and promising field of investigation in sociolinguistics (much of which is done by anthropologists), anthropology, and sociology (where ethnomethodology presents what is in effect an ethnographic theory). At the other end of the scale, reconsideration of the macrounit of study, a culture, promises to reshape ethnographic theory. We talk about "a culture-bearing unit" sharing a "cognitive code" which it passes down through the generations; yet in a number of recent studies researchers have shown that cultural boundaries are not simply the outcome of differential transmission of tradition, but are also produced and maintained in interaction between social groups. Ethnographic theory must account for these boundaries. To do so it must assume a perspective that encompasses a number of neighboring "cultures," a regional perspective. Several investigators, especially in the field of economic anthropology, have been focusing on regional systems. This perspective poses problems not only for ethnographic theory, but also for method and technique in a multilingual, multicultural context.

The most telling indictment against the new ethnography is that it has not been notably successful in producing ethnographies. Like current linguistic theory, it has succeeded in revealing the complexities of relatively simple and restricted domains to such an extent that it is difficult to envision anything like a complete description of a total system under the paradigm. For those who see the value of ethnography as being limited to theory testing, ethnography in the old sense of going out and recording for posterity what's there loses its justification. I am enough of an old ethnographer, however, to be reluctant to dismiss our obligation to record the range of human cultural variability in some fashion. Current theorists rely heavily on data from old ethnographies written with very different theoretical objectives. There is no reason to suppose that future theorists will be any less dependent on current ethnographic statements. Yet the ethnographic record of the world is woefully incomplete. Almost every author of a research proposal in anthropology, no matter what the problem or where the field site, claims he or she will make a contribution to a poorly understood problem in a little-known area of the world. In most cases such claims are perfectly true — especially when made in reference to our own society.

Ethnography and Cognition
Michael Agar

The Basic Arguments

... In my view, ethnography is essentially a decoding operation. Beginning with the observation that some group successfully intercommunicates in a manner not understandable to an outsider, the ethnographer asks what knowledge is necessary to interpret correctly the verbal and nonverbal messages.

Such a conception of ethnography fits nicely with Goodenough's (1967) definition of culture:

> What does a person need to have learned if he is to understand events in a strange community as its members understand them and if he is to conduct himself in ways that they accept as conforming to their expectations of one another? To describe the contents of such a body of knowledge is to describe a community's culture. (p. 1203)

A description of shared knowledge, or cognition, enables us to decode the observed behavior.

Most ethnographers who investigate cognition suggest a focus on language. Language is a well-organized system of relatively few units which is used to talk about numerous areas of human knowledge. Frake (1962a: 75) argues that:

> Culturally significant cognitive features must be communicable in one of the standard symbolic systems of the culture. A major share of these features will undoubtedly be codable in a society's most flexible and productive communication device, its language.

Language may be examined on any number of levels. "Discourse stages," "exchanges," and "utterances" are only three examples of analyzable chunks of language (Frake 1964c:130). The usual language unit singled out in cognitively oriented work is the *lexeme,* or a "meaningful form whose signification cannot be inferred from a knowledge of anything else in the language" (Conklin 1969:43). Although the "theoretical definition and operational isolation" of lexemic units remain problematical (Kay 1966), the lexeme is usually used as the primary inroad to cognitive systems.

From *Ripping and Running: A Formal Ethnography of Urban Heroin Addicts,* by Michael Agar. Copyright © 1973 by Seminar Press. Reprinted by permission of the author and Academic Press.

This is not an arbitrary choice. In cognitive psychology, the basic unit of cognition is the "concept" (Bruner *et al.* 1956). Although different definitions of "concept" exist, the notion, as used here, indicates a class of discriminable objects or events which are considered to be equivalent on the basis of certain shared properties. As we have seen, such sets are often talked about in a language. There is evidence to indicate that concepts that are frequently communicated, or culturally important, or most "available," will have atomic, linguistic labels (lexemes).

Cognitive anthropology has taken those concepts labeled by lexemes as the basic units of data. Recall that the ethnographer's task is to describe the knowledge necessary to behave appropriately. Relating the cognitive approach to this goal, we find that it has been attained only in a limited sense. The output of a cognitive study presents the knowledge necessary to name a new instance of that concept. This is necessary, but obviously not sufficient, to achieve the broader goal. As Frake (1964c:127) notes:

> Our stranger requires more than a grammar and a lexicon; he needs what Hymes (1962) has called an ethnography of speaking: a specification of what kinds of things to say in what message forms to what kinds of people in what kinds of situations.

Attempts have been made to discuss the cognition underlying larger behavioral segments. Attempts by Frake and by Metzger and Williams are discussed in detail in the next section. Other approaches have been posited. Some are grounded in analogies between language structure and culture-cognitive structure.

Although two well-known approaches of this type exist, neither has been very productive. Pike (1967) has suggested the "behavioreme" concept to isolate units of analysis. Hall (1959) offers the "isolate-set-pattern" scheme, based on an analogy with the linguistic phonology, morphology, and syntax. Both attempt to define units of culture that have applications beyond the lexical level. Two reasons might be offered for their nonproductivity. First, language behavior is, as noted earlier, a tightly organized system of relatively few units. Possibilities expand rapidly as the behavior segment becomes more inclusive. Second, linguistic theory developed only after numerous emic studies were available. To posit a cultural theory on the linguistic analogy, when we do not know what an emic cultural study looks like, is a bit premature.

Similar criticisms could be leveled against other attempts to deal with large units of behavior. Barker and Wright's (1954) "behavior stream," Goffman's (1961b) "focused interaction," Miller, Galanter, and Pribram's (1960) "plans," Newcomb's (1953) "A-B-X" model, and Hymes's (1964) components of a communication situation all represent such attempts. While they are all useful in directing our attention to behavioral analysis at a level above the lexeme, the analytic distinctions, although suggestive, are a priori and tentative. The distinctions usually raise more questions about their relationship to actual behavior than they answer.

To summarize, several authors have proposed conceptual frameworks for the analysis of ongoing behavior. To segment the behavior, different concepts have been offered — for example, "focused interaction," "mutual co-orientation," "behavior stream," and "behavioreme." An overriding problem is the etic nature of these concepts. While there is nothing inherently wrong with an etic concept, difficulties arise when the etic concept cannot be unambiguously mapped into the emic concepts of the culture in question.

The problem is similar to that faced by earlier linguists when the concepts of Latin grammar were mapped into non-European language systems. Learning from their experience, one strategy might be to search for emic segmentations of ongoing behavior rather than using a priori concepts. In fact, the study of emics with a view toward an etic metalanguage has been advanced as a fundamental strategy of cognitive anthropology (Kay 1970, Sturtevant 1964).

Now, assuming that cultural members do segment ongoing behavior into identifiable chunks, we would expect some of this segmentation to be conceptualized in the member's cognitive apparatus (Frake 1969). From this assumption, it is a quick argument to reassert the relationships between lexical labels and culturally significant categories. This is an interesting conclusion: Perhaps a good way to study behavior above the lexical level is to study lexically labeled categories. We are simply moving the lexical study to a higher conceptual level. In the next section, attempts to move in this direction will be discussed.

Cognition and Events

In his study of Subanun religion, Frake (1964a) defines a goal of "descriptive adequacy" which is met when "ethnographic statements" included in the "theory of cultural behavior" can be used by a stranger to "appropriately anticipate the scenes of the society" (112). Based on this, the minimal tasks in producing an ethnographic statement are outlined (Frake 1964a:112):

1. Discovering the major categories of events or scenes of the culture.
2. Defining scenes so that observed interactions, acts, objects, and places can be assigned to their proper scenes as roles, routines, paraphernalia, and settings.
3. Stating the distribution of scenes with respect to one another, that is, providing instructions for anticipating or planning for scenes.

A Subanun "offering" event is then discussed in terms of its settings, provisions, paraphernalia, participants, and routines (Frake 1964a: 115–122).

Whereas this is an insightful intuitive outline to the emic segmentation of ongoing behavior, there are some difficulties in his formulation. First, how do we know that the members of a labeled category are something similar to an "event"? Second, do the units of the "constituent structure" (Frake:115) constitute formal universals of an event grammar? Third, is the distribution of scenes a simple linear sequence, or does it include relationships among contiguous events? These questions can be discussed one at a time.

The notion of "event" is difficult to define precisely; I shall adopt the strategy here of taking it as a primitive term. There are, nevertheless, some comments on "event" that may be useful. First, we would expect many lexically encoded events to be verbs, or expressable as verbs through some derivational process. More specifically, we will be interested in "action-process" verbs (Chafe 1970); that is, verbs that encode an "actor" engaging in some "act," which is also a "process" acting on some "patient."

The problem of constituent structure remains to be dealt with. Frake offers etic classifications which apparently have emic equivalents when related to scenes ("interactions" become "roles," "acts" become "routines," etc.). The issue is confused a bit when he uses structural units (i.e., "provisions") in the emic analysis which were not present in the initial etic formulation, and conversely.

At any rate, the proposed constituent units of events, though of heuristic value, seem a bit premature at this point. First, the problem of definition faces us with the units as it did with the term "event." Second, the constituent units could lead us to define behavioral segments as culturally significant to a scene when, in fact, they are not. In a later study of Yakan law, this problem is considered with reference to the irrelevance of physical setting to a litigation event (Frake 1969:156). Finally, the units are not independent. For example, some routines could determine the role, setting, and paraphernalia. Because of such problems, it is probably best to set aside the design of a constituent structure format for events.

A third question involves the distributional frame. To what extent does the occurrence of a scene depend on the preceding scene, or on anticipations of the following scene? Three criteria for frame description are given (Frake 1964a:124):

> (1) the probability of the events that comprise the frame, (2) the alternative scenes . . . that can be anticipated to occur in the same frame, (3) the alternative kinds of ceremonies that can be anticipated to occur given the occurrence of a ceremony.

Metzger and Williams (1963:1077) also discuss the distributional frame in their study of Ladino wedding ceremonies in a Mexican community:

> While the ceremonies are clearly defined in their distinctive features
> and in their order of time, there is structural alternation . . . on several
> levels, two of which may be mentioned at this point: (1) one or more
> ceremonies may be omitted from the series; and (2) within the cere-
> mony, a constituent feature is present as one or another of a set of
> mutually exclusive alternants, or, may be omitted entirely.

Note the relationship between Metzger and Williams's point 1 and Frake's
points 1 and 2, and between the former's point 2 and Frake's point 3. Each
is saying two things: first, that a slot can be filled in different ways with
differing degrees of probability; second, that the same event that fills the
slot can be realized in different ways.

Both studies indicate that events must be related to events if we are to
understand their meaning to participants, although both treat the distributional frame as a simple linear string. The interrelationships among events
in a sequence are only mentioned briefly.

The problem is essentially twofold. First, what is it about one event that
entails the occurrence of another? Second, what kind of decision making
underlies the empirical distribution of event sequences?

Both studies deal with these problems to some extent. In the first problem, we are looking for determined event sequences, or sequences of high
probability. Ceremonies of this type are characterized as "scheduled ceremonies." "Thus the annual occurrence of a given kind of scheduled ceremony is highly probable and learning that a given scheduled ceremony has
indeed occurred is not very informative (it is not 'news') to the person who
knows the culture" (Frake 1964c:482). The study of Ladino weddings also
shows that certain events in the ceremonial sequence must occur (i.e., are
determined), while others may or may not occur with varying degrees of
probability (Metzger and Williams 1963:1096).

In view of the fact that certain events are determined, we are still unsure of what it is about one event that determines, or is determined by, the
next. In some cases, the sequence may simply be an accepted tradition with
no perceived logical relationship. There is another possibility: "If there is
a legitimizing occasion and the necessary components are procurable, a
festive meal is staged" (Frake 1964a:113). This statement is important.
The person who engages in an event will often need certain prerequisites
before he can attain the event outcome. One kind of event interrelationship,
then, might have to do with prerequisites. For example, part of the analysis
suggests that the harvest is closely related to the staging of a ceremony
(Frake 1964a:124). Without attempting to second guess Frake, we can
safely assume that a harvest produces food, and food is a prerequisite for
a festive meal, which is in turn one feature of a ceremony. Summarized
diagrammatically, the relationship might look like this:

$$\text{Harvest} \xrightarrow{\quad \textit{food} \quad} \text{Ceremony}$$

In this case, one event outcome provides a prerequisite for the other to occur.

Similarly in Metzger and Williams's work (1963:1082), a prerequisite for the *matrimonio* is the *novios oficiales*. These, in turn, are provided by the *pedida*. Again, to summarize:

$$\text{Pedida} \xrightarrow{\quad \textit{novios oficiales} \quad} \text{Matrimonio}$$

Those two events are also related by a prerequisite. By looking at such interrelationships, the relationship of events may be more understandable.

Careful consideration of the prerequisite link also suggests a possible confusion between cognition and behavior. The outcome-prerequisite link is a logical link between event concepts. It does not necessarily imply that events actually occur in that sequence empirically. Previous studies mention the probability of occurrence of an event in a given slot. Predicting actual occurrence is an important question, but it is different from the question of cognitive structure. At present we are exclusively concerned with structure; in subsequent sections, we will ask how the structure relates to actual performances of the conceptualized event and its prerequisite linkages to other events.

In the "normal" course of events, a person who wants to engage in an event needs prerequisites. Frake's (1964a) discussion of "unscheduled" events implies another principle. "The distributive frames of many ceremonies are composed of unscheduled events that disrupt the ordinary routine of activities" (125). Here again, a focus on prerequisites might be useful. If one wants to block the occurrence of "disruptive" events, one strategy might be to block the occurrence of prerequisites for such events.

The discussion of sickness contains an example of this principle. One possible prerequisite of a sickness event is a debt to a supernatural creditor. "Sooner or later, the Subanun who has neglected a ritual debt becomes ill" (Frake 1964a:126–127). Clearly, then, one strategy for the prevention of the disruptive sickness event is to block the prerequisite by exercising one's ritual obligations. This principle, too, will be valuable in later sections.

The second problem, decision making, raises two separate issues. The first has to do with the selection of alternative forms in producing an event, as exemplified in the alternative realizations of the *matrimonio*. Many of the decisions here are made after assessing the virginity of the *novia*, the presence of death in a family, etc. In the later study of Yakan law, discussions of "conditions" (Frake 1969:152) and "procedures," and "schedules"

(Frake 1969:164) also indicate how variant forms of the same event can occur.

The second issue involves selection of prerequisites. One prerequisite of the *matrimonio* is food, and several possible kinds of meals can serve as prerequisites. Some of the factors that enter into a decision on what kind of meals to serve are outlined, such as the appearance of wealth, and the social expectations of others. These two factors, among others, interact in decision making with the output being a selection of the kind of meal. Neither study separates these two aspects of decision making. Although both are manifested in ongoing behavior, one is a result of selection among prerequisites; the other, a result of selection among alternative realizations of a given event. These distinctions will be put to use in the analyses that appear in later sections.

To recapitulate, Frake's and Metzger and Williams's studies offer several suggestions for the analysis of emic segmentation of ongoing behavior. Key entry points, in such a study, are the lexical labels of event categories. As in any such analysis, the shared properties of the category members can be described. However, since one or more aspects of an event are related to human behavior, and since human behavior is productive, we may expect alternative manifestations of these behavioral properties.

Furthermore, to understand an event, we must also understand its relationship to other events. One possible linkage between events may lie in the notion of prerequisites. Two events may be cognitively related in that the outcome of one provides a prerequisite for the next. By looking at the decision making related to the events as well, we can increase our understanding of fairly inclusive behavior segments.

Events and Addict Culture

To summarize the preceding sections, the ethnographer attempts to describe a body of knowledge or cognition. This knowledge will enable him to understand behavior that he originally could not properly interpret in a manner acceptable to members of the community. Although many efforts in cognitive anthropology have accounted for naming behavior, the approaches of Frake and Metzger and Williams suggest ways to describe systematically the knowledge related to larger behavioral segments.

This general viewpoint suggests an approach to the study of urban heroin addicts. Any *square* who observes *street junkie* interaction soon learns that two *junkies* who have not previously met and who are of different regions, races, or ages can converse over a wide range of topics in a manner not understandable to an outsider. Such a fact is a manifestation of a shared culture. A description of the knowledge necessary to understand a particular segment of interaction would be a partial description of the culture.

As a first step in the description, the addict argot was collected. An understanding of the argot, such that acceptable paraphrases of any sentence could be given, was insufficient for the complete understanding of longer segments of behavior. Following the argument in the preceding section, I examined the argot and listened to addict speech in a search for lexically encoded events. Three lexemes in particular struck me as promising starting points because of their high frequency of occurrence. Logically enough, the three encoded highly significant, central events in the life of the street junkie. The three were *hustle* ("obtain money illegally"), *cop* ("buy heroin"), and *get-off* ("inject heroin").

Straightforward elicitation of folk definitions indicated that meaning was almost always specified in terms of the desired outcome of the encoded event (Frake 1969:153). A junkie *hustles* to get *bread* ("money"); he *cops* to obtain *stuff* ("heroin"); and he *gets-off* to get *straight* ("not-sick"). [G]*etting straight* is the most important outcome in the context of this discussion. The manner of definition suggests a way to talk about the distribution in terms of prerequisite links. Notice that the outcome of one event is also the prerequisite for another.

The outcome of *hustling* is *bread,* which is a prerequisite for *copping.* The outcome of *copping* is *stuff,* which is a prerequisite for *getting-off.* The outcome of *getting-off* is to be *straight,* which is a prerequisite for *hustling.* The three events are logically linked together by a relationship between the outcome of one and the prerequisite of another. This cognitive linkage, as mentioned in the preceding section, is not to be confused with behavior.

In day-to-day life, prerequisites can be obtained in other ways. For example, *bread* could come from a legitimate job, or from parents, rather than from a *hustle. Stuff* could be found in a gutter where it had been ditched, or stolen from another *junkie.* A *junkie* could get *straight* by swallowing large amounts of codeine cough syrup rather than injecting heroin. All of these can and do occur, but the links described here are the usual or "unmarked" ones for the *street junkie.*

Another possible confusion of the cognitive structure with behavior might lie in the actual temporal distribution of events as they are performed. Nothing in the structure says that the *junkie* will first *hustle,* then *cop,* then *get-off,* then *hustle* again. If he has a large amount of money, the *junkie* might *cop* three or four times in succession, then stay in his *crib* ("residence") for a few days and repeatedly *get-off.* If he is *straight,* the *junkie* might go to a party rather than immediately *hustle.* The structure does say that a *junkie* needs *bread* to *cop,* and that if he does not have it, the most frequent way to get it is to *hustle.* The same holds, *mutatis mutandis,* for the other events.

The logical relationships between events can be summarized in Figure 1. Whereas this simple structure was the starting point of my ethnographic

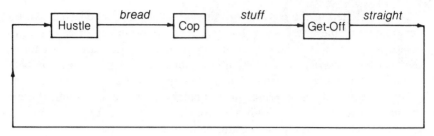

Figure 1

work, I want to anticipate some of the later conclusions for purposes of clarity. . . .

The first problem in the simple structure of Figure 1 is that other prerequisites are necessary to engage in the events. At this point, our focus will be restricted to *copping* and *getting-off* . . . To *cop*, the *junkie* needs *bread*, but he also needs a *dealer* from whom to *cop*. To *get-off*, he needs a place and some *works* ("implements used to inject heroin") in addition to *stuff*. By adding these prerequisites to the simple structure, we obtain Figure 2.

Recall that events with undesired outcomes were mentioned by Frake in his article. This idea is important here as well. As the *junkie* accumulates prerequisites for events that he wants to produce, he is also accumulating prerequisites for events that he wants to prevent. For example, when the *bread* and *dealer* prerequisites for *copping* exist, the prerequisites for a *burn* also exist. A *burn* occurs when insufficient *stuff* is given for the amount of *bread* spent. Consequently, while he engages in *copping*, he will also worry about preventing a *burn*.

When the *junkie* has either *bread* or *stuff*, he is subject to a *rip-off* ("physical confrontation to steal person's goods"). If there is another *junkie* who might *rip* him *off*, and if he has *bread* or *stuff*, he will worry

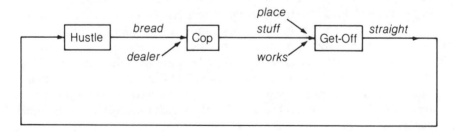

Figure 2

about this possibility. Similarly, if the *junkie* has either *works* or *stuff,* these could become prerequisites for a *bust* ("arrest"). Consequently, if the *junkie* has either of these in his possession, and if there is another person who might be the *man* ("law enforcement officer") or a *snitch* ("informer"), he may worry about a *bust.* Indicating the links between prerequisites and undesired events, we obtain the structure shown in Figure 3. . . .

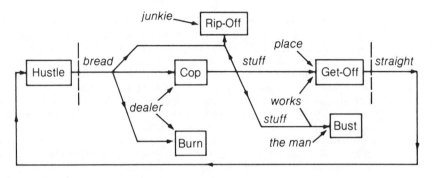

Figure 3

By focusing on a definition of culture as cognition and drawing on suggestions explicit and implicit in earlier studies of lexically labeled events, we have obtained a structure that links together different events important to the *street junkie.*

Telling the Convict Code

D. Lawrence Wieder

In the following pages Wieder analyzes the nature and course of his efforts to carry out fieldwork in a halfway house for paroled ex-addicts in East Los Angeles. From his very first contacts in the house Wieder found that residents referred to the same "convict code" that researchers had described as fundamental to prison subcultures. Wieder identified the following specific "maxims" that made up the code: (1) do not snitch (inform); (2) do not cop out (admit that you have done anything illegal or against the house rules); (3) do not take advantage of other residents; (4) share what you have; (5) help other residents; (6) do not mess with other residents' interests; (7) do not trust staff — staff is heat; and (8) show your loyalty to the residents (Wieder 1974:115–118). In the materials included here Wieder examines the various ways this "convict code" was invoked and used by all those present in the halfway house setting — residents, staff, and researcher alike — to structure and create meaning in routine activities.

RME

Interactional Uses of the Code

The Code as Told by Residents

My first contact with the project came about because I was looking for some kind of research position on a project dealing with deviance. I had heard through colleagues that the Department of Corrections might have something, so I called them. I was invited to their research offices in downtown Los Angeles and told that they had a position open. My colleague-to-be, Mr. Don Miller, said that his section of the Research Division had been charged with studying the halfway house in East Los Angeles. They had already made outcome studies and, therefore, knew that a stay at the halfway house did not improve a parolee-addict's chances of abstaining from drug use. However, they did not know why this was the case. Miller and some of the members of the administration of the department thought that an exploratory study of the structure of the organization and of the lives of the residents might shed light on why the organization was not "working." The job promised considerable freedom, and it appeared quite appealing to me, so I arranged to take it.

From *Language and Social Reality: The Case of Telling the Convict Code*, by D. Lawrence Wieder. Copyright © 1974 in The Netherlands. Mouton & Co. N. V., Publishers, The Hague. Reprinted by permission of the publisher.

I want to stress that I knew nothing about correctional establishments, that I had read none of the literature in this area, and at that point decided with other researchers in the Department of Corrections research office (Don Miller and Al Himmelson) that it would be desirable, at least at first, for me to remain ignorant in that regard. We felt that my ignorance was desirable, because equipped with the literature, my observations might be pushed in the direction of the results of previous studies. However, we did have brief discussions concerning the possibility of the existence of some kind of oppositional subculture in the halfway house and that that was one of the things I might look for.

Miller, who had already spent one day a week at the halfway house for six months or so, took me there and introduced me to the staff and a few of the residents he had come to know. I was given an office in the upstairs of the building in an area where none of the staff had their offices. I had planned to try to avoid identification as a staff member, to observe what I could of the organization by being around it in as many places as I could, and to become friends with residents so as to spend time with them in order to see what it was that they were doing and saying. To assist in doing this, I wore casual clothes, i.e., a sport shirt and cotton slacks, while the staff wore coat and tie, and intended not to locate myself next to staff while in the presence of the residents.

My first contact with the residents was provided by Miller, who introduced me to a resident with whom he had become friendly. He told the resident, whom I will call Sanchez, that I was going to study what was going on at the halfway house. Sanchez said that he would like to help, so the next time I was at the halfway house, I asked him to come to my office to tell me about the place. After he had sketched out the program for me and explained the difficulty in finding jobs for ex-convicts, I asked him how the residents got along with one another; particularly, were there things that they should do and should not do. He said that "guys" should not snitch (inform on each other) or steal from one another. I asked if there were anything else, and he replied that, yes, there was more to *the code* than that. When I first heard that, I wondered if he had had so much contact with researchers that they had taught him to speak about moral expectations as forming a code, although later experience with other informants, who said essentially the same thing, led me to think that that was not the explanation. In any case, I was struck with the extent to which those expectations were verbally formalized.

I tried to get my informant to tell me more. For example, were there parts of the code that had to do with the use of drugs in the house. I said that I had heard that there were a lot of drugs at the halfway house. What had seemed up to that point to be a conversation that was filled with "good rapport" and was teaching me much, suddenly was destroyed. For a moment he said nothing. Then he told me that I could not ask that — at least not now. He said that for me to do research in the halfway house would require my making it clear that I was on the side of the residents. He suggested that I should publicly argue with the staff about their treatment of the residents, that I should not spend time with the staff, and that I should take guys out for beer and the like. I later came to see that he was telling me to behave like a good resident by showing my loyalty to the residents. He suggested that if I followed his instructions, then perhaps after several weeks I might find out something. Even then, however, he was unsure about the possibility of learning very much from the residents. After giving me this piece of advice, he then said he had to go set up the tables for dinner, and the conversation which had lasted for nearly an hour ended. I realized later that the very matters being talked about in the conversation with Sanchez made the course of that conversation understandable as a rule-governed dialogue. I saw why the conversation had halted — because for him to tell me about drug use would have amounted to or come close to snitching.

Following Sanchez's advice, in part, I then began my attempts at observing life at the halfway house. I went to the meetings the residents went to, sitting as they sat, and saying nothing. I went to lunch and dinner with them. I stayed with them when they washed the dishes and did other work around the house, sat on the front porch with them, and talked with them in the front room. When it seemed appropriate, I asked them to join me for a beer outside the house, though this was not a common occurrence. . . .

. . . [M]y contact with the residents was erratic at best. The very routines of the halfway house made contact difficult. The residents were rarely there when they did not have to be. This meant that during the day, only those that were at the house to work off board and room were typically there. The others would come in for dinner, sometimes for lunch, and for meetings, and then leave until curfew. I could never count on seeing a particular resident, since anyone with whom I had already talked would most likely not be around again except at meetings and meals.

Nevertheless, some halting and some extensive conversations were held, especially with residents who were working around the house, and sometimes with others immediately before dinner and after meetings. When these conversations did occur, I found the residents very ready to tell me something of their history, their complaints about parole, the halfway house, the police, the difficulty in finding good jobs, and what it was like in prison, but exceedingly little about life in the halfway house aside from relations with staff, and practically nothing at all about relations between residents and what the particular resident was doing besides working or looking for work.

. . . I began to see that the difficulty I was experiencing was produced by the same phenomenon that I was trying to investigate. I came to see that my experience of not being able to join conversations over the dinner table, although conversations were going on all around me, was being produced by the code that I was trying to explicate. When I was having a conversation with a resident and other residents passed by and said something in Spanish to him, followed by the conversation coming to a quick halt, I came to understand that this too was a sanctioning of the code.

In the third to fourth week of the study, my understanding of the code as it applied to me (that it applied to me and how it applied to me) was strengthened by some residents who explicitly pointed out the relevance of the code in and for their dealings with me. A point I wish to emphasize is that resident recitations of the code, or some element of it, were done in such a way that the residents were not simply describing a set of rules to me, but were also simultaneously sanctioning my conduct by such a recitation. I experienced their "telling the code" as an attempt to constrain my conduct by telling me what I could and could not appropriately do. In particular, they were often engaged in persuading me that some questions I might ask and some questions I did ask were "out of order" and that there were some areas of resident "underlife" that I should not attempt to explore. To show this in more detail, some concrete examples will be cited.

In my fifth or sixth week at the house, I encountered a younger resident, whom I will call Arnaldo, in the hall, who asked me if I knew of any jobs that were available. We were walking down the hall toward his dormitory, and both of us walked into it, when I said that I didn't know of any. Then he began to tell me of the pressure staff was putting on him because he was not yet employed. We talked about the ways staff was suspicious of him because he had not yet found work and what his social life was like without any money. The house manager came past and asked us to help unload a truck of toys for the annual Christmas party. While we unloaded the truck, Arnaldo told me about "kiss asses" who volunteered to do favors for staff, which, he explained, unloading the truck was not, since he was more or less ordered to do it. After we finished the unloading, I asked him if he would like a beer, and he said, "Sure, if you're buying." We continued our talk about "regulars," "snitching," and "kiss asses," and about getting stopped by the police because one lives at a halfway house, while we walked to a nearby tavern which reputedly catered to addicts. Though our conversation had been long and friendly, when I started to ask him about the clientele of the bar and the fact that I had heard that there were lots of guys "holding" (possessing drugs) there, Arnaldo said, "I don't know, but you'd be the last one I'd tell if I did." I was taken aback by this remark, for our talk during the past two hours had led me to think that I could ask such a question. I did not know what to say and did not press the matter further, as I might have done by asking him why I would be the last one he would tell. "The reason" seemed immediately obvious, since we had been talking about the code — for him to have told me would have bordered on snitching. He changed the topic by asking me if I had read a lot of books about addicts, and what I thought about what they had to say. At that point another resident, whom I will call Miguel, popped his head in the door for a moment and then left. We had resumed talking, when Miguel returned and came in. I said hello to him, at which point Arnaldo said that he had to get back to the house to set up for dinner, leaving me with Miguel, who sat down at the bar next to me.

I said that I had seen him just a moment ago, to which he replied that he had seen me, decided that he did not want to be "grouped" by me, and started to leave, but had seen the "fuzz" (police) patrolling the block outside and decided to come back, even if that meant talking to me. I had talked to Miguel several times in the house prior to this. I said, "What do you mean, be 'grouped' by me?" He said that when he was in the house talking to me that other guys would come past and say to him in Spanish, "Hey man, cut loose of that guy or he'll group you," which meant "talk to you about what is your business and none of his." At about this point, a girl he knew came up and started talking to him, and though he introduced me to her, when he turned to talk to her, I was not part of their conversation. A resident who was a parolee-at-large (one who breaks parole by deliberately avoiding all contact with his agent) walked in, spotted me, and left. I said to my "informant" Miguel that I was sorry that I could not convince residents that I would not let the staff know I had seen them, to which he replied, "Do you think that they would believe you?," as if to say that, of course, they would not. I said that I supposed they could not afford to. I asked him if he could tell me more about that, but we had to leave if we were to eat dinner at the halfway house. I suggested that we might go out for a beer that evening, and he said "Fine; we can talk more about your work then."

... [After dinner, when Miguel was ready to leave] I asked him where he would like to go, and he said that he would prefer somewhere outside the neighborhood, because my presence in a local bar would make other guys uncomfortable, and he did not want to be seen with me there. So we "headed" for a bar near the place where he worked. The ride in my car to the bar provided a stream of conversational topics — that he got a ride to work every day from another employee of the place where he worked; that he had that guy pick him up a block away from the halfway house so that his friend would not see him coming out of the halfway house; what kind of a bar we were going to; its bikini-clad waitresses; and, when we arrived, the fact that aside from the waitresses, there were no women in the bar. Then he turned his attention to what I was doing in the halfway house. He said that I was "fucking up" and "ranking" my job by talking to guys about themselves and the house. He said it was foolish to try to talk to convicts about personal matters like that, unless I knew them very well, and that that would not happen because guys were not there long enough. When I asked him what I could do, if that were the case, his response indicated that it was not "really" a problem of "establishing rapport," as he had previously seemed to indicate. Instead, he said that my "problem" was the kind of event it was for residents to be talking to me in the setting of the halfway house as that conversation would be construed by other residents. That is, it was an issue of residents' being seen by other residents as violating maxims of the code or appearing to be about to violate maxims of the code, especially prohibitions against snitching, copping out, and messing with other residents' interests, and prescriptions calling for a show of loyalty among residents and a show of distrust for staff.

He said that guys would rather not lie to me if they could help it, so they would try to steer clear of me if they could. He said that what I had been told was largely a lot of "bullshit." When I asked what was going on that kept guys from talking to me, he replied that they would tell each other not to talk to me, but more than that, every one of them had the following fear, though he, Miguel, talked to me in spite of it: every ex-con knows that he is very likely to go back to prison sometime, and that is especially so for addicts. On the return trip, the ex-con might meet others he had seen and known at the halfway house. That other guy might be there on a fifteen-year sentence and count himself as dead, that is, he would not care what happened to him. If the "dead man" recalled that someone had spoken to me at the halfway house, he could take that as an instance of someone's gossiping to me about the "dead man's" business and, in turn, attack and perhaps kill the supposed gossip. Therefore, it was dangerous to talk to a researcher. My attempts to get people to talk to me were "stupid" and were endangering persons who were helpful to me. . . .

. . . My data gathering efforts with the residents altered the character of my own circumstances as I knew them. As I obtained new materials about the residents' social world, my own field of action was progressively developed. By "telling the code," residents gave me a schema for seeing the sensible, factual, and stable properties of that part of my social world which intersected theirs. Residents' "telling the code" was consequential for the ways in which I saw my research circumstances. In this consequentiality, "telling the code" was not merely about the halfway house and events in it but was, as well, an active element of that same setting. . . .

The Code as Told by Staff

As I continued my observational work, I increasingly watched staff-resident encounters, the round of staff's activities, and the character of staff's talk. These observations showed me that staff had been taught the code by residents and each other and employed it in ways that both paralleled its uses by sociologists and by residents and inmates. Staff "told the code" in describing, interpreting, explaining, and finding the patterned character of resident conduct. They also used the code in giving advice to each other, in devising strategies, and in justifying their own actions and decisions. For staff, "telling the code" identified the meaning of resident behavior, portrayed situations from the point of view of residents, and defined staff's own situation and the meaning of staff's actions.

Some of my conversations with staff were tape recorded. Excerpts from . . . these conversations[1] show some of the ways that staff "knew" and "told" the code.

> W: Suppose a guy discovered that his jeweled watch had been stolen from him here in the house; what do you think he should do about it?
> PA: I think he should do a little investigating on his own and find out who took it. Okay, and then after he did that, he should confront the guy with it and tell him to give back his watch, or otherwise he will take care of the justice himself. I do not think he should tell staff.
> W: Okay; why?
> PA: Okay, well, if he tells staff about it, he's going to be branded as a fink. The majority of them [the residents] would think that way. Any time you tell staff anything like that, you're a fink, you know.
> W: What consequences do you see for him?
> PA: Oh, you know, he's liable to get killed. Yeah, that's a sixty-forty possibility. There's a sixty-forty possibility he'd be a — his status in the eyes of the rest of the people — it would diminish because he did something you're not supposed to do, and staff would have feelings about it too. They wouldn't know whether they should take his side or say, "What the hell is the matter with you — you violated the rules."

The parole agent's response is almost identical to resident advice about the same matter. Staff elaborated the meaning of the situation from the standpoint of the residents by invoking the code as relevant to the possible alternatives a victim of theft would face. The moral and consequential meanings of a situation of action — what to do about a stolen watch — are generated by imagining the possible actions that a resident could take and then assessing those actions in terms of their likely meanings when defined by reference to the code.

. . . Like residents and sociologists, staff "told the code" to identify or name individual acts and patterns of repetitive action and to collect diverse actions under the rubric of a single motive and, in turn, to name them as the same kind of act. They rendered resident action sensible or rational by noting the ways in which resident action was rule-governed and directed toward achieving goals that were specified by the code. In this way staff offered a folk version of Weber's adequate causal analysis by showing that the typical patterned actions of residents followed from a "correct" course of reasoning. Staff portrayed the reasonable character of resident action by using the code and its elements to define the residents' situation. By "telling

---

[1] I encountered innumerable instances of staff's "telling the code." For a more lengthy presentation of tape-recorded protocols of staff's "telling the code" and an analysis of the varieties of the modes of "telling the code," see Wieder (1969:235–250).

the code" as the residents' definition of their situation, staff showed that patterns of resident action had Durkheim's social-fact properties of exteriority and constraint. Residents' actions were reasonable in the sense that they had no choice but to behave in the fashion that they did.

In "telling the code," staff implicitly and explicitly used a wide range of social scientific conceptions, e.g., rule-governed action, goal-directed action, the distinction between the intended and unintended outcomes of action, the distinction between normatively required and normatively optional means of achieving a morally valued end, roles, role-bound behaviors, and definition of the situation. The use of these ethno-social scientific conceptions in "telling the code" structured staff's environment. It did this by identifying the meaning of a resident's act by placing it in the context of a pattern. An equivocal act then becomes "clear" in the way that it obtains its sense as typical, repetitive, and more or less uniform, i.e., its sense as an *instance* of the kind of action with which staff was already familiar. Staff's environment was also structured by the flexibility of "telling the code," which could render nearly any equivocal act sensible in such a way that it was experienced as something familiar, even though the act might not be "expected" or "predicted" in any precise meaning of those terms. For example, when the parole agent portrayed a diverse collection of actions — a resident's ridiculing the agent and other group members in a committee meeting, being late to the meeting, giving inadequate excuses, never siding with staff on any issue, and playing one staff member off against another — as instances of a familiar pattern of behavior (demonstrating one's opposition to staff as a display of one's loyalty), he made them parts of an already known pattern, even though the specific behaviors might not have been predicted. "Telling the code" also structured staff's environment by *connecting* a given act to its possible goal or to some specific consequence of the act among its many consequences. For example, one staff member identified a case of a resident's (possibly accidental) burning his own mattress as an attack on staff. This consequence was only one among many consequences, e.g., it created much smoke that would bother his dorm mates, and it could have served as a "cover" for some illegitimate activity. By seeing the potential code-relevance of the act as an attack on staff, the staff member identified "the" specific meaning of the act. Acts were also rendered sensible by connecting them to the activities of others (especially staff) in terms of role-bound reciprocities.

. . . Staff's "telling the code" also rendered important features of staff's environment *trans-situational* and *non-situation specific* in character. It rendered parts of staff's environment trans-situational by depicting them as recurrent and produced by a constantly operative set of motives (provided by the code) which were acted upon in every staff-resident encounter. Non-situation specificity was an accompaniment of trans-situationality, for in staff's hands, "telling the code" drew attention away from the specific features of the situation of an act (e.g., that it was *this* resident acting toward a specific staff member who had treated him in a particular way), while giving it a trans-situational explanation. By explaining the varieties of unpleasant gestures that residents directed toward them in terms of "the (trans-situational) principles by which these men live," staff "avoided" the possible interpretation of those unpleasant actions in such situation-specific terms as "getting back at a staff member for the way he treated the resident the day before" or "responding to an obvious attack on the resident's integrity." . . .

"Telling the code" among staff occurred with greatest regularity when residents were doing something troublesome or unusual. On the occasion that a staff member had to tell of the trouble, explain it, or propose some remedy for it, the code was frequently invoked to account for the source of the trouble. The most common trouble staff was called on to explain was the lack of progress in committees and groups. Once a week, a staff meeting was held in which the staff members who led committees reported on what their committee had done. When a staff member reported that his committee had not accomplished much, he explained that the residents could not and would not participate in any active way and that there was nothing that staff could do to alter that fact. Therefore, whatever the committee could accomplish had to be done by staff, and staff did not have enough time. Frequently other staff members would join in with sympathetic remarks (such as, "They regard group as a crock of shit," "They think it's square to participate in committees," "They say going to a pool tournament at halfway house is for kids"), showing that they understood that the men would not participate and that they were deliberately motivated not to participate. When those in charge attempted to reject these accounts, they did so not by arguing against the claim that residents refused to cooperate, but by arguing against the claim that staff did not have enough time to do what residents would not do. In many cases, a staff member's explanation for nonproductivity which was based on resident refusal to participate was accepted and obtained the acknowledgment of others that the staff member was properly doing his job, even though his committee had not accomplished anything.

. . . Through these examples, it can be seen that the code was usable by staff in explaining, describing, and strategizing about resident behavior, not only in talking with the researcher, but also in dealings between themselves. On the occasions in which the code, its categories, and analogues of the code were offered by staff to staff, they were accepted as factual. That is, "telling the code" was unquestioned, and to the extent it suggested action, it was usable as the socially sanctioned grounds of action.

Through these accounts, staff identified actual or anticipated actions and events as instances of the same kinds of troublesome occurrences they had seen before and already knew how to deal with. Couching the accounts in the language of the code portrays the occurrences as independent of the particular resident personnel that were involved, e.g., it was not simply that those particular ten new residents were "testing the limits," but that any group of new residents would "test the limits." The occurrences were also thereby characterized as independent of the particular issues over which they had occurred, e.g., resident resistance to a committee was independent of the particular work of that committee, or disputes with staff over transportation were independent of residents' actual needs for transportation money, etc. The occurrences that were accounted for by use of the code and its analogues were also thereby seen as independent of the staff member who was involved. That is, it was not that this particular staff member had done something to the residents that obtained hostility or resistance in response. Instead, the code account provided that residents would behave that way toward any staff member.

The trans-situational and non-situation specific character of "telling the code" made it useful for staff in managing their relationships with each other. It served to relieve staff members of some of their responsibilities for motivating residents to participate in the program. It accounted for the relative lack of productivity in those aspects of the program which called for staff and residents to work together. It served to defend staff and staff ideas against the complaints of residents. It did these things by focusing attention away from the substance of the interactions, the substance of staff-resident work, and the substance of resident complaints about staff and staff programs. By "telling the code," staff could discount resident talk and action as not "really" substantive complaints and resistance to something in particular. Instead, they could interpret that talk and action as compelled by the residents' code-required need to show their loyalty to each other and to show their lack of trust in staff. . . .

Persuasive and Reflexive Formulation:
The Code as About and a Part of the Setting

One *could* say that the "telling of the code" was a formulation of the organized character of resident life which residents and staff provided as a narrative which accompanied their affairs. The fact that the code was titled would make it appear to be some kind of "oral tradition" which had the moral force to govern the affairs of contemporary residents. Indeed, as I have indicated, residents spoke of the long-standing, "what-I-was-taught-as-a-child" character of the code. It was also the case that the code was "told" in showing the organized character of resident life. This was so in the ways that the reciting of the code "formulated" a particular occurrence being presently talked about as an instance of a typical occurrence. For example, the staff-aide's resistance to going to a neighborhood bar with parole agents was a show of his loyalty to the residents and was analyzed by him as an instance of avoiding the possibility of being seen as a snitch or other kind of turncoat.

It would appear that one *could* speak of the code as an "oral tradition" which was employed to instruct outsiders (like myself and staff) as to the organized character of what they had seen, were seeing, or would see. That is, one *could* say that residents employed this narrative to point out that an event, or "our relationship," or the behavior of that other resident, or the resident's own behavior were instances of patterns which were long-standing, which had been seen before, and which would be seen again. One would also then say that residents were "telling the code" in showing, or perhaps to show, that the particular event under consideration would have been enacted by "any resident," because persons who were residents were morally constrained to act in that fashion. That is, the code was employed to explain why someone had acted as they had and that that way of acting was necessary under the circumstances. In brief, one would be saying that the code was employed by residents to analyze for outsiders and perhaps for themselves the "social-fact" character of their circumstances, for they were noting particular occurrences as instances of regular-patterns-of-action-which-are-produced-by-compliance-to-a-normative-order.

While one *could* propose such an analysis of the code as an exegetical organizing narrative, that would be something like a narrative which is offered by the tour guide of a museum or the narration for a travelogue film, to do so would be misleading. Such an analysis, if it simply left the matter here, would be misleading in precisely the ways that a travelogue narrative differs from the "telling of the code." Since I find the travelogue narrative helpful by contrast, let me indicate what I understand as its features. In the travelogue story of a voyage, one encounters the story shown on the screen and the identifications, explanations, and descriptions of the narrative heard over a loud speaker as discrete occurrences — narrative and picture. One hears the narrative as an outside commentary on the events depicted visually. In the case of "purely narrative films," the sound track never cuts to ongoing conversation or other sounds of events shown visually. Whatever talk comes over the loudspeaker, and all of that which comes over the loudspeaker, is narrative. The narrative begins with the beginning of the film and "completes itself" by the end. Whoever speaks on the soundtrack is doing narration. Typically, explanations are temporally juxtaposed to the scenic occurrences they explain. Finally, one listens to the narration and sees the film passively as a depicted scene for one's enjoyment or edification, not as an object that one must necessarily actively encounter and immediately deal with. Coupled with the feature of the passive audience, the narrator speaks for whomever listens. The parties hearing him are unknown to him, do not act upon his fate, and indeed have no involvement with him beyond their listening.

"Telling the code" contrasts with each of the above enumerated features of the travelogue narration. The crucial difference is that the code was not encountered "outside" the scene it was purportedly describing, but was told within that scene as a continuous, connected part of that scene by being manifested as an active consequential act within it.

The talk occurring in the halfway house that invoked the code, referred to the code, or relied on the code for its intelligibility, then, was not simply or merely a description of life in a halfway house. Instead, this talk was at the same time part of life in the halfway house, and it was a part that was itself included within the scope of things over which the code had jurisdiction. It is in this sense that talk involving the code was reflexive within the setting of its occurrence. . . .

"Telling the code" was not heard as a "disinterested" report delivered in the manner of a narrator who was speaking to unknown and distant persons about matters upon which they could not act. Instead, the code was being "told" about matters which were critical to hearer and listener, because "the telling" formulated and fed into their joint action. In contrast to that sort of narrative which is a description of the events displayed on a screen, the code was often "told" about the immediate behavior of the hearer and teller. It was multi-formulative and multi-consequential in the immediate interaction in which it was told and multi-formulative and multi-consequential in and for the occurrence of that interaction as an aspect of the social organization of the halfway house.

As a first step in explicating this multi-consequential and multi-formulative character of "telling the code," let us examine the range of "work" that a single utterance can accomplish. When talking with residents, staff and I often had a relatively friendly line of conversation terminated by a resident's saying, "You know I won't snitch." Hearing such an utterance functioned to recrystalize the immediate interaction as the present center of one's experiential world. "You know I won't snitch," multi-formulated the immediate environment, its surrounding social structures, and the connections between this interaction and the surrounding social structures. It (a) told what had just happened — e.g., "You just asked me to snitch." It (b) formulated what the resident was doing in saying that phrase — e.g., "I am saying that this is my answer to your question. My answer is not to answer." It (c) formulated the resident's motives for saying what he was saying and doing what he was doing — e.g., "I'm not answering in order to avoid snitching." Since snitching was morally inappropriate for residents, the utterance, therefore, formulated the sensible and proper grounds of the refusal to answer the question. It (d) formulated (in the fashion of pointing to) the immediate relationship between the listener (staff or myself) and teller (resident) by relocating the conversation in the context of the persisting role relationships between the parties — e.g., "For *you* to ask *me* that, would be asking me to snitch." Thus saying, "You know I won't snitch," operated as a renunciation, or a reminder of the role relationships

involved and the appropriate relations between members of those categories. It placed the ongoing occasion in the context of what both parties
knew about their overriding trans-situational relationships. It (e) was *one
more* formulation of the features of the persisting role relationship between
hearer and teller — e.g., "You are an agent (or state researcher) and I am
a resident-parolee. Some things you might ask me involve informing on my
fellow residents. Residents do not inform on their fellows. We call that
snitching." Besides reminding the participants of a trans-situational role
relationship, the features of that trans-situational role relationship were
originally and continuously formulated through such utterances as, "You
know I won't snitch."

Beyond the multi-formulative character of this single utterance, it was
also a consequential move in the very "game" that it formulated. As a
move in that field of action which it formulated, it pointed to the con-
tingencies in that field as they were altered by *this* move. Furthermore, the
utterance as a move obtained its sense and impact from those altered con-
tingencies. Much of the persuasiveness of "telling the code" consisted in
its character as a move in the field of action which it also defined. By saying,
"You know I won't snitch," (a) the resident negatively sanctioned the prior
conduct of the staff member or myself. Saying that the question called for
snitching was morally evaluating it and rebuffing me or the staff. The utterance (b) called for and almost always obtained a cessation of that line
of the conversation. It was, therefore, consequential in terminating that
line of talk. In terminating that line of talk, it (c) left me or staff ignorant
of what we would have learned by the question had it been answered.
And it (d) signaled the consequences of rejecting the resident's utterance
or the course of action it suggested. By saying, "You *know* I *won't* snitch,"
the resident pointed to what he would do if the staff persisted. He "said"
he would not comply, irrespective of the staff's wishes. He thereby warned
that the conversation would turn nasty if staff or I did not retreat from the
question. He also pointed to the staff's obligation (or my obligation) to
be competent in the affairs of residents. To refuse to acknowledge the sense
and appropriateness of the resident's response was to risk being seen as
incompetent in the eyes of all other residents and staff. Finally, by noting
that what was being requested was *snitching,* a resident pointed to the
consequences for himself if he were to go ahead and answer the question.
The potential consequences for him could include beatings and even death.
Since staff was obliged to protect residents, this fate was also consequential
for them. The potential consequences of refusing to accept the credibility
of the resident's response made that response persuasive.

II

Theory and Evidence in Field Research

Introduction

Kathy Charmaz
The Grounded Theory Method:
An Explication and Interpretation

Jack Katz
A Theory of Qualitative Methodology:
The Social System of Analytic Fieldwork

Egon Bittner
Realism in Field Research

Michael J. Bloor
Notes on Member Validation

Introduction

Field research begins rather than ends with "setting down the meaning particular social actions have for the actors whose actions they are" (Geertz, this volume, p. 57). For those who engage in field research seek to move beyond these particular meanings to identify general patterns and regularities in social life. This is the aim of theory — what Geertz terms "specification" or "diagnosis" — "stating, as explicitly as we can manage, what the knowledge thus attained demonstrates about the society in which it is found and, beyond that, about social life as such" (this volume, page 57). Fieldworkers ultimately attempt to arrive at theoretical statements of general scope and applicability, yet at the same time they try to keep these theories close to the distinctive meanings of actual social life.

This dual commitment — to develop general theoretical analyses and yet to tie such analyses closely to specific observations of social life — has placed fieldwork in a state of tension with the modes of theorizing and assessing evidence that prevail in the social sciences. On the one hand, the standard logico-deductive approaches to theory do not apply to the analysis of the field data. Such deductive approaches view theorizing as a procedure in which formal hypotheses are derived from existing theoretical propositions and then checked against data collected specifically to test their validity. In contrast, in fieldwork, theorizing depends on concepts derived from the data rather than on deduction from received theory. The goal is to arrive at theoretical propositions after having looked at the social world, not before. Hence, prevalent procedures for verifying theoretical propositions are by and large of little use in field research. For such procedures presuppose prespecified, fixed designs for the collection of the data needed to test hypotheses. The hallmark of fieldwork methods is flexibility. Fieldworkers must modify and adapt their procedures to the exigencies of the settings in which they work.

Field researchers have always struggled with these issues: how to develop theory that stays close to the events analyzed, and how to assess the evidence for theoretical conclusions when it is inevitably assembled by methods that are not fixed and are often difficult even to specify. The struggle continues, marked now by the growing conviction that standard social science models have limited relevance and may even represent serious obstacles, to adequate solutions to these issues.

In this section I will examine a number of contemporary expressions of these struggles, including (1) ways to develop theory close to the events analyzed, and (2) different ways to appraise the credibility of fieldwork findings.

The Analysis of Field Data

Contemporary approaches to generating theory from field data share several concerns. First, all such approaches insist that the goal is to develop theoretical propositions that are "grounded" in or reflect "intimate familiarity" (Lofland 1976) with the setting or events under study. Theory is grounded when it grows out of, and is directly relevant to, activities occurring in the setting under study.

Second, such concepts are best developed from field data if the researcher avoids a premature commitment to any theory, a priori concept, or system for classifying field data. Glaser and Strauss (1967:33) advocate that the fieldworker go to a research setting as nearly tabula rosa as possible "without any preconceived theory that dictates . . . 'relevancies' in concepts and hypotheses," although not without a more general sociological perspective, question, or focus. Others take a somewhat less extreme position, suggesting that the process is more one of being open to new theoretical possibilities, of minimizing a commitment to see the situation in the conceptual categories the fieldworker brings to the settings.

Finally, in field research, analysis is not a separate, distinct stage of the research process; it occurs at all points of the study as data are collected, recorded, and coded into analytic categories. The collection, coding, and analysis of data are inextricably bound up with each other, a feature of field methods that maximizes flexible pursuit of theoretical leads discovered in the field.

In combination, these concerns render the qualitative analysis of field data "simultaneously deductive and inductive" (Lofland 1976:66). Field research does not involve a strictly inductive process (if such is possible) but rather exhibits a feature that has been termed a "double fitting" of fact to theory and theory to fact. Baldamus (1972:295) has suggested that this procedure:

> may be envisaged by imagining a carpenter alternately altering the shape of a door *and* the shape of the door-frame to obtain a better fit; . . . [in the same way] the investigator simultaneously manipulates the thing he wants to explain as well as his explanatory framework.

Bulmer (1979:660) characterizes this combination of inductive and deductive procedures, also termed "retroduction," in the following terms:

> A theory is not pieced together from observed phenomena; it is rather what makes it possible to observe phenomena as being of a certain sort, and related to other phenomena. Theories put phenomena into systems. They are built up "in reverse" — retroductively.

This moving back and forth between observations and theory, modifying original theoretical statements to fit observations and seeking observations relevant to the emerging theory, characterizes the analytic process in field research.

Beneath these common concerns, however, lie a number of different strategies for developing theory in fieldwork. These differences will be traced out in three current approaches: *grounded theory* (Glaser and Strauss 1967; Schatzman and Strauss 1973; Glaser 1978; and Charmaz, the following reading); *analytic induction* (Bloor 1978; Manning 1978; Katz, whose 1982 essay follows); and the *strategic interaction* analysis of John Lofland (1971, 1976).

Grounded Theory

Grounded theory rests on the claim that the discovery and elaboration of theory are distinct and separate enterprises from its verification. Writing in 1967, Glaser and Strauss proposed grounded theory as a corrective to "an overemphasis in current sociology on the verification of theory, and a resultant de-emphasis on the prior step of discovering what concepts and hypotheses are relevant for the area that one wishes to research" (1967: 1–2). The concern with verification, they felt, often inhibited theoretical originality, leading the fieldworker to turn prematurely from the full development and elaboration of theory to testing its validity (28). Procedures for verifying theoretical propositions proceed on a different logic than those involved in the development of theory. For example, in the process of verification the researcher seeks to come up with a yes or no decision on whether the data support a particular theoretical proposition or hypothesis. In discovering theory, in contrast, the researcher continuously modifies theoretical propositions so that they fit the data, thereby elaborating, extending, and deepening received theory. To develop theory in this way the process of theorizing must be pursued unfettered by the restrictions of verification. Citing a number of studies, Glaser and Strauss concluded (1967:27):

> These researchers ... do not seem to have focused directly on how their theory emerged; as a result, they have not explored how they could have generated more of it more systematically, and with more conceptual generality and scope. A focus on testing can thus easily block the generation of a more rounded and more dense theory.

As an alternative to pursuing verification, Glaser and Strauss recommended a sustained focus on the process of discovering and elaborating complex, interesting theory. The theorist seeks to produce a rich set of analytic propositions that identify and relate many diverse themes rather than establishing the relation between a few key variables decided in advance. Theory is generated in two main ways. First, through *constant comparison* of the data the researcher develops conceptual categories and identifies their properties. Second, additional data are collected using *theoretical sampling,* where new observations are made in order to pursue analytically relevant concerns rather than to establish the frequency or distribution of phenomena. The impetus behind theoretical sampling is thus the elaboration rather than the verification of theory:

> Theoretical sampling is, then, used as a way of checking on the emerging conceptual framework rather than being used for the verification of preconceived hypotheses. Comparisons are made continually between kinds of information to generate qualifying conditions, not disprove hypotheses. While in the field, the researcher continually asks questions as to fit, relevance and workability about the emerging categories and relationships between them. By raising questions at this point in time the researcher checks those issues while he still has access to the data. As a result, he continually fits his analysis to the data by checking as he proceeds. (Glaser 1978:39)

Several general criticisms have been made of the grounded theory approach. Some researchers have suggested that grounded theorists' insistence on deriving concepts from data without reference to established concepts or theories flirts with pure induction. Yet a purely inductive development of theory from data is not possible, as concepts are inevitably involved and presupposed in making sense of data (Bulmer 1979:667–668). Other fieldworkers contend that grounded theorists treat the notion of field "data" in an overly empiricist and unproblematic fashion. Grounded theorists tend to view data and theory as distinct phenomena: theory, once generated, may suggest where to collect data and what kinds of data to collect, but is not seen as inherent in the very notion of data in the first place. Field data, however, are never theoretically "pure," but are always products of prior interpretive and conceptual decisions made by the fieldworker in the ways considered previously in Part I. The grounded theory approach ignores these processes whereby "data" are assembled, processes which build concepts into the data from the very start.[1]

Finally, grounded theory has been criticized for drawing a radical separation between procedures for discovering and for verifying theory. Recent

---

[1] Grounded theorists not only devote little attention to the fieldworker's implicit or explicit concepts used to classify and record events as data in the first place; they also give little or no consideration to the relation of field data to actors' meanings and first-order theories. For they emphasize the grounding of theory *in the data,* not in members' meanings or definitions. And while such data may reflect members' meanings, this sort of "grounding" is neither necessary nor essential (see Charmaz, this volume, pages 112–113).

writers in the philosophy of science, for example, do not confine themselves to the argument that "discovery" and "justification" are "equally important to science . . . and must be given equal weight" (Feyerabend 1975:167). These writers contend more fundamentally that the very distinction is invalid and useless since "we are dealing with a single uniform domain of procedures all of which are equally important for the growth of science" (Feyerabend 1975:167). One consequence of grounded theorists' insistence on this distinction is particularly significant: while grounded theory glorifies and tries to further generate theory in its own right, it also treats discovery as a stage prior to verification. This rigid divorce between discovery and verification lends support to the critique of fieldwork as insightful but not rigorous (see Katz, this volume, pages 128–130).

Analytic Induction

In *Method of Sociology* (1934), Florian Znaniecki proposed the method of analytic induction as a rigorous, systematic means for deriving theoretical propositions from empirical data. Znaniecki contrasted analytic induction with statistical "enumerative induction," where conceptual categories and empirical generalizations are formulated from an existing pool of cases. Proponents of analytic induction, in contrast, begin with a rough formulation of the phenomenon to be explained and an initial hypothesis explaining the phenomenon, then go to a small number of cases (even a single case) to see if the hypothesis fits that case. If not, either the hypothesis or the phenomenon to be explained is reformulated so that the case is accounted for. The procedure then continues, with the researcher examining cases and producing reformulations of these sorts whenever negative cases are encountered, until *all cases* can be explained (see Katz, this volume, page 130*ff*). In this way analytic induction "abstracts from a given concrete case the features that are essential, and generalizes them" (Bulmer 1979: 661).

The two classic instances of field research using the analytic induction procedure are Lindesmith's study of opiate addiction (1947) and Cressey's study of embezzlement (1953). In each instance the research moved through a series of successive reformulations of both what was to be explained and the hypotheses offered as explanation. Consider, for example, the stages of reformulation made by Cressey.

First, Cressey noted that since the category of convicted embezzlers included both con artists and passers of bad checks, and did not include some offenders who had in fact embezzled (e.g., a bank teller convicted of forgery but not embezzlement for forging a customer's name to a check), it was not useful sociologically. He thus redefined his phenomenon as persons who had "accepted a position of trust in good faith . . . [and then] violated that trust by committing a crime" (1953:20).

Cressey's explanation of such violations of trust began with the hypothesis that such violations occurred when those in positions of trust came to see theft as merely "technical violations." He rejected this notion on finding convicted embezzlers who admitted knowing that their behavior had been wrong and illegal. Next he explored the possibility that violations occurred when a worker "defines a need for extra funds or extended use of property as an 'emergency' which cannot be met by legal means" (28). But some violators noted even greater emergencies in the past but no violation, and others reported no financial emergency ever. The revised hypothesis focused on psychological isolation, often tied to gambling losses: "persons become trust violators when they conceive of themselves as having incurred financial obligations which are considered as non-socially sanctionable and which, consequently, must be satisfied by a private or secret means" (28). But negative cases appeared in which there were no financial obligations and hence that condition was modified to more general "non-shareable problems" seen as solvable by trust violation. The final negative case occurred with violators who met the above conditions but who had not earlier embezzled because of their ideas of right and wrong. Changing his hypothesis to incorporate these cases, Cressey came to the following final theory:

> Trusted persons become trust violators when they conceive of themselves as having a financial problem which is non-shareable, are aware that this problem can be secretly resolved by violation of the position of financial trust, and are able to apply to their own conduct in that situation verbalizations which enable them to adjust their conceptions of themselves as trusted persons with their conceptions of themselves as users of the entrusted funds or property. (30)

Analytic induction theories have been criticized in several ways. Most relevantly, Turner (1953:606) argued that despite claims to universal explanation, Cressey's theory cannot be used to predict who will and will not embezzle, since it does not indicate when and how a problem becomes nonshareable, when embezzlement comes to be seen as a solution, or which violators will be able to rationalize their behavior. Turner also noted that the causes of embezzlement Cressey pointed out cannot be fully specified apart from the outcomes they presumably produced. As he asked: "Is it possible, for example, to assert that a problem is nonshareable *until* a person embezzles to get around it?" (606)

The selection by Katz seeks to revitalize and extend the procedure of analytic induction as a distinctively qualitative yet rigorous way for analyzing field data. Katz locates the search for negative cases and the modification of analytic propositions to incorporate such negative cases as the essential processes in theorizing with field data; he suggests that they can be pursued without claiming universal explanation.

Finally, to return to the critical difference between analytic induction and grounded theory: analytic induction seeks to produce a total explanation of the phenomena observed in a way that responds to the requirements of verification. Whereas grounded theory separates the processes of explanation and verification in theory in order to pursue the former more intensely, analytic induction, particularly as expressed in Katz's statement of the approach, asserts that qualitative analysis has a distinctive rigorous, systematic quality in its own right, and is not merely the insightful precursor to ultimately more important verification.

Interactional Strategy Analysis

John Lofland (1971, 1976) urged that the development of theoretical generalizations in field research be pursued with the substantive theoretical framework he termed "qualitative strategy analysis" of social interaction. This framework builds upon analysis of distinctive types of "interactional *strategies*" used by actors in different social *situations* (1976: Chapters 3 and 4). The goal is to move from topical or substantive concepts of strategy and situation to more generic conceptions. As Lofland noted in reference to situations (1976:31):

> To conceive of a situation generically is to discriminate and bring forward social aspects that possess more generalized, more common, more universal relevance. A given situation is scrutinized in terms of the *kinds* of general human concerns that are being coped with and acted toward. The analyst attempts to answer the question: "Of what abstract, sociologically conceived *class* of situation is this particular situation an instance?" Or, "What are the abstract features of this kind of situation?" Or, "What kind of situation is this?" To answer questions such as these is to offer a generic conception of a situation.

Lofland emphasized that the fieldworker approaches data with such concepts rather than without theoretical commitment. As he sketched the process (1976:66):

> The analyst
> 1. begins with an abstract sense of what a generic situation is and what generic strategies are;
> 2. immerses himself in the concrete items of the actual social life under study;
> 3. develops and constructs a generically framed analysis of situations and strategies from the organic intertwining of items 1 and 2.

Finally, rather than urging varied comparisons and theoretical sampling within one study, risking one-shot and superficial observations, Lofland advocated a process of conceptual accumulation, in which successive studies "addressed to the same generic situation" are compared, typologized, and integrated into a more comprehensive set of analytic statements and generalizations. Lofland emphasized the necessity of completing sustained fieldwork in a variety of specific settings, and only then making systematic comparisons. He warned of the dangers of "short-circuiting" that arise otherwise from trying to generalize without adequate data (1976:93–94).

Problems of Evidence and Credibility

In quantitative social science research problems of verification, and, more generally, of the adequacy of theory and evidence, are addressed through procedures for assessing *validity* and *reliability*. These procedures cannot be directly carried over to the assessment of qualitative analysis and data, since they presuppose preset research designs that are at odds with the flexibility so intrinsic to field methods. Fieldworkers have thus developed a variety of different procedures for trying to assess the adequacy of their theories and evidence.

External and Internal Validity

One response has been to try to develop more or less rough analogs to quantitative measures of validity and reliability that would apply to qualitative data analysis. Denzin (1970:185–218) provided one leading example of this effort, suggesting that the verification of theoretical propositions hinges on questions of external validity — "Can the observations of the participant observer be generalized to other populations?" — and internal validity — "Do the observations represent real differences, or are they artifacts of the observational process?" (199) External validity — the representativeness of a particular field study — requires the fieldworker to demonstrate that the cases studied "are representative of the class of units to which generalizations are made" (200). This process is facilitated by the sort of specification of the phenomenon of interest that occurs with analytic induction.

Problems of internal validity are more pressing in fieldwork. As Denzin set up the task: "Internal validity sensitizes the observer to the biasing and distorting effects of the following intrinsic factors: historical factors, subject maturation, subject bias, subject mortality, reactive effects of the observer, changes in the observer, and peculiar aspects of the situations in which the observations were conducted" (201). Reactive effects — the ways in which the presence and actions of the observer affect and change the setting under observation — are particularly critical to detect; they can be identified both by directly checking with key informants and by careful review of notes about field relations.

The Credibility of Field Data

Denzin drew heavily on the approach developed by Howard Becker and his coworkers and reported in a series of influential writings on fieldwork methods (many reprinted in Becker 1970a). Generally avoiding the terms validity and reliability, Becker addressed the question, "how credible are the conclusions derived from data gathered by fieldwork?" (1970a:39). In examining this question Becker gave special attention to the problem of reactivity, that is, persons' tendency to behave in ways that are direct responses to the presence and actions of the observer. From the perspective of quantitative methods, field data appear particularly subject to reactive effects since they are not collected by pre-specified, fixed procedures. In fact, Becker argued, fieldwork data are less artifactual or reactive than either experimental or survey data because they are subject to the social constraints which naturally operate in the situation studied. Whereas the experiment creates a social situation with experimenter-defined parameters, and survey research relies on a short and again artificial interview, field-workers study people in their natural habitats subject to the everyday constraints operating there (1970a:46):

> They are enmeshed in social relationships important to them, at work, in community life, wherever. The events they participate in matter to them. The opinions and actions of the people they interact with must be taken into account, because they affect those events. All the constraints that affect them in their ordinary lives continue to operate while the observer observes.

Becker argued furthermore that fieldwork conclusions are highly credible in that they rest on "rich detailed data." As he emphasized, such data (1970a:52):

> ... counter the twin dangers of respondent duplicity and observer bias by making it difficult for respondents to produce data that uniformly support a mistaken conclusion, just as they make it difficult for the observer to restrict his observations so that he sees only what supports his prejudices and expectations.

Rich data are a product of the fact that the fieldworker spends a long period of time studying the particular setting, collecting a variety of observations on any particular topic, and using many different procedures. Any particular conclusion or interpretation the fieldworker comes to "has therefore been subjected to hundreds and thousands of tests" (1970a:53), which may not be readily apparent, however, in the formal presentation of the results.

Becker also proposed more specific procedures for assessing fieldwork evidence. In the first place, data are more credible when they come to the observer as a "volunteered statement" rather than in response to a question put by the observer (1970a:30): "The volunteered statement seems likely to reflect the observer's preoccupations and possible biases less than one which is made in response to some action of the observer, for the observer's very question may direct the informant into giving an answer which might never occur to him otherwise." Second, the interpretation of particular pieces of evidence will depend upon the group context in which they were observed. What people say and do in the presence of the observer alone may not be what they say or do in the presence of the observer and their own colleagues. Becker cited the instance of medical students, who "express deeply 'idealistic' sentiments about medicine when alone with the observer, but behave and talk in a very 'cynical' way when surrounded by fellow students" (30). Finally, the credibility of fieldwork evidence depends on the "credibility of informants." Much evidence consists of statements members offer to the fieldworker, and the meaning and import of these statements must be assessed by answering such questions as: "Does the informant have reason to lie or conceal some of what he sees as the truth?" (29).

Toward "The Social System of Analytic Fieldwork"

As Katz suggests in his discussion of qualitative methodology (this volume, page 128), at several critical points Becker's approach to fieldwork evidence remains wedded to more positivist, quantitative models of validity or reliability. In particular, Becker often conceptualized reactivity in terms drawn from these models. He tended to treat reactive effects, for example, primarily as sources of distortion and bias and hence as factors that should if possible be eliminated from field observation.[2] Yet many fieldworkers have come to advance a different conception of reactivity, one that emphasizes becoming aware of rather than eliminating reactive effects. Gussow (1964:231) provided one of the first and clearest statements of this position: "Ordinarily, in good fieldwork, researchers are not greatly concerned about whether they have disturbed the natural field or not, provided that they can analyze how they affected it structurally. Indeed, by affecting it, they often get to know better what it is they are studying." In this view, "the investigator is conceptualized as part of the reality being studied. Here, it is taken for granted that the observer alters that which is observed; but these alterations are the subject of study . . . in the first [view], the alterations, resulting from the effect of the observer upon that which is observed, are interference; in the second, they are data" (Cassell and Wax 1980:261).

As Pollner and Emerson argue (this volume, page 236), fieldwork is unavoidably interactional in character, and the fieldworker is necessarily consequential for those studied. Solutions to reactivity thus lie not in restricting, cutting off, or regularizing field interactions, but in trying to

---

[2] At times, for example, Becker wrote as if totally nonreactive field methods are possible. One of his main arguments, after all, is that those observed are constrained to act in ways they would were no observer present. This argument thus holds up a model of "pure" field data uncontaminated by the presence of the observer. It is this model that has been rejected by the changed conception of reactivity discussed here.

become sensitive to and perceptive of how one is perceived and treated by others. The researcher, in Clarke's phrase, is viewed as "a source for the result, [not] as a contaminant of it" (1975:99). It is this conception of reactivity that Katz incorporates in his analysis of the evidentiary strength of field methods.

A second positivist carryover appears at points in Becker's discussions of evaluating the credibility of informants. Becker often emphasized the need to determine the "truth value" of statements made by informants; specifically, he suggested that volunteered statements have more such value than directed statements, or that statements made to a locally powerless observer are worth more than statements made to an observer perceived as significant in the local setting. In effect, Becker was suggesting that we give simple yes/no answers to questions of the credibility of field data; yes, it is valid, no, it is not valid. But in doing fieldwork, researchers are often concerned more with what a particular statement means for the social world in which it was made than simply with whether it is true or false. As Becker himself emphasized in another context (discussing the apparently conflicting "idealistic" and "cynical" statements of medical students) (1970a:48): "We would err if we interpreted one or the other of these expressions as the 'real' one, dismissing the other as mere cover-up."

The fieldworker has to assess the validity of the data collected. This means that the fieldworker has to decide whether a particular observation is typical, a lie, a distortion, or whatever. But the point of making such determinations is not to throw out those pieces of data now counted as false or incorrect, or even to be categorizing them in those terms. Rather, once having made these determinations, the fieldworker must trace out their connections with the forms of social and interactional life in which they occur. In this respect, the lie, once detected, may be even more interesting than the truth, since it opens up a social phenomenon to be explored, understood, and explained. The fieldworker's task has only begun once a statement comes to be interpreted as a lie; a critical stage of fieldwork inquiry then takes place as an effort is made to understand why the lie was told and what it indicates about social relations in that setting or about relations between the informant and the researcher.

Finally, determining the credibility of informants is a much more complex and embedded process than many discussions of fieldwork methods acknowledge. There are no formulae for deciding whether or not to believe what those in the field tell us or others. Moreover, to conclude that a particular informant lied is only possible as the result of having spent time observing in a setting and learning something about the ways and concerns of those observed. When we first start, we cannot tell the lies from the truths or discern what is said cynically to please superiors from what is said in good-faith community with coworkers.

"Natural History" of the Research
and Explicating One's Methods

The revised conception of reactivity, seeing the researcher as unavoidably part of the reality under study, encourages new approaches to assessing the adequacy of fieldwork findings.[3] One such approach emerging in contemporary field research recommends making explicit the actual procedures, analytic assumptions, and interpretive devices used to collect, make sense of, and communicate field reports. While Becker (1970a) suggested a "natural history" of the field project along these lines (see also Glaser and Strauss 1967:230–231), Cicourel (1964, 1978) has most explicitly advanced this proposal. Cicourel recommended that the fieldworker be as explicit as possible in describing how he or she came to a particular interpretation of observed events and incidents. This in turn involves several different procedures. First, the fieldworker, like members, relies heavily on various kinds of "background knowledge" in deciding the import and meaning of any particular scene or action. Some of this background knowledge derives from familiarity with the setting studied and the people in it; other parts come from the more global, common-sense knowledge about social life we possess as members of society. Cicourel often uses a procedure of trying to fill in as exactly as he can manage the kinds of background knowledge he has used to come to his interpretation (see Cicourel 1968). A second key to specifying the fieldworker's interpretive practices lies in identifying the implicit "model of the actor" (1974a:27) that informs and determines the attribution of meanings to specific incidents.

In addition to trying to self-consciously explicate and communicate one's interpretive practices, Cicourel also sought to put fieldwork methods on a more solid ground by trying to study the ways in which observations and experiences get transformed into field "data" in the first place. More specifically, Cicourel has begun to examine the complex informational processing whereby researchers compile their major data base of written field notes. Inevitably fieldworkers selectively comprehend, interpret, and code in memory ongoing social activities in ways that depend on their conceptual presuppositions, general cultural knowledge, prior experiences in, and particular knowledge of the setting. Written field notes involve subsequent "summarizations" of these recalled exchanges, and hence reflect

[3] New approaches become desirable because of the following considerations: Under more positivist conceptions, the adequacy of fieldwork methods and of the findings these methods produce were to be assessed by determining how closely these findings correspond to "events in the real world." But when all findings are seen as inevitably dependent upon the methods used to discover them, there is no way of obtaining access to such "events in the real world" without recourse to some other method. Adequacy, then, can be determined less by correspondence than by comparison of the results of different methods, a procedure usually termed "triangulation" (e.g., Denzin 1970:297ff).

the structure of *memory* processes. Cicourel has examined these processes by comparing the transcripts of medical interviews with physicians' written summaries (1974b). More precise field data can be collected, he maintains, through "the explicit study of interpretational and summarization procedures, as they occur during interaction, interviews, and taking notes or elaborating upon them" (1978:29).

Appraising Ethnographic Accounts

Appraising theory and evidence in ethnographic accounts raises a set of additional issues. For ethnographic analyses take as their basic commitment to convey the subjective realities of those studied. To talk about the relationship between "data" and findings is one thing; to talk about findings as somehow reflecting or capturing members' meanings is something else again.

One standard way in which ethnographers try to establish that their descriptions are credible is to emphasize the fieldworker's closeness to and familiarity with the life and culture under study. Immersion, proximity, or at least some sort of social and psychological intimacy, are thus used not only as a method, but also as a way of claiming validity or credibility for findings. The claim is made, usually implicitly but sometimes explicitly, "I was there and I know how it is." It is this sort of stance that Bittner terms "realism" in the selection included here.[4]

Bittner argues that the claim, "I know because I was there and have come to see things from the members' perspective," assumes that the fieldworker's experience of members' worlds is essentially isomorphic with the members' own experiences. It is this claimed identity of experience or perspective that many ethnographic accounts invoke on behalf of the credibility of their findings. Bittner, however, insists that the ethnographer can never completely adopt the actor's perspective and attitude, but can only approximate it. In part this results from the limitation that the ethnographer's experience can never exactly duplicate that of a member. In some cases, for example, the member has grown up in that culture, whereas the fieldworker comes upon that culture as a "second culture" apprehended in light of his or her first culture. In addition, the fieldworker is in the setting only temporarily, and knows that the research will eventually end. The fieldworker's experience is thus freer, a product ultimately of choice and decision; the experience of the member, and even of the stranger who has come to stay in a new culture, is surrounded by necessity. As Karp and Kendall note (1982:257):

[4] Marcus and Cushman (1982) analyze the similar but more elaborated tradition of "ethnographic realism" in anthropological fieldwork, examining ethnographies produced in this mold as an established literary form with its own distinctive "genre conventions" for conveying plausibility and a sense of having "been there."

Fieldworkers . . . are not subject to the same constraints, and this must inevitably affect the quality of their experience. Rosemary Firth (1972) recounts a nightmare she had shortly before leaving the field. She dreamt that she really was a Malay woman, "squatting in front of a smokey fire." The participation that the fieldworker gives is neither as committed nor as constrained as the native's.

This lack of commitment and constraint, Bittner contends, becomes reflected at a deep level in the ethnographer's concern with the "actor's perspective." Bittner points out that the very formulation of members' realities and concerns as "perspectives" involves a fundamental distortion. It leads the fieldworker to slip "in and out of points of view," treating the "meanings of objects as more or less freely conjured" by members (this volume, page 154). Description in terms of the actor's perspective tends to depict social life as *perceived* events and meanings, ignoring or distorting the lived reality of members' worlds which are characterized by "traits of depth, stability, and necessity that people recognize as actually inherent in the circumstances of their existence" (this volume, page 155). As Geertz (1976:224) suggested, what the ethnographer *sees* as a "concept" the native *experiences* more immediately:

> People use experience-near concepts spontaneously, unselfconsciously, as it were colloquially; they do not, except fleetingly and on occasion, recognize that there are any "concepts" involved at all. That is what experience-near means — that ideas and the realities they inform are naturally and indissolubly bound up together. What else could you call a hippopotamus?

The implication is clear: "The ethnographer does not, and, in my opinion, largely cannot, perceive what his informants perceive" (Geertz 1976:224). The ethnographer, then, does not grasp the members' perspective "in itself," but as mediated through his or her own theoretical, cultural, and personal constructs and concerns. The ethnographer, finally, does not produce description from the members' point of view, but description of a member's point of view from the point of view of a researcher.[5]

Several strategies have been proposed to ensure a more direct verification of ethnographic accounts that are cognizant of the distinction between

[5] This is true even if the observer seeks to empathize with members' concerns and meanings. Geertz (1976:236–237) considers the limits of empathy and of efforts to gain "acceptance" by those studied in the following passage:

> . . . whatever accurate or half-accurate sense one gets of what one's informants are, as the phrase goes, really like, does not come from the experience of that acceptance as such, which is part of one's own biography, not of theirs. It comes from the ability to construe their modes of expression, what I would call their symbol systems, that such an acceptance allows one to work toward developing. Understanding the form and pressure of, to use the dangerous word one more time, natives' inner lives is more like grasping a proverb, catching an illusion, seeing a joke — or, as I have suggested, reading a poem — than it is like achieving communion.

members' realities and the fieldworker's descriptions of those realities. First, in line with the view of culture as what a person has to know in order to act appropriately in the eyes of its members, a number of fieldworkers have proposed that ethnographic accounts can be verified by being used as instructions to an outsider attempting to pass as a member. Douglas (1976:123), for example, held that tests of "interaction effectiveness" provide presumptive evidence of the fieldworker's grasp of appropriate behavior in the setting and hence of field findings. Wiseman (1970:280–281) reported that she "tested" her findings on skid row life by having several novices read her descriptions and then "successfully" pass as skid row drunks for short periods of time. Yet it may be possible to "pass" as a member without actually performing as a competent insider (due to the politeness or face-saving graces of members, for example).

A second procedure seeks to verify fieldwork findings by taking them back to the members whose worlds they describe and analyze to see if members recognize and hence "validate" such accounts. Such a procedure has been variously termed "member validation" (Gould et al. 1974), "member tests of validity" (Douglas 1976), or "host verification" (Schatzman and Strauss 1973). As Bloor's essay indicates, this procedure must recognize that fieldwork accounts are second-order constructs, formulated for different purposes and to different ends than member accounts. We should thus expect not that the accounts will be absolutely identical, but rather that "members recognize, understand, and accept one's description of the setting" (Douglas 1976:131). Yet even here, as Bloor explains, difficulties arise. In particular, the fieldworker must inevitably interpret the meaning and import of members' evaluations of his or her findings. As Bloor suggests, positive member reaction may come to be seen as the product of friendship, disinterest, or civility, negative reaction as the result of ideological preconceptions or local institutional commitment. Under these conditions, member support or rejection of fieldwork findings may reveal very little about the "validity" of these findings and a great deal about what is significant and meaningful to members.

There is, finally, a danger that fieldworkers will understand and use these procedures in too rigidly a positivist way, literally as tests of validity. Exposing findings to the scrutiny and response of those studied does not produce absolute "truth" against which to measure and evaluate those findings, but only another statement whose meaning must be inferred or determined by the fieldworker.

The Grounded Theory Method: An Explication and Interpretation

Kathy Charmaz

Publication of Glaser and Strauss' pioneering book, *The Discovery of Grounded Theory* (1967), provided a strong intellectual rationale for using qualitative research to develop theoretical analyses. The authors were protesting against a methodological climate in which qualitative research typically was viewed as only a helpful preliminary to the "real" methodologies of quantitative research (see, for examples, Hyman et al. 1954; Lazarsfeld 1944; and Stouffer 1962). In addition to providing a powerful rhetoric for qualitative analysis per se, in the *Discovery* book Glaser and Strauss also began articulating research strategies to codify the analytic process throughout the research project. In the decade that followed, other qualitative researchers who held different perspectives, notably Douglas (1976), Johnson (1975), Katz (this volume), Lofland (1971), Lofland and Lofland (in press), and Schatzman and Strauss (1973) contributed to the growing literature on collecting and rendering qualitative materials.

Both the assumptions and analytic methods of grounded theory have been criticized by some qualitative researchers on a number of counts. Lofland and Lofland (in press), for example, suggest that grounded theorists fail to give proper attention both to data collection techniques and to the quality of the gathered materials. From Katz's (this volume) perspective, discovery and verification are inseparable and the grounded theory contrast between them in some sense perpetuates the notion that qualitative research is preliminary. These criticisms misinterpret the aims and methods of grounded theory. Unfortunately, several features of the grounded theory method have contributed to such misinterpretation. First, the language of the grounded theory method relies on terms commonly used in quantitative research and, I believe, this language lags behind actual development of the method. To illustrate, the terms such as coding, comparison groups, and theoretical sampling reflect the language of quantitative research and often elicit images of logical deductive quantitative

Used by permission of the author. Copyright © 1983 by Kathy Charmaz.

I am indebted to members of the Bay Area SWS writing group for their comments on an earlier draft of this paper, with special thanks to Gail Hornstein for her careful review of it. I also appreciate the critiques provided by Adele Clarke, Robert M. Emerson, Marilyn Little, and Susan Leigh Star.

procedures.[1] Second, the method arises from and, to date, relies on Chicago school sociology, which, as Rock suggested (1979), depended heavily on an oral tradition implicitly transmitted to students. I view grounded theory similarly as a practice learned largely through apprenticeship. Although Glaser's (1978) work is a critical step forward in explicating the oral tradition in grounded theory, the work contains many tacit assumptions and speaks most directly to students who worked closely with him or Strauss.

In response to these criticisms and misunderstandings of the grounded theory method, I aim to: (1) explicate key analytic procedures and assumptions often left implicit in earlier statements; (2) offer interpretations which suggest varying approaches to the method; and (3) provide substantive applications of the method to illustrate how it can be used during the analytic process. Because I aim to explicate and interpret the method, I draw heavily on approaches developed by Glaser (1978). Throughout the discussion, I will provide examples and illustrations from my own past and current research using this method.

A Preliminary Statement of the Grounded Theory Method

The grounded theory method stresses discovery and theory development rather than logical deductive reasoning which relies on prior theoretical frameworks. These two aspects of the method lead the grounded theorist to certain distinctive strategies. First, data collection and analysis proceed simultaneously (see Glaser and Strauss 1967). Since grounded theorists intend to construct theory from the data itself, they need to work with solid, rich data that can be used to elicit thorough development of analytic issues (see Lofland and Lofland, in press). Grounded theorists shape their data collection from their analytic interpretations and discoveries, and therefore, sharpen their observations. Additionally, they check and fill out emerging ideas by collecting further data. These strategies serve to strengthen both the quality of the data and the ideas developed from it.

Second, both the processes and products of research are shaped from the data rather than from preconceived logically deduced theoretical frameworks (see, for example, Biernacki, forthcoming; Broadhead, in press; and Wiener 1981). Grounded theorists rely heavily on studying their data and reading in other fields during the initial stages of research (see Glaser 1978). They do not rely directly on the literature to shape their ideas, since they believe that they should develop their own analyses independently. From the grounded theory perspective, researchers who pour their data into someone else's theoretical framework or substantive analysis add

---

[1] No doubt this reflects Glaser's rigorous quantitative methodological training at Columbia. To date, the language of grounded theory is largely the language Glaser adopted.

little innovation and also may perpetuate ideas that could be further re-fined, transcended, or discarded.

Third, grounded theorists do not follow the traditional quantitative canons of verification. They do, however, check their developing ideas with further specific observations, make systematic comparisons between observations, and, often, take their research beyond the confines of one topic, setting, or issue. Perhaps because they make systematic efforts to check and refine emerging categories, their efforts may be confused with traditional verification. From the grounded theory perspective, the method does not preclude verification by other types of researchers; it merely in-dicates a division of labor.

Fourth, not only do grounded theorists study *process,* they assume that making theoretical sense of social life is itself a process. As such, theoretical analyses may be transcended by further work either by the original or a later theorist by bringing more and different questions to the data (see Glaser 1978). In keeping with their foundations in pragmatism, then, grounded theorists aim to develop fresh theoretical interpretations of the data rather than explicitly aim for any final or complete interpretation of it (see Schwartz and Jacobs 1979).

Coding

Coding, the initial phase of the analytic method, is simply the process of *categorizing* and *sorting* data. Codes then serve as shorthand devices to *label, separate, compile,* and *organize* data. Codes range from simple, con-crete, and topical categories to more general, abstract conceptual categories for an emerging theory.[2] In qualitative coding, researchers develop codes out of their field notes, interviews, case histories, or other collected ma-terials (these could include diaries by participants, journals, interactional maps, historical documents, and so forth). Examples of codes I have used in my studies of chronic illness include self-esteem, sources of support, discovering illness, defining limitations, transitory self-pity, identifying mo-ment, and identity questioning. These codes range from lesser to greater complexity as the analytic process proceeds.

Codes may be treated as conceptual categories when they are developed analytically. This means the researcher defines them carefully, delineates their properties, explicates their causes, demonstrates the conditions under which they operate, and spells out their consequences. A descriptive cate-

---

[2] Qualitative coding is not the same as quantitative coding. The term itself pro-vides a case in point in which the language may obscure meaning and method. Quantitative coding requires preconceived, logically deduced codes into which the data are placed. Qualitative coding, in contrast, means *creating* categories from inter-pretation of the data. Rather than relying on preconceived categories and standard-ized procedures, qualitative coding has its own distinctive structure, logic and pur-pose (see Glaser and Strauss 1967, Glaser 1978).

gory such as defining illness applies to the substantive area studied. A theoretical category such as transforming identity, in contrast, is part of a theoretical scheme, and may be applied across diverse substantive areas.

Codes serve to summarize, synthesize, and sort many observations made of the data. By providing the pivotal link between the data collection and its conceptual rendering, coding becomes the fundamental *means* of developing the analysis. Hence, the categorizing and sorting inherent in coding are more than simply assigning subject headings or topics to data. Researchers use codes to pull together and categorize a series of otherwise discrete events, statements, and observations which they identify in the data.[3] Researchers make the codes fit the data, rather than forcing the data into codes. By doing so, they gain a clearer rendering of the materials and greater accuracy. When reading the data, grounded theorists ask: "What do I see going on here?" To illustrate, when reading a number of interviews with widows who had been housewives, I noted that these women repeatedly mentioned the pressures to establish social and economic independence that they confronted due to their husbands' deaths. Although they later enjoyed their new pursuits, they initially were fearful and reluctant to begin independent lives. Here, I coined the term "forced independence" to code their experience into a more abstract *conceptual category* that described and analyzed the widows' experience (Charmaz 1980a).

Grounded theorists code for *processes* that are fundamental in ongoing social life. These processes may be at organizational or social psychological levels, depending on the researcher's training and interests. To find these processes, grounded theorists carefully scrutinize participants' statements and actions for patterns, inconsistencies, contradictions, and intended and unintended consequences. The initial questions they ask are: What are people doing? What is happening? (See Glaser 1978). What the researcher views the participants as doing may not be the same as what participants claim to do. For example, in a treatment unit, participants may claim that their actions are devoted fundamentally to treating patients, yet the researcher may decide an intense jockeying for power underlies their actions, and thus, is the more significant process to pursue.

The *assumptions* that participants hold provide a fertile field for coding. Seeking to discover, identify, and ask questions about these assumptions keeps the researcher thinking critically and defining what is implicit in the

---

[3] Glaser and Strauss (1967) imply that the data speak for themselves. They don't. Since researchers pose questions to the data, the codes they develop directly reflect the questions posed. Similarly, Glaser and Strauss often seem to take a partly objectivist view of the researcher's role. While they encourage researchers to build on their prior experience, they frequently seem to assume that researchers are interchangeable and remain unaffected by their commitments, interests, expertise, and personal histories. My interpretation and use of the method is more distinctively phenomenological (see Blumer 1969).

data. The researcher then defines how participants act upon their assumptions in the specific setting, which, of course, helps the researcher convert topics into processes. Further, rather than viewing the participants' assumptions as truth itself, the researcher gains some distance on his or her materials. In this way too the researcher avoids overimmersion, which may lead to taking over the views of participants as one's own. For example, a medical sociologist who uncritically accepts the practitioners' discourse of meaning may shape his or her research around terms such as "coping," "stress," and "stress-reduction" without looking at their underlying assumptions.

When looking for processes, the researcher also must ask: What kind of events are at issue here? How are they constructed? What do these events mean? By looking for major processes, researchers delineate how events are related to each other. In a particular study, a researcher may identify several major processes. If so, then grounded theorists code for all of them and may decide later which ones to pursue. Importantly, a grounded theorist sticks with his or her interpretations of the data and follows leads from them, even when they lead to surprising new research problems.

At times, researchers readily identify basic processes, for example, when they are so visible, stark, and direct that even a naive researcher quickly defines them. But other major processes remain much more implicit and covert. Those which are tacitly shared but remain unspoken sometimes are difficult to pull out. This is particularly the case when participants themselves cannot articulate the assumptions and meanings that they, in fact, hold and act upon. In an earlier project on a rehabilitation institution for the physically disabled, I discovered that middle-class staff held markedly different conceptions of time than most of the lower-class patients whom they served. Professional staff held a linear progressive view of time, with the realization of goals in the future. Yet they worked with patients who generally held a cyclic view of time, situated in the present. For the patients, time moved from present to present, from crisis to crisis. Repeatedly, staff became frustrated by these patients' failure to use time in the institution to work on the small incremental gains toward a distant goal that staff viewed as both medically and personally appropriate. Instead, patients simply passed time, waited for change, or killed time with unsanctioned pursuits until discharged (Calkins 1970).

Initial Coding

Coding is a two-phase process: an *initial* searching phase precedes a later phase of *focused* coding (Glaser 1978). In the initial phase, researchers look for what they can define and discover in the data. They then look for leads, ideas, and issues *in* the data themselves. Glaser (1978) advocates line by line coding to gain a full theoretical accounting of the data. This prompts the researcher to look at the data with a theoretical eye from the start and actively encourages playing with and developing ideas.

Although every researcher brings to his or her research general preconceptions founded in expertise, theory, method, and experience, using the grounded theory method necessitates that the researcher look at the data from as many vantage points as possible. At this point, the rule for the researcher to follow is: *study your emerging data.* At first, the data may appear to be a mass of confusing, unrelated accounts. But by studying and coding (often I code the same materials several times just after collecting them), the researcher begins to create order.[4] If researchers think that the data suggest more questions than they can answer, then they need to collect more data while simultaneously coding them. Sometimes, neither the data actually collected nor the researcher's emerging ideas are related to the original research objectives or topics. In this case, the researcher either continues with the material on hand or finds more appropriate sources of data for the original topic. In my chronic illness interviews, for instance, I had not anticipated covering either self-pity or social support. Yet both these topics were repeated themes so I followed up on them.

Several further suggestions from my experience may help. First, I attend to the general context, central participants and their roles, timing and structuring of events, and the relative emphasis participants place on various issues in the data.[5] I also look for connections between individuals' special situations and problems and their interpretations of their experience.[6] For example the problems of leading independent lives become magnified for young adults with serious chronic illnesses who seek simultaneously to develop intimate relationships and to prepare themselves for jobs.

Second, I construct codes to note what participants lack, gloss over, or ignore, as well as what they stress. For example, I note the kinds of information patients possessed or lacked about their illnesses when they first were diagnosed. Also, since I am interested in time perspective, I note the lack of awareness of time when respondents tell me that they did not think about time at all as well as other respondents' descriptions of an intensified

---

[4] If the confusion is not worked through analytically, piles of thin, undeveloped data result. Hence, it is important to keep studying and coding data even though it may seem easier to simply collect more. Another problem may occur: In dispelling initial confusion, early analysis may induce an erroneous sense of familiarity with the setting or issue. The fieldworker must persist in efforts to ferret out negative cases, account for variations, and explore the consequences of ideas. In this respect, premature publication is a potential hazard of the method.

[5] By context I mean the range of historical, political, economic, and organizational issues relevant to these particular data. The researcher needs to address context (1) to place the study in perspective, (2) to collect and understand the data, and (3) to minimize reifying ideas.

[6] Glaser (1978) also warns the researcher not to assume that face sheet data are important (age, sex, race, religion, occupation, number of years employed, etc.) until they show up in the data in patterned ways. Thus, face sheet data, like other categories, must also be grounded in the data to merit inclusion in the completed analysis.

awareness of time. On a more concrete level, I code for the absence of attention and assistance from intimates when it is observed, implied, or reported, besides coding the detailed accounts of other patients who had available intimates to visit and help.

Third, I scrutinize the data for in vivo codes. Research participants sometimes describe their experiences with imagery and power that far transcend their individual situations. One young diabetic described himself as trying to become "super-normal," an experience that many newly and/ or younger chronically ill persons shared. Later, I took the term super-normal identity and raised it to a conceptual level to treat analytically (Charmaz 1973). Many of the chronically ill talked about the significance of others "being there." Subsequently, I took the term "being there" as a code and devised subcodes to pull out its underlying meanings and assumptions.

Fourth, I try to identify succinctly the process that the data indicates. Here the onus is on the researcher to identify, through coding, what the data *mean*. For example, some respondents who said they had been "depressed" or "felt bad about myself" described these feelings in ways that were strikingly similar to those who explicitly defined their feelings as self-pity (Charmaz 1980a). *Comparing* bits of data with other data for their similarities and differences helps enormously in developing codes. For example, both "negative" feelings such as self-pity and elusive topics such as experiencing time sometimes prove to be difficult subjects for a respondent to address. So, I compare responses to help me identify what is implicit in one set of data but explicit in another. Then, I may decide to return to earlier respondents with more detailed queries.[7]

Examples of Initial Coding

In the following examples, I show the kind of diversity and number of codes developed in initial coding when the researcher pursues as many diverse avenues as he or she can create. The interview statements below are made by persons with different chronic illnesses. My study centers on experiences of time and self of the chronically ill.

---

[7] Furthermore, developing an explicit category for the experience allows the researcher to go back to respondents and ask direct questions. I built rapport with many of my respondents, and I found that I could go back to them to explore many sensitive topics directly. The following statement illustrates the kind of direct response I got when I went back to one woman and asked her if she had experienced self-pity. She replied:

Oh, yes. How tragic! Why me? Yeah, it's not fair. I get a disease I've never heard of; does anybody else have it? I mean I'm nice to small children and animals. I thought I had good Karma and then I grow up with allergies, get colitis, have back injuries and have migraines. Why do all these other people who are not as nice and far more deserve to be sick, why not them? (See Charmaz 1980a:126)

Codes	*Interview Statements*
	A 29-year-old man with renal failure was discussing his high school years, and events that occurred long before he was diagnosed.

Self-perception
Awareness of difference
Identifying self through
  ill health
Comparing health to
  others'
	... I knew I was different. I caught colds very easily and my resistance was very low, and so I knew that generally speaking my health wasn't as good as everybody else's, but I tried to do all the things that everybody else was doing.

	A 29-year-old woman with colitis was recounting her first episode of illness.

Normalizing context of
  illness
Self-esteem:
  feelings of failure
  failure of self
Reality contradicts
  idealized experience
	... I was under a great deal of stress as a result of all this bouncing around and trying to get a job and trying not to have to go home to my parents and admit that I had failed. [I] failed at life. I had left college, and left there saying, "Gee, I can do it on my own," so I was trying this exciting existence I read about and there was something wrong; I had all this pain. I didn't know what to do about it.

	A 54-year-old woman who had had cancer and currently had a crippling collagen disease was explaining her view on why she had had a recurrence of cancer.

Self in retrospect
Self-esteem
Outcome of timed
  struggle
Improving self-esteem as
  treatment goal
	... When I look back on my second bout of cancer, I was not feeling good about myself and the whole struggle of the last three years put me into X (a cancer institute) to try to get me to feel better about myself.

Focused Coding

Focused coding is the second, selective and conceptual, phase of the coding process. In focused coding, the researcher takes a limited set of codes that were developed in the initial phase and applies them to large amounts of data. The process is selective because the researcher has already weeded through the materials to develop a useful set of categories. It is conceptual because the codes employed raise the sorting of data to an *analytic* level rather than one that is used to summarize large amounts of information.

Focused coding forces the researcher to develop categories rather than simply to label topics. Categories may be taken either from the natural language of the participants (an in vivo code) or from the researcher's analytic interest. For example, I took the term self-pity and treated it as a category (Charmaz 1980a). Then I defined it by analyzing the data systematically. I developed another category out of my analytic interests: "identifying moments." This was not part of the natural language of my respondents. Instead, it reflected my categorization of those moments when participants instantly defined clear meanings about their present identities. Since I was generally interested in relationships between time and identity, I looked for material in the data which illuminated connections between the two. I had heard a number of accounts of moments when identity was at issue before I created a category that reflected the described events.

The purpose of focused coding is to build and clarify a category by examining all the data it covers and variations from it. Frequently, this means going back through the data and resifting it in relation to the newly devised category. New categories may subsume earlier materials that were left uncoded or were coded in different ways.

Researchers also use focused coding to break up the category. They develop subcategories which explicate and exhaust the more general category. I broke my category of "identifying moment" into the rather obvious subcategories of positive and negative identifying moments and coded for them (after I witnessed moments when ill persons were identified positively). *Properties* must be identified for the categories developed through focused coding. The properties define the category, delineate its characteristics, and demonstrate the conditions when it develops. For example, a major property of "identifying moment" is the immediate, direct social identification one interactant confers upon another.

After developing their set of focused codes, the researchers may use knowledge of the literature to expand and clarify the codes and to sensitize themselves to ways of exploring the emerging analysis. Pretend, for example, a group of organizational researchers in a hospital find that nurse participants show much concern about "professionalism" but assume that everyone shares their implied meanings of it. The researchers need to discover precisely which meanings these nurses and other professionals hold. After collecting first-hand data, they may use the literature to compare meanings attributed to the term and the criteria invoked to indicate it with their data. The range of meanings of "professionalism" include: maintaining an objective distant attitude, realizing high-quality craftsmanship with criteria set by members of the occupation themselves, and claiming a high status while simultaneously dissociating from those who cannot also claim it. In this instance, researchers need to portray the meanings of the term held in the setting they study. Hence, they use the literature to help outline and compare these meanings rather than to force them into "correct" interpretations. In other instances, the literature can be used as direct data for focused coding. In both cases, the researcher uses the literature as a source of *questions* and *comparisons* rather than as a measure of truth.

Since the grounded theory approach heavily emphasizes process, the categories developed are not treated separately as single topics; rather, grounded theorists weave them together into a *processual analysis* through which they can abstract and explicate experience. Thus, returning to my earlier example, defining self-pity through data analysis was just the first step.

After categorizing types of self-pity and its social sources, I then developed the processual categories of becoming immersed in self-pity and reversing self-pity which were vivid when I directed questions toward them, but only implicitly related in the early data before I systematically explored these areas.

Focused coding helps the researcher to outline a framework that preserves the complexities of everyday life. By showing relationships between categories in ways that explain the issues and events studied, focused coding helps to provide the groundwork for developing explanations and predictions.

When researchers begin to question their data analytically, they are beginning to *use* it, rather than simply relate it to an audience. For example, when organizational researchers investigate a topic such as staff turnovers, they would first define exactly what is meant by the term and cite the conditions under which such turnovers occur. Then they would use their data and their knowledge of the situation to help them determine which leads to follow up from there. Under which structural conditions do turnovers increase? Under which do they decrease? How do supervisors view turnovers? How do staff view them? What effects, if any, do they have on staff and client morale? Are there any subtle properties of turnovers that have direct effects on other parts of the organizational structure? Do supervisors change supervisory styles after a run of turnovers? What are the consequences of turnovers? What are the consequences of turnovers for direct client service? Are turnovers the "real" organizational issue or are they reflections of something else? (See Katz's essay, which follows.)

Many, if not most, researchers do develop or adopt "families" of codes that shape their emerging analyses (Glaser 1978). Among them are those that specify process, causation, degree, dimension, type, or a particular type of ordering such as structural, temporal, or generality (see Glaser 1978). By becoming aware of the elements of the code family invoked, one can raise more questions in research and become a better critic of other research works.

A final comment is in order. When the data are rich and full, the researcher may mine the information repeatedly for diverse foci (see Glaser and Strauss 1965, 1968). What may have been implicit to the researcher becomes explicit when he or she reexamines the data with new focused codes. For example, my interests in the chronically ill were primarily directed to issues concerning identity and time. Although I amassed considerable data concerning social support or its absence, I initially did not look at this topic systematically. As I began to study support and recognized its relationship to trust, I also realized that betrayal was a crucial code for understanding the experience of one group of chronically ill persons (Charmaz 1982). Then I categorized types of betrayal and their consequences. In short, the researcher may engage in focused coding of the same data multiple times as he or she identifies new questions to put to it.

Examples of Focused Coding

In the following examples, I provide several focused codes with their corresponding data. The codes show the selective nature of focused coding.

Code	Interview Statements
	A young woman who had had a serious flare-up of colitis recalled:
	... During this time I was under constant care by an intern who later thought I should see a different psychiatrist when I got out of the hospital because he thought I was coming on sexually to him and the odd thing about that was that I found him not
Identifying moment	sexually attractive at all — that was sort of an interesting twist to that thing. I mean when you are
Critical failure of self	not in a very good place to be told that you have failed with your psychiatrist is like the parting blow. You know it was awful.
	A woman with intensive experience in undergoing bureaucratic evaluations responded to my questions about how she felt about being scrutinized.
	... All I can do is dissolve in tears — there's nothing I can do. I just get *immobilized* — you
Relation of interactional sources of self-pity and self-blame	just sort of reach a point, you can't improve, can't remedy the situation, and you're told you aren't in the right category for getting the services you need and can't get for yourself. It makes me madder and madder at myself for being in the situation in the first place.
	The following observations were made during an interview with a retired college professor and his wife, both of whom had chronic illness.
	... I asked, "Did you keep up with professional work after you retired?" He said: "I used to teach extension courses but with the budget and that governor, there isn't any money for extension courses." She [his wife] cut in [to me], "Andrei used to be an extremely successful speaker; partly his enthusiasm, partly his articulateness, but with the speech problems, he can't do it ..." [He, slowly
Negative identifying moment	and painfully] "The schools don't have any money ... I can't speak very well."
	I felt desperately sorry for him at this point. Whether or not both factors were at play at the point when they stopped calling him for extension teaching, this was a terrible moment for him when she said it. Regardless of the real reason, at this precise moment knowing what she thought of his deteriorating competence was critical to him. Participating in this short sequence was like watching

*someone who was observing his own identity
crumbling away — it was painful both for him
and for me, although I got the impression that she
was so caught up in her perceptions of accuracy
that she actually didn't see how it defaced him . . .
Acknowledging that he can't speak very well was
said like an admission of guilt or inferiority that
was previously hidden from view.*[8]

Memo Writing

Memos are written elaborations of ideas about the data and the coded
categories. Memos represent the development of codes from which they are
derived. An intermediate step between coding and writing the first draft of
the analysis, memo writing then connects the barebones analytic framework
that coding provides with the polished ideas developed in the finished draft.
By making memos systematically while coding, the researcher fills out and
builds the categories. Thus, the researcher constructs the form and substance toward a finished piece of work and develops the depth and scope
of the materials.

Through memo writing the questions developed in coding are put into
analytic context. The memo tells what the code is about; it raises the code
to a category to be treated analytically. To differentiate between descriptive
and analytic categories, consider the topic of "friends." Descriptive treatment might focus on the link between friends, and their shared activities.
Analytic treatment, in contrast, might focus on the implicit criteria for
qualifying to be a "friend," the rhetorical uses of the term, the conditions
for elevating someone from an acquaintance to a friend, the converse conditions for reducing a friend to an acquaintance or former friend, the mutual obligations necessary to sustain friendship, and the consequences of
friendship for other relationships and activities. When treating the topic
analytically, the researcher likely generates a set of categories which are
more abstract than the original topic, and yet explicate underlying assumptions and processes.

Memo writing takes place throughout the research process starting with
the first interviews or observations. These early memos shape aspects of
subsequent data collection; they point to areas the researcher could explore

---

[8] As I watched Andrei's response to his wife's commentary, I saw him blanch and
almost reel as if he had been physically struck. Her statements were so direct that he
seemed caught by them, as if there was no escape then as well as in the future.
The defeated tone in his voice when he admitted he could not speak suggested to me
how deeply this brief episode affected him. Prior to the interview, I had learned
from the couple's physician, who took an unusual personal interest in this elderly
couple, that Andrei's speech impairment was never discussed openly. The physician
felt that Andrei hid the extent of his loss from himself, which was striking in view
of his degree of speech impairment compared with his prior eloquence. (From
original field notes.)

further. They also encourage the researcher both to play with ideas and to make early assessments about which ideas to develop. Additionally, early memos provide concrete sources for comparison with materials gathered later. By writing memos throughout the research process, researchers avoid being paralyzed by mountains of unanalyzed data and immobilized by the prospect of needing to complete final papers and reports. As a crucial correction to such problems, writing memos throughout the research process sharpens and directs data collection and coding.

Since it fosters a theoretical rendering of the data, memo writing is a useful strategy at various levels of theoretical development. Some grounded theorists construct many short memos on diverse categories. They gradually build up levels of abstraction. Others write fewer memos but work at a more abstract, comprehensive level from the start. Although each reflects a working style, novices frequently discover that writing many memos helps to expand their theoretical grasp of the materials, keeps their analyses flexible, and provides sharper, clearer guidelines for data collection. Also, developing memos through rewriting gives the novice practice in systematically raising the analytic level of the ideas. A developed memo may become a whole section of a paper since it renders and synthesizes part of the data.

Writing is only one part of the grounded theorist's work with memos. Sorting and integrating memos follows memo writing. These two steps may themselves spark new ideas which, in turn, lead to more memos.

Writing Initial Memos

The first step in writing memos is to take codes and treat them as topics or categories. At the beginning of the memo, the author should title it and describe what it is about. If the grounded theorist already has a precise definition of the category, he or she provides it. If the category is concrete and visible, the researcher likely constructs a precise and immediate definition. If the memo is about some more abstract or ambiguous category — such as transforming identities — then the researcher may develop a precise definition later in the analysis. However, at this point, researchers should explore ideas during the memo-writing process. By keeping work flexible, the researcher may create more innovative and denser (many ideas integrated together) pieces of work.

When a category explicates a major pattern, grounded theorists stop and cite the conditions under which it operates and when it varies. What are the structural conditions giving rise to increased turnovers? What are the structural conditions under which a policy about turnovers is articulated or is reorganized? When writing memos, grounded theorists sometimes discover that they define new patterns and ideas that do not initially tie into their coded topic or category. Even when these connections are not apparent, they pursue the idea anyway but put the memo aside and reexamine it after finishing several other memos. (The ideas may make sense in another section of the work.)

Grounded theorists also explain how the code is related to other previously developed categories and codes. Spelling out the connections between categories assists in creating an integrated "whole," helps to reduce rambling, and aids in identifying implicit links, all of which tighten the work considerably.

Whenever writing a memo, researchers describe and discuss the category by delineating its properties as they are reflected in the data the category represents, or at least note the page and date of the properties in the data so quick retrieval is possible later (see Glaser 1978).

Grounded theorists make comparisons explicit through memo writing. They often compare several observations in order to demonstrate the existence of the category they are talking about. For example, I composed a stack of accounts of feelings about illness when I was developing my material on self-pity to separate what constituted self-pity from other responses.

As more data accumulate, grounded theorists refine the earlier memos to account for greater variation, to gain a firmer grasp of the general context, and to understand the specific conditions under which the category works. By this time, the grounded theorist may also understand when the category changes and what its consequences are. For example, by examining the accounts of many patients, I was able to outline what contributed to moving away from self-pity, as well as the consequences of remaining immersed in it.

Sorting Memos

Sorting memos simply means putting those that elucidate the same category together in order to clarify its dimensions and to distinguish it from other categories. By going through accumulated memos and sorting them, researchers gain insight into what the core variables, key phases in a process, or major issues are in the research.

When analyzing a process, the researcher quickly sorts the memos into phases of that process. Sometimes researchers discover that they actually have several issues or processes that can be covered separately. In that case, sorting keeps the researcher from muddling categories that are logically, if not experientially, distinct. Conversely, an important dimension of sorting is to increase analytic precision in handling experientially mixed and muddy categories. In my work on chronic illness, for example, I analyzed the sources of loss of self (Charmaz, forthcoming). Living a restricted life results in loss of self. So does being devalued. Yet several people voluntarily restricted their lives to avoid devaluation. The categories are not entirely distinct, hence sorting helps to provide an analytic handle for communicating the categories in writing.

Grounded theorists sort for both the *content* of the memos and the *ordering* of them. The ordering of the memos, which forms the core of the paper, often reflects the ordering of experiences the data represent. The ordering may be explicitly grounded in the data as the researcher discusses steps in a process such as recruiting new workers. Or it may be implicitly grounded through the researcher's own sense of logic. For example, the organizational researcher might order memos on supervising by sorting for its properties, when it varies, its implications for morale, and its significance for getting the actual work done.

Integrating Memos

Sorting the memos helps to prepare for their subsequent integration. By integrating the memos the researcher reveals the relationships between categories. Such integration does not always occur spontaneously; often the researcher has to demonstrate the integration explicitly. Although analyses of processes sort and integrate readily into phases, other analyses require the imposition of a logical order. After writing, sorting, and integrating memos, I sometimes share them with interested respondents to see how my analysis fits with their experiences and views (see Huber 1973).

In the following two memos, I treat the category "identifying moment." The first memo is an initial description of the category as I first developed it when working on my dissertation. The second memo refines and extends the earlier materials; it also takes into account substantial further data collection. In the second memo, I include raw data to illustrate the analytic points. That memo appears in almost identical form in the published paper (see Charmaz 1980a).

An Initial Memo on "Identifying Moments" [9]

Identifying moments, in which the individual is treated in ways which designate new definitions of who he really is, may be captured and dramatized in the person's mind. When the disparity is great between prior valuations of self and present treatment such as of being a person worthy of *respect* and the entire procedure is characterized by *disrespect,* from the long wait to being shunted around and having one's identity questioned and categorized, conditions exist for these individuals to feel that they are losing control of their selves and the form of their existence.

Further, identifying moments when the individual is being defined and categorized may instantaneously flash images of the future and

[9] This memo synthesizes the accounts of patients who described their encounters with agency and hospital clinic personnel. These patients had been financially independent while working but now felt they needed assistance temporarily for medical and/or living expenses.

heretofore *unforeseen identity*. Consider the impact on the unsuspecting individual who hopes to remobilize later to be told the only category into which he fits is that for the "totally disabled."

A Later Memo on "Identifying Moments"

It became clear to me that how a particular chronically ill person was identified by others sometimes became revealed to them in the course of a moment's encounter or interaction. These moments gave the ill individual *new reflections* of self, often revealing that he (or she) is not the person he felt he was. Hence, within the course of a few moments, someone's self-image may be radically called into question.

Moments that call into question previously held definitions of self may be identified as either negative or positive, although data describing negative moments are much more extensive (identifying moments may also reconfirm assumptions about self, although these are less likely to be recounted since they are not problematic).

Negative identifying moments are those shrouded in *embarrassment* and *devaluation*. They often lead to self-pity and self-blame: self-pity because of the implications of the definitions of the other; self-blame because of being in the situation in the first place. One woman described a demeaning encounter with a social service agency when in the course of a moment, she saw herself as being defined as someone not worth helping. She said,

> All I can do is dissolve in tears — there's nothing I can do. I just get *immobilized* — you sort of reach a point, you can't improve, can't remedy the situation, and you're told you aren't in the right category for getting the services you need and can't get for yourself. It makes me madder and madder at myself for being in the situation in the first place.

Negative identifying moments that occur in intimate relations are likely to be even more devastating. If ill persons can no longer claim preferred identities in other worlds in the present, although they may have possessed extraordinary identities in the past, they may feel that no recourse exists but to accept the identity thrust upon them since it was defined by those who know them most intimately.

(The observation of the elderly professor and his wife which occurs on pages 119–120 directly follows.)

Theoretical Sampling

Theoretical sampling means sampling aimed toward the development of the emerging theory (Glaser 1978; Glaser and Strauss 1967). As researchers analyze their materials and develop theoretical categories, they frequently discover that they need to sample more data to elaborate a category. Because researchers only develop theoretical categories through the analytic process, they do not know in advance what they will be sampling. Thus, theoretical sampling differs from the kind of selective initial sampling most qualitative researchers engage in as they set criteria for their research problem (see Schatzman and Strauss 1973).

As an inductive technique, theoretical sampling exemplifies the inductive logic of the grounded theory approach. Since grounded theorists systematically build their theoretical frameworks out of their observations, theoretical sampling is part of the progressive stages of analysis. It becomes necessary to use theoretical sampling when the analyst's present data do not exhaust the theoretical category the researcher is developing. At this point, then, more data are needed to fill out, saturate, and exhaust the category. Subsequently, the researcher samples whichever groups or events will provide the relevant material for the category. Comparison groups are chosen only for their theoretical relevance in theoretical sampling (see Glaser and Strauss 1967). Since I focus upon the chronically ill, I return to them when I use theoretical sampling. The theoretical category gains more scope, however, if the researcher chooses other comparative groups.

The need for theoretical sampling means that the conceptual categories that were inductively constructed have become sufficiently developed and abstract that the researcher can construct specific questions about them. Theoretical sampling then becomes a means for checking out hunches and raising specific questions. Furthermore, it provides a way to check the scope as well as the depth of a category.

Conclusion

The above explication of the grounded theory approach derives from the original methods that Glaser and Strauss (1967) and Glaser (1978) have delineated. Although I attempt to be faithful to the form and logic of their approach, over the years I have developed my own style of using grounded theory. Each researcher who adopts the approach likely develops his or her own variations of technique.

Basically, however, any researcher who claims to use the grounded theory approach endorses the following fundamental strategies. First, discovering and analyzing social and social psychological processes structures inquiry. Second, data collection and analysis phases of research proceed simultaneously. Third, analytic processes prompt discovery and theory development rather than verification of preexisting theories. Fourth, theoretical sampling refines, elaborates, and exhausts conceptual categories. And last, systematic application of grounded theory analytic methods progressively leads to more abstract analytic levels.

Although I have outlined how to do substantive analysis using a grounded theory approach, analysis need not remain at the substantive level. By taking the analysis to higher levels of abstraction and conceptual integration, grounded theory methods provide the means to develop formal theories (Glaser and Strauss 1971; Strauss 1978). To do so, the grounded theorist takes the comparative methods further. After developing conceptual categories, he or she refines and reworks the emerging theory by comparing concept with concept. Developing formal theories necessitates sampling a variety of different situational contexts and groups in which the concept applies. That way the theorist analyzes the boundaries and applications of the developing theoretical framework. To date, however, the grounded theory approach has been used primarily to develop rich substantive analyses. A theoretical analysis at the substantive level, though more modest in scope and power than formal theory, gives the analyst tools for explaining his or her data as well as tools for making predictions.

A Theory of Qualitative Methodology: The Social System of Analytic Fieldwork

Jack Katz

Introduction

Readers of qualitative field studies repeatedly raise four questions about evidence. They may be characterized as four "R's" that haunt participant observers in sociology. I will illustrate these evidentiary questions as they might be addressed to a field study I conducted on civil lawyers for the poor. These illustrations will then provide a point of departure for a re-analysis of the methodological issues involved more generally in the assessment of fieldwork evidence.

1. *Representativeness.* I studied the legal assistance programs in Chicago through historical documents, organizational files, and eighteen months of fieldwork in 1972 and 1973. Since 1973, I have had numerous interviews with lawyers who have worked in Legal Services programs in Chicago, Connecticut, and California, but my report primarily covers experiences and events in Chicago in the early seventies. The study may have some value as a historical document of local interest, but I offer it as a general institutional analysis of the careers of legal assistance lawyers and their organizations. Can such generalization be justified?

2. *Reactivity.* In Chicago, I observed and talked with staff lawyers sometimes for minutes, sometimes for hours; in court, their offices, their homes; without anything approximating a fixed questionnaire. Perhaps the differences I report in the data simply reflect differences in my behavior. I might be asked, "How do you know it looks the way you describe it when you're not there looking?"

3. *Reliability.* I typed up about 2,000 pages of field and interview notes, presented only a fraction in the final report, and have not specified the criteria I used to select those data I published. A sympathetic but concerned reader might well observe and ask, "There is an infinite amount of background context that you could have included or excluded from your original field notes and the final text. The meaning of the behavior described would change with a change in the description of its context. How can you say your descriptions are the right ones?" A less kind

Adapted, with minor editorial changes, from "A Theory of Qualitative Methodology: The Social System of Analytic Fieldwork," in *Poor People's Lawyers in Transition* by Jack Katz, pp. 197–218. Copyright © 1982 by Rutgers, The State University of New Jersey. Reprinted by permission of the publisher.

reader might put it, "How do we know you didn't overlook disconfirming data, or even make it all up?"

4. *Replicability.* I began the study at a time when I learned that the legal assistance organizations in Chicago were about to merge. My initial interests were twofold. "Merger" seemed an attractively elusive phenomenon, one on which there seemed little useful sociological literature. The other interest was in the analysis of personal and collective careers and their relations. This interest grew out of my fascination with Georg Simmel's writings, and from my training in symbolic interaction, with its perspective on the processes in which people shape individual and collective identities.

I began by interviewing organizational leaders, asking about their personal careers and their expectations for the merger. Then I began sitting in on lawyer-client interviews. When meetings began at the merged organization, I attended. I recorded my observations and interviews, sometimes contemporaneously, sometimes within an hour or two, often that night, occasionally weeks or even months later. The "career interviews" were loosely structured, to say the least. I would typically begin with questions about how the lawyer came to the job, move to initial experiences, then encourage a recollection of stages and changes in internal career, and finish by asking about expectations for the future. I changed the focus of my observations and interview questions in innumerable, unrecorded moves.

In light of such broadly formulated interests and inconstant methods, one might well ask, "If we wanted to test your analysis by repeating your research, how would we know what to do?"

Qualitative field studies appear especially vulnerable to criticism because they do not proceed from fixed designs. They do not use formats for sampling that could produce statistics on the representativeness of data. They abjure coding books that might enhance reliability by spelling out in advance the criteria for analyzing data. They fail to give detailed instructions for interviews — the questions to ask, their order, when to give cues and when to probe — that might give the reader faith that differences in subjects' responses were not due to variations in the researcher's behavior. Because of their emphasis on informal and flexible methods, qualitative field studies seem to make replication impossible.

Unfortunately, qualitative researchers have customarily conceded fundamental methodological weaknesses when faced with the four "R's." [1] Not

---

[1] "Qualitative" researchers have often called for a reorientation of methodological thinking, but they have not transcended the conventional approaches. Becker and others (1961:33–45) have proposed a *post-hoc* application, to informally gathered data, of methods used to guide the collection of data in more formalized research. For example, their remedy for reactivity is to count up all field notes bearing on a given proposition and to assign greater weight to observations of behavior in group

displaying significant statistics, they acknowledge the "merely exploratory" status of their "case" studies. Citing the importance of "getting close to the data," participant observation fieldworkers concede risks of reactivity (Scott 1965:266). Symbolic interactionists discard coding books, and along with them the goal of verification, as a necessary cost of developing "grounded" theory (Glaser and Strauss, 1967). As for replicability, some qualitative methodologists recommend reporting a natural history of the study but ultimately attribute success to "having the gift" (Lofland 1976: 318).

Something important is missing from methodological thinking.[2] On the one hand, as both Becker (1970:6–7) and Glaser and Strauss (1967:12) have noted, the sociological community, despite its neglect of the rationale for qualitative methods, frequently rewards qualitative empirical research. On the other hand, forceful questions have been raised as to whether formal research designs ever could be implemented according to their prescriptions. In fact, the argument increasingly goes, research designs never do anticipate fully the social relations that emerge in the research process. However random the sample, research subjects are never chosen through logical deduction from the theory purportedly tested (Camilleri 1962). Inevitably there are unscheduled influences on the understanding by respondents of the questions or stimuli (Cicourel 1964). Unexplicated bases for interpretation are ubiquitous (Garfinkel 1960), and they undermine the effort to establish that one has performed a replicable study.

These considerations raise two sets of related questions. Are not the methodologies of social surveys and experiments premised on a substantive sociological claim that supposedly pre-fixed features of the research, such as plans for probability sampling and coding rules, can actually determine and accurately predict the social relations established by the researcher with subjects, readers, and subsequent researchers? What is the methodological value of the formal research design if it does not in fact govern re-

---

settings than to reports of one-to-one encounters between researcher and research subject. They also recommend a *post-hoc* quantification procedure to create evidence on representativeness. These steps lead to the acceptance of a proposition about a group if the total number of observations and the ratio of positive-to-negative observations exceed arbitrary standards.

These are, at best, second-best solutions. When enumerated data are offered as the product of surveys and experiments, they purport to describe the precise number of instances underlying the substantive analysis, and they treat each datum as having a discernible weight on the analysis. The observational researcher who has directly entered, diffusely experienced, and variously recorded a natural setting cannot support this claim. Some field notes are, after all, based on observations covering seconds, others on a day's experience. . . .

[2] Despite the rhetoric of discovery and exploration, we are asked to attend to qualitative studies not merely on the claim that they develop attractive ideas but on an assertion that something "out there" has been discovered — on an empirical assertion that the theory is in fact "grounded." For a vigorous critique of the distinction between discovery and verification, see Feyerabend (1975:165–169).

search? This essay takes up the converse set of questions. If qualitative field research can produce what the scientific community is willing to regard as valuable results, must there not be methodologically valuable empirical implications of the qualitative field researcher's behavior? Perhaps we should look for the methodological strength of qualitative fieldwork not by comparing it with an image of research from fixed designs but by examining the social relations which may be built up with research subjects, readers, and subsequent researchers by the fieldworker's conduct, from initial entry into the field to the final write-up.

This essay outlines a sociological theory for evaluating qualitative field research. It takes three substantial rhetorical risks. The first is to offer a general theory of a distinctive social system that can be constructed by field research. Some may prefer a more "grounded" approach, specifically illustrating with elaborate qualifications one subset of hypotheses. But my immediate objective is to undermine a habitual critical perspective, and for this the emphasis is best kept on the possibility of a comprehensive alternative methodological stance. The second risk is to ignore diversity in methods and focus on one qualitative research strategy, analytic induction. . . . The third risky decision is to formulate the distinctive strengths of qualitative field research in the standard terminology of methodological discussion, e.g., in discussions of the four "R's." To some readers, the argument in places may appear simply to be giving a different meaning to established standards so that field research will look good where it has looked bad in contrast to surveys and experiments, and vice versa. In a sense, that is precisely the contribution the essay attempts to make to the literature of field methods, from which it admittedly borrows and rebottles much. As indicated by the opening paragraphs, my motivating concern has been a practical dilemma, the need for a rhetoric with which to respond more directly to standard methodological questions than claims of "discovery rather than verification" and "pretesting" allow. The need is to outline an alternative perspective for interpreting such issues as representativeness, reactivity, reliability, and replicability, and simultaneously to indicate that the customary readings are at best arbitrary.

Analytic Induction Revisited

The fundamentals of analytic induction can be stated simply. The researcher is committed to form a perfect relation between data and explanation. When encountering a "negative case" — evidence contradicting the current explanation — the researcher must transform it into a confirming case by revising the definition of either the explaining or the explained phenomenon. The researcher is enjoined to seek negative cases and the resulting opportunity to modify the explanation. There is no methodological value in piling up data of a sort already determined to be consistent with the theory. Quantification therefore plays no logical role.[3]

I used analytic induction throughout my research on the careers of legal assistance lawyers. Legal assistance leaders had often complained about "high turnover" and staff lawyers had often remarked that "two years" represented a benchmark for assessing their careers. Was there, I wondered, a common process of leaving the institution, or "burning out," as the lawyers put it? Was there a concise explanation of when and why staff lawyers would burn out?

My first step was to allocate into groups of short and long tenure all the lawyers who had entered the organization at least two years before the date of my analysis. In effect, the two-year point represented the initial definition of the thing to be explained. Then I looked for background features unique and common to those who remained more than two years, such as education, age, prior experience, political philosophy, work location, ethnicity, and sex. In effect I was looking for factors that would perfectly explain why lawyers were on one list or the other. This did not work, but instead of abandoning the effort I took an obviously artificial tack: I excluded all the confusing cases and drew up two neat lists for comparison, one with lawyers who had stayed more than two years and who had been "activists" before joining legal services, and another with lawyers who had left within two years and who had not been activists. Then I considered "exceptions" one by one, modifying the definition of the explanadum or the explanans in order to fit the "exception." I was manipulating the meaning of the concepts distinguishing the lists in order to restore the perfect correlation which initially characterized them.

It quickly became apparent that I could not hope to explain the difference between those who did and did not stay more than two years. Some lawyers who had stayed more than two years were miserable, as unhappy as some who had left within a few months. Idiosyncratic factors, such as the chance appearance of job offers, might be what really distinguished the two. So I changed the definition of the explanadum to "desiring to stay two years." This definition of the problem provoked new analytic difficulties. Legal Services programs offered staff lawyers a great variety of work set-

---

[3] Because of the irrelevance of quantification to the logic of analytic induction and because of the search for qualitative variation implicit in the hunt for negative cases, the following discussion frequently contrasts "qualitative" and "quantitative" research. In fact many, perhaps all, researchers use a combination of quantitative and qualitative methods. The possibilities for mutually beneficial combinations have been argued by Zelditch (1962), Reiss (1968), Sieber (1973), and Myers (1977), among others. The claim usually is that quantitative methods offer evidence or proof; qualitative methods, validity or insight. Whatever the merits of these conciliatory positions, they have failed to explain how qualitative methods can be rigorous in their own right.

tings, from administrative posts, to jobs supervising major litigation, to assignments in neighborhood offices serving walk-in clients. It appeared unlikely that in all of these quite different jobs the same factors would explain the persistence of the desire to remain. So I delimited the explanadum by qualifying it as a "desire to stay in a frustrating place." Through confronting a series of exceptions the explanadum changed again to "involvement in a frustrating place," and then finally to "involvement in an insignificant status." Likewise the definition of the explanans was changed from features of pre-organizational biography to methods of transcending pressures to take on insignificant or routine work, including the use of legal strategies for reform and participation in a collective culture that celebrated the significance of reform work.

After working this way with sketches of biographies, I developed the concepts further in a two-step process of coding field materials. In this part of the research operation, the codes represented the concepts of the explanation, and problems in making coding decisions represented problems in the explanation. First, I altered the codes to fit one-sentence summaries previously made from typed interview and field notes. Then in writing the text, I adjusted the analysis when the quotes extracted directly from the original notes were not what the summaries had led me to expect. When a quotation showed both the presence and absence of involvement in a lawyer's experience at the same time, the concept of involvement had to be further refined; when a section of an interview showed the presence of involvement and the absence of the condition stipulated as explanatory, the explanation had to be revised. Theoretical development continued from early in the research throughout the writing.

Analytic induction used in these ways is a distinctively qualitative methodology, clearly distinguished from methods requiring pre-fixed designs. True, the overriding commitment to seek negative cases is a pre-fixed feature. But the injunction to alter the contents of the theory during data collection gives the research process a distinctive openness. In practice, one does not begin with an hypothesis and then encounter exceptions one by one. Instead, one begins with multiple hypotheses and is confronted with a mass of hostile evidence. Analytic induction permits the researcher to flounder interminably in the choices of: which hypothesis to select out and stick with; then which datum in the disconfirming mass to select as an "exception" while consciously ignoring temporarily the discouragement of the rest; and then whether to alter the explanans or the explanadum. . . .

Field researchers generally have not embraced analytic induction as a doctrine.[4] This reluctance appears related to problems historically but not

---

[4] Since Turner's (1953) review of the handful of studies then recognized as examples of analytic induction, there has been virtually no explicit discussion of the method. An exception is the extensive treatment in Lindesmith (1968) and Manning (1978); see also Moskos (1967:104–105). . . .

necessarily associated with the method. As originally proposed, analytic induction claimed a superiority over "enumerative induction" by promising perfect correlations and "universal" explanations rather than probabilistic findings. But then very few if any perfect explanations appeared. Yet this embarrassment misconceives the methodology. Analytic induction ought to be evaluated in the same way in which field researchers practically gauge the value of their work. The test is not whether a final state of perfect explanation has been achieved but the *distance* that has been traveled over negative cases and through consequent qualifications from an initial state of knowledge. Analytic induction's quest for perfect explanation, or "universals," should be understood as a strategy for research rather than as the ultimate measure of the method. Analytic induction is a method for conducting social research, not a perspective from which to evaluate findings. . . .

In addition to their claim of "universal" explanation, early proponents of analytic induction (in particular, Znaniecki 1968) unnecessarily raised hackles by arguing its superiority over "statistical enumeration" for developing "genuinely causal laws." Against this background, Turner's critique — essentially that the concepts of explaining and explained phenomena in studies using analytic induction shade into each other and suggest tautology — was especially forceful. Analytic induction appeared to produce good definitions at best, not causal explanations.

The case for analytic induction can be made stronger with a number of revisions. If we view social life as a continuous symbolic process, we expect our concepts to have vague boundaries. If analytic induction follows the contours of experience, it will have ambiguous conceptual fringes. Its independent and dependent variables will inevitably shade into each other, suggesting tautology. But this weakness is only remarkable if exceptional claims are made for the method. Analytic induction and enumerative induction (in other words, survey statistics) differ in the form, not the fact, of uncertain results. For the statistical researcher, practical uncertainty is represented by statements of probabilistic relations; for the analyst of social process, by ambiguities when trying to code borderline cases into one or the other of the "explaining" or "explained" categories. In application to given cases, predictions on the basis of probabilistic explanations will sometimes be wrong, and predictions on the basis of explanations of social process sometimes so indeterminate as to be useless. (Turner did not claim that all explanations of analytic induction would be circular, nor that all its predictions would be indeterminate. See note 5.) . . .

A final difficulty for using the tradition of analytic induction is its apparent emphasis on an epistemology of "induction." What field researchers actually do when they use analytic induction would be described more properly by philosophers of science as "retroduction" than as induction: a "double fitting" or alternating shaping of both observation and explanation, rather than an *ex post facto* discovery of explanatory ideas (Hanson 1958:85ff; Baldamus 1972). To signal both my departure from several aspects of the tradition of analytic induction and my debt to the tradition's essential guide to research practice — the injunction to search exclusively for negative cases — I drop the reference to "induction" in favor of the rubric *analytic research*.

Analytic field studies will not produce "proof," i.e., artifacts of evidence which speak in a standard language or specialized fashion about representativeness, reliability, and so forth. The exclusive commitment to search for negative cases implies that there ought to be a different conceptual point for each reported phenomenon. Each datum reported should make its own substantive and not solely evidentiary contribution to the analysis. But analytic fieldwork does create an elaborate framework which can be used by researchers to assess how well they are doing and by readers to make evaluations. That framework is a social system, of which I sketch the following aspects.

Applied consistently in field research, the search for negative cases will: force the researcher to focus on social process as experienced from within; induce research subjects to act toward the researcher as a meaningful member of the native world; enfranchise readers as colleagues competent to make an independent analysis of the relation between data and explanation; and shape a role which subsequent researchers can readily take up for testing substantive findings. I suggest that this is a social system distinctively constructed by analytic fieldwork, in contrast with quantitative social research from fixed designs, and that this social system can be invoked to spell out answers to a wide variety of methodological questions frequently asked of qualitative field studies. This system of social research relations promotes generalizability, reduces the problem of reactivity, establishes constraints toward reliability, and enhances replicability.

Representativeness

The strategy of analytic research is to expand constantly the domain to which an explanation validly can be generalized. The sequential process in which theory is altered upon discovery of a negative case, in turn changing the meaning of a "negative case," allows each new datum to function as a rival hypothesis. This method invests research energy with maximum efficiency to improve the generalizability of theory.

Analytic research rests the external validity of a study on its internal variety. The more differences discovered within the data, the greater the number of possible negative cases, and thus the more broadly valid the resulting theory. From a perspective on the sociology of social research, the analytic method, if it is followed, actually promotes the discovery of internal variety and thus its logic for establishing external validity.

In practice, the analytic method shapes a particular researcher perspective on research subjects. It leads researchers inexorably to examine social process as subjects experience it from within. Once researchers have been led to examine the emergence in subjects' experience of the phenomena to be explained, they find that their basis for generalization — qualitative variation — has expanded vastly. . . .

This has in fact happened in every known instance in which analytic induction has been used expressly to discipline social research. At the start, the researcher's conceptual units have often been static background factors and discrete acts. As the study has developed, the units have become processes with vague boundaries.[5] Lindesmith (1968) discovered that he could not explain the first act of taking opiates, only addiction, a sustained use. Rejecting explanations by personality type, he offered a motive developed in the process of use, a "craving." In my study, an early concern was to explain turnover among poverty lawyers. This was a focus on an *act* of leaving an organization. I ended with an explanation of "involvement," a perspective on continuing a line of activity as intrinsically compelling.[6] . . .

If this hypothesis on the effects of the use of the analytic method on the researcher's perspective is true, it implies a principle to guide qualitative research. Given the strategy of exploiting internal variety in order to warrant generalizability, the ideal site is one that is both in a period of historical change and has the most differentiated members. These do not appear to have been the principles typically guiding the selection of sites for qualitative research.

Critics might respond that the fact that a site is distinctive in the heterogeneity of its members and in the drama of its historical change makes it

---

[5] Cressey's (1953) use of analytic induction to explain embezzlement is an exception that proves the rule. Although narrower than the legal definition, the embezzlement to be explained by the theory was treated as a discrete act. Cressey was obliged to specify the occurrence of something precisely connected with the criminal act. Turner (1953:606) seized on this point of vulnerability in his critique, noting that the explanatory conditions — having a nonsharable financial problem, recognizing embezzlement as a solution and rationalizing it — would seem always to have existed for some time before the embezzlement occurred. Significantly, Turner explicitly softens his argument in turning to Lindesmith's theory, noting only problems ("in some cases") at the boundaries of explanans and explanandum.

[6] See also Becker (1953). Understandably but paradoxically, most studies using analytic induction have begun as attempts to explain social problems: Lindesmith, opiate addiction; Cressey, embezzlement; I began with an attempt to explain "staying more than two years," or the problem of "turnover" about which legal assistance leaders had so frequently complained. In pursuit of a perfect explanation, the researcher must initially rely on an outsider's view of what is homogenous when choosing a phenomenon for study, and "deviance" by definition has already been singled out as such. Yet a consistent contribution of such research is to establish the inaccuracy of the outsider's perspective by redefining the phenomenon in terms of homogeneity from the *inside*. A major difference between the view of social problems held by outsiders and insiders is that outsiders pick out discrete acts for sanction or regret whereas insiders experience a process with vague boundaries.

unrepresentative. The researcher's naturalistic focus on symbolic social process suggests a strategy to work on this problem. Take the charge that unique features of the research site — extreme differentiation of members, large scale of organization, rapid change in collective character — bias all the data collected. The qualitative researcher can examine the range and fluctuations of members' situated experiences and may discover tests for the rival hypotheses. If the objection is that a smaller, more homogeneous and static context would alter members' behavior, the researcher may locate exceptional members who, for a time at least, were situated in a homogeneous subunit isolated from the influences of a general historical trend.

To use this logic, one must assume that there are not complete discontinuities on the dimension at issue between the case studied and the place or time invoked in the rival hypothesis.[7] For example, I tried to explain involvement and alienation from work among poverty lawyers by studying organizations in Chicago in the early 1970s. I would like to determine whether my theory requires qualification when applied to lawyers working in rural California poverty law offices, but I have no direct data. Is it reasonable to reject the hypothesis that the theory cannot be extended to the rural California site by examining the exceptional experiences of a lawyer who worked in Chicago's Mexican-American neighborhood legal assistance office and cultivated vineyards in abandoned West Side lots in preparation for a move to a poverty law job in his native Northern California? I would also like to test the validity of my theory for lawyers currently assisting the poor. One might object that political commitment and its collective mobilization was unusually strong and pervasive among poverty lawyers during my fieldwork, in the early seventies, and that there is a general malaise now. But is the contrast so complete that a close examination of the experiences of the earlier group *could not* have encountered instances of the currently dominant perspective? By definition, no researcher can prove continuity between what he has and what he has not studied, but the analytic method points a way for thinking the problem through. . . .

Quantitative and qualitative strategies toward generalizability strike different bargains with the existential limitations of social research. In attempts to establish statistical significance, the more the researcher sees data as heterogeneous (the greater the number of variables examined in a given number of data), the less likely it is that levels of significance will be reached. The goal of specifying the explanation by testing it against rival hypotheses through partial correlation or elaboration analysis may be pursued only at the cost of weakening the argument that the patterns examined

---

[7] A general evaluation of the capacity of analytic induction to warrant generalizations thus hinges on theoretical contentions about discontinuities across societies and over history. For some provocative questioning of several once-accepted discontinuities, see Riesman (1976).

are significantly representative of a larger population (see Camilleri 1962). Statistical evidence of representativeness depends on restricting a depiction of qualitative richness in the experience of the people studied. A similar practical trade-off confronts those who do inductive research, but it forces the opposite choice. By searching for data that differ in kind from instances previously recorded, analytic research creates a picture of the scene researched that is strategically biased toward much greater variation than random sampling would reveal. Brilliant qualitative studies such as Goffman's *Asylums* (1961) overrepresent the richness of everyday life in the place actually observed in order better to represent social life outside of the research site.

Reactivity

... I have asserted as an empirical proposition (or perhaps more accurately, reasserted after Blumer [1969:82]) that when sociologists committed to hunt for negative cases examine theories that explain discrete acts by background psychological or social characteristics, they will inevitably transform their theoretical perspective into a focus on social process as experienced from within. When this research perspective is used in direct contact with subjects, it becomes a form of participant observation. Participant observation appears to exacerbate the problem of reactivity — subjects' responses to a study's methods that confound substantive findings. Among approaches to participant observation, the analytic method might appear the worst.... Flexibility and fluctuation in research behavior are required. A participant observer committed to search exclusively for negative cases might constantly change the content of questions or the angle of observation; and as a result, any difference in the behavior of research subjects could be attributed to a change in the researcher's behavior.

Spokesmen for participant observation have taken a defensive position on the issue, noting dangers for "objectivity" (Scott 1965:266) and for "contaminating" the scene examined (McCall 1969). Reasonably courageous sociologists might well be frightened off by such metaphoric warnings. To use participant observation appears to risk not only destruction of the scientific self but the pollution of society!

But interaction between variations in research methods and variations in members' behavior does not necessarily produce a methodological problem. It does when the resulting behavior is irrelevant to the researcher's objectives, or when the researcher fails to interpret correctly how he is perceived by members. Yet it is precisely on these grounds that analytic field research shows distinctive methodological strength. In contrast to research that attempts to fix the researcher's behavior with a design for gathering data, the analytic field method makes valuable substantive data out of the responses of members to the researcher's methods. Moreover, this qualitative approach distinctively creates opportunities for testing the meaning to members of the researcher's presence.

It is my thesis that in order to recognize the strength of qualitative field methods in matters of reactivity, we must develop a sociology of social research. A key virtue of the analytic field researcher's lack of preset methods is that it deters the presentation of a "scientific" self. If the researcher influences members, it will not necessarily be as a "researcher." Members have reason not to take as a "researcher" the sociologist whose methods take shape in response to native concerns.

In relations with researchers, members will take what is to them significant action by identifying researchers as significant others. To consider participant observers significant, a member must cast them into identities rich with indigenous meaning. In field studies of communities or organizations, researchers may be grilled as informants, sworn in as confidants, and debated as representatives of the views of various groups and leaders. In these relations, members reveal their concerns, not about the world of social science research as understood by the researcher, but about everyday aspects of their own social lives. If by their presence analytic field researchers change the scenes in which they participate, the data they take out are still about those communities and organizations.

By *not* insisting on a uniform meaning for the research role, the analytic field researcher minimizes the problem of creating irrelevant, "artificial" data. Conversely, the use of fixed methods to combat reactivity paradoxically exacerbates the problem. By attempting to control the research setting rigidly, so that differences in members' behavior cannot be attributed to variations in research methods, experimental and survey researchers define artificial "research" settings and induce members to become hypersensitive to accidental and unplanned variations in researcher behavior (Becker 1970:44). . . .

Analytic field methods not only minimize the risk that members will act "artificially" as research subjects; it lets them shape an identity for the researcher that itself provides valuable substantive data. Two distinct sources of data are made available. One source has been recognized in a classic social science tradition that seeks to understand members' social lives by examining the researcher's subjective experiences in trying to shed an alien "research" role. Anthropologists have long taken their emergent problems in learning how to act as natives for substantive data on the implicit rules of a society (for a recent statement, see Wallace 1962).

The other source of data, one more neglected by field researchers, is member efforts to define a role for the researcher.[8] Consider the question of access. It is usually discussed as a problem faced only at the start of a study, before substantive data gathering can begin. In fact, the negotiation

---

[8] An exception is Gussow (1964). Psychiatrists exploit these phenomena as "transference."

of access is ongoing, continuing from situation to situation and from the beginning to the end of each interview, in the researcher's efforts to establish and maintain rapport. Indeed, once the process of developing rapport is over and researchers with fixed questionnaires are ready to begin serious interviewing, qualitative researchers are often ready to leave. By this point they have realized which questions make no sense to an interviewee and have found substitutes that do. An appreciation of such qualitative distinctions is more important for the analytic researcher than learning which way the questions are answered this time.

Rich data are available in members' efforts to place a field researcher in a role and at a distance useful for native purposes. A process through which members attempt to keep the researcher further out is revealing of the nature of the scene studied. So are ploys by members to draw the researcher further in. On the former: For virtually the entire course of an eighteen-month field study, Wieder (1974) failed to build rapport with the residents of a halfway house for parolee-addicts. By examining his frustrations in "learning the code," and by investigating similarities in the alien roles residents shaped for him and for the staff, Wieder detailed the techniques used by residents for achieving segregation. The very fact that the residents persisted in reacting to the researcher as nothing more than an irrelevant researcher provided relevant data on the dominant culture in the institution. On the latter: Gusfield (1955) turned into data the sometimes frustrating reactions of Woman's Christian Temperance Union leaders to his efforts at maintaining a formal interview role. Cast by them not as an indifferent, neutral, scientific "researcher" but as an informed member of the public, he was berated and subjected to proselytizing efforts. The concerns of members about the boundary between outsiders and insiders and their ability to define it are significant features of all social systems.

Of course proffered interpretation of the meaning of members' behavior toward researchers may be wrong. But member behavior that has been shaped in response to the researcher's methods is not necessarily more problematic as substantive data than behavior shaped in any other interaction. Field researchers have missed this point. Common topics in the literature on participant observation concern whether members are lying, being superficial, or showing racial deference to the researcher. There is no fundamental difference between these problems of interpretation and those about whether members are lying, being superficial, or showing racial deference to each other. . . .

Reliability

. . . Quantitative sociologists have developed complex measures of reliability, many of which have been described in the annual American Sociological Association publications of *Sociological Methodology*. One old and relatively simple quantitative strategy for providing evidence of reliability suffices to indicate the apparently unreliable nature of qualitative field methods. If rules for coding are specified before data are gathered, the researcher can produce specialized, statistical evidence on the extent of agreement among "judges" who independently apply the scheme to the same data. This strategy is inconsistent with qualitative research. By definition, so long as a researcher's encounters with data are governed by preset coding rules, they cannot be exploited to develop qualifications in substantive analytic categories.

But qualitative research is not necessarily "impressionistic." The search for negative cases leads the qualitative researcher to a holistic analysis that binds propositions and data into an intricate network.[9] Seen within the social relations analytic observers develop with members and readers, the network constrains the researcher toward consistency in selecting and interpreting data. Such a network holds together my thesis on the careers of lawyers for the poor.

I have argued that the social environment presented to legal assistance lawyers — clients, adverse parties, courts — characteristically defines the problems of the poor as insignificant. In turn, poor people's lawyers typically experience expectations that their work should be routine. To maintain intense involvement in client representation, the lawyers must struggle to treat problems as significant by doing a specific kind of work: reform. Because the environment calls for routine, their maintenance of involvement depends on reform.

An elaborate network of analysis and data underlies this summary statement. There are two main themes in the analysis, a warp and a woof, each of which has multiple strands. Thus "the environment" includes the expectations presented by clients and by the adversaries and court settings brought in their wake. The "reform" activities of the lawyers include not only litigation objectives but the creation of an everyday intraoffice culture that resists and transforms "routine" messages received from outside.

Each of these propositional strands is itself a combination of evidentiary threads. I support the assertion of a judicial expectation for routine treatment by direct evidence. For example, I quote a poverty lawyer's account

---

[9] Holistic studies are usually thought of as case studies that try to comprehend an entire organizational or community social system. I am indebted to Diesing (1971) for his empirical research on the methodology of such studies. I believe that analytic induction takes on a holistic character even when it seeks to explain a particular line of action and that therefore the following methodological comments are applicable to analytic induction in general. Of his attempt to explain opiate addiction, Lindesmith (1947:15) wrote: "The actual process of the study may best be described as an analysis of a series of crucial cases which led to successive revisions of the guiding theory and to a broader and broader perception of the implications of that theory. Isolated bits of information and apparent paradoxes one after the other seemed to form integral parts of a consistent whole."

of an instance in which a state court judge responded to his argument of a far-reaching constitutional issue literally by throwing the pleadings out of court. I treat some data as neutral on the proposition, for example, reports of courteous judicial hearings of routine motions. I offer many types of indirectly supporting evidence, for example, explanations by legal aid lawyers that a court's failure to comprehend routine arguments represents judicial senility or alcoholism or prejudice against the poor. *A fortiori*, judges experienced as having such incompetencies would appear to be unresponsive audiences for complex arguments. Similarly, varied evidence bears on the characterization of the expectations of clients and opposing counsel.

To convert disconfirming into confirming data, it was necessary to qualify concepts and generate explanatory propositions. On the generation of explanation: If the environment defines the lawyers' work as routine, then one should find that the lawyers' development of reform strategies is a necessary condition for their involvement in work. Further, if some lawyers who are litigating reform issues describe themselves as disengaged and demoralized, then another necessary condition must be added to the explanation. This second condition was found to be participating in a peer-sustained culture that expresses a reform perspective. On qualifying concepts: If lawyers who are not litigating for reform nevertheless recount extended periods of immersion in work, the theory must be refined by elaborating the meaning of "being in the institution's environment." I found that these lawyers were occupied with internal leadership projects of institution building such as training other lawyers, not with directly representing clients in an adversarial setting. The result: A complex analytic framework supports any proposition, although the framework is illustrated by what may seem superficially to be casually selected "anecdotes."

However unconvincing the reader may judge this institutional analysis of routine and reform to be, my point is to indicate the many ways in which it could be embarrassed. There is no insurance that analytic researchers will make rigorous interpretations, but readers can easily guard against being misled. As a result, as a practical matter the researcher faces strong constraints toward reliability. On the mundane level of mechanics, self-deception and biased selectivity in recording data will involve substantial difficulties.

Considering the social relations created in the research process, there are several methodologically salutary features of participant observing. Analytic field study builds relations such that the researcher will often be unable to grasp immediately whether what he is recording is supporting or contradicting his current analysis. I assume I share the following experiences with other qualitative fieldworkers. In the field I often wonder whether I should be elated or depressed for my theory in response to the course an interview or observation is taking. Group scenes usually contain much that is obvious to members but challenging for me to comprehend. In interviews I must restrain analytic commentary in order to remain respectfully attentive and in order to provoke respondents to keep responding. I have no forms on which observations can be checked off and no set formulas for probes. A fieldworker inclined to ignore disconfirming data and record only confirming data often could not easily make the discrimination.

Once the qualitative researcher is out of the field and constructing a text, the social relationship of writer to reader presents elaborate constraints against inconsistent and unexplicated interpretations. If the qualitative data-gathering and text-construction process seems inarticulate, even mysterious, it helps to recognize that, irrespective of how unruly the analytic researcher's practices, the reader has rules available to detect error in the text. Blumer's classic critique of *The Polish Peasant* (1939) demonstrated the multiple objections that a discerning reader could make to qualitative research reports. Charges of a lack of fit between data and analysis may come from many sources: from multiple interpretations by the reader of the data presented; from the apparent irrelevance of the member's meaning to the analyst's point; from the connection between the analysis and the data being made through interpretive commentary rather than through the data itself; and from inconsistent implications of data presented in different parts of the text.

The weblike character of the text means that each datum will ramify in implications throughout. To insulate a careless analysis from critical readers, the researcher would have to engage in a laborious process. Each quote or episode would have to be edited carefully so that it might avoid contradiction elsewhere in the analytic framework. For example, if I had characterized the legal assistance lawyer's professional environment loosely as disreputable or demeaning (one of my earliest hypotheses), then I would have had to purge, from all quotes, any indication that a local judge or opposing counsel may have acted respectfully. To protect the initial, casual analysis, an extensive chopping up of quotes would have been essential, and further, a meticulous effort would have been necessary to avoid the appearance of chopped data.

Authors of qualitative field research reports cannot escape a dialectical evidentiary bind. The analysis must be made dense to make the data representative, to claim, in other words, that the study is generally useful. If the network of field materials and propositions is very limited, it would be easy to indulge inclinations not to report inconsistent data. Of course this could be done, but after a point the deceit would become self-defeating. Who would care? The study then would not pretend to be very useful or significant.

Given the possibilities of misfit, a biased selection of data that would convince a careful reader is not easily achieved. Given the emergent character of the analysis, if a confirming quote is hard to find or invent, the alternative readily available is to alter the analysis so that the data at hand will suffice. The everyday stuff of writing qualitative analysis consists of an ongoing series of retroductive shifts: trying to convince oneself that a quote or episode can be interpreted to fit the analysis until frustration is sufficient to make stepping back and modifying the analysis seem the easier course. . . .

In the traditional view, qualitative fieldworkers seem relatively free of practical constraints on recording and interpreting data wishfully and carelessly. Analytic research must be kept small scale in its human organization. Arrangements to deploy numerous researchers and coordinate their activities would compromise the method by requiring a prespecification of the data that they are to look for. Thus little if any mutual consent must be achieved to invent qualitative field notes. Qualitative research produces bulky field notes recorded with abbreviations meaningful only to the researcher. The interpretation of field notes often depends on a knowledge of context supplied by prior field notes or known but not recorded by the researcher. Field notes cannot as readily be transferred to other sociologists in original state as can responses to fixed-choice questionnaires because they cannot as easily be masked to preserve confidentiality without altering their meaning. The analytic strategy, which never separates data gathering from inspection of "results," may tease the qualitative researcher to disregard disconfirming data selectively, perhaps through an unconsciously biased inability to understand "inarticulate" responses. In contrast, the collection of quantitative data from a preset design may block the researcher's awareness of what findings would be disconfirming until data collection is complete and the computer has finished its run. The rules which preset the meaning of data to be gathered through surveys are used in large-scale research as a framework for an organizational hierarchy which gets the work done. An elaborate conspiracy might be necessary to manufacture findings. Moreover, the frequent practice in survey research of hiring specialized data gatherers who lack responsibility for analysis would appear to insure motivational neutrality.

On the other hand, this arrangement carries the risk of building alienation and indifference into a study at its most basic level (Roth 1966). In contrast, the close relationship between field researcher and subjects should make it more likely that the researcher will take the people studied as significant others. This audience can provide powerful constraints on reliability. To dismiss their objections to interpretations, the researcher might have to renounce an emotionally significant segment of his or her life. It would also seem to be easier to alter the number in a category than to invent quotations that sound like seventy-five different research subjects. Working with hypotheses, one could specify statistics on significance and correlations which would be confirming. One could instruct a machine to figure elegant equations backwards and manufacture the data necessary to make the math succeed. Just as it would be easier to change the number entered in a category than to invent a quote, it would be easier to figure out what that number should be.

My purpose is not to impugn the integrity of statistical researchers but to outline an empirical theory for evaluating reliability in analytic field studies. I have used the issue of manufacturing data as a way of short-cutting a more lengthy argument that would cover in detail allegations of morally lesser methodological sins. If there are constraints inherent in analytic field research which automatically place the dishonorable researcher between the Scylla of apparent unreliability and the Charybdis of apparent insignificance, *a fortiori* the merely careless analytic researcher should be found in the same straits. To develop in detail a theory of the constraints against fraud in qualitative and quantitative social research, one might examine real cases of serious allegations.[10] But for the present, if the methodological strength of research depends on the social system it actually fashions, qualitative field researchers need not be deferential in evidentiary debate.

Replicability

To the extent that researchers pre-fix their decisions for gathering data, they can easily present readers with a format for testing findings by repeating the study. Questionnaires and sampling procedures defining the boundaries of the relevant population may be included in an appendix; the coding book and written instructions for administering the survey instrument may be copied and mailed to subsequent researchers. Apparently inviting replication, psychology experiments traditionally have been reported in articles that neatly separate the description of methods and findings. The format takes the posture: You don't believe it? Go see yourself.

Analytic field research changes procedures for gathering data in order to encounter negative cases, then changes the analysis, and so on, in an interactive relation of method and substance. Innumerable *ad hoc* judgments are made in the field, decisions on when to visit the research site and when to move from observing one situation to another, decisions on when and how to probe in interviews. They could be reported, if detected, only through retrospective reconstruction. Because standards of substantive relevance change rapidly within the research process, much of the data considered will not be reported nor even recorded. The difficulties of specifying the research procedures used and of accounting for all the data considered add up to an inability to define what a replication would be.

---

[10] In an informal note, Mel Pollner suggests to me that the inquiry might start with a comparison of the controversies around the work of anthropologist Carlos Castaneda (Strachan 1979) and psychologist Cyril Burt (Hearnshaw 1979).

Despite these facts, the analytic field research strategy promotes relations with other researchers that facilitate the subsequent testing of substantive findings. . . . [T]he claim in analytic research that no negative case can be found invites the testing of findings without repeating the original research. A subsequent researcher can simply pick up where the study left off, looking for a single contradiction.

If the costs of subsequently testing qualitative field research findings are relatively low, so the rewards are relatively high. It has been notoriously difficult to publish failures to reject null hypotheses. Publishing criteria are biased toward disconfirming and innovative results. An attempt to replicate a study with a fixed design and determinate findings runs the risk of becoming nothing more than an unpublishable confirmation. The risk is a significant deterrent. In contrast, subsequent tests of qualitative field studies will never be merely attempts at disconfirmation. If only because the original research fails to specify what an exact repetition would be, a subsequent researcher should be confident of documenting new types of phenomena, valuable for other theoretical purposes, in his search for disconfirming cases.

Analytic field research also more democratically empowers readers to become subsequent testers. . . . Qualitative research reports properly may be regarded as good to the extent that readers test them in application to new data in the very process of reading. Underlying the reader's experience in "recognizing" as valid or rejecting as "artificial" an analytic formulation in a qualitative text is an implicit application to phenomena within the reader's experience, to new data existing beyond the reach of the original research.

To appreciate the reality of such testing, compare the implications of two allegations, that when writing *Asylums,* Goffman invented his portrait of the mental institution; and that Hollingshead and Redlich invented the survey responses and the computations presented in *Social Class and Mental Illness* (1958). Assume it is 1961, and follow-up studies have not yet been attempted. Readers of both works would, I submit, respond differently. There is a sense in which a reader would judge that the former charge could not be true. If Goffman was never a participant-observer in St. Elizabeth's Hospital, as he said he was, he must have been in some other mental hospital; or he must have talked to people who were; or read accounts by people who were. Ignorant of his methodology, one takes his results as evidence that he did something right. One can judge the value of his text immediately with as wide a variety of methods as he *might* have used. For the quantified survey study, the allegation of dishonestly reported methods and fabricated findings is much more crucial. One can readily imagine how the allegation could be true; if one wants to test it, one faces a sizable task; and if one believes the allegation, the work is worthless. To evaluate such claims requires an accurate and detailed account of how the findings were produced from a pre-fixed design.

In a fundamental way, the allegation of fictive data is less meaningful when applied to qualitative field studies. In fact, many of the best interweave observational and interview data with excerpts from novels written by earlier participant observers. An example is the use of Melville's *White Jacket* in Goffman's *Asylums* (1961:33–34). Another legitimate use of fictive data is illustrated in a book by Rosett and Cressey (1976). Drawing on wide but unspecified prior research and participant observation experience, they invent a criminal case, a cast of players, and a multistage decisional process — a whole social organizational setting and drama — in order to demonstrate the collective construction of guilty pleas. . . .

When such authors blur the line between fiction and data in their texts, they are obeying tendencies natural to their methodology. Phenomenologically, the distinction between "created" and "recalled" data becomes ambiguous in qualitative field research. Observations can be recorded at any time, contemporaneously or long after they are made. No rules govern the timing. Researchers can credit as data their own experiences in interaction with members.[11] Given this methodologically sanctioned freedom, the researcher may often be unable to assert confidently whether his image of a research scene is recalled or "made up."

But given the relation between author and subsequent researcher, this is a very constraining freedom. Qualitative researchers obtain no license from their affinity to the novelist. After all, the analogy between the novel and the participant observer's qualitative text is not complete. The requirement for an explicit analysis that is more general than the case under study, plus the discipline of the negative case, breed a compelling concern that one is not manufacturing data. On what else other than the accuracy of his analysis in the scene researched can the author rely to avoid a subsequent researcher's discovery of disconfirming data and the consequent charge that the analysis offered exists only in its author's mind? For the analytic researcher, methodological constraints are experienced as existential matters, not as matters of methodical convention.[12]

Researchers' Social Relations and the Evaluation of Analytic Fieldwork

By recommending a sociological perspective on methodology, I mean to call attention to implications for the evaluation of findings that may be

[11] See Glaser and Strauss (1967:252) for a defense of one such instance: Fred Davis's article "The Cabdriver and His Fare" (1959), which was based on personal experience but written long after Davis left cab driving and without benefit of contemporaneous field notes.

[12] Compare the distinction drawn by W. James (1970) between truth as "reflection" and a "pragmatic" theory of truth.

discovered by examining the system of social relations created in the research process. I have proposed hypotheses on the social relations created by analytic field research with reference to four familiar standards of evaluation. First, representativeness. By searching exclusively for negative cases, a researcher gives distinctive shape to his or her perspective on the people studied. To avoid contradiction by negative cases, analysis inevitably turns to the examination of social process as experienced from within. Continued study of a given segment of social life turns up increasingly refined discriminations between states of phenomena as they emerge in and vanish from experience. . . .

Researchers who gather data from fixed designs acknowledge that statistics on significance measure only the uncertainties of extrapolating from the data examined to the specific population sampled, not the prospects for extrapolating to later times and other places. Since any use of the findings of a study will necessarily be in application to a different population, a showing of statistical representativeness is necessarily an incomplete achievement. Analytic research cannot measure the uncertainty with which the scene it describes reflects any larger population, but its single-minded pursuit of qualifications in order to enhance the prospects of accurate application to other times and places raises the question whether this failing should be troublesome.

In its present state, the methodological literature assumes that reactivity in participant observation is a contaminating problem. But if we examine how research procedures shape the meaning of the study to members, we may conclude that field research without a formal design makes interaction between researcher and member into a substantive data resource. In a sense, analytic field research dissolves the problem of reactivity, whereas formally rigorous methods actually create it by enhancing the appearance of "research" and by limiting variation in the meaning of the research process to members.

Qualitative researchers typically concede an inability to verify the reliability of their interpretations of data. Yet even sociologists who labor to show high levels of statistical agreement among indicators acknowledge a logical gap between indicators and what is indicated (Blalock 1968). True, field researchers make themselves vulnerable in special ways to questions of objective interpretation by elaborating a network of idiosyncratic observations and informally fabricated explanations. But does this imply methodological weakness? From a sociological perspective on the relation between researcher and reader, the analytic method confers on readers unique powers to make their own judgments on reliability from independent encounters with data. Is that not preferable? Unlike statistical measures of the relations between several items in an index, or of agreement scores on a given item administered at different times, the analytic qualitative approach does not separate the evaluation of reliability, or consistency in interpretation, from the evaluation of validity, or the mesh between the researcher's concepts and the meanings expressed by subjects. Is that not preferable?

Qualitative researchers often admit to an inability to describe what would have to be done to repeat a study. They also have questioned whether a study is ever so disciplined by pre-fixed designs that, by adopting a published account of social research, anyone could ever really repeat it. The strength of analytic field research for replicability lies in the relationship it creates between original and subsequent researchers. When used in participant observation, the analytic method induces the researcher to credit as data his or her own experience as a member, minimizing the barriers to subsequent researchers for continuing the verification process. If qualitative field research offers no insurance that the researcher did not make up findings, it also raises the question of whether social research need be conducted in such a way that fabricated data can become a meaningful problem.

The analytic approach to fieldwork maintains an interaction between method and substance, breaking down their separation. Analytic field studies will not produce "proof," or artifacts which stand apart from substantive findings and can measure, or otherwise speak in a standard language about, representativeness, reliability, and so forth. The process and perspective for evaluation must be different. Acting within a system of social relations constructed in the research process, readers can make evaluations and researchers can assess how well they are doing.

Applied consistently in field research, the search for negative cases will force the researcher to focus on social process as experienced from within; induce research subjects to act toward the researcher as a meaningful member of the native world; enfranchise readers as colleagues competent to make independent assessments of the trustworthiness and general significance of the analysis; and facilitate subsequent tests of the findings by readers. This social system, which contains dimensions that have been barely outlined in this preliminary essay, can be invoked to spell out answers to numerous methodological questions frequently asked of qualitative field studies. For each qualitative field report, readers can assess how richly the researcher has perceived internal variation in the data; how radically the researcher varied his approaches to subjects; the density into which data and analysis have been interwoven; and the practical ease of testing the theoretical claims on new data.

Realism in Field Research

Egon Bittner

... [T]he taking of leave from objectivism was heralded as a genuine return to what is generally accepted to be the fundamental percept of all social science inquiry, the recognition of the relevance of the perspective of the actor. Above all, however, the newly liberated research stood for the revival, or the reinstatement into its rightful place, of *realism* in sociology of the kind associated with the celebrated achievements of the Chicago School in the 1920s.[1] The claim to realism — of faithfulness to reality — is important because its consideration makes available for analysis the manner in which objects come into view and are seen as objects of research interest, and realism can therefore be considered as the methodological equivalent of positivist objectivity.

The work to which the foregoing remarks allude consists mainly of a number of urban ethnographies.[2] Characteristically, to carry out their studies the researchers rely exclusively on those competences and resources they possess as members of society. To be sure, experience and a tutored subtlety of perception are highly valued, but the only thing that might be considered to be a required intellectual posture in this sort of fieldwork is total immersion in the life studied. Accordingly, fieldworkers find putting themselves into the picture they are drawing not only unavoidable but also a welcome obligation. The obligation to make clear who is talking draws its validity from the highest authority. "There is no absolutely 'objective' analysis of culture — or perhaps more narrowly but certainly not essentially different for our purposes — of 'social phenomena' independent of special and 'one-sided' viewpoints according to which — expressly or tacitly, consciously or subconsciously — they are selected, analyzed and organized for expository purposes." And later from the

From "Objectivity and Realism in Sociology," by Egon Bittner, in George Psathas, ed., *Phenomenological Sociology: Issues and Applications.* Copyright © 1973 by John Wiley & Sons, Inc. Reprinted by permission of John Wiley & Sons, Inc.

[1] I use the term "realism" to refer to the fieldworkers' efforts to discover and describe the full complexity and actual import of the features of settings as they are appreciated by persons to whom these settings are the circumstances of their lives. The use is not intended to contain any implications linking it with the old nominalist-realist controversy.

[2] A very large number of studies would qualify for inclusion here; some are Cavan (1966); Humphreys (1970); Polsky (1967); Scott (1968); and a collection of shorter studies, Douglas (ed.) (1970).

same source, "All knowledge of cultural reality, as may be seen, is always knowledge from *particular points of view*" (Weber 1949:72, 81).

It follows necessarily from these percepts that if anything said about social reality is to make sense, especially if it is to make unambiguous sense, it must be said in ways such that the point of view is either implicitly obvious or explicitly explained. The question is, of course, whether the researcher's immersion in the reality he studies and his emergence into the description he renders satisfied the requirement of making his point of view explicit. The question has not been studied with the care it deserves. Indeed it is not too difficult to sense in reading the urban ethnographies mentioned that the practice of writing in the "as-I-see-it" manner is more plucky than considered. Pluck is a virtue, especially in this case, but it does not set all things right.

The truth is that there attaches a spirit of adventure to fieldwork such that questions concerning realism of perception and description are decided by how one feels about it. This personal aspect of fieldwork is ill-concealed by referring to it as a method of research on par with, let us say, survey analysis or laboratory experimentation, a reference that is probably best understood by treating it as an expression of a live and let live attitude. Unfortunately the combination of personal enthusiasm and compromise, taken together with the ethnographer's notorious disdain for hypercomplicated, metacritical hair-splitting, are not very hospitable to analysis. Yet if the fieldworker's claim to realism and to respect for the perspective of the actor are to be given serious credence, then it will have to be made clear what form they assume when they are a function not of a natural attitude of the actor but of a deliberately appropriated "natural attitude" of the observer. That is, if it is true that the quality of an object or event — its meaning — does not attach to them objectively but is instead discernible only within the frameworks of socially organized settings, and there only from a perspective of specially oriented interest (for instance, the meaning of the remark "you old son-of-a-bitch" is something to which those between whom it passes have, on the occasion of its passage, a uniquely privileged access) then a fieldworker must somehow *contrive* an appreciation for these objects and events, since they do not constitute the actual circumstances of *his* life and therefore do not matter to *him* in ways he must nevertheless recognize them as mattering, regardless how participating a participant-observer he might succeed in being. In other words, the fieldworker re-turns to seeing things as they appear to those who live their lives in their midst, and thereby appears to take re-course to an objectiveness that rests on directly intuited facticity for its warrant. Whereas this turn to reality does not call for an argued defense when it occurs in the natural course, *choosing* it as a preferred way of seeing things does require justification.

Fieldworkers are, of course, not unaware of the need to *contrive* access to information and explanation, but they tend to view it as a matter of maintaining trustful relations with people whose activities and lives they study and of cultivating open-mindedness and perceptual subtlety on their own part. In fact, how to achieve these objectives is a matter of very considerable concern among fieldworkers and is usually treated in connection with ethical questions; there is a good deal of practical lore available on these matters. The concentration on how to do fieldwork well and how to get it done, laudable as it is, not only fails to cast light on the epistemological problem underlying realism but actually obscures it. The greater the effort to enhance the adequacy of observation on counts such as acceptance, transfer of trust, subtlety, perspicacity, open-mindedness, patience, and scope, the less likely that serious, searching questions will be asked about that which has come to view by means of all this loving care. That is, the more satisfied the fieldworker is about having done all in his power to solve procedural research problems, the less likely he is to note, and if noted attribute significance to, the fact that the reality he has seen and is describing is of a special kind, no matter how closely it resembles the "real" reality. The aim of contrivance is the approximation of authenticity, thus the more successful the outcome, the less likely that it will be remembered as contrived. In fact, however, the nature of reality the fieldworker attends to and, by extension, the realism embodied in his observations have nothing at all to do with the particulars of research technique. It is not whether he observes well or poorly that matters but the circumstance of his being an outside observer with all the consequences issuing from it.

Perhaps the best way to capture and render the actual reality in fieldwork is to consider the reality it *seeks* to capture, namely, the reality of everyday life. It is important to emphasize that the term "world of everyday life" refers to a zone of reality that is not limited, as the terms might be mistakenly taken to imply, to the ordinary, routine, broadly common aspects of existence from which the rare, the celebrated, the dramatic have been excluded. The feature that defines the world of everyday life is not its familiarity — familiar though it surely is! — but that it is the zone in which "*my* life takes place," the zone in which "*my* existence is actually located." There exist certain other "realities" (finite provinces of meaning), as we all know, but "*this one is my home.*" [3] Here is where I dream about being elsewhere, here is where I play being Hamlet, here is where I expect to cash in on promises made to me, and here is where I will have to live up to promises I made. It is impossible to overestimate

---

[3] The following discussion draws to the extent required by the present argument on the "constitutive phenomenology of the natural standpoint," as taught by Alfred Schutz; cf. his *The Phenomenology of the Social World,* translated by G. Walsh and F. Lehnert, Northwestern University Press, Evanston, Ill., 1967, p. 44, where the sentence in which the phrase occurs is unfortunately somewhat garbled.

the *centrality of the subject* for the phenomenal constitution of the world of everyday life. *But* while I am undeniably the center, the "null-point," toward which the world of everyday life is structured, I recognize within this world, through the office of the *general thesis of the alter ego,* you, him, them, all "null-points" in their own rights.[4] And so the world of everyday life is above all *our* home in which we live, in some ways identically, similarly, jointly, reciprocally, according to arrangements some of which we claim to have authored, whereas others appear to belong to preexisting realities.

Although this is not the place to go into details concerning the constitution of the world of everyday life, stopping the discussion at this point leaves open the possibility of a most serious misunderstanding (which actually exists in the minds of many people who profess a phenomenological outlook). To say that the world of everyday life is organized relative to the perceiving subject seems to imply that its meaning structures are freely determined at this "null-point." To counteract this possible implication it will be worthwhile to draw attention to the ways in which the factual reality of the world actually impresses its hold on the subject.

First, I, the perceiving subject who faces the world knowingly, know that as an object among objects I enjoy no special privilege. I come into being, endure, and perish as a thing among things and even if I have it within me to look forward to redemption, it will not be in this world. However much I may have taken charge of my own life, the bare fact of my existence is just that, a fact over which I have no control. Moreover, a great many of the features of my existence are also given in just the same way as the fact of existence itself. And all of this is prior to either stoic calm or *Angst* about it.

Second, despite the fact that I have (together with the rest of mankind, of course) an enormous span of control over the world surrounding me and can arrange my life so as to avoid, evade, master, or harness whatever I will not abide in its natural form, it remains a melancholy truth that the world as a whole will always have its way with me, in the long run. What the length of my tether and the scope of my options might turn out to be will undoubtedly depend to a large degree on my own initiative. But wisdom in the exercise of freedom — or simply reasonableness — consists of aligning one's will with the immutable urgencies that inhere in the realities of circumstance. What else is folly if not the neglect of or oblivion to the intractabilities of the world?

Third, and finally, the preceding two points could be viewed as expressions of someone's personal philosophy of life. But they were re-

---

[4] Concerning the matter of the subject's "null-point" position in the world of everyday life see Alfred Schultz (1962:127); on the "general thesis of the alter ego" cf. Schutz (1967: Chapter 3).

counted here as also describing the outlook of people whose professed beliefs run counter to them. We are not now interested in professed beliefs, however, but in that outlook which takes over when something must be done, for example, when someone must do what needs doing to success-fully take a plane across the country. The point here is that when someone has business with the world, or any part of it, he must be prepared to deal on the world's terms. What these terms are is not reliably taken from what the timid have to say. Instead, the terms are, from case to case, in what even the most radical of the radical comes to see when he sees that sometimes some things *have* to be done, and sometimes there is no getting around certain things, no matter what, in spite of all rational considerations.

Now, into this setting moves the fieldworker, a visitor whose main interest in things is to *see* them, and to whom, accordingly, all things are primarily *exhibits*. His orientation to the setting of his study is one of unrelieved and undifferentiated curiosity, and if he is good at it he will soon be able to see things appropriately to their situated meanings. But he will only be able to learn *that* they are this or that, not to recognize them *as* themselves. Thus, for example, he might learn to recognize the amusing without being amused by it; and even if he permits himself the joy of amusement, either indulgently or in remorseless exploitation of his own responses, he cannot appreciate it in its natural sense while remaining faithful to his aims as a fieldworker. For he must never relax the guard of skepticism about his own responses. After all, *his* sense of humor is not a guide to be trusted!

The paramount fact about the reality bounded by an ethnographic fieldwork project is that it is not the fieldworker's own, actual life situa-tion. This is so not because he might disdain accepting it as his own world, nor because he somehow fails in his attempts to make it his world, but because he *cedes* it as not being his world. He has deliberately under-taken to view it as the world of others. He is the only person in the set-ting who is solely and specifically interested in what things are for "them," and who controls his own feelings and judgment lest they interfere with his project. Of course, a good fieldworker learns quickly to recognize things according to the sense assigned to them within the field of his study. And he could probably impersonate a native well enough to get away with it. But even at the very height of his field competence, perhaps especially then, he cannot yield and be responsive to the sense things naturally im-portune. In other words, for the fieldworker things are never naturally themselves but only *specimens* of themselves. Specimens, because he sees them subsisting outside the natural subject-object relation within which alone they have founded meaning.

Since the fieldworker, as fieldworker of course, always sees things from a freely chosen vantage point — chosen, to be sure, from among actually taken vantage points — he tends to experience reality as being of subjective origin to a far greater extent than is typical in the natural attitude. Slipping in and out of points of view, he cannot avoid appreciating meanings of objects as more or less freely conjured. Thus he will read signs of the future from entrails of animals, believe that the distance objects fall is a function of the square of time, accept money in return for valuables, and do almost anything else along this line; but the perceived reality of it will be that it is so because someone is so seeing it, and it could be and probably is altogether different for someone else, because whatever necessity there is in a thing being what it seems to be is wholly contained in the mind of the perceiving subject. Hence, without it ever becoming entirely clear, the accent of the fieldworker's interest shifts from the object to the subject.

It is in this shift of interest that the fieldworker encounters phenomenology, which he correctly identifies as the major school of thought dedicated to the systematic study of subjectivity in a descriptive, although not empirical sense. But it appears that the availability of phenomenology at this point is somewhat of a mixed blessing. On the one hand, phenomenology, especially in the version contained in the writings of the late Alfred Schutz, offers an enormously fruitful theory of social reality. On the other hand, there is the risk that phenomenological teaching could be mistaken as encouraging descriptions consisting of unanalyzed impressions.

The promise contained in the work of Schutz is well known: Phenomenological sociology builds on an understanding of the constitution of meaning in the solitary ego, moves to the exploration of conditions that account for interpersonally shared meaning, and leads to a full-fledged study of the phenomena of objective culture like law, language, and above all that "ideal of community life which has the power to sustain itself through time in the minds of members" [5], society. Though these meaning structures have their locus in consciousness and are in this sense "subjective objects" (Gurwitsch 1966:141–147), they are phenomenally outside the perceiving subject and confronted by him. The retention of this sense of "objectiveness" of social reality — the retention of an unbiased interest in *things as they actually present themselves* to the perceiving subject — is the foundation of *realism in fieldwork*. For this, however, the fieldworker needs not only a good grasp of the perspectives of those he studies but also a good understanding of the distortive tendencies his own special perspective tends to introduce.

The risk alluded to as the second alternative is commonly neglected. It involves a self-indulgent concentration on what in theology is called *fides qua creditur* (subjective faith) to the exclusion of interest in *fides quae creditur* (the object of faith) (Lindstrom 1967:228–243). That is, one takes phenomenology to be the study of the actual appearing of reality in

---

[5] These remarks are an attempt to state the teachings of Schutz in a few words. The remarkable quote is from van de Vate (1971:149).

consciousness. Now, there is a certain ordinary reasonableness in thinking that all phenomenology calls for is describing what this or that thing seems to him who does the relating.

The risk that the teachings of phenomenology on the topic of subjectivity will be taken to urge the uncritical acceptance of variously occasioned impressions as the last word concerning the meaning structures of the social world is probably no greater in the case of fieldworkers than any others, but it is more serious. For the fieldworker, as noted earlier, forever confronts "someone's social reality." And even when he dwells on the fact that this reality is to "them" incontrovertibly real in just the way "they" perceive it, he knows that to some "others" it may seem altogether different, and that, in fact, the most impressive feature of "the" social world is its colorful plurality. Indeed, the more seriously he takes this observation, the more he relies on his sensitivity as an observer who has seen firsthand how variously things can be perceived, the less likely he is to perceive those traits of depth, stability, and necessity that people recognize as actually inherent in the circumstances of their existence. Moreover, since he finds the perceived features of social reality to be perceived as they are because of certain psychological dispositions people acquire as members of their cultures, he renders them in ways that far from being realistic are actually heavily intellectualized constructions that partake more of the character of theoretical formulation than of realistic description.[6]

The risk of an abortive phenomenology has another aspect worth mentioning. Not only does it constitute a failure of realism and thus become, in effect, a factor in the estrangement between man and the world, but it also signals a retreat from unity among men. For this unity depends in part on the sharing of circumstances of existence constituted as a meaningful environment. And to the extent that the abortive phenomenology of social reality seeps into modern consciousness, taking the form of a pallid ideology of cultural relativism, it attenuates the natural bonds of human community.

By the same token, however, it is only by means of a genuine phenomenological analysis that the special epoché of the observer of social reality can be understood in all its ramifications. And it is only within the framework of this understanding that the fieldworkers' observations can be assigned their proper relevance.

[6] Concerning constructive analysis and the process of formulating cf. Garfinkel and Sacks (1970).

Notes on Member Validation   *Michael J. Bloor*

Introduction

In the natural sciences findings are usually regarded as validated when they are replicated by a second investigator who repeats the initial investigator's experiment. In the social sciences validation is conventionally equated with a different sort of replication (sometimes called "triangulation," see Denzin 1970), the use by the investigator of different methods to produce the same findings. These validation procedures are themselves of problematic validity. For instance, it is difficult to see the warrant for rejecting findings that are the product of a seemingly appropriate method simply because they are not "triangulated" by additional findings generated by seemingly less appropriate methods.

In contrast to this replicatory approach, various social scientists hold an analysis to have been validated when a correspondence is demonstrated between the investigator's description and the descriptions of members of the collectivity that is being investigated. One such procedure was reported by the anthropologist Frake (1964b): the validation of the investigator's taxonomies by the attempted prediction of members' descriptions in the situation of their use in field settings. Frake (1961) checked his glossary of the diagnostic classifications of the Subanun people in this manner. A related procedure (also recommended by Frake) is that of validation via the attempted prediction of members' reactions to hypothetical cases constructed by the investigator. Finally, it has been argued that for a researcher to "pass" as a member may demonstrate the adequacy of his or her grasp of members' perspectives (Douglas 1976:123–124). None of these various procedures is free of difficulties. For example, merely "passing" as a participant in a field setting need not demonstrate the validity of the researcher's ethnography since members may tolerate a considerable degree of deviance in fellow members (critical discussions of these procedures can be found in Emerson 1981:362–363; and McKeganey and Bloor 1981: 66–67).

Used by permission of the author. Copyright © 1983 by Michael J. Bloor.
Both of the research projects described in this paper were supported by the Medical Research Council. I wish to thank Robert M. Emerson, Gordon Horobin, Neil McKeganey, and Patrick West for their criticisms of an earlier draft. The paper has also benefited greatly from my reading of an unpublished paper by Emerson and Pollner (1982) reporting on a member validation exercise that they conducted.

In addition to proposing techniques involving replication, prediction, and passing, a number of sociologists have recommended "member validation" as a procedure for assessing the validity of qualitative findings (see Schatzman and Strauss 1973; Gould et al. 1974; Douglas 1976; Emerson 1981). With this approach, it is suggested that qualitative findings are validated to the extent that collectivity members recognize and endorse the sociologist's account of their social world.

Although member validation involves treating lay assessments as the validators of professional judgments, it should be emphasized that this is not merely a matter of juxtaposing the researcher's and members' accounts: the two sets of accounts will normally differ too greatly in character to admit direct comparison of their content. As Alfred Schutz (1967) has argued, while laymen produce their own distinctive sociological accounts of their social worlds, these accounts will inevitably differ from the accounts provided by sociological researchers since each is formulated in light of different purposes at hand. A member's sociological account will only have that degree of clarity, consistency, and elaborateness required by the member's purpose at hand, and hence cannot be directly compared with a sociologist's description compiled for different purposes, emphasizing "completeness," consistency, and so on. Equally, some descriptions furnished by sociologists may seem sketchy and elliptical when reviewed in the light of members' interests and purposes.

Since direct comparison is not feasible, the task of member validation procedures is not to elicit comparable members' accounts, but rather to discover "if the members recognize, understand, and accept one's description of the setting" (Douglas 1976:131). In effect, the member is asked to judge whether or not he or she recognizes the sociologist's account as a legitimate elaboration and systematization of the member's account. The member judges whether or not the sociologist's account seems familiar in that it refers to, and originates in, elements similar to those in the member's stock of common-sense knowledge. However, validation exercises in which researchers try to elicit such judgments from members are inevitably subject to various difficulties and uncertainties. In this essay I will illustrate and elaborate these difficulties by reporting on two contrasting member validation exercises.

The Adeno-Tonsillectomy Study

The first validation exercise occurred in a study of regional variations in rates of surgery for adeno-tonsillectomy (the removal of the tonsils and/or the adenoids separately or conjointly) in two regions of Scotland. Under the British National Health Service, Ear, Nose and Throat surgeons act as the "gatekeepers" to this particular operation. Children with ear, nose, or throat problems are seen in the first instance by their family's General

Practitioner (GP). If the GP thinks adeno-tonsillectomy might help the child then he may refer the child to a surgeon's outpatient clinic; no child receives an outpatient appointment without a referral from a GP. At the clinic the surgeon assesses the child's history and conducts a clinical examination; if he or she feels that an operation is indicated then the child is placed on the surgical waiting list.

The study was designed to discover whether regional variations in operation rates reflected different surgical assessment practices. This task required developing detailed descriptions of each surgeon's routinized criteria for accepting children for adeno-tonsillectomy. Treating each surgeon's clinics separately, I sat in a series of clinics and noted the history taken for each relevant case, the examination findings, and the results of any ancillary investigations such as X-rays. I noted any comments the surgeons made to me on cases and asked questions on their reasons for taking particular disposal decisions when I got the chance. I also made some use of the surgeon's casenote materials and of general conversations during tea-breaks and similar occasions. I conducted a separate analysis of the clinic population of each surgeon in which I attempted to construct inductively the decision-making criteria that accounted for the disposal of all the surgeon's cases.[1]

Comparison of the different surgeons' decision-making criteria indicated a number of parameters of intersurgeon variation in routine assessment practices which would account for regional differences in tonsillectomy rates. Thus there were variations between surgeons in the *search procedures* used in the examination. Some surgeons took a much broader spectrum of clinical signs into account than did their colleagues. Further, surgeons not only differed as to *which* signs they thought it relevant to search for, they also differed concerning the *importance* given to clinical findings as opposed to reports of the patient's history. Surgeons' search procedures used in the history-taking varied in specificity, extensiveness, and the degree to which these search procedures allowed the surgeon to assess the symptomatology independently of the assessments of the parent and the GP. There were similar differences — of specificity, extensiveness, and independence — in surgeons' *decision rules* pertaining to the history. Finally, surgeons differed in the degree to which they would restrict access to tonsillectomy for younger children, and in the particular age-range over which these restrictive criteria were employed.

During the period of data collection all of the surgeons had been told that I hoped to discuss my findings with them in due course. On completion of my analysis of the data a typed report was sent to each of the eleven surgeons in the study detailing what I took to be his or her criteria for adeno-tonsillectomy. Each report was accompanied by near-identical cov-

---

[1] Fuller accounts of the adeno-tonsillectomy study, the analytic method, and the findings can be found in Bloor 1976, 1978.

ering letters suggesting a meeting to discuss the report and containing the following passage:

> I would very much appreciate an opportunity to discuss the findings with you, in order to discover to what extent they correspond to your impression of your clinic practice . . .

A sense of the contents of the reports can be gleaned from the following extract (with case illustrations excluded):

> It was noted that preschool children and children who had attended school for a year or less were more likely to obtain a conservative (i.e., nonsurgical) disposal than older children with equivalent symptoms.
>
> Broadly speaking, the disposal of younger children with a parental history of sore throats was determined by the severity of attacks suffered as defined by the number of days of bedrest (if any) and the number of days off school (if any). Children who had suffered both recurrent and very severe attacks, i.e., attacks necessitating three or four days in bed or longer, were listed for surgery at first visit. Children who had suffered less severe attacks, i.e., attacks necessitating a couple of days in bed or just a few days off school, were recommended for chemotherapy and reviewed unless they were already receiving chemotherapy in which case the children were discharged. Children who had never suffered severe attacks, i.e., had never been off school, were discharged. . . .
>
> Children who had suffered sore throats of intermediate severity would be listed for immediate adeno-tonsillectomy or tonsillectomy (rather than be recommended for chemotherapy and reviewed) if one or more of the following circumstances obtained:
>
> (a) If a child's other symptoms were such that attendance as an in-patient was necessary in any case in order for a middle ear suction or an adenoidectomy to be performed.
> (b) If a child had previously received a conservative disposal and subsequently reattended as a new patient with a reoccurrence of previous symptoms.
> (c) If a child's cervical glands indicated that the child's tonsils were chronically infected.
> (d) There was some indirect evidence that children of servicemen might be listed for surgery at first visit although their symptoms were consistent with a decision to review the case, but this possibility could not be adequately explored in the present study sample.

At a later date I conducted a tape-recorded interview with each surgeon in his or her office, focusing on the report.[2]

---

[2] My wish to validate my findings was only one of the factors which impinged on the interview encounters with the surgeons. There were certain gaps in the analysis that I wanted to repair: children with certain symptoms or combinations of symptoms were missing from the samples of some surgeon's clinics, so I had no opportunity to ascertain what the surgeons' operating criteria were in such cases. Additionally, I wished to give the surgeons some individual feedback on the study as a matter of courtesy and as a way of expressing my gratitude for access to their clinics.

These interviews provided some evidence in seeming support of the descriptions offered in the reports, although it was clear that, while my accounts were recognizable to members, they were not isomorphic with their common-sense knowledge of their work practices. Thus, one surgeon talked of recognizing familiar, taken-for-granted practices in my description of his clinic work, but indicated that he himself had never explicitly formulated just such a description:

> ... I think it was a fair assessment, a fair summary. It put into words many of the things which we do which are more second nature I think. You know, I think you've done quite well summarizing (laughter) me. Some of these things, "Well," I think, "You know, that *is* right," when I see it written down. And when you're doing it, well I suppose you have these things in the back of the mind but ...

Equally gratifying was the readiness of several surgeons to dispute particular points in the report in such a manner that I was able to correct the analysis subsequently. For example, one surgeon disputed my statement that he did not put children suffering from secretory otitis media on the waiting list for adenoidectomy unless they had associated hearing loss. He said he would review such cases, but if the secretory otitis media was seen to be persisting at later clinic appointments, then he would operate despite the child's unimpaired hearing. On returning to my data I found that no children with unimpaired hearing but with persistent secretory otitis media had been present in my sample of his cases, so I felt justified in qualifying the analysis in this respect.[3]

Beyond these disagreements over particular points, there was one surgeon who substantially disagreed with my report of his practices, arguing that I had underestimated the importance he attached to the examination findings relative to historical criteria:

> There are of course — and naturally — a lot of things that go through the mind of the ... of the doctor when he's examining these children and [they] don't perhaps come out. You have made the points of a number of indications, or contra-indications, or what-have-you, and none of it can possibly take in the clinical impression, the visual impression of the state of the tonsils on the surgeon which, err, doesn't perhaps appear ... So these ... these points, they cannot appear in a

---

Finally, there was the consideration that some means of sustaining the surgeons' cooperation would need to be found if the study was to be developed (at that time a parallel study of GPs' assessment practices was being contemplated). To ignore these different purposes and their differential effects on the data may lead to distortions in subsequent analyses.

[3] It was a natural consequence of the methods adopted that my analysis would pertain largely to common combinations of symptoms, while the surgeons would qualify my analysis by referring to cases they had encountered with uncommon (and therefore memorable) combinations of symptoms.

normal sitting-in and watching. (Yeah) You know, even ... and all I would write down in a casenote would be "tonsils moderate, glands++" or whatever ...

I ... I thought it was a good report but I felt that ... you know, it's an objective report from the point of view of what you saw, which is fair enough. But if you were sitting in a corner, after all, you really couldn't see.

So you're really left I think entirely — partly on the history, I pay a lot of attention to the history and the way it's presented to me — but basically on a clinical impression of the tonsils.

On consideration, there seemed to me to be every likelihood that my description of his practice had been ill-founded. Unlike most of the surgeons he had not verbalized his examination findings in the clinics for my benefit (I had obtained them later — in abbreviated form — from the casenotes), and so data collection and subsequent analysis had arguably been biased toward the historical evidence.

Yet despite the fact that some surgeons ostensibly were validating my analysis, either in general terms or by making corrections that implicitly left the rest of the analysis intact, the exercise seemed unsatisfactory in a number of respects. Firstly, in certain interviews I began to suspect that the surgeons concerned had not read the report in the "right" critical spirit. I had unthinkingly assumed, in framing the exercise, that the surgeons would scrutinize the reports in a manner analogous to that of an academic colleague criticizing a draft paper, or that of a teacher assessing a student's essay. Moreover, I had assumed that, since the papers described their own decision-making activities, the surgeons would be greatly interested in the reports and their contents. I came to realize that a number of the surgeons had reacted differently on one or both counts. The following excerpt illustrates an apparent lack of preparation and interest typical of some encounters:

Bloor: Err, you got the report that ...

Surgeon: ... Yes, I read it: I have it up there actually (reaches for the report). It's something to what I imagined it would be, that pattern of things you know (Yeah). Uh-huh.

Bloor: Were there any specific points about that?

Surgeon: No, no. No, nothing ... special.

Bloor: It corresponded more or less to your own impressions?

Surgeon: Yes, uh-huh, uh-huh.

Bloor: Ah ... (....) was there anything that you disagreed with specifically?

Surgeon: No, I don't think so.

Bloor: Or anything that ...

Surgeon: ... Can't recall disagreeing with anything, er ...

Bloor: Or anything that I'd omitted?

Surgeon: No I don't think so. Do you think there's enough cases here to form any ...? Err ... There's one thing on [paragraph] twelve ...

Some of the surgeons, then, had read their report with only very limited interest, without sufficient commitment to the research topic to wish to compare my findings with their own impressions of their practice. It should also be noted that surgeons are more centrally concerned with events in the operating theater than events in the outpatient clinic: clinical assessment, especially for a routine surgical procedure like adeno-tonsillectomy, is not a prime interest.

Note also how the surgeon in the above excerpt initially found nothing in the report with which he would disagree, but when he started to "reread" the report he found several items to dispute. Only in the unfolding context of the interview, taking his cue from the interviewer, did the surgeon find it a relevant pursuit to apprise the report in a critical fashion. It therefore seems that the critical points that the surgeon went on to voice were, in a sense, an artifice of the interview situation, framed by the respondent at the insistent prompting of the interviewer. Such occurrences are particularly likely if the respondent has little initial interest in the interview topic.

Other contextual influences apparently affected the content of the interviews. Some surgeons, for example, appeared reluctant to voice, or debate, aspects of my report with which they disagreed. This reluctance may have had its roots in an exaggerated respect for the "scientific" status of my findings, in a kindly wish to reassure a young researcher apparently racked with doubts about his findings, or in common courtesy. An interview is a species of conversation and, as such, it follows the implicit rules of polite conversation in which open disagreement is minimized. In the following exchange both parties struggled to maintain harmony despite a dispute over an assertion in my report that the surgeon was prepared to operate on children whose parents denied a history of sore throats provided that the children had examination evidence of tonsillar infection:

> *Surgeon:* . . . But I would be very surprised at this. And very reluctant to talk people into an operation.
> *Bloor:* Yes. There were . . . I got the impression that it wasn't so much cases where the parents manifested reluctance, but where they denied a history of sore throats say, but the symptomatology was of what they would call recurrent colds or something of that nature.
> *Surgeon:* Um. Fair enough, okay.
> *Bloor:* Well, I'm, I'm, er . . .
> *Surgeon:* (laughter) Well, I don't know. But seeing it in cold print like that . . . I, I say: "Did I, in the absence of a history of sore throats, say that the tonsils have got to come out?" Must have done, must have done, obviously.
> *Bloor:* But that's, that's the sort of . . .
> *Surgeon:* . . . That's an interesting point . . .
> *Bloor:* . . . But it's your impressions of that report, whether you feel it corresponds to your own impressions of your practice that I'm looking for. So . . .

> *Surgeon:* Yeah. I would have thought I would say "Oh well there's nothing really of any trouble — you can run along dear." *But* if you have observed this, then this is of value. . . . I know what you mean: there's often, sometimes . . . they say "Oh he's not had any trouble with his throat." And yet they've arrived on your doorstep. So they must have something wrong (um), their own doctor must . . . (um). Never mind, okay, leave it.
>
> *Bloor:* Well . . .
>
> *Surgeon:* . . . Does that? . . . No, leave it, this is quite valuable to us, I mean. Because, if you . . . (well) this is your . . . this synthesis . . .

The respondent was faced with a "reality disjuncture" (Pollner 1975) — my contradiction of his experience of his world — which he sought to deal with in a variety of ways. He tried to close down the discussion and move on to a less contentious topic ("Um. Fair enough, okay . . . Never mind, okay, leave it."). Additionally, he was prepared, at least for conversational purposes, to abandon his prior sense of his clinic procedures and embrace my "scientific" version ("Must have done, must have done, obviously . . ."). Further, he proffered an alternative version which could serve to dissolve the disjuncture, namely that lack of a history of sore throats from the parents might reflect parental misdiagnosis ("they say 'Oh he's not had any trouble with his throat' "), such that a child might be listed for tonsillectomy with a history of sore throats from the referring General Practitioner but no *parental* history. Reality disjunctures of this nature pose deep threats to interaction and normally call forth such conversational repair-work; in this instance the surgeon's stance had the effect of resolving the disjuncture while endorsing the validity of my report.

Such consensus-seeking behavior is by no means confined to the interviewee: I too proffered an alternative version of the disputed events to which the surgeon could give his assent ("I got the impression that . . .")! I have already noted my concern with maintaining rapport with members to smooth the path for an anticipated, related study. Further, it would be idle to pretend that in the interviews I was unconscious of the status gap between me and the respondents. Where the purpose of the interview is the conducting of a validation exercise, then the researcher (and possibly the respondent) may be orienting his or her behavior toward the negotiation of a consensual view of that particular social reality under examination. The nature of this exercise intends the result. Emerson and Pollner (1982), reporting on a member validation exercise they conducted, ruefully recognized that the transcript of their interview showed them attempting to refocus the discussion on what they viewed as the central aspects of their report and eagerly encouraging the respondent's attempts to restate and assent to those central aspects.

Difficulties of this nature are not simply confined to those interviews that were felt to be unsatisfactory, nor can they be corrected in any fundamental sense by "improvements" in interviewing technique. These problems apply with equal force to interviews I earlier described as ostensibly satisfactory: they are native to the method. The contents of the interview cannot be simply decontextualised to constitute a test of validity: the contents are influenced by the immediate circumstances of the interview context.

A further analytical difficulty centers on the occasioned and temporally bounded nature of the validation exercise. In my attempt at member validation I implicitly assumed the surgeon's views to be invariant rather than being provisional, contingent, and subject to change over time. That this implicit assumption was unwarranted is illustrated by the fact that the surgeon whom I quoted earlier ("I think it was a fair assessment, a fair summary . . .") wrote a letter to my research director following the publication of my comparative analysis violently denouncing the study. Ideally, members' reactions should perhaps be monitored on several occasions over time; this would also allow members to assent to revised analyses intended for publication.

In sum, the validation exercise fell victim to some major problems: an inadequate reading by some surgeons; a lack of strong interest; contextual influences on the interviews; the consensus-oriented nature of the project; and the essentially provisional character of members' reactions. Yet the validation exercise concerned itself with monitoring the reactions of only one of the groups party to the outpatient clinic assessments: the views of parents, nurses, and children were not sought. The second validation exercise I wish to describe occurred as part of a study of a psychiatric day hospital run as a therapeutic community. In it I attempted to get two different groups of members (staff and patients) with rather dissimilar perceptions of the hospital to validate my description of the patient culture in that institution. Under these circumstances the previously analyzed problems of member validation are multiplied and intensified.

The Psychiatric Day Hospital Study

In the day hospital study, I focused on the problematic relationship of the informal patient culture to the hospital's group therapy program. While the principles of therapeutic community practice emphasize mobilizing the patient culture as an instrument of therapy, that culture may also subvert the formal treatment program in favor of patients' situated needs and gratifications. The study identified various aspects of patients' behavior that the day hospital staff viewed as beneficial to therapy, for example, continuing the work of the group therapy sessions through informal patient discussions centered on perceived difficulties, or providing comfort and support to fellow patients undergoing the stresses and strains of treatment (which might otherwise lead many patients to default from treatment). Additionally, the study identified aspects of patients' behavior that the staff thought were detrimental to therapy, for example, becoming interested in the difficulties of other patients as a substitute for examining their own problems, or the formation of cliques that would buttress patients' resistance to discussing their difficulties in the formal groups.

The study highlighted what may already be evident to an alert reader, namely, that staff prescriptions for patient behavior were incipiently conflicting. Essentially similar patient activities could be interpreted in opposite ways as beneficial or as detrimental to therapy: informal patient discussions could be seen as extending the work of the formal groups or as providing a forum for the manipulative activities of "patient therapists"; provision of comfort and support to other patients could be seen as keeping patients in treatment or as bolstering their resistance to group therapy; and so on.[4]

Further, the study focused on staff reactions to patients' complaints that their behavior was "misunderstood," that they were subject to contradictory expectations, and so forth. In such circumstances the staff freely admitted inconsistencies but simultaneously drew patients' attention to the widespread occurrence of limitations and contradictions in expectations in daily life. Staff commonly made their own inconsistency an occasion for therapeutic work, insisting that patients learn new and nonpathogenic ways of reacting to limitations and contradictions in expectations.

The data were collected by participant observation, ordered into two stages: the first stage involved extensive participation in informal patient activities, and the second stage involved participation in the staff meetings and review groups.[5]

At the outset of the study I had told staff and patients that if access were granted then it was my intention to circulate a draft report of my findings and gather reactions to it. In the course of fieldwork I had agreed to send a copy of my draft report to several patients who had expressed an interest in what I was doing and at the end of my fieldwork I reiterated my intention of circulating a draft report in due course. Some months later, on completion of the draft report (subsequently revised and published: Bloor 1980), I arranged for two tape-recorded group discussions to take place, focused on reactions to the precirculated draft. The group discussion format was selected because of my dissatisfaction with the interview format

[4] There are some similarities here between the use for accounting purposes of the activities of the informal patient culture, and the use of the "convict code" as an interpretive scheme for a wide variety of occurrences with the halfway house studied by Wieder (1974; and this volume pages 78–90).

[5] Fuller accounts of the day hospital, the study methods, and the findings can be found in Bloor 1980; Bloor 1981; and Bloor and Fonkert 1982.

adopted in the adeno-tonsillectomy study: I hoped to be less active and influential as a participant in the group discussions than I had been as an interviewer in the previous study.

One of the discussions took place with the day hospital staff and the other with a group of ex-patients. The latter group were all people to whom I had become close during fieldwork; I had remained in contact with them after they had completed their "course" of treatment and had discharged themselves.[6] Thus they were highly committed, either to the research topic, to the research process itself, or to the researcher. This degree of commitment brought difficulties in its wake. As Emerson and Pollner (1982:23) point out, the researcher who trades on his friendships with members to solicit their cooperation in a validation exercise is prestructuring the encounter within a "friendship framework." Members' reactions to the research findings may owe something to the personal relations that have grown up over time between researcher and researched.

It was from the outset an unexamined assumption, by me and by members alike, that the staff and patient discussions of my report should take place separately. This assumption reflected an acknowledged divergence between staff and patient perspectives on the day hospital treatment program. This divergence of perspectives poses almost insuperable problems for a validation exercise insofar as it suggests that certain aspects of an ethnographic description may be endorsed by some members but contested by others. Additionally, the researcher may, on occasion, find himself in an intermediary position, lacking endorsement from holders of both (opposing) perspectives. In the extract below there was general agreement among staff members that I had underemphasized the degree of informal interaction between patients and nursing staff:

> I do think the informal situation in a therapeutic community is, par excellence, the therapeutic situation. This is why the nurse's role, as opposed to the traditional hospital, the nurse's role in a therapeutic community is so much a key role, simply because they are available outside the formal groups to make relationships, to mix with patients outside formal groupings.

Yet in the ex-patient group discussion one of the ex-patients denied that such nurse-patient contacts were ever "informal":

> *Bloor:* . . . One point of substance which they [staff] disagreed with was that they felt that — and I think they're probably right — that I gave insufficient attention to the way that nurses, in particular, could mix informally with patients. You know, in

---

[6] I also tried to contact a number of ex-patients who had defaulted from treatment and whose reactions to the day hospital might have been expected to be more critical than those of other ex-patients. However, only one of the defaulting group said he was willing to give me his reactions to the report, which I collected in a tape-recorded interview (not used here).

the corridors, at lunchtime, in the work groups and so on. And chat informally to patients/

Harry: /I was never aware of them doing that (. . .) I still felt it was "them and us." I never really felt that it was "informal": I really did feel that they were apart from us.

Phyllis: There was one time Edith [staff] and some of us were in the kitchen . . .

Ellen: That's right, aye (. . .) I remember doing the daffodils with Oliver [staff] that day and I didn't feel any . . . And even playing golf with Tam [staff]

Harry: Aye well there were these occasions but I never really felt they were . . . (laughter)

Furthermore, since members recognized the lack of a universality of viewpoint, acknowledging that staff and patients often held very different perspectives, some appeared to endorse my report, not so much because it reflected their own viewpoint, but because they saw the report as representing — or mediating between — opposing viewpoints:

I didn't pick up anything, I mean I couldn't pick on [i.e., disagree with] any one thing, because you've always put the both sides to each case, or explained it from both (aye) points of view (aye).

However, there was general agreement among members of the staff group that this balance of viewpoints had been inadequately struck in the report:

. . . I think it's a . . . a courageous thing to do really, because, err, it's like being in the middle of the road — you get run down by both sides of the traffic (laughter). You can't win. But, er. Yeah . . . I don't think . . . I still think that, taking that as your vantage point for writing this, this I think on the whole is a very reassuring document. I take . . . I acknowledge what Patrick was saying about . . . I didn't think you were being cynical (mebbe not the right word) but there may be some flavor of . . . Mebbe you were more easily sharing the patient point-of-view than the staff point-of-view. And mebbe we are more defensive as staff than we . . . [7]

Staff members traced the source of this inadequate balance to the stresses and strains of a participant-observer role, and particularly to the difficulties engendered by the changeover from being a participant in informal patient activities to being a participant in the staff group. Here a good deal of the staff discussion involved reference to passages in the report to interpret my feelings about the day hospital and its staff:

Can I come in there? (um) you see, I started . . . After I'd read this a few times I thought, I'll have to put something down that's more together. And so I just jotted down one or two things and I've got:

---

[7] One of the ex-patients also tasted this "flavor" of bias:
Um, that's what I thought. I almost thought there were many occasions when you were *prepared* (aha) to say what the staff said as well (laughs).

> "Terms used are cold." And I felt, you know, the change . . . when you
> left the patient participation and joined the staff part of it, it seemed
> to me as if you were talking at one point very much at a feeling
> level — when you were around the patients — you weren't picking up
> that when you were in the staff part. . . .

Additionally, some of the staff group (a minority) found the report not
just unbalanced, but also defective, in that it failed to reflect their psychodynamic concerns:

> The first time I read it my overall impression was that . . . err, I mean,
> I was pleased with the paper but I wasn't sure whether you were
> gullible. Then my impression was: it seemed to be naive, that was my
> feeling. 'Cos there was a lot that almost . . . it almost . . . almost needed
> to be said that "Yes, there's a great deal of other work on this." Ehm.
> It was almost as though I saw myself being rather silly in behaving in
> the way I did, as though I didn't quite understand it (yes). I did have
> a feeling that I understood it. That was my first impression, that was
> the feeling I had: I felt that a lot of the . . . I think, well-understood
> concepts that I base the way I work on weren't being acknowledged
> (yes, yes) . . . Can I . . . ? Can I say that my comment about naivete
> is on the basis of what I conceive of as what I'm doing? . . . . I'm not
> saying that the paper's naive. The concepts that I hold, it seems, we
> didn't share.

Here is an unequivocal statement that I had missed the underlying meanings and purposes of someone's actions, meanings, and concerns tied to
their psychodynamic framework and concepts. Without reference to these
concerns, my accounts appear "gullible," "naive." Yet even this criticism
implicitly recognizes and honors the parallel but separate nature of our
two accounts, each a product of our respective purposes at hand.

While some of the reactions of both staff and patients were critical, they
were far from uniformly so. Indeed, one of the analytical difficulties of this
exercise lies in the interweaving of positive and negative reactions, even by
the same individual. For example, the same member of staff who sought to
lay bare my alleged "cold" feelings toward staff also volunteered the following remarks:

> I must say the thing that struck me first of all, Mick, was how you had
> put it together at the end. People often ask me to say what happens
> at the day hospital and I haven't been able to tell them. I think very
> much you have put into the words the kind of thing I would have
> wanted to say. That bit I liked.[8]

[8] The speaker is probably referring to the final paragraph of the report:
In effect, patients are inducted into a world of warm, caring relationships where
judgments are suspended and a wide range of deviant behavior is permitted,
only to slowly realize that in the day hospital, as in the outside world, there
are contradictions — limits to care, limits to what is permitted. When a patient
suggested that I couldn't really care less about her since I only turned up at
the hospital three days a week, a staff member replied that I couldn't attend
more often and that was the unchangeable reality. "No one can give you 110

Here the speaker apparently finds the researcher's description so satisfactory that it is fit for re-use in other contexts: the researcher's account may become a substitute for members' accounts. Where such substitution of descriptions occurs, the new description reflexively reconstitutes the social reality it purports to describe. This reality-constructing aspect of the researcher's description can be seen even more clearly in the following extract where an ex-patient links her reactions to the report to her developing retrospective understanding of events in the day hospital:

> It explained a lot of the ... the confusion in the group, and the ... contradictions all the time, and how, so often, you left the group at the end of the day and you didn't know what had been going on. But now it's beginning to sink in. It explains how that's the way it's got to be, that's the only way it can work (um), although you're always trying to make it better. But at the time, you know, when I left the group ... Now I'm understanding it.

The speaker has used the report to redefine, give new meaning to, previously imperfectly understood events; the report has become incorporated into her experience of the world.

Relatedly, another ex-patient seemed to accord my description of events primacy over his own memories, which appeared to him by comparison to be selective and defective:

> I think there are certain things in there that I really don't want to remember. But having read it, it brought it back!
> Yeah, but are you not ... are you not a little bit embarrassed about reading about taking part in some of these things? To be reminded of them? Because I tended to look back on the group and what went on with all of us as ... great times (laughter). And it wasn't really (laughter).
> ... You know, I found it pretty brutally honest and, as I say, I felt a bit embarrassed with a lot of the things, you know, reading them again. Ehm, but I think ... I think you've done a good job with this. And simply because you got that reaction from me.

Thus, not only do members' purposes at hand produce particular accounts, but they also produce distinctive member readings of and reactions to the sociologist's account. In validation exercises members will often assess sociological accounts in light of their own purposes and interests as members rather than in light of the sociologist's purposes. To expect otherwise is to require the member, in a rather ethnocentric manner, to suspend his own various interests in his activities and enter into the sociologist's selective frame in order to respond to the report. Members, then, may even come to

---

percent care." It is the staff belief that as patients are forced to come to terms with these contradictions and accept these limits, then they are adopting patterns of behavior which will equip them to deal with life outside the day hospital more adequately than formerly, to recognize and accept the contradictions and qualifications of everyday life. (Bloor 1980:27)

incorporate the researcher's account into their own stock of knowledge of the world because of its relevance and adequacy for their interests; such incorporation may possibly be interpreted as evidence of validity. Alternatively, it may be objected that the researcher is validating his analysis only in a rather perverse way, by making the world over in the image of his analysis!

On occasion, however, members' endorsement (or even incorporation) of a researcher's account may be discounted for validation purposes. This is the case where the member strongly endorses elements in the report which the researcher feels to be only of incidental importance, and where the supposedly central elements of the report are passed over.[9] For example, one ex-patient made only passing comment on what I regarded as the central element in the report — incipiently contradictory prescriptions for informal patient behavior — but returned repeatedly to a "minor" point I had made concerning the value of interpatient interaction in providing patients with reassurance and encouragement in the course of therapy:

> I think the great thing ... I found ... You know, one thing that you said was the sort-of-congratulating the patient on actually getting somewhere sort-of-thing. And I thought that was really important. Because it seems that ... you can almost get into a routine that people have got to get something bad out of their system, you know, to be crying, upset, you know, trying to get their problems out sort-of-thing. You know, I liked the way that you saw it was necessary also to give something back. To say, "That was good," or "Well done" ...

Once again, it is necessary to recall that a member is unlikely to be able to simply juxtapose, template-like, his or her member's description with the researcher's: the member's description is likely to be composed of a number of discrete clusters of ideas, and the researcher's description is likely only to touch centrally on some of these clusters and perhaps will only touch elliptically, or not at all, on some clusters with which the member is most centrally concerned. It may be that this discrete property of members' descriptions (mirroring members' diverse descriptive purposes) explains the interweaving of positive and negative reactions that was noted earlier: unqualified endorsement of a researcher's description is unlikely, since the report may correspond to certain discrete members' ideas only at the expense of underemphasising, ignoring, or implicitly contradicting others. As Emerson and Pollner (1982:19) point out, a member may see from the ethnographer's description "how one does something like that, but not only or distinctively that."

A final caveat relates to the impact of the group discussion format on the content of the discussions. The group discussion format was adopted in

---

[9] Emerson and Pollner (1982:18) actually found their respondent endorsing part of their ethnography in terms that were quite contrary to their own understanding of what they had written!

this study primarily because of my dissatisfaction with the way that the interview format in the adeno-tonsillectomy study had shaped the content of the interviews with the surgeons. Certainly, the group discussion format has the apparent advantage that the researcher is much less a participant in the discussion than in the interview and is thus less likely to take a lead in negotiating a consensus in the manner described earlier. However, in both these group discussions one participant (the senior staff member in one instance and an older ex-patient in the other) emerged as a refocusser of the discussion and a qualifier of critical remarks. It may be that one of the participants may naturally gravitate toward the negotiating role that the researcher thought had been abandoned along with the interview format. Consequently, certain remarks may read as expressions of mediating intentions rather than, or in addition to, being merely reactions to the findings. For example:

> Well, I think some of my, err, colleagues have a number of specific points they want to raise with you and I'd rather that they personally did that (um). I think as far as I personally am concerned, and from what I hear from my colleagues who'd read your draft first . . . would be well, on the whole we are happy with this. I certainly felt happy with it for a number of reasons. So I think that the overview is a very positive one as far as we are concerned. And mebbe we'd better make that absolutely clear in case you think we're now going to niggle (laughter). And we probably are! (laughter)

Such chairman-like behavior indicates that the group discussions, like the interviews, were not free of contextual influences.

Conclusion

Evidently then, members' reactions to sociological findings (whether elicited in group discussion or interviews) are not immaculately produced but rather are shaped and constrained by the circumstances of their production: by the relations between researcher and researched, by the exigencies of polite conversation, by the search for consensus, and so on. Moreover, member validation exercises are necessarily bedeviled by differences between the purposes at hand of members and of the sociologist. These differences of purpose not only lead to differences in the structuring of lay and professional accounts which eliminate any possibility of a simple matching of accounts, but they may also generate other problems such as: limited member interest in the validation exercise; an intermingling of positive and negative reactions; tensions between requiring the member to enter into the sociologist's selective frame or allowing members to focus on issues that the sociologist may consider secondary or elliptical; and so forth. Further difficulties have also been noted, including the essentially provisional character of members' reactions and a possible lack of agreement among members in their lay descriptions of social reality.

Nevertheless, it would be a mistake to view member validation exercises as valueless. Several benefits attached to such exercises can be identified. Stating an intention to conduct a member validation exercise may ease the negotiation of access into some sensitive research settings. Members see the advantage of obtaining direct feedback and they are reassured by the knowledge that they will get a sight of the findings prior to publication. Some researchers may feel it is, in any case, a matter of ethics or etiquette to furnish their research subjects with a full report of their findings.

Beyond these practical and ethical advantages, members' comments on reports of findings remain *relevant* to the issue of the veracity of those findings. While the previous analysis shows that members' pronouncements on findings cannot be treated as a test of validity, it should also be clear that a member validation exercise can generate material that is highly pertinent to the researcher's analysis. This additional material must be treated as data, not as a test, and subjected to interpretation and analysis in order to discover its meaning; following such evaluation the additional material may enrich and extend the findings. Not only should the new material from the validation exercise be examined, but the original data should be reexamined in the light of this new material. In particular, negative reactions from members should be a stimulus for a reanalysis: the researcher is obliged to try and ascertain whether these negative reactions are merely a situated product of the validation exercise itself, or whether they reflect deficiencies in the original analysis. Ironically, but inevitably, negative member reactions may act as a spur to reanalysis, but positive member reactions cannot be taken to indicate that the analyst's task is completed. By attempting to incorporate members' caveats and criticisms into a reworked analysis the researcher may broaden his or her analysis in a manner similar to that claimed for analytic induction (Katz, this volume, pages 127–148). As Emerson (1981:362) has argued, "taking findings back to the field is not a test but an opportunity for reflexive elaboration," an opportunity for the extension and enrichment of the fieldworker's original analysis.

III

Relational and Personal Processes in Fieldwork

Introduction

Rosalie H. Wax
The Ambiguities of Fieldwork

John H. Johnson
Trust and Personal Involvements in Fieldwork

Barrie Thorne
Political Activist as Participant Observer: Conflicts of Commitment in a Study of the Draft Resistance Movement of the 1960s

Melvin Pollner and Robert M. Emerson
The Dynamics of Inclusion and Distance in Fieldwork Relations

Introduction

While field researchers have traditionally sought to explore and analyze the social relations and worlds of others, contemporary practitioners also call for close attention to the social processes of fieldwork itself. Field methods possess a strikingly social character; as Cassell has noted, "the interaction is the method; the ethnographer is the research instrument" (1980:36). In this respect, both specific items of data and deeper appreciative understanding derive from immediate social interactions and from longer-term relations the fieldworker establishes with those studied. Understanding these interactions and relationships provides a critical task for contemporary fieldworkers:

> Good fieldwork . . . depends crucially upon discovering the meaning of social relations, and not just those characterizing the "natives'" relations with each other. It depends equally upon discovering the meanings of anthropologists' relations with the people they study. (Karp and Kendall 1982:250)

Close examination of the social processes involved in fieldwork has been accompanied by explicit concern with the personal dimensions and consequences of the fieldwork experience. As the resocialization imagery of fieldwork implies, fieldwork may profoundly affect and transform the researcher. Many fieldworkers now strongly insist on the need to acknowledge and to analyze self-consciously such personal consequences of fieldwork. As Clarke has argued (1975:118):

> We must accept that social scientific research involves the researcher relating to those he investigates, and that the result is the outcome of their relationship, a relationship which, like all relationships, will change both parties. The knowledge thus gained from these relationships not only changes the knower; it becomes part of the knower. We must look then to the knower as much as to his field if we would understand what he is saying, and recognize that he has a valid part to play as a person, not just as a manipulator of techniques, in the acquisition of knowledge.

In this chapter I will examine the relational and personal processes that have received such attention from reflective field researchers. Several topics are critical here, including: the ongoing course and character of field relations, with specific attention to the details of what fieldworkers actually do when in the field; the details of the interactional transactions between fieldworker and those studied; and the inevitable personal and emotional reactions of the fieldworker which shape both the character of these transactions and their interpretation.

Relational Issues in Fieldwork

Social interaction and personal relations produce field data and understanding in at least two ways: First, it is only by establishing such relations that the fieldworker can gain access to these happenings and settings that are of interest. The process of gaining entree, which involves a continuing, progressive series of negotiations rather than a one-shot agreement (Johnson 1975), puts the fieldworker in the presence of the ongoing social life to be observed. Second, once some sort of relation has been created, the character of that particular relationship determines what sorts of experiences and hence what kinds of experiential and intuitive insights the fieldworker will gain.

Attention to the nature and course of field relations is not "merely" a pragmatic issue that every fieldworker confronts in simply going about getting the research done. There are two other, more general, grounds for close, reflective analysis of these relations and interactions. First, as emphasized in Part II, the methods that the fieldworker actually employs provide a critical point of departure for assessing the quality of both the data collected and the analysis made of that data. If data, description, and analysis are products of the modes of participation in a broad sense, then understanding those modes of participation is central to evaluating the substantive and analytic claims of any particular field research project.

Second, the very processes of getting on in the field, of dealing with recurrent problems such as entree, access, and rapport, reveal critical substantive and theoretically relevant features of the setting under study. Cicourel (1964:65) noted, for example, that "the participant observer interested in obtaining 'good' contacts in the field and the social scientist interested in studying basic patterns of social interaction" share a concern with the styles of interaction and social types found in any particular setting, although for different ends. The fieldworker's concerns with these social types is practical: "how to identify them, enter into relationships with them, and engage their support." Theorists are concerned with these types as ends in themselves. Methodological procedures are inseparable from substantive findings in fieldwork, as the previous selection from Wieder has illustrated.

Fieldwork Roles

The character and import of field relations have traditionally been analyzed in terms of fieldwork roles. In a key statement of this approach, Gold (1958) suggested that such roles fall along a continuum from complete observation (at an extreme, observing from behind a one-way mirror) to complete participation (the researcher gone native). Gold emphasized the different qualities of the two roles falling at the midpoints of this continuum, the observer as participant and the participant as observer.

A number of researchers question the appropriateness of this sort of fixed role imagery for analyzing field relations. Schatzman and Strauss (1973:58–63), for example, have talked not about mutually exclusive roles but about distinct modes of participation in ongoing situations, including: watching from outside; passive presence in the situation; limited interaction (aimed at clarifying actors' intents and meanings); active control; full participation as a researcher; and participation with a hidden identity. They view these modes of involvement not as mutually exclusive options (except for the last), but as tactical choices, all of which may be selected at different times and occasions in the course of a particular study.

Others have proposed that the nature of participation, rather than the extent of that participation, provides the critical dimension of field relations. Whether the fieldworker is overtly identified as a researcher or has covertly assumed a role natural to that setting marks the crucial distinction here. Thus, Lofland (1971:93–101) contrasted the *unknown* with the *known observer* as the two basic fieldwork styles, while Schwartz and Jacobs (1979:57) held that whether others think the researcher is a "scientist" or a "bona fide member" is a critical variable in field relations. The latter also suggested that whether a role is overt or covert does not automatically determine how the researcher participates in the setting; either actor may make more detached observations or participate in "normal, natural" ways.

Finally, standard accounts have often described field relations in overly circumscribed and rationalistic terms. While some researchers have depicted the techniques used to establish researcher role as highly impersonal, actual field relations proceed with a much fuller mixture of research and personal concerns (Johnson, this volume; Clarke 1975:103). Fieldwork roles are established only through the collaborative efforts of fieldworker and those studied. This process, marked by continuous negotiation and mutually beneficial exchange, is often unpredictable, and can generate unique role alignments, as Rosalie Wax emphasizes in the selection that follows. In addition, standard accounts of field relations have often ignored the impact of local settings, as actual field relations vary from situation to situation, person to person, and over time, all in ways only marginally under the control of the researcher, as Johnson shows in the reading included here.

Closeness and Distance in Fieldwork

The goal of most field researchers is to get as close as possible to the on-going life and events that they wish to understand and analyze. The fieldworker seeks "immersion in the natural situation" as a means to the rich, "direct experience" of everyday life that is the basis for reliable data (Douglas 1976:123). Immersion in this prolonged, intensive manner can confer a deep and accurate sense of the concerns and meanings of those studied that is often not apparent to the outsider or detached observer. Van Maanen (1981:210–211) provided a revealing example of this possibility, relying on his experiences in police training and working the streets (see "The Moral Fix" in Part IV) to explore the subtleties of meaning of a "good car shake":

> I had heard this phrase bandied about frequently in Union City from virtually my first day in the field to my last. Initially, I had thought it applied *post hoc* to those vehicle stops in which contraband of some kind was discovered and, hence, an arrest enacted. However, after working patrol for several months, I began to see that all partnerships used the notion to refer to those cars seen on the road that were thought to have a higher probability than others of simply turning up something interesting, criminal or otherwise. For instance, to many of the men, a "good car shake" was an automobile occupied by one or more pretty young women. Where police matters were concerned, however, the "good car shake" took on more specific connotations, although its meaning varied greatly from one patrolman to another. For example, to some officers a "good car shake" was a late model Cadillac carrying a carload of young black men. To others, it was a battered passenger van with out-of-state plates and being driven by a shaggy and dishevelled young man . . .
>
> This is not to say that all "good shakes" are stopped and checked. The vast majority of them are not. Indeed, "good shakes" are seldom discussed between the men once a partnership has worked out an understanding of what the phrase means to each person. But . . . the notion itself is important to patrolmen and hence relevant to the fieldworker. Yet, since the use of the notion rests on assumptions that derive from a person's particular biography and associations in the organization, the fieldworker can easily be misled as to its meaning — as I was initially.

Although often strongly advocated as an ideal mode of research participation, immersion by itself is in fact impractical on several grounds. First, as Rosalie Wax emphasizes, in most situations the notion of literally becoming a member and taking on a native identity is a romantic illusion at best and a self-deceptive barrier to effective fieldwork at worst. In cross-cultural research in particular, the fieldworker cannot become a member, and is best advised to accept the inevitable cultural and social differences between him and his hosts even while trying to gain some active, participatory place in their daily rounds of life. Second, even where something approaching total immersion is possible, fieldwork requires a contrary stance of detachment and distance. Good fieldwork is characterized by a paradoxical and "peculiar combination of engrossment and distance" (Karp and Kendall 1982:261), both of which are necessary in order to deeply comprehend others' realities. To understand others' ways of life requires the use of experience-distant as well as experience-near concepts, and this in turn demands at least partial disengagement from the immediacy of this life.[1]

Many fieldworkers achieve this combination of involvement and detachment by first immersing themselves in and then withdrawing from the social world under study. But as Pollner and Emerson point out in their paper concluding this section, balancing participation and distance must also be managed during the ongoing course of fieldwork encounters at the level of concrete interactions. Those studied act not only to exclude, but also to incorporate the fieldworker into their social worlds and routine rounds of activities. Thus fieldwork often demands interactional devices and strategies that allow the fieldworker to stay on the edges of unfolding social scenes rather than being drawn into their midsts as a central actor. In this respect distance as well as closeness in fieldwork is a jointly accomplished activity, one dependent upon the obligingness of those observed to allow the fieldworker to be physically present but socially marginal.

Finally, for some fieldworkers, examining some kinds of field settings, immersion and its assumption of common interest between fieldworker and those studied are fundamentally inappropriate goals. Douglas (1976:55) in particular has proposed that much fieldwork is more appropriately conducted on a conflict model which assumes that:

> many of the people one deals with, perhaps all people to some extent, have good reason to hide from others what they are doing and even to lie to them. Instead of trusting people and expecting trust in return, one suspects others and expects others to suspect him. Conflict is the reality of life; suspicion is the guiding principle.

---

[1] Distance may be urged for other reasons as well — as a corrective to bias and overrapport brought on by too strong an identification with those studied. Douglas (1972:26), for example, urges that fieldwork involvement be limited to empathy and kept short of full sympathy:

> Empathy is an ability to *feel with,* to see things from the standpoint or perspective of the individual being studied rather than to identify with or act from this standpoint. There is no reason whatsoever to believe that to understand is to sympathize with or to agree with, although this may be necessary for certain individuals because of their own feelings, identifications, and so on.

Douglas has subsequently questioned the adequacy of this distinction, suggesting that it is overly simple and too polarized, but he still insists on limited rather than total involvement (1976:99).

Douglas termed this alternative field method "investigative field research," and he emphasized the ways in which such a method must penetrate the various fronts, lies, and evasions that informants put up to keep the fieldworker from learning the truth. Much fieldwork carried out in this antagonistic style employs covert roles; the fieldworker tries to pass as a member in order to gain access to settings assumed unlikely to let an openly identified researcher enter. Particularly in research in groups with strong ideological commitments, it may be very difficult for an openly identified fieldworker to negotiate access and entree.

Covert Roles and Reactivity

Covert field roles have long been assumed to offer a critical advantage beyond access — the likelihood of minimizing reactive effects. If the fieldworker is not known to be a researcher, he or she will be treated as just another member in the setting (although the covert role will limit the fieldworker's ability to pursue explicit research questions; Lofland 1971:93–101). Covert fieldworkers can presumably discount and ignore any effects of their presence or behavior because, after all, these effects are simply those that any member would produce and hence are "natural" in and to this setting.

There have been a number of telling criticisms of these methodological justifications of covert methods. Cassell (1980:34–37), expanding Erikson's (1967) earlier observations, contended that covert procedures in fact inhibit the fieldworker's sensitivity to reactive effects: "the investigator who presents a 'false' self is affecting both the ability to judge what is going on and the course of interaction by the need for constant monitoring of one's 'act' or 'front'" (36). Erikson (1967:371–372) suggested the concrete difficulties that may arise along these lines by considering an incident reported in the study *When Prophecy Fails* by Festinger et al. (1956), in which a number of researchers posed as converts to an apocalyptic religious group:

> At one point in the study, two observers arrived at one of the group's meeting places under instructions to tell quite ordinary stories about their experience in spiritualism in order to create as little commotion as possible. A few days afterwards, however, the leader of the group was overheard explaining that the two observers had appeared upset, excited, confused, and unsure of their errand at the time of their original visit, all of which helped confirm her suspicion that they had somehow been "sent" from another planet. In one sense, of course, this incident offered the observers an intriguing view of the belief structure of the cult, but in another sense, the leader's assessment of the situation was very shrewd: after all, the observers *had* been sent from another world, if not another planet, and she may have been quite right to sense that they were a bit confused and unsure of their errand during their early moments in the new job. "In both cases," the report informs us, the visits of the observers "were given as illustrations

that 'strange things are happening.' " Indeed, strange things *were* happening; yet we have no idea how strange they really were. It is almost impossible to evaluate the reaction of the group to the appearance of the pair of observers because we do not know whether they were seen as ordinary converts or as extraordinary beings. And it makes a difference, for in the first instance the investigators would be observing a response which fell within the normal range of the group's experience, while in the second instance they would be observing a response which would never have taken place had the life of the group been allowed to run its own course.

The Issue of "Trust"

Whether mere empathy is sufficient to produce perceptive field data, or whether some closer, sympathetic identification is also needed, the field-worker needs to develop rapport or trust with those studied. While much of the literature on trust and rapport is practical and strategic in character (e.g., Berk and Adams 1970; Schatzman and Strauss 1973), it is also motivated by deeper methodological concerns. For as Johnson (1975:84) has noted, "There is a widespread consensus among field researchers that the rapport or trust between the observer and the members is an essential ingredient for the production of valid, objective observations." Johnson also suggests that in most fieldwork literature "trust" is conceived as "magically opening a door to collection of valid and reliable data" (1975: 119). Once rapport develops, it is believed that people in the setting will reveal previously concealed information and even intimate secrets to the fieldworker.

Such accounts exaggerate and distort the significance of trust. First, trust is never universal: Some people may never trust the fieldworker for personal reasons, while in other situations the researcher's efforts to establish close ties with some people will inevitably antagonize others. Second, the imagery that trust creates a "magic moment" in which prior evasions, distancing, and suspicion finally drop away is fundamentally misleading (Johnson, this volume, p. 204). All field relations are social relations and as such are patterned and regulated in various ways. These patterns and regulations mean that there is no totally free, transcendent way to study natural events in social life: any and all methods are constrained by the inevitable social character of the relations they rely upon. Trust, then, is never absolute; it involves not transcendence, but merely achieving a different sort of relation than one had before. This remains a role arrangement with its own distinctive patterns for conveying and withholding information.[2]

---

[2] Since trust (and rapport) involve social relationships, they could well be analyzed sociologically as phenomena in their own right. Levy's (1968) fieldwork on whites in the Southern civil rights movement in the 1960s moves in exactly this direction. Levy departs from the premise that "the nature of trust appears most clearly when its absence can be examined" (viii) to analyze the processes by which northern whites

Consider several specific examples. First, Warren and Rasmussen (1977: 354) argued that in a study of massage parlors, the latter author's gender and sexual status (available) had critical effects on field relations: "As a youthful, divorced, and attractive male, Rasmussen was a *threat* to some of the respondents — mostly males — and a *prize* to others — mostly females. Therefore, his ease of access to data was greatest for female masseuses, and least for male parlor owners, customers, and intimates of the masseuses." Yet this held only as a general trend, for "intimacy" with the masseuses *both generated access to some sort of data and restricted access to others.* As a result of his "role of boyfriend," for example, "(t)he women in the parlor were somewhat reluctant to tell the whole truth about their sexual involvements" (354). For "boyfriends" were not told everything (or sometimes even anything) about these sexual activities (see also Douglas 1976). Even (or perhaps, especially) romantic intimacy fails to lead to total, "magical" trust.

Similar problems have hindered the efforts of various "indigenous" or "third world anthropologists" to develop alternatives to the "outside" descriptions and analyses of Western anthropologists by doing field studies of their own cultures (Fahim and Helmer 1980:646). Exactly because they are involved in a set of relations with important local implications, indigenous fieldworkers often encountered resistances that the "powerless and neutral stranger" did not. For example: "the local anthropologist may not be taken seriously by informants if he probes types of behavior that informants view as commonly shared knowledge, such as marriage customs, or he may be considered intolerably crude in broaching other topics, such as sexual practices" (Fahim and Helmer 1980:646). Two issues are involved here. In the first place, there is the problem of who can ask what of whom. The cultural alien has real advantages in being able to ask questions proper to few local people (except children and other marginal sorts).[3] Second, there is the problem of what it is appropriate for someone of a particular local status to ask about. In one case a Norwegian anthropologist was able to complete an ethnographic study of Nubian people in the Sudan whereas an Egyptian anthropologist was unable to do so, since the latter was distrusted by the Nubians because of his sponsorship by the Egyptian government and his cultural view of the Nubians as a low status group (Fahim and Helmer 1980:646–647).

---

became aware of and tried to manage the pervasive expressions of deep mistrust they received from southern Blacks. Here again methodological problems (Levy himself was such a mistrusted northern white) have been turned into a topic for substantive analysis.

[3] Platt (1981) experienced just these sorts of problems in her efforts to interview sociologists about their own research projects: For example, her questions appeared incongruous when respondents knew that she knew many of the things she was asking about.

In sum, neither indigenousness, hard-won rapport, nor even "intimacy" provide transcendent access to all aspects of the lives and concerns of others. Every access is relationally situated, and hence inevitably partial. There is no way of learning all the secrets of another, since telling secrets as well as keeping them is fundamentally relationally bound. Trust provides not transcendent but situated access — to some secrets, including some that may be critical to understanding that particular scene — but inevitably not to all secrets.

Simultaneous Researcher/Member Roles

Some contemporary fieldworkers seek to participate as both a researcher and a member in the setting studied, a more common occurrence in sociological than anthropological fieldwork. Researchers make deep, long-term commitments to becoming active members, as illustrated by Thorne's decision to become a draft counselor in her study of the draft resistance and by Van Maanen's participation in police training in order to conduct fieldwork (both in this volume). These instances differ from covert fieldwork in that the research effort is explicitly identified: the fieldworker is both (simultaneously) researcher and member.[4] Fieldworkers advocate this method of full participation less to gain entree than as a means of gaining deeper appreciation of the group and its way of life; they insist that different levels of insight are gained from actually doing an activity rather than simply watching it being done, no matter how empathetically. Jules-Rosette (1975), for example, contends that the understandings she acquired of ritual in an African apostolic sect could come only through participation in such rituals as a good faith member. Only by actually going through conversion, for example, could she come to appreciate the inner meaning and significance of the activities involved.

It is difficult but nonetheless important to clarify the specific kinds of insights and sensitivities that accrue from becoming a member, actually doing activities, as opposed to simply observing these processes from an outside, detached perspective. Following Bittner's argument in the preceding section, the experience of even the member-researcher cannot be exactly that of the ordinary member. Nonetheless, it may provide a much closer approximation, one conferring immediate experience of at least some of the constraints experienced by ordinary members. It may also provide a grounded appreciation of the practical skills and intuitive judgments some members develop and employ in going about their routines and jobs; some such appreciation appears to inform Van Maanen's writings about the po-

---

[4] Fieldwork thus comes almost full circle to the classic Chicago School trait of combining member and research roles (Introduction), but with the interesting twist: Whereas Nels Anderson, for example, was hobo first and fieldworker subsequently, contemporary member-researchers reverse this sequence.

lice, for example.[5] In this way, actually performing members' functions in good faith may diminish or entirely do away with a kind of facile criticism that sometimes appears in field research.

Personal Dimensions of Fieldwork

In the past the personal dimensions of field research have been regarded as only marginally relevant and either omitted altogether or relegated to brief mention in introductions or appendices. Reflecting "a formal hiatus between the researcher and his facts" (Clarke 1975:118), descriptions of how methodological procedures produce data typically excluded consideration of the fieldworker's involvement as a person.

In contrast, contemporary fieldwork accounts often deal more overtly with a variety of personal and emotional processes that have affected both the course of the research and the life of the researcher. In general, the highly personal character of field relations has received increasing acknowledgment. The imagery of the fieldworker as only scientist/researcher has been discredited as the complexity of actual field relations has been emphasized. As Clarke (1975:104) has noted, "research, 'science,' data collection, synthesis testing, professional rivalry, social-emotional needs, identity, integrity, age, sex, status, and culture, are all integrated in the person of the researcher," and it is to some such mixture of traits, rather than to just those of "scientist," that those studied react. Actual fieldwork is not carried out in a highly pre-planned rational manner (although methodological accounts may suggest some such rational schema after the fact), but rather involves an emerging process of "creative trial and blunder" (Karp and Kendall 1982:260). Decisions made in the field are as likely to be motivated by "personal or subjective factors" as by strictly research concerns (Johnson 1975:90). Fieldwork, in sum, is a deeply personal as well as a scientific project, and the subjective, emotional experiences of doing fieldwork are intricately tied to the interpretations and theories ultimately produced.

The Personal and Social Attributes of the Fieldworker

The personal and social characteristics of the fieldworker are of immediate and central pertinence to those studied (see Pollner and Emerson, this volume, pages 237–242) and consequently affect the nature and kinds of data that can be obtained in the field. Johnson (1975:91), in particular, has emphasized the critical if often unnoted relevance of both "the observer's biographically unique personal experiences" and "the observer's

---

[5] I am suggesting neither that such appreciation *inevitably* results from doing in good faith what members do, nor that such doings are the *only* means of coming to this appreciation; only that the good-faith experience increases the possibility of discovering, for example, such skills and intuitions.

sexual status, racial status, socioeconomic background, appearance, abilities, goals" in shaping the way those studied define, evaluate, and react to the researcher. Elements of the fieldworker's personal biography are not only socially relevant to those studied, but also fundamentally shape the researcher's interpretive and theoretical interests in the field setting in ways that are not usually examined (but see Seeley 1964). For the fieldworker attends to issues and events in the field through a lens structured by past experiences, both personal and professional (a distinction that becomes highly problematic in fieldwork).[6]

The almost always relevant effects of gender have received attention in many discussions of field research methods. Golde (1970), in identifying recurrent themes in the fieldwork accounts of women anthropologists, emphasized that there is a frequent concern with *protecting* the female fieldworker. A stance of protection reflects both the perceived vulnerability and "provocativeness" of the woman's position (Golde 1970:5–7). "Protection, then, has a double aim — the direct need to insure the safety of the woman, and the protection of others through the prevention of situations that might provoke others to exploit her" (5–6). The result can often be severe restrictions in the fieldworker's freedom of movement in the field.

Yet such restrictions are always specific, reflecting the particular social understandings about gender (and age) that prevail in that locale. Women in general, and women fieldworkers in particular, while excluded from entire realms of activity that are male-dominated, have unique access to other activities that are considered appropriate to women. Rosalie Wax (1979) provides a case in point, which also illustrates at a somewhat deeper level how the very questions one can "appropriately" ask presuppose and reveal the implicit relevance of gender for the organization of social interaction. The Waxes had begun a participant-observation study of education in a Sioux Indian Reservation. After noting the rigid gender segregation of social worlds and activities in this community, the Waxes came upon another problem (R. Wax 1979:510):

> We also found that when either of us approached an older man and asked a question like, "Is there anything that your children particularly like about the schools?" he invariably ignored our question and proceeded to deliver an oration on the general value of education. Though eloquent, these speeches did not tell us what we wanted to

[6] Karp and Kendall (1982:252–253) argue that each fieldworker brings "a singular mixture of presuppositions, personal penchants, and past histories into the field, and these factors cannot help but color interpretations made there. They influence interpretations both because they predispose individual fieldworkers toward particular ideological or theoretical positions, and because they figure in the manner in which fieldworkers present themselves to the populations they study." These authors also suggest that a researcher's earlier fieldwork experiences will influence interpretations and understandings made in subsequent field studies. Particularly in anthropology the second culture studied by the fieldworker is often understood by contrast with the first one studied (and both by contrast with the researcher's native culture).

know. When we approached younger married men and asked similar questions they looked away bashfully and changed the subject. We soon discovered that only ignorant White People would put such questions to men. For among the traditional Sioux, all matters involving children or child-rearing — at home or in the school — were culturally defined as women's business. Young men simply did not talk about children. Old men were expected to take only a general benevolent interest in the welfare of the young.

There is some danger, however, of overemphasizing the rigidity of gender-appropriate behavior. Women fieldworkers have frequently been able to establish highly unconventional field relations in which they fairly consistently ignore or violate local gender-appropriate forms of behavior, in this sense negotiating a way to get their questions asked and their observations made. The cost, however, can often be loss of standing as a competent performer on that social scene. Daniels (1967) has supplied an illustration in her research involving interviews with U.S. Army officers. A "low-caste stranger" in this all-male, hierarchically organized world, Daniels was able to make a social position for herself which enabled her to collect her data. The position is well typified in the following exchange (1967:285–286):

> On another occasion, at a convention meeting, I joined a group of officers at a party. One member of the group was not known to me. He asked the person standing next to him who I was. That officer clapped us both on the back and said: "What? You don't know Arlene? Then you ought to meet her. She's a great girl. She's our mascot. She studies us."

As Daniels (295) concluded, "I became, after three years, an amusing and ornamental mascot, treated with friendly affection but little respect." [7]

Issues of racial identities have received somewhat less attention than those of gender. Liebow's (1967) reflections on the nature of his fieldwork among Black streetcorner men are among the most sensitive available in any field account. Liebow noted that the racial difference was always present (1967:248), and in all likelihood more markedly so for the men studied than for himself: "When four of us sat around a kitchen table, for example, I saw three Negroes; each of them saw two Negroes and a white man." Yet on occasion, particularly in the field, he felt that the racial differences had been transcended:

> Sometimes, when the word "nigger" was being used easily and conversationally or when, standing on the corner with several men, one would have a few words with a white passerby and call him a "white mother-fucker," I used to play with the idea that maybe I wasn't as much of an outsider as I thought. (248–249)

[7] Note the relevance of these observations for Kanter's (1977) later and more general analysis of the adaptations to being a *token* in an organizational setting.

But on closer reflection, and on reviewing his field notes, Liebow concluded that view represented a "touch of vanity." Even conversations in which his Black friends would talk openly of the irrelevance of his being white ultimately served to call attention to the distance race created (see the two incidents on pages 249–250). As Liebow concluded (250–251):

> ... the wall between us remained, or better, the chain-link fence, since despite the barriers we were able to look at each other, walk alongside each other, talk and occasionally touch fingers. When two people stand up close to the fence on either side, without touching it, they can look through the interstices and forget that they are looking through a fence.

Two brief, concluding remarks on the relevance of such social attributes in field relations are appropriate. First, it seems likely that female fieldworkers much more frequently have the experience of being a "low-caste" researcher in their particular setting. In general male fieldworkers will tend to be of higher status than those they study more often than female fieldworkers (e.g., Liebow), and they may have to work consciously at reducing their threatening qualities as a result. In contrast, in many settings women will have to work forcefully and explicitly to be taken seriously.

Second, while social attributes exercise a fundamental and pervasive influence over the nature of field relations, I see no principled way of deciding whether the shared attributes of fieldworker and those studied should be minimized or maximized.

Personal and Emotional Effects of Fieldwork

Fieldwork, Rosalie Wax has noted (1971:20), is essentially a process of "relearning and resocialization" (see also Briggs 1970) that inevitably engenders deep feelings of insecurity, anxiety, loneliness, frustration, and confusion. These personal and subjective motives and feelings arising during fieldwork may significantly affect research outcomes. Extending Schwartz and Schwartz's earlier analysis (1955) of the distortive effects of intense anxiety on participant observation, Gans (1968) identified a number of subjective processes specific to field relations that lead to overidentification with those studied, including the experience of irremediable marginality from the group and guilt from the subtly deceptive stance assumed toward its members.

Field researchers have explored in greater detail the dynamics and consequences of such personal involvement and identification with those studied (Wolff 1964, 1976; R. Wax 1971; Jules-Rosette 1975; Thorne, this volume, pages 216–234). A number of these accounts have suggested that personal involvement produces bias or distortion in observation and interpretation. R. Wax examined the changing course of her strong identification with several ideological factions in relocation camps (1971:118–162), yet she suggested that continual exposure to different groups in the field gradually corrected initial biases (141). Douglas urged fieldworkers to avoid studying issues "too close to their hearts" or in which they have intense and unresolved emotional conflicts (1976:93–103).

Other fieldworkers have emphasized that subjective experience is not only a source of bias, but also a source of insight and understanding, both of those studied and of oneself. Wolff (1964) in particular has insisted that successful fieldwork ultimately requires *surrender* to the culture and community studied. This stance requires "total involvement, suspension of received notions, pertinence of everything, identification, and risk of being hurt" (1964:237), and produces strong subjective engagement with the life concerns of those studied. This engagement leads to a deep understanding of these concerns. The fieldworker's emotional and subjective reactions to specific settings and events in the field can also lead to fuller appreciation of members' lives and experiences. Reinharz (1979) advocates such an approach in what she terms "experiential analysis," a concept that evolved from fieldwork conducted on how families living in an Israeli town subject to terrorist shelling coped with this ever-present threat. In coming to this town to begin her research, Reinharz has first to make what provisions she could for her own physical security. In so doing she came to realize that her own strategies and reactions to the shelling were comparable to those of the Israeli families (1979:336):

> Early in the process . . . I uncovered my previously unknown and unexamined responses to potential disaster. I found myself recording my own feelings to the same problem to which the families' responses were being studied. . . . I no longer considered these personal reactions internal noise that disturbed the research process. Rather, I looked to my reactions as an indicator of general patterns for coping with the continuous threat of potential destruction.

The subjective and emotional experiences of doing fieldwork affect not only the interpretations made of those studied, but also, often at a profound level, the very self of the fieldworker. Particularly when venturing into other cultures, fieldworkers are exposed to "the impact of a new way of thought and life upon their own" (Clarke 1975:104), an exposure that may fundamentally transform their sense of who and what they are. Even in less exotic field settings, personal values and beliefs are frequently challenged and questioned, and attitudes drastically changed as a result (Clarke 1975; Johnson 1975). Indeed, going into the field may lead to resocialization or even conversion experiences that deeply affect the fieldworker's personal identity. Zola (1982) provides a striking account of the impact of fieldwork on researcher identity in discussing his personal experiences in a village for the physically handicapped in The Netherlands. This field experience not only radically transformed his sociological understanding of the world of the handicapped, but also had profound personal consequences, as he came to fully recognize and embrace rather than to distance himself from his own longstanding physical impairment. Indeed, in some instances fieldwork may be pursued as a way of working through troubling identity-related issues. Hughes (1971:566–576) has suggested, for example, that a number of graduate students at the University of Chicago found in fieldwork a means of "sympathetic emancipation" from the immigrant culture or occupational background of their parents.

Fieldworkers face a number of unresolved issues in their handling of these field-based emotional and personal experiences. First, to what extent is full disclosure of the personal experiences of fieldwork a realistic possibility? Lofland (1971:132), while highly sympathetic to personal dimensions of fieldwork, has suggested that fieldworkers, particularly the young and professionally unestablished, will inevitably shy away from full disclosure. In the selection included here, Johnson echoes these reservations and explores a number of factors that portend something less than full disclosure.

Second, to what extent is full disclosure necessary? Clarke has warned against the dangers of "vulgarization and distortion posed by highly personal accounts," and advised against including "every passing emotion" in field reports (1975:120). One minimal criterion might restrict inclusion to those personal and emotional experiences that significantly affect the researcher's understanding of the setting in general or of critical activities within it. In this regard, Thorne's article and postscript offer a number of reflections on the linkage of intense personal experience with wider sociological understanding.

The Ambiguities of Fieldwork

Rosalie H. Wax

While a graduate student in anthropology at the University of California at Berkeley in 1943, Rosalie Wax began an extended fieldwork study of the Japanese relocation centers located at Gila and Tule Lake. Some years later, she conducted fieldwork with her husband, Murray Wax, on formal education on the American Indian reservation at Thrashing Buffalo. In this selection Wax draws upon these two field projects to examine a number of the relational processes and problems fundamental to doing fieldwork. RME

It is very difficult to appreciate and understand what goes on in another culture in the terms of the people who live in that culture. It is even more difficult to communicate such an appreciation and understanding — once it is acquired — to members either of one's own culture or of yet a third culture. But it is even more difficult to understand and describe what goes on in a field situation, because many of the most important things that occur are not explicable in terms of the meanings, concepts, or definitions of either culture. One consequence of this is that certain of the more important utterances of fieldworkers about fieldwork may be understood at once by their experienced colleagues, but they may be misleading or ambiguous to inexperienced people who do not know what it is like to live and work in the limbo between two cultures or societies.

Immersion

When an experienced participant observer reads that a fieldworker "immerses himself into the native scene" (Lowie 1937:232), "steps into another society" (Powdermaker 1966:19), or becomes "physically and morally a part of the community" (Evans-Pritchard 1964:77–79), he nods his head in understanding because he knows from personal experience and in depth what these professionals mean by the terms they use. But a person who has never tried to "live with" an alien people does not know what these terms mean, and should he read the existential accounts given us by Whyte, Lowie, Carpenter, and others, he may reasonably conclude that terms like "immersion" or "becoming a member" need a good deal of qualification. For example, a human being may immerse himself in a book, a game of

Reprinted from *Doing Fieldwork: Warnings and Advice* by Rosalie H. Wax by permission of The University of Chicago Press and the author. Copyright © 1971 by The University of Chicago.

chess, in the study of Arabic, or in a bathtub. He may even, like some great historians, immerse himself in the literature and culture of an ancient people so as to become intimately acquainted with this people's *Weltanschauung* or their world of meanings. But he cannot, by his own will and determination alone, immerse himself in another *living* group or society. If he manages to squeeze, step, or even dip into a group of living people, it is because the people who are already there invite or let him in or, at least, move over and give him a place to stand. Immersion or stepping into, or becoming a member of, a society or culture of living people is always a *joint* process, involving numerous accommodations and adjustments by both the fieldworker and the people who "accept" him.

On another level, many fieldworkers, and especially inexperienced researchers, do "become immersed in" or, perhaps it would be better to say obsessed with the impulse to get themselves totally accepted by, the host people. This, they mistakenly think, is what "developing rapport" means. In extreme form, this obsession may take the form of the fieldworker's trying to divorce himself from his own people and developing the delusion that he is rapidly becoming a native. If there is any value to this practice I have not discovered it. Still, it may be a stage through which novice researchers must pass — just as some adolescents get pimples and some graduate students attack the pet notions of their professors. Perhaps, illusion though it is, the conviction that a fieldworker is "in" may serve as a crutch and comfort during the initial period when he must sometimes live in an almost total social limbo. Later, when he becomes more genuinely "involved," he can dispense with illusions and accept the fact that he is and will always remain a non-native.

There are other and more genuine forms of "immersion." For example, a fieldworker may become so fascinated by the new, exciting, and significant things he is learning, that he may spend months passionately and persistently thinking of nothing else. Simultaneously, he will find himself becoming personally or socially involved in the community, not only because of his developing relationships with acquaintances, employees, and friends, but because, to some degree at least, he is now really beginning to lose touch with his own people and with the world outside. After many months or, perhaps, several years of concentrated study of what was once an "alien community," this activity, for the time being, has become his life. By this time, of course, the community is no longer alien.

The symptoms of this kind of immersion are various. I, for example, find that as soon as I become personally or intellectually involved in a field situation, I cannot concentrate on any problem that does not concern this immediate situation. Each time I have gone into the field I have taken along a box of academic tomes, but I have never read any of them. During the first part of the field trip I was too worried and anxious to concentrate; during the later part I was too busy. My husband, on the other hand, is able to do fieldwork and also to read and think about many "outside" things. Indeed, at Thrashing Buffalo, during the spells of cold weather that kept us housebound for a week or more, he "surfaced himself" quite easily and rewrote a long paper dealing with a subject which had nothing to do with Indian education. For this feat I still feel a kind of awe.

During my first difficult months at Gila I threw myself so furiously into my attempts to "get data" that I almost forgot the existence of the world outside the center and outside the interests of the Evacuation and Resettlement Study. When the American army invaded Italy, I did not hear the news until a Japanese acquaintance told me about it. This, I realized, was going too far, and I subscribed to a daily newspaper and forced myself to read it at my solitary meals. Twenty years later, when we went to Thrashing Buffalo, I urged my husband to subscribe to a number of newspapers and periodicals. Even so, during the Cold War flareup of late 1962, I was once startled by an Indian grandmother, who, though she could barely speak English, opened our discussion of education by asking in a loud voice, ringing with joyful anticipation: "Has the war started yet?"

There is another and deeper kind of immersion which may occur after a fieldworker has truly become involved with the "living people" in the society he is studying. Indeed, he may be unaware that he is "immersed" until he is given the opportunity to leave the field for a pleasant vacation and finds that he does not want to go. Sometimes, his new and hard-won social ties and relations may mean, or seem to mean, more to him than his ties with his own people. He may even come at times to feel that his own people are "the outsiders." After becoming involved in the political activities at Tule Lake, I found leaving, even for short staff conferences, extremely difficult. Life "outside" had become almost unbearably dull. Leaving Thrashing Buffalo after only seven months of work proved to be almost as much of a wrench, even though I had been complaining loudly and regularly about the "hardships" and the "isolation." William F. Whyte tells us that after he had lived and worked in Cornerville for three years, he applied for another grant of three years, since he felt that there were many important areas of Cornerville life about which he as yet knew little. As Evans-Pritchard remarks, "An anthropologist has failed unless, when he says goodby to the natives there is on both sides the sorrow of parting" (1964:77–79).

Perhaps I should digress here to remark that every time I have been in the field and become truly involved I have had to struggle with an impulse to stay longer than I should have stayed. By this I mean that I felt an almost irresistible urge to gather more data rather than face the grim task of organizing and reporting on the data I had. But in every case, the longer I stayed, the less time I had to write, and the poorer became my final report. Indeed, most of the data gathered at the expense of the time I had allowed for writing is still languishing in my files. It is a horrid but inescapable fact that it usually takes *more* time to organize, write, and present material well than it takes to gather it. The notion that one can work in the field for a year and then write a good report while one is carrying a full- or part-time teaching load is idiotic. (People do write in this fashion, but this is one reason why so many monographs are uninspired.) The sensible researcher will allow as much free time to write his report as he spent in the field. If he is really astute and can get away with it, he will allow himself more.

Membership

Some enthusiastic participant observers assert or imply that a fieldworker must become a member or, at least, a quasi member of the group which he expects to study. Like the notion of immersion, this notion of membership can be ambiguous and misleading. It ignores or glosses over two crucial facts: (1) that it is the group that defines the terms of acceptance or rejection of new members; (2) that groups vary enormously in the ways in and the extent to which they will permit an outsider to "become one of them." In a complex culture there are groups or societies that solicit membership, and a fieldworker will have no trouble at all in becoming a participating member if he is willing to pay the expected price of money or time. There are also many aggregates or categories into which an unfortunate or unaggressive person may be pushed. Thus, a researcher who loses his job may join the unemployed, he may become sick and study a hospital, he may get himself arrested and imprisoned and study a prison. Complex societies also offer a variety of jobs, occupations, or statuses into which a fieldworker may be admitted in whole or in part, if he learns the ropes, keeps to the codes, and behaves with reasonable circumspection. But they also contain many groups, organizations, and professions which grant membership only after a long and arduous apprenticeship (which virtually no fieldworker can endure or afford to undergo), and they contain at least some ethnic and religious groups into which one must be born and reared in order to be accepted as "one of us." Folk or tribal societies may not be quite so complicated, but they vary a great deal in their practices of accepting an outsider as a member. Some peoples seem to have a tolerant or casual attitude toward "outsiders." They may accept a fieldworker, not as one of themselves to be sure, but as an outsider who is willing to learn, understand, and respect their ways. Other tribal societies may permit an outsider to live near or even with them, provided that he comport himself discreetly, like a wise cat in a house full of dogs; but they would consider ludicrous and contrary to nature the idea that he might become "one of them." Still other peoples define any outsider as an enemy, and the fieldworker who tries to push his way in and "join" them is asking for disaster.

Moreover — and this is a point which most people who write about fieldwork do not sufficiently emphasize — many tribal or folk societies not only maintain a strict division of labor between the sexes and ages, but the people who fall into these different categories do not converse freely or spontaneously with each other even when they eat, sleep, and live in the same dwelling. For example, a young male anthropologist might live in an Indian household and even carry on with the Indian girls and yet learn very little about what women — old or young — think, say, or do. Similarly, William Foote Whyte, in his study of a street corner society, seems to have learned a very great deal about the young men, but he tells us virtually nothing about the Italian girls or about local family life. Conversely, I, as a middle-aged woman, was never able to converse openly or informally with either the old or the young Indian men at Thrashing Buffalo. The older men, even when I knew them fairly well, would tend to deliver lectures to me; the younger men, as was proper, were always too bashful or formally respectful to say much. With the Indian matrons, on the other hand, I could talk for hours.

Since this is what groups or societies are like, the researcher who wishes to do at least some participating will do well to bear in mind that the quality and depth of his participation or his "membership" will be determined by a series of understandings, agreements, and new situations, worked out by his hosts and by himself. If he joins a group that welcomes new members, he may find himself pressured into acts or undertakings in which he does not wish to involve himself and find it necessary to insist that he can be only a partial or incomplete participant. If he joins a group that admits useful hangers-on, he may be pressured into roles that contribute very little to his research, for example, rich feast-giver, unpaid taxi-driver, pampered and secluded guest. If he tries to obtain membership in an elite group, like physicians, big business executives, Orthodox Jews, or American Indians, he will soon "observe" that most doors are firmly closed in his face. If he is permitted to attach himself to a suppressed, subordinate, or persecuted group, he will find that he must reciprocate by keeping his mouth shut. But whatever the area or depth of his research, he will, as he gains experience and trust, be offered opportunities to enlarge the scope of his participation and his "membership," and this usually means that he will be able to enlarge the scope of his investigation.

Identity

Perhaps the most egregious error that a fieldworker can commit is to assume that he can win the immediate regard of his hosts by telling them that he wants to "become one of them" or by implying, by word or act, that the fact that they tolerate his presence means that he *is* one of them. Indeed, this is the mistake that all experienced fieldworkers warn against.

William F. Whyte ([1943] 1955:304) tells us that early in his investigation he tried to enter into the spirit of his friends' conversation by cutting loose with a string of obscenities and profanity. The boys looked at him in surprise. Doc shook his head and said: "Bill, you're not supposed to talk like that. That doesn't sound like you." "I tried to explain that I was using terms that were common on the street corner. Doc insisted, however, that I was different and they wanted me to be that way."

Powdermaker (1966:263) does not seem to have suffered from the impulse to assume a native identity. But she gives us several examples of how foolish and impractical the notion is. Africans, she emphasizes, do not expect any European to become an African or to follow tribal customs. But they want to be treated "properly," with respect. "The absence of this attitude in many Europeans caused bitterness and hostility." She relates how, on one occasion when she was driving in the compound, the hat of an African riding a bicycle blew off and fell directly in front of her car. She stopped her car, whereupon the African retrieved his hat, saying, "You are a proper European." By proper he meant "someone who treated others with respect and had a sense of etiquette, i.e. politeness and good taste; it was a valued trait in tribal society." She also tells us a pertinent anecdote (1966: 119) about a couple of anthropologists who worked in South America:

> The wife decided that she wanted to "go native" and left her husband for a short time to live with an Indian family. She slept in their house, dressed as they did, ate the same food, and, in general, tried to live the native life. At the end of an agreed-upon period, her husband and his colleague called for her. As she climbed into the truck with a sigh of relief, her Indian host winked broadly at her husband. He and his family had been humoring her play-acting.

Ned Polsky (1967:124), who has done fieldwork among hustlers, beats, and other persons classed as criminals, speaks with even more emphasis against trying to "become one of them":

> In doing field research on criminals you damned well better *not* pretend to be "one of them," because they will test this claim out and one of two things will happen: either you will . . . get sucked into "participant" observation of the sort you would rather not undertake, or you will be exposed, with still greater negative consequences. You must let the criminals know who you are; and if it is done properly . . . , it does not sabotage the research.

William Stringfellow (1966:24–25), a young white lawyer who took up residence in the Harlem slums, tells us that, after he had lived there several weeks, a Negro acquaintance from the neighborhood suggested that they have a cup of coffee. Over the coffee, the Negro remarked that Stringfellow was still shining his shoes. "He said that he knew that this represented the continuation, in my new life in Harlem, of the life that I had formerly lived and he added that he was glad of it, because it meant that I had remained myself and had not contrived to change, just because I had moved into a different environment." Stringfellow interpreted these words to mean that "to be accepted by others, a man must first of all know himself and accept himself and be himself wherever he happens to be. In that way, others are also free to be themselves."

These comments and examples suggest that the wise and well-balanced fieldworker strives to maintain a consciousness and respect for *what he is* and a consciousness and respect for *what his hosts are.* Clumsy and amateurish attempts to alter or adjust his identity make him look silly, phony, and mendacious. Besides, many people will interpret his assurances that he is one of them as rude, presumptuous, insulting, or threatening.

Perhaps good fieldwork is more like play or playacting than most of us are willing to admit. Respondents rarely resent a fieldworker's "acting like them" or "learning their ways" so long as the fieldworker makes it clear that he knows that he is only playing a part and that his newly acquired skills do not entitle him to any privileges which they are not willing to offer him. What people do resent — sometimes very deeply — is the amateurish notion that the acquisition of a few tricks or a sentimental statement about universal brotherhood will, almost automatically, turn a clumsy and ignorant outsider into an experienced, hardened, expert, or sacred person like themselves.

Among our acquaintances are a number of men who have put much effort into establishing an identity as an American Indian. They convince many white people that they are Indians, but, rarely, if ever, do they convince the Indians. The latter tell humorous anecdotes about them and laugh behind their backs. Ironically, another white man, married to an Indian woman, is sometimes affectionately called an Indian by his Indian relatives (Wax, Wax, and Dumont 1964:56), for, though he makes no claims to Indian status, he talks to all of the Indians in friendly and unassuming fashion. Indeed, his mother-in-law remarks that he is "just as much an Indian" as her daughter "even though he is a white man."

The disposition to assume an identity with the people of quite a different society or culture is, I suspect, related to the fact that our complex contemporary culture contains so many groups or societies that permit or encourage "joining" or voluntary membership. Besides, our notion of progress is closely related to the notion that man changes his "self" (though not his identity), and from infancy we are taught not only that we can but that we must change and "develop" ourselves. In consequence — even if we take many courses in anthropology or sociology — it is difficult for most of us to grasp the point of view of peoples who are unable to conceive of the idea of the changing self.[1] On the other hand, many of the young people in our contemporary society are undergoing "a crisis of identity" and do not know what they are. Some of these young folk search for their missing sense of identity in a strange or alien group. To what degree their search

---

[1] Illuminating discussions of conceptions of the self may be found in Lee (1949) and Wright (1966).

helps them I do not know. But I doubt that it helps the host group or contributes much to a general knowledge and understanding of mankind.

Attached or Instrumental Membership

With rare exceptions a fieldworker cannot become an autochthonous, aboriginal, or organic member of a tribal or ethnic group. Nor, except in rare cases, can he slip neatly into a long-established traditional role. Nevertheless, there is a special sense in which a fieldworker who lives near or with the people he is studying does become a member of the group. But what he becomes is an attached or instrumental member, a person who, though he always *is* and *remains* an outsider or non-native, may function *in the society* in a manner that is useful and agreeable to his hosts. An excellent example of this kind of instrumental membership is the case of Peter Freuchen. Freuchen lived with the Eskimos, off and on, for half a century. He took an Eskimo wife and had children by her. His Eskimo "friends" called him "the man who thinks for us," and, in many ways, treated him as *if* he were one of them. He played many useful roles in the community, serving his hosts as trader, explorer, arbitrator, and as mediator between them and the white men. But these roles, it should be noted, were not those of the traditional Eskimo man. Nor is there any indication in Freuchen's voluminous writings that the Eskimo ever came to regard him as a fellow Eskimo or that he ever thought of himself as an Eskimo.

An extremely perceptive and helpful discussion of what it means to be an attached member, a friend, but always an outsider, is given us by Elliot Liebow in his study of Negro street corner men. He tells us (1967:248–251) that the

> brute fact of color, as they understood it in their experience and as I understood it in mine, irrevocably and absolutely relegated me to the status of outsider. I am not certain, but I have a hunch that they were more continuously aware of the color difference than I was. . . .
>
> Whenever the fact of my being white was openly introduced, it pointed up the distance between me and the other person, even when the intent of introducing it was, I believe, to narrow that distance. . . .
>
> Once I was with Richard in his hometown. It was his first visit in five years. We arrived in the middle of the night and had to leave before daybreak because Richard was wanted by the local police. We were in his grandmother's house. Besides Richard, there were his grandmother, his aunt, and two unrelated men, both long-time friends of Richard.
>
> The group was discussing the possibility of Richard's coming home to stay and weighing the probable consequences. In the middle of the discussion, Richard interrupted and nodded at me. "Now Ellix here is white, as you can see, but he's one of my best friends. Him and me are real tight. You can say anything you want, right to his face. He's real nice." "Well," said his Aunt Pearl, "I always did say there are some nice white people."

Though Murray and I lived on the Thrashing Buffalo reservation for only seven months, our Indian neighbors gently or not so gently nudged us into roles for which, in their opinion, we were particularly suited. To begin with, of course, we were "claimed" by one family and propelled into the already well-established role of white thrill seekers or Indian lovers who would pay their hosts large sums of money for the opportunity to participate in "genuine fullblood life." Having escaped from this cul-de-sac, we were "adopted" by and established a more edifying relationship with one of the reputable families of the community, playing the role of eccentric but reasonably decent employers. Other reputable and not so reputable families then made overtures to us, letting us know that they too had bright sons or daughters who knew how to type or who had graduated from high school. We hired some of these young people as we needed them, and if this caused any conflict within the community, we did not hear of it. (Though had we given a good job to any rival of the ChargingBear family there might have been trouble.) Other families called on us, sometimes as a formal courtesy, sometimes out of curiosity, and more frequently to sell us beadwork. We bought a good deal of beadwork, partly because our neighbors needed a little cash, and our purchases were a way by which we could share our wealth and yet maintain a principle of reciprocity. Besides, the beadwork was often very beautiful. We also learned much because we attended most of the ceremonial events, dances, weddings, bingo parties, giveaways, and even the forty-year-old movies (which were shown by an itinerant missionary lady from the Crow reservation). We were tolerably welcome at these events because we minded our manners, did not "poke fun" (laugh at Indian ways), were not shocked by bingo playing or lively jokes, and because, like well-mannered rich visitors, we shared with the community by making seemly gifts and contributions. Besides, by attending these affairs we showed our respect for the community and unostentatiously demonstrated that we were not like "the other stuck-up white people and mixedbloods" who pointedly avoided appearing at fullblood ceremonials or events. In a sense, Murray came, in a small way, to act as a "chief" in the traditional Indian pattern of patronage, but not, of course in the sense of the moral leader or organizer. He also began to be approached by people in the community who wanted expert advice on how their children, now in high school, might obtain the kind of higher education they desired, for this, everyone conceded, was the area in which he was truly knowledgeable.

We also learned much because we allowed the schoolchildren of our local community to wait inside our house for the school bus. They soon began to arrive long before the bus was due, and they often stopped in for a return visit in the afternoon. These visits were sometimes hard on us, but they provided an opportunity to observe the children in a situation where no adult was organizing or controlling them. We also learned many interesting things because we were the only white people for miles around who would let Indian neighbors use their telephone. In this way we were apprised of local scandals, travels, and accidents (though of course I learned most of these through visiting the women), and we were also able to observe how the fullblood Indians use the Indian police force. On the other hand, we learned relatively little by functioning as chauffeur for some of our neighbors, though our willingness to pick up people and help them in an emergency gave us a general reputation as generous folk, and the Thrashing Buffalo, unlike some other peoples, do not despise casual or unconditional generosity.

Role Playing

Some experienced fieldworkers speak of role playing in fieldwork as if the fieldworker's roles were ready and waiting for him in the society he wishes to study. All he has to do is find the roles and "assume" them. In point of fact, in the field, many of the researcher's most useful roles are spontaneously invented and developed by the combined efforts of his respondents and himself. These new relationships are sometimes peculiar or even fantastic, and they rarely fit precisely into the social structure of either of the participants. But hybrid devices though they may be, they serve as social ties which the involved parties find mutually profitable and satisfactory.[2]

I would not have been able to do fieldwork in Gila and Tule Lake if my respondents and I had not been able, jointly, to invent and maintain many of these relationships. Some Japanese Americans felt more comfortable if they could treat me like a sympathetic newspaper reporter. I knew very little about how a reporter behaved (indeed, I had never seen or spoken with one), but I responded and we were able to converse more easily. In Tule Lake the superpatriots and agitators found it easier to talk to me once they had convinced themselves that I was a German "Nisei," "full of the courageous German spirit." I found this fantasy personally embarrassing, but I did not make a point of denying my German ancestry. Finally, I was not a geisha, even though a shrewd Issei once suggested that it was because I functioned as one that I was able to find out so much of what happened at Tule Lake. His explanation was that Japanese men — and especially Japanese politicians — do not discuss their plans or achievements with other men or with their wives, but they are culturally conditioned to speak of such matters with intelligent and witty women. Though vanity has tempted me to accept the Issei's hypothesis, I think it would be more accu-

---

[2] Readers interested in this point will enjoy a perceptive article by R. O. Haak (1970). Haak suggests that "when groups are forced into confrontation each takes what it needs from that confrontation and does not perceive it in the same way even when both are moving toward a satisfactory rapprochement. Far from representing this as a lapse in communication, I would generalize that a happy outcome requires each faction to salvage its self-esteem under the common umbrella of mutual misunderstanding."

rate to say that the Japanese agitators and I developed a new role which fitted their temperaments and mine. This role had no precise place in either the Japanese or the American culture, but in Tule Lake it permitted us to converse with considerable mutual satisfaction and enlightenment.

During the course of my fieldwork, respondents and I have spontaneously constructed many of these mutually profitable roles. But the experience I remember most vividly is one that occurred before I attended a university or became interested in anthropology.

During the depression, from about 1930 to 1938, my family — two brothers, two sisters, my mother, and myself — lived in a Mexican neighborhood in Los Angeles. We met several pleasant Mexican youths at a settlement house and invited them to join us at our house for some sessions of poker. We played for stakes of atomic minuteness, but even so, we soon became aware that our new friends were cheating. Embarrassed, we pointed out that we didn't play that way. The Mexican boys smiled amiably and said, "But this is the way we always play. We can't play any other way." So we *gringos* held a discussion and decided that we too would cheat. But this worked out very badly for us because we were very clumsy cheaters. Besides, we had played our kind of poker for so long that we could not really enjoy cheating even when we got away with it. So we held another discussion. This time the Mexican boys suggested that we all play as usual. They would cheat with might and main and we would play fair. But if one of us caught one of them cheating, the catcher would get all the cheater's chips. This new set of rules worked marvelously well. The Mexicans outdid themselves in clever deceptions, and we, in the course of many sessions, became phenomenally expert at detecting "aberrations" in their play. Best of all, the new system evened out the odds, so that neither of us won consistently from the other. Occasionally, fascinating moral dilemmas arose. Our dog once snapped at the seat of a Mexican youth's pants just as he was sliding an ace between himself and his chair. My sister contended that she should get the pot by reason of the alertness of our dog; the Mexican youth contended that she ought to be penalized because her dog had not behaved like a sportsman. The debate was so wonderfully entertaining and lasted so long a time that I do not remember how it was resolved.

I do not intend to suggest that roles in most field situations are developed as easily and with as much open discussion as was the procedure in this culturally mixed poker game. Nevertheless, the fundamental principles and mutual assumptions of both situations are similar. While the two parties may be willing to play together, yet each carries with himself a set of habits or skills that he is unwilling or unable to abandon. The very process of their interaction may lead to the emergence of a new game with new rules. (The situation in a cross-cultural schoolroom or in cross-cultural medical practice seems to me to be quite similar. Dumont [1971] remarks that, in a successful classroom, "cooperation was lodged within this framework and the development of it required an environment in which choice and compromise was the norm." See also Marriott [1955].)

Perhaps the most useful thing to say about involvement, membership, or role playing in an alien community is that the value of a role, for the participant observer or social scientist, does not depend on its traditional genuineness or *Echtheit* but on the vantage point that it gives to the observer or participant who plays it. If the role gives him the opportunity to observe what he wishes to observe, to communicate with and understand the people about whom he wishes to learn, in a manner and fashion to which they do not object, it is a *good* role.

Trust and Personal Involvements in Fieldwork

John M. Johnson

In the following reading John Johnson reflects on his field relations with Child Welfare Services (CWS) social workers in district offices of two metropolitan departments of public welfare. Most of the fieldwork was conducted at one of these offices, Metro, between July 1970 and May 1971. From the very start Johnson paid special attention to the research process in its own right, keeping careful notes and making detailed observations on his social and personal experiences in the course of doing fieldwork. In this excerpt he focuses on the nature of trust and personal involvement in these field relations. RME

The Problematics and Limitations of Trust

For over six months at Metro I had presumed that whatever trust was, eventually it would be possible to apprehend its basic character and develop it. Throughout this period, however, it had been obvious that my personal relations with the social workers were different and variable. This fact did not seem to be a falsification of my presumptions, only a limitation of them. I assumed that the reasons why relations of trust had not developed in particular instances were to be found in my procedures for demonstrating trustworthiness to the members. My presumptions began to change when I grasped what was, in retrospect, an equally obvious truth: the agency members experienced their relations *with one another* problematically. Once this was articulated, it continually surprised me that I had spent over six months believing in my presumptions about trust. They were invalidated on prima facie grounds every day, yet I had failed to turn this truth back on them.

This is not to say that in general the members at Metro *dis*trusted one another. There were some instances of this, but for the most part individuals trusted some more than others, trusted some not at all, and often trusted some for some purposes but not for others. During my first six months I witnessed friendships and romances created and dissolved, and committees in every stage from originating idea to dissolution or atrophy. There were alliances, coalitions, and interoffice political factions. They were put together for the purposes at hand and dissolved when victories or defeats were consummated. And yet throughout these observations I thought I

Reprinted with permission of Macmillan Publishing Co., Inc. from *Doing Field Research* by John M. Johnson. Copyright © 1975 by The Free Press, a Division of Macmillan Publishing Co., Inc.

would be developing relations of trust in such a fashion that, at a magic moment, it would be possible to know these phenomena independently of the daily flux. I additionally assumed that at this magic moment what is called the problem of going native in the field-research literature would emerge as another, but different, problematic.

I would have to say in candor that I always knew people experience their relations with one another problematically. It isn't necessary to conduct field research to learn that. The essence of my seventh-month insight — the sort of revelation that other field researchers have termed an "ah-ha experience" — was the realization that I had failed to translate this common understanding into my thinking about the methods of social research. As soon as I did, an entire range of new problems emerged for further study. . . .

Prior to applying the obvious truth noted above to the research setting, I assumed that at some point in the inquiry I would try to delineate procedural rules for developing the trust of various types of informants in terms of the kind and quality of data collected. The idea that this is what one does is implicit in many of the traditional field-research writings. It is explicit in some (Cicourel 1964:54–66). It appears to be a reasonable inference to draw from the seemingly uncommonsensical writings of Erving Goffman that all one has to do to develop trust is penetrate the front regions of a setting or in some manner get behind the daily appearances of things (Goffman 1959). From the research experiences reported here, it is clear the problems aren't this simple. This is especially evident in instances of inside dopesters, freeze-outs, and attempted manipulations of the observer (see Johnson 1975:122–131).

Even in those instances where a sense of trust developed between myself and the social workers, the relations were more fluid, emergent, and situational than any definitive set of procedural rules could possibly articulate. At the most mundane level, individuals had bad days, or sometimes only bad mornings or bad afternoons. These were slices of experiential time when individuals not only didn't want to talk to the affable researcher but didn't want to talk to others in the setting either. The cues for recognizing such moments were typically individually specific. They included furrowed brows, blank stares, sharp or curt methods of talking, and so forth. Such cues constituted important bits of tacit knowledge used by the members to organize the setting. Often they would pick up on the cues as indices of the way an individual was feeling that day. An example is a comment like "Looks like that first call got Bill off on the wrong foot today. He'll be testy for the rest of the day."

Some daily variations related to how individuals were feeling. Others had to do with situations occurring earlier, like having a flat tire on the way to work, running out of gas, or being confronted with a crisis before having an eye-opening cup of coffee. Other variations resulted from events from one's private life, like discovering that one's fiancé had been wed over the weekend or that one's house had been burglarized. Eventually I termed these kinds of occurrences the *mini-dialectic* of personal relations in field research. I concluded it was impossible to elaborate an absolute set of procedural rules for learning about such occurrences. The important criteria for recognizing these features were situational. Even if possible to elaborate, however, the rules would be of dubious utility for methodological purposes.

The *maxi-dialectic* of personal relations in field research is more important methodologically, but it is equally difficult to describe these relations. Earlier materials described the changing nature of my personal relations with some of the CWS workers, including the inside dopester, the freeze-outs, the manipulative supervisor, and others. There were other changes too. Several of these will be briefly illustrated.

I was in the process of establishing relations of trust with one social worker, or so I thought, when all of a sudden the bottom fell out of our relationship. A close friend of his later reported the worker was "put off" because he thought I was winning the favor of an attractive woman who had previously rebuffed his advances. The woman was actually one of the inside informants of the research, a close friend of my wife. The CWS worker did not know this at the time, however.

There were several situations where actions taken to befriend one worker incurred the antagonism of others. In the case of the supervisor who tried unsuccessfully to have the research terminated during the tenth month, the most common explanation put forth by the other workers was that I had befriended the blind social worker (see page 212). In a similar situation, my befriending of one worker became redefined as possible complicity by others opposing him in an interoffice political struggle. In another situation my methodology inspired the moral indignation of an older woman. To establish trust with one of the male workers, I had used a procedure known as throwing a roaring drunk, at a few infamous brothels of a neighboring community. In the subsequent storytelling the woman remarked to a friend that she thought I would have been "above" doing the kinds of things Frank was known to do. Little did she know.

These illustrations emphasize two major points about the conduct of field research. First, in any complex social setting the personal relations between an observer and the individuals he studies will emerge gradually and will be problematic. The personal relations are subject to changes, and it is incumbent on the investigator to assess the influences of these changes. Second, the complicated personal relations involved in a field-research project will necessarily create patterns in the field observations. To say this, however, is not necessarily to say the research is less objective. For example, the development of relations of trust constitutes a pattern which could actually result in more objective observations.

There appear to be several distinctive relations between the patterns of my observations and the patterns' effects. In some cases, independent evidence warrants judgment either that a given pattern is irrelevant to questions about the intersubjectivity of the observations or that the influence is minuscule. In other cases, independent evidence warrants a judgment that the objectivity of the research has been affected. For most of the patterns existent in my field observations, however, a fundamental uncertainty remains about their influences, if any. There are two important implications of this. The first is that it is impossible to rationalize social science knowledge in any absolute sense; when all is said and done, an element of mystery remains. The second important implication concerns the relations of the field observations, records, notes, and analyses to what gets reported as the research findings. . . .

The following materials will briefly depict the possible relations which may exist between the patterns of my research observations and their effects. I will describe, first, one pattern and note the reasons why it was judged irrelevant to the issue of the objectivity of the project. Then other patterns will be noted, and the reasons why they were considered as affecting the observations. These illustrations show that there are fundamental limitations of field-research observations even in those instances where relations of trust are developed.

In an interview conducted during the final week of the observations at Metro, I asked one female CWS worker if she thought my sex made a difference in her actions throughout the research. I asked if she thought she might have done anything differently if I had been a woman. She said my being male did make a difference. Then she paused momentarily, gave the question more thought, and said she wasn't certain what the difference was. She advanced the supposition that she engaged in more "woman-talk" when in the company of other women. She observed that she had done less of this on those days we had been together. I then recalled her earlier observation about a home call where she felt restrained in discussing the client's sex life. I asked if she thought this situation would have been different with a woman researcher along. She replied that it was hard to say for sure, but it might not have made any difference. She said the crucial factor was just having another person along with her; it might have been the same even if the other person had been a woman. She concluded this portion of the interview by saying she could not make a definitive judgment about this.

In retrospect, I've developed a sense that the ambiguous differences hinted at by this social worker are indeed real ones. With an admittedly limited understanding of "woman-talk," however, my conclusion is that the kind of information one gets from engaging in it is not directly related to the knowledge I sought during the research. My conclusions support one of S. M. Miller's (1952) observations; on many occasions I was availed of more information than I needed to have, and on many others more information than I expected or wanted to have.

Another pattern of the observations was also judged irrelevant for the research. It involved the workers' geographical selection of the home visits to which they would take me. Often, when the workers wanted to make a visit to a home in one of the outlying areas, they went there directly from home in the morning to reduce driving time. They often made calls on the way home in the evening for the same reason. This meant there were several cases in each worker's caseload I never observed. But since the worker's homes were spread out over an equal area, I concluded there was no basis for thinking that the research included any kind of geographical bias.

Independently obtained evidence suggests that other observational patterns produced what could be accurately termed a bias in the research. In one pattern, for example, I was systematically excluded from observing situations when the CWS workers had planned in advance to use what they defined as procedures for sanctioning welfare clients.[1] The three most commonly used expressions for these procedures were "coming on strong," "leaning on a client," and "pulling the rug out" (from under a client). This pattern applies mainly to the observations at Metro. Here the CWS workers were dealing with nonadjudicated cases. They were not formally deputized by the county. In three of the other offices the CWS workers were deputized, albeit with more limited mandates than police or probation officers. Here the workers dealt with adjudicated cases only. And these workers did not engage in the same efforts to keep the researcher from observing their coming-on-strong activities. On several occasions a worker from one of the latter three offices allowed me to witness such actions on the very first visit.

As early as the tenth week of the research at Metro I became aware of the possibility of such a bias. As I returned from a home visit one day, I met another worker in the parking lot. He called me aside and said he had something to tell me. He related comments of two other workers he had overheard in the office that morning. These two workers agreed they wouldn't be taking "the charming field researcher" to see certain kinds of situations. My intimate added that since he and I were close, he wanted to explain this to me. He told me I should not interpret this as an indication of any personal animosity. He informed me that with certain welfare cases it was sometimes necessary to come on strong — "to lean on them a bit" — to motivate the clients to take actions which would benefit them in the long run. He remarked, "Sometimes these things get a little messy." It wouldn't be reasonable to expect many workers to take me along on these occasions. He said it could be that none of them would ever do so.

During this conversation, as I remember it, I agreed with his judgment that this was reasonable, but I really didn't think his suppositions would prove correct. If his observations about what would happen to me in this regard were correct at the time, I thought, the others' apprehensions would

[1] It should be underscored that I am referring here only to what the social workers defined as sanctions; whatever the various welfare clients might have perceived or experienced as sanctionable or a sanction is an entirely different issue altogether.

disappear over time, after I had more opportunity to demonstrate my general trustworthiness.

The truth of my intimate's observations was established persuasively over the next eight months. Several of those with whom I later established relations of trust subsequently made similar observations. During an interview conducted in the final week of the field observations, one worker remarked that she liked me very much personally, thought I was pleasant and personable, and said she hated to see the field research concluded. She said she had thoroughly enjoyed the days we had spent together, a feeling which was mutual. She then went on to say that she had not taken me to see any situations where she thought it necessary to "pull the rug out" from under a client. She added that there were other situations too. These included several intimate friendships she had developed with clients over the years. She remarked that she kept some of these cases "on reserve," meaning that they afforded her a place to go when she wasn't feeling too well or didn't feel like discussing anyone's private troubles.

Why did this systematic exclusion occur? I concluded there were two major reasons. The first is relatively obvious. Such exclusion results from the irremediable paradox of mixing the metaphorical language of scientifically objective social casework, a dubious result of decades of attempts to transform political and moral problems into managerial ones, with oppositional metaphors like "coming on strong," clearly suggestive of uses of power independent of moral or ethical considerations. But this isn't the whole truth of the matter.

The second major reason for the systematic exclusion is that the realization of one's intention to come on strong in a given instance is thoroughly problematic. I was able to observe several situations where the worker's intentions before the home call were altered drastically. Several went in like lions but came out like lambs. From my limited observations and many discussions with social workers about this, I concluded the problematic nature of the sanctioning practices was equally as important a reason why the social workers systematically excluded me from observing these events.

While the firsthand field observations of the preplanned sanctioning practices were few, I was able to learn about these actions. As soon as I realized the limitation of the field observations, I invoked a strategy of second-guessing. This was utilized during several of the many coffee-room conversations in which I participated. It was intended to elicit accounts of the sanctioning practices, to draw the workers out. To do this, I constructed fictitious accounts of sanctioning events which I claimed to have witnessed recently. I would then solicit the worker's evaluations of the typicality or familiarity of the account. This was a practical method for eliciting the worker's observations and reflections. A typical response to my fictitious account involved a worker in relaying the details of one of his or her casework experiences. I also used this method for drawing out the social workers' knowledge on other occasions. I did not, however, consider these accounts as appropriate substitutes for actual observations.

One might be tempted to consider some of the illustrations in this chapter as interesting field-research anecdotes. But they raise important theoretical and methodological questions. If relations of trust in a field-research project are indeed problematic and if the problematics entail limitations of the research observations, an assessment of these facts as they affect the validity of the observational findings is called for. With respect to the validity of my observations of social welfare activities, one conclusion to be drawn is that my systematic exclusion from situations involving the use of sanctioning procedures introduced a certain *routinization bias* into the research.[2] Since this bias involves features of the setting which were *not* observed, there remains a fundamental uncertainty in attempts to assess the exact nature of it. With respect to the situations where workers padded their caseloads or held cases in reserve, there are similar grounds warranting a conclusion that the observations include a *public-morality bias.* As stated earlier, this means the observations do not include welfare activities intentionally used for thoroughly private purposes. One intimate informed me privately, for example, that from time to time he "had some things going for him" in his caseload. This was a reference to sexual liaisons between him and his clients. He never, of course, took me along to witness these occasional realities of public welfare. On several occasions intimates described how and under what conditions formal rules and regulations of the agency could be, and were, manipulated for personal financial gain. On no occasion did I actually witness this, though. There is a lesson to be learned from these illustrations: even if a sociological field researcher feels confident that he has given his all to develop personal relations of trust in order to obtain valid intersubjective observational data, this does not set everything right. It is still necessary to assess the influences of the relations on the research data. . . .

Feelings and Personal Involvements

The overformalized rationalistic instrumentality which appears as the public account of one's "methods" is never the whole story of the research. Our discussions to this point document two ways an observer's personal feelings become fused with the rational accounts — through the initial anxieties at the start of the research and one's gut-level reactions to the situation at hand. A third way, decidedly more important, involves one's ongoing personal relations with the persons in the setting where the research

---

[2] In his long-term research investigation of the police, Jerome Skolnick concluded that he had been systematically excluded from witnessing those actions which could plausibly be interpreted as police brutality, violations of another's rights, and the like. See his *Justice without Trial* (New York: Wiley, 1966).

is conducted. All field investigations which penetrate the rational appearances of the public front of a setting, which involve relations of trust with the individuals there to obtain a truthful, empathetic, valid, and reliable understanding of the actions occurring there, will inevitably involve complicated personal feelings between the observer and the members. Instead of being dependent on one's gut-level reactions to an immediate situation, many of these feelings are of a transsituational character, and some accrue glacially over time, perhaps without explicit awareness. But this does not mean these dimensions of feeling are less primordial than the others or that they necessarily transcend the gut level because of the time involved. In substantive terms, some of the inhabitants of this realm of feeling are sympathy, love, hate, friendship, resentment, admiration, respect, infatuation, identification, and dislike. Such feelings are the meaningful stuff of which the problems of overrapport and going native are made, to use the euphemisms of the field-research writings.

The complicated feelings between an observer and the persons among whom the investigation is conducted may involve, as Kurt Wolff (1964) has taught us, cognitive elements, even a cognitive love. Based on my reflections, the conception of cognitive love precisely characterizes my feelings toward one of the CWS social workers at Metro, and one other worker at another office. It cannot be said that the CWS worker at Metro and I immediately hit it off as a result of some personal compatibility. He was the one who lodged the first accusation that I might be a spy from the governor's office at the initial meeting of the two CWS units. For the first couple of months our interactions with one another were cordial but cool. Eventually we became friends, largely as a consequence of our generally compatible personalities, demeanors, past experiences, interests, and so forth. Personally I liked him and felt certain about communicating such sentiments, and he responded accordingly. In retrospect, this particular friendship might have been anticipated, even though it wasn't. It might have been anticipated because, in the terms used in the traditional field-research literature to categorize types of informants one is likely to find in a given setting, this CWS worker was a "natural" (Dean 1954), that is, one of those rare reflective individuals capable of very insightful analyses of daily events. As we were around each other more and more, he gradually became even more inclined to see his practical CWS actions as exhibits for analysis. By the end of my stay at Metro he referred to these analyses as *his* participant-observation research, and it is my judgment that I successfully "turned him out" as an analyst of everyday affairs. On several occasions I told him it was unfortunate that he was not the observer for the field investigation of CWS. And I meant it. A number of the insightful ideas I subsequently reported were, quite frankly, stolen from him.

In addition to being a natural, this CWS social worker happened to occupy *the* key position in the two CWS units with respect to information control and caseload referral. Also, he single-handedly altered or subverted several existing official policies or practices directly affecting the character of the CWS work at Metro. Several of these actions were clandestine, and others patently illegal.[3] This may have been one of the reasons for his initial apprehension about admitting an outsider access to the official public secrets. In short, it would have been impossible to obtain a valid understanding of what occurred at Metro CWS without befriending this worker. In this respect, I consider my friendship with him as very fortuitous for the research.

Wolff's abstract definition of the core meaning of "surrender" as "cognitive love" does make some sense, then. On other counts, however, the idealization fails miserably in telling us how affective and interactional elements of action are involved in the research process, and hence distorts our understanding. Conspicuously absent is any mention of the nonrational grounds of some of our pettier feelings. Take the two freeze-outs I encountered during the field observations at Metro. One was the girl who told her friends she was "horrified" by my presence. I agonized over this situation for months and months, resolutely rejecting others' explanations of it by invoking some typification of her personality, continually thinking of ways to put her at ease, and worrying about what I must be doing wrong. What emerged out of all this was a private irrational fear of her. I *still* don't know why it came, but the feelings of fear were real ones.

My relations with the second freeze-out mellowed over time, but they were none too friendly at best. In contrast to the first instance, where my private feelings could be said to have epitomized an Adlai Stevenson consciousness almost until the end, my private feelings about this fellow were less charitable. Frankly, I thought he was a "betty," although I think I successfully masked that sentiment during the research.

Petty feelings emerged in other situations. On one or two occasions I just got bored and fabricated some excuse to escape for a desired respite from boredom. As noted earlier, on one occasion an older woman directed moral indignation at me because I had "lowered myself" by going with one of the male social workers to throw a glorious drunk at several infamous brothels of a neighboring community. I spoke deferentially in my response to her, but my private feelings consisted of "deleted expletives." I wasn't in the mood for that kind of social wrath at the time. Wolff's emphasis on the cognitive character of one's affect ignores all these petty feelings, but they are all only too recognizable in our everyday actions.

The experiences of my social welfare research included several friendships. Some originated before the research, and some have continued for

---

[3] These references are further elucidated in my "The Social Construction of Official Information," unpublished Ph.D. dissertation, University of California, San Diego, 1973, especially chaps. 3, 7, and 8.

years afterward. Others came to bloom during the observations but have atrophied over time. Only on one occasion did I have a sense that a friendship presented a problem for the research. This situation involved the personal struggle between one CWS supervisor and the CWS social worker who was legally blind. The supervisor didn't think blind persons should be in CWS. She set out to build a case against him, a preliminary to having him dismissed. Because of his reliance on a paid driver for transportation, the blind worker was caught in a bind. He feared his presence in the office during the working day would be used to constitute part of the case against him. He solicited my assistance as his cover for a period of about three weeks. Without hesitation I agreed. This meant that I went with him on many more home calls during this time than I otherwise would have done. The problematic character of this, for me at least, consisted of the conflict between this course of action and the specific welfare activities I wanted to concentrate on at the time. It is doubtful whether my actions introduced any additional elements of selectivity into the research observations, but with different options I would have chosen otherwise.

A claim that field research involves feelings of friendship is one that deserves considered reflection. One issue raised by this is the possibility of a conflict between one's personal feelings and a rational course of action intended to effect the best observational results. This issue is raised by the comments in the preceding paragraph. If or when such a conflict occurs, it is incumbent on the observer to use his sociological competencies to evaluate the effects. But there are other potential conflicts inherent in friendships, and these are little appreciated. The most obvious possibility is that of a conflict between the substantively rational sentiments of friendship and a formally rational body of codified rules such as legal statutes.

Having spent much of my time for the past decade lingering in and about official state bureaucracies, notably universities, welfare agencies, and military commands, it is very difficult for me to believe there are many adults who are *not* technically guilty of periodic violations of official rules, such as laws. Illegal drug use, for example, is very common in these settings.[4] And yet one almost never hears of an instance where one colleague calls in the police on another or uses the "hot line" to Washington. Unauthorized sexual liaisons are frequent. Some members don't even know what the official rules are about these, and not surprisingly; the rules are rarely in-

---

[4] In the course of my research a questionnaire distributed to the social workers at Metro by the local Social Services Union said that about one-third of the workers used barbiturates during their work activities. I knew there were even several "pushers" in the office, in the sense of persons who kept bottles of phenobarbital in their desks which others could draw upon as they wished. Personally, I never felt certain that what the questionnaire reported was correct, but there was no apparent reason why anyone would exaggerate about this.

voked.[5] Playing around with the entries on official records and reports is common. These public secrets rarely inspire moral indignation. The potential for conflicts between the absolutism of the formally rational legal codes and the moral pluralism of substantively rational family, friendship, and colleague sentiments is obvious in these settings. When a conflict actually occurs, the members invariably elect a moral or ethical view over a legalistic one, at least with respect to *their own* or their friends' actions. This would be no news to many parents; the game is typically "no holds barred" when one is called to the police station in the middle of the night to extricate a son or daughter from the clutches of the officials. My personal thinking has been undeniably colored by these kinds of experiences. But I am also aware that the situation is very different in other settings. Among the BaMbuti in Africa, for example, the possibility of such conflicts would not arise because of the homogeneity and uncodified nature of their moral sentiments (Turnbull 1962). Even in our own teeming, conglomerated societies there are pockets of moral isolation where it is possible to live without dealing with these complexities on a day-to-day basis, such as the Amish communities of northern Indiana and many university laboratories.

I am aware of many others who do not share my views on this subject.[6] Whether or not my suppositions are correct, however, if one were to view my field-research conduct in the welfare agencies from a legalistic perspective, it would be seen that my actions involved complicity in, or "guilty knowledge" of, literally hundreds and hundreds of illegal activities. The relevant legal categorizations would include being an accessory before and after the fact of an illegal act, misprision of felonies and misdemeanors, obstructing justice, and others. From my understanding of the field-research literature, but especially from my many conversations and "debriefings" with colleagues in sociology, it was, and still is, inconceivable to me to report such actions to the legal authorities.[7] I regarded my ethical position on this particular issue as an absolute one; I was prepared to go to jail before violating the confidentiality of the research information. And I still feel that way. To put this in the vernacular popularized by the Watergate

---

[5] To give just one example, at my present place of employment many of my colleagues are unaware of a state statute which specifically proscribes the sexual liaisons of university professors.

[6] This fact was dramatically emphasized to me through some of the prepublication journal reviews I received when I tried to publish several papers describing the field investigation. In his rejection of one paper, for example, one of the anonymous reviewers for *Social Problems* judged me as having a "perverted sense of morality," and this was the only basis cited for the rejection. One of the few available public accounts of these phenomena is contained in Don Martindale's (1973) illuminating discussion of the academic reviews he received about one of his recent analyses.

[7] In citing the research literature here, I am specifically indebted to the exceptional analysis by Ned Polsky, "Research Method, Morality, and Criminology," in his *Hustlers, Beats, and Others* (1967).

follies, I was, and am, prepared to "stonewall it" to the end. It comes as a surprise to me, then, to learn that this is not the position taken by other sociological researchers.[8]

Observers of all kinds have remarked about the strength and pervasiveness of sexual desire for aeons. Modern psychology elevates this tidbit of common-sense knowledge to scientific status and calls the desire a drive. And yet when one reviews the methodological writings in the social sciences, the implicit instruction is to believe one of two things about this: either one must be a eunuch to conduct scientific research, or, in the vein of Wolff's argument, the desires of scientists involve only (or primarily) cognitive elements. My research experiences, and my other experiences, do not support this naive view. One example (although I shall mask the specific details) is a series of events that occurred near the end of my investigations. They involved what has been called the eternal triangle for centuries in literature, the third party being one of the inside informants for the research and a close personal friend of my wife. The resolution involved feelings of bitterness, betrayal, hate, resentment, and shattered friendships. It produced a severe crisis for me personally and delayed the writing of the research reports. The situation involved a considerable amount of "hurt," which is one of the elements of Wolff's definition of surrender. But it would be pure casuistry for me to consider the prime mover of these events as the *cognitive* element of social action!

In one sense, the present discussion only brings out in the open some of the public secrets of scientific conduct which many have understood for a long time. John Lofland aptly captures this common understanding, and some of the reasons for masking one's research account. He writes (1971: 132–133):

> One of my mentors has commented that what typically goes into "how the study was done" are "the second worst things that happened." I am inclined to believe that his generalization is correct. What person with an eye to his future, and who wishes others to think positively of him, is going to relate anything about himself that is morally or professionally discrediting in any important way? This is especially the case since fieldwork tends to be performed by youngish persons who have longer futures to think about and less security about the shape of those futures. We delude ourselves if we expect very many fieldworkers actually to "tell all" in print.

During the Watergate investigations, our brother sociologist Richard M. Nixon coined a phrase which expresses Lofland's observations in a more

[8] This reference is specifically to the discussion by Carl B. Klockars (1974) of his "research bargains" with professional fences, or receivers of stolen goods. Klockars tells us that the research agreements he worked out with "Vincent" included the understanding that if Klockars were to be hauled into court by a subpoena of his research information, he would reveal his information and sources before going to jail.

parsimonious fashion. When his aides were called on by others to reveal the methodological protocol of certain past events, as it were, he advised a "limited hangout." My experiences and reflections tend to support the wisdom of sociologists Lofland and Nixon. I think the best we can expect from the methodological literature is a limited hangout.

The complicated fusions of feelings and rational thoughts which become intertwined in any scientific investigation raise two major theoretical questions. The first is whether some form of direct participation by an observer with the members of the social group being studied introduces any greater degree of bias or error into an investigation than would obtain from an observer's reliance on his own common-sense thinking based on no direct personal involvement. The evidence on this is mixed, but it is clear that a "detached" investigation based on no direct participation contains a great potential for not being true. Others have previously addressed this question (e.g., Douglas 1972:3–33), so it will not be dealt with in detail here.

The second major question is related to the issue of establishing relations of trust in anthropological and sociological field research. Many analysts agree that trusting relations are the essential ingredients if the research report is to be a true one. The question is whether the sentiments resulting from the observer's personal relations with the individuals in the setting necessarily mean that the research report will be biased. This does seem to be a distinct possibility, but there is clearly no *a priori* reason for thinking that it will necessarily occur. These personal sentiments would appear to become a potentially biasing feature of the research when the observer's intentions to *empathize* with the individuals in the setting, that is, to truthfully understand the situation from the actors' perspective, become transformed into a *sympathetic* stance. A sympathetic stance exists where the observer takes the side of, or promotes the perspective of, the group he studies.[9] Such a distinction is often less than clearcut. The understanding of this leads some analysts to advise the wisdom of reading all field-research reports with an eye to its tenuous nature (Scott 1965: 272–282). The same understanding exists in common-sense thought. It is commonly expressed by the remark that one always looks at one's loved ones with rose-colored glasses.

[9] This discussion of the distinction between empathy and sympathy borrows from the analysis by Douglas (1972).

Political Activist as Participant Observer: Conflicts of Commitment in a Study of the Draft Resistance Movement of the 1960s

Barrie Thorne

Participant observation, it has often been noted, involves a problematic balance, a dialectic between being an insider, a participant in the world one studies, and an outsider, observing and reporting on that world. Researchers are cautioned to avoid too much involvement, commitment, or rapport (e.g., Miller 1952; Gold 1958); to strive for neutrality (Gans 1968; Vidich 1955) and for empathy rather than sympathy (Douglas 1972; Johnson 1975). These cautionary statements prescribe a moderate dose of involvement, and like all general prescriptions, they tend to gloss over the varied experiences and possibilities of actual field research (Glazer 1972, is a noteworthy exception).

Field settings vary, for example, in the degree to which neutrality or moderate involvement is possible, and researchers vary in the ways in which they are drawn into participation in the group being studied. My experience as a participant observer in the draft resistance movement of the late 1960s sharpened my sense of such variation. The Resistance was a strongly partisan social world, and intense commitment was expected from those who participated in more than a fleeting way. I was a participant in the movement, committed to the goals of ending the Vietnam War and the draft, before I decided to also approach the movement as a sociologist gathering data for a dissertation. The conflicts I experienced between my position as an active and committed participant in the Resistance, and as a sociologist studying the movement, point to specific issues bound up in the general problem of conflicting loyalties in field research: the issue of how one's daily activities are allocated; questions of risk and the consequences of one's actions; and conflicts over definitions of experience and the casting of knowledge. These sorts of conflicts can never be fully anticipated when research begins; analysis of them may shed light both on characteristics of the particular world one is observing, and on the nature of field research (including the political and institutional context of the social sciences) as a way of being in and experiencing the world.

Reprinted by permission of the publisher from *Symbolic Interaction*, V. 2, n. 1, Spring 1978, pp. 73–88. Copyright © 1979 by JAI Press Inc.

I would like to thank Everett C. Hughes and Kurt H. Wolff, whose wise counsel and insight into the vicissitudes of field research helped sustain this project. Peter Lyman, Gaye Tuchman, Murray S. Davis, Charles S. Fisher, and Malcolm Spector also made helpful comments on various drafts of this paper. Discussions with Robert M. Emerson were central to the development of ideas in the postscript.

Studying the Draft Resistance Movement

I initially ventured into the draft resistance movement in Boston in March, 1968, because I was strongly opposed to the Vietnam War and wanted to be part of organized protest. During the previous summer I had been involved in a project called Vietnam Summer, and had helped canvass neighborhoods to discuss peoples' attitudes to the war. I returned to antiwar activities when a friend told me about the draft counseling projects of the Boston Draft Resistance Group, and I started training as a counselor. At the same period of time I was looking around for a thesis topic, and after about a month of contact with the draft resistance movement, learning to be a draft counselor and participating in demonstrations, I decided to become a sociological observer, as well as a participant committed to the goals of the movement. I anticipated conflict between these dual purposes — although nothing as intense as I eventually experienced — but felt good about being able to gather material for a thesis while also acting on my political commitments. My effort to combine political commitment with sociological observing was helped all along the way by the flexible attitude of my thesis advisers, who did not minimize the dilemmas but were always helpful as I tried to sort them out.

As a point of principle, I wanted to avoid disguised research. From the start, I explained my research intentions to those I saw on a regular basis, as well as reassuring them that I shared their political commitments; their responses to my research activity ranged from hostility to mild tolerance. Overall, I was allowed to hang around (often, as will be explained later, under a spectre of suspicion) because I did movement work and professed commitment to the goals of ending the war and the draft.

Two factors ran against my efforts to avoid disguised research. Like other field researchers (Glazer 1972; Gans 1968) I discovered that people I had told tended to forget about my sociologist's role; when I realized this was happening, I felt guilt mingled with relief at the comfort of full acceptance. Furthermore, in the course of draft counseling, going on movement expeditions, marching in demonstrations, and attending meetings, I encountered many people whom I had no chance to tell about my research intentions. In these situations I was, in effect, a disguised researcher; as Roth (1962) observes, secrecy is a matter of degree.

Chronology and Rhythms of Involvement

There were two draft resistance organizations in Boston; they shared a common origin and ideology, but differed in tactics. The Boston Draft Resistance Group (B.D.R.G.) focused on draft counseling and community organizing; the New England Resistance (N.E.R.) developed around the tactic of non-cooperation with the draft, encouraging registrants to sever ties with the Selective Service, and staging events like draft card turn-ins, demonstrations for those refusing induction, and symbolic sanctuaries for resisters coming to trial (for more detailed comparison of these tactics see Thorne 1975b; on the history of the Resistance, see Ferber and Lynd 1971; Useem 1973; Thorne 1971). From the beginning I sought to be part of both organizations, partly because I was new to intensive movement activity and did not have a preference of tactics, but mainly because I wanted to get a rounded view of the movement and observe the range of its contexts and settings for the sake of my study.[1]

In the early stages of my involvement it was relatively easy to float between the two groups, drawing on the license newcomers are often granted as they get established in a new social world. Because newcomers tend to be thrust into a watching and listening role, I also found it psychologically easier to be an intent observer early in the study. For the first few months I found my way around the B.D.R.G. by training to be a draft counselor, going on early morning expeditions to draft boards to talk about the war and the draft with registrants waiting to be transported to the army base for their pre-induction physicals, and by attending weekly steering committee meetings. At the same time, I began hanging around the New England Resistance, helping with typing in the office, attending Monday night dinners which were a regular occasion for sociability among N.E.R. activists, and participating in public events like demonstrations and draft card turn-ins.

As I got to know, and be known by, people active in both groups, I became more fully involved in various projects. My contacts with the B.D.R.G., in keeping with the tempo of the group's activities, tended to be steady and routine, paced around regular stints as a draft counselor, early morning visits to draft boards, and regular meetings. The N.E.R. was less routinized; it moved from event to event in an apocalyptic spirit, building up for periodic crescendos of activity. At such periods, it was almost impossible to be only marginally involved. One of those times of white-heat activity, in which I joined fully, although at night I forced myself to undertake the daily routine of typing field notes, was in April, when a big Resistance draft card turn-in coincided with Johnson's decision not to seek re-election and was followed by Martin Luther King's death. I participated in the daily marches, rallies, and emotional meetings that marked those events, and in spare moments I helped put out special editions of the N.E.R. newspaper; this was the period in which I was most active in the New England Resistance. Over the summer I continued to work on the newspaper, which gave me access to the ongoing office life and public

---

[1] Douglas (1976) notes that the extent of a researcher's participation, which is tied to the question of how representative and contextualized the findings are, is somewhat different from the *degree or depth* of one's involvement.

events of the N.E.R. At the same time, I continued my more routinized involvement in the B.D.R.G.

By the fall of 1968 the newspaper venture had largely folded, and the N.E.R. was in a state of internal dissension. The N.E.R. had gradually moved away from organizing around the draft and had begun to focus on trying to radicalize soldiers and high school students, activities which interested me less (both politically, and in terms of my research focus) than did antiwar work. Through regular stints as a draft counselor at the B.D.R.G., I had gradually become (and become known as) "experienced" at counseling. I felt more knowledgeable politically as well as about draft details, and realized that my sense of strategy, tactics, and political style fit more closely with the B.D.R.G. than with the New England Resistance. By November I had gradually shifted primary affiliation from the N.E.R. to the B.D.R.G., and although I still attended some N.E.R. events, I got more caught up in B.D.R.G. activities such as organizing early morning visits to draft boards.

In the spring of 1969 I became bored with draft counseling. The fact that I had by then accumulated extensive data on the draft counseling process contributed to the lessened interest; in addition, persuaded by movement criticisms of the tactic, I began to doubt its political value. I also tired of my role in organizing visits to draft boards and gradually withdrew from the position of project head. By that time many of the B.D.R.G. old-timers had gone on to other political activities and groups, the N.E.R. had evolved into a small group of activists mainly working with soldiers and high school students, and around both groups there was general talk about the "death" of draft resistance. My involvement tapered off as the movement itself dispersed, though I had contact with both groups until they finally disbanded (the New England Resistance in July 1969; the Boston Draft Resistance Group in October 1969).[2]

During my daily involvement with the Resistance, I continually faced two problems: first, how to respond in a situation where I wanted freedom of movement as an observer, but was forced to take sides as a member; and second, the related question of priorities, of how, in my daily allocation of time and effort, to balance my political goals with the needs and demands of research.

Partisanship

At every level the draft resistance movement demanded partisanship. Among the active members there was no tolerance for neutrality on the

[2] When to leave the field is an issue much discussed among participant observers. In this study, when the movement dispersed, the field left me. The quick tempo and rapidly shifting quality of Resistance events made me wish I were omnipresent; I felt anxious when I missed a particular event because the rapid turnover of tactics and membership gave daily movement life a non-repetitive flavor.

issues of the war and the draft, and the issues assumed crisis proportions. Within the movement individuals were pressured to join specific groups, and, partly because there was disagreement about tactics, multiple membership was difficult to maintain. Only people with valued resources could freelance (without inciting suspicion) as full participants in the B.D.R.G., the N.E.R., and other organizations in the antiwar spectrum. The notable examples of approved freelancers were a black man whose race was an asset in such all-white radical groupings, and a resister who had already served a jail sentence for refusing induction and whose experience and proved commitment became shared resources. My efforts to straddle the B.D.R.G. and the N.E.R. were regarded with mistrust, and I felt constant pressure to take sides.

Although the B.D.R.G. and the N.E.R. shared an early history, an overlapping set of issues, and a general loyalty when confronting the outside, they differed on points of strategy, tactics, and general style. Relations were competitive and sometimes strained. It was easier to be a partial member of the B.D.R.G. than of the New England Resistance, but even B.D.R.G. people mistrusted anyone who attempted to belong to both groups.

As a newcomer, I could wander in and out of both organizations, but after that phase, I felt continually forced into a choice. People in the antiwar movement often inquired and commented about the affiliations of individual activists. My self-identification shifted as the year wore on. Sometimes I tried a complicated formula which approximated how I felt ("I'm working on the Resistance newspaper and I draft counsel at the B.D.R.G."), but the approved slots were less complex. During the summer several B.D.R.G. people indicated they regarded me as a member of the New England Resistance, even though I was a regular B.D.R.G. counselor. But by the fall, I felt more thoroughly "B.D.R.G." and introduced myself as such. At a demonstration in September, an N.E.R. activist came over and said, "Hello B.D.R.G." In March 1969, I went to a national Resistance conference as a representative of the Boston Draft Resistance Group; people from the New England Resistance also attended.

Conflict Over Priorities

In choosing how to spend each day — what meetings to attend, projects to work on, events to join — I acted not only out of political conviction, but also out of my interest in observing the workings of the Resistance movement. Initially I felt relatively detached and went to every kind of Resistance activity; the goal of observation was primary. But as I became more comfortable with the issues, rhetoric, and style of the radical movement, and as I became absorbed in the goals and strategies of the Resistance, I slipped more fully into the role of participant.

I still observed and recorded whatever I was involved in, but the decision to be *there* (draft counseling instead of planning a draft card turn-in; on an early morning visit to a draft board instead of in the middle of a sanctuary) increasingly involved tension between personal political, and research considerations. There was continuous debate about tactics, about whether draft counseling, draft card turn-ins, and sanctuaries were the most useful activities. I thought through each issue on political grounds, and eventually came to oppose both card turn-ins and sanctuaries and to support draft counseling as a major direction of effort. This position both led to and grew out of my closer involvement with the B.D.R.G. during the late summer and fall of 1968. The B.D.R.G. continually argued against and only minimally participated in draft card turn-ins and sanctuaries, which for a time were the central activities of the New England Resistance. By early 1969, I, along with many B.D.R.G. activists, had also become skeptical about the political effectiveness of draft counseling; our doubts contributed to the demise of the group.

Apart from the larger issues, there were smaller decisions about how to allocate time and effort, and my interest in observing entered into these choices. Wanting to get a rounded view of the movement, to see it from as many vantage points as possible, I poked in and out of a range of situations. The ongoing life of both the N.E.R. and the B.D.R.G. included many little expeditions: visiting draft boards to try to get information about dates of physicals and inductions; ventures to bus stations and inside the army base to leaflet and talk with soldiers; setting up anti-recruitment tables when the Marines came around to colleges. I was a perpetual and eager volunteer for these expeditions, mainly because they gave me a change to see the Resistance movement in a variety of situations (and hence, I believed, enhanced the representativeness of my data).

While on these expeditions I participated fully: accosting soldiers to engage them in discussion about the war; doing impromptu draft-counseling on every occasion; debating with the Marine recruiters in front of a group of junior college students. But from the point of view of the movement and its political goals, my time might have been better spent in other activities such as organizing projects at the office. I was more a gadfly than a patient organizer. In my efforts to experience as many different settings as possible, and in my attempts to straddle group boundaries, I was running against the organizational and purposive grain of the draft resistance movement.

My style of participation was partly shaped by my role as observer, and that outlook set me apart from full participants. I was a committed participant, but with limits related to temperament and reluctance to give up my outside involvements; both of these limits were bound up in the way I defined my research role. Throughout the experience I had a residue of safety, a horizon of options that most of the participants lacked. The role of observer provided a defense against experiences I found fearful; it provided me a measure of control in a situation which I was both strongly drawn to and cautious about. My experience might be seen as an example of a general option social scientists have created: fieldwork as controlled adventure.[3]

Fieldwork as Controlled Adventure: Conflicts Over Risk-Taking

No matter how fully I participated in the Resistance, and even in the final days when I was seen as an experienced draft counselor and old-timer, I still retained a dimension of marginality. In contrast with anthropologists in foreign cultures and sociologists crossing lines of class, race, or deviance, this dimension was relatively small. I came from the native population, the central constituency of the draft resistance movement: white, middle-class, young, college-educated, part of the subculture of metropolitan-hip-university centers. Without these various attributes, especially youth and comfort with the counter-culture, I would not have been accepted in the daily activities of the Resistance.

But in other ways I was marginal, and as my involvement progressed, I found myself relying on this sense of marginality not only to lend a degree of detachment, but also to provide immunity from some of the risks which went along with Resistance activities.

My marginality was based partly on sex. The Resistance had a sexual division of labor which placed women in a subordinate and derivative position (Thorne 1975a). Exempted from conscription, women did not personally confront choices about the draft, and they were, at least initially, exempted from some of the pressures toward risk-taking that were directed at men. If I had been a male participant observer, especially in the N.E.R., I would have been under continual pressure to turn in my draft card and risk jail. As a woman, I entered with relative distance and immunity from risk, although not with as much immunity as I had anticipated.

My strongest marginal trait was my position as a graduate student, a role which evoked suspicion and mistrust. In the first place, many of the central Resistance people had dropped out of college and were extremely critical of the careerist, business-as-usual, Establishment overtones of being a student (and especially a graduate student). Some of them had particular mistrust for social scientists. But perhaps most important was the fact that my being a student gave me an outside set of involvements and options which ran against the Resistance sense of collectivity and demand for full commitment and risk-taking.

The central activists of the Resistance movement constituted a community of fate. To varying degrees they had severed other careers or possible futures and come to regard their lot as being cast with the Resistance, or more broadly, with the radical movement. They were enmeshed in a fateful situation: taking the risk of turning in draft cards, refusing induction, har-

[3] Larry Rosenberg suggested this term to me.

boring deserters, setting up sanctuaries, aiding and abetting violation of the Selective Service law. They also confronted hostile political antagonists (hecklers, rather terrifying threats from right-wing organizations), and continually suspected the presence of Feds (it was presumed that there were infiltrators from the F.B.I. or the police, that the phone was tapped and the mail watched).

An atmosphere of risk, uncertainty, and danger infused the daily life of the Resistance movement, especially the New England Resistance. The B.D.R.G., though also assuming tapped lines and infiltrators and working in possible violation of the legal proscription against counseling to resist, was more bureaucratic, pragmatic, and cautious about taking risks. I felt ready to take whatever consequences might result from draft counseling, proselytizing in front of draft boards, and participating in demonstrations and marches. But beyond that commitment, I did not throw my fate in with the Resistance. Of course, I did not have a draft card to turn in, but I also avoided any activities which appeared to involve uncertain and high stakes (such as the first sanctuary and working with deserters). Nor did I drop out of school, an action which many Resistance people felt should accompany radicalization. Unlike those who faced uncertain futures and probably jail, I could (and fully intended to) go back to having a safe career as an academic. And I always preserved that option; I was reluctant to place it in jeopardy.

The first sanctuary showed me dramatically that I was ultimately in a different world from fully involved Resistance people. The Arlington Street Church sanctuary in May 1968 was the first, not only in Boston, but also the first in the country. It was a new tactic for dramatizing the dilemma of conscience of antiwar draftees and trying to build support around them. A draft resister and an AWOL soldier were declared in symbolic sanctuary, and a large and spectacular, week-long event was built around the occasion, while everyone waited for the government to respond. It was anticipated that there would be mass arrests, since the sanctuary technically violated laws concerning aiding and abetting deserters, as well as the Selective Service law. The choice of entering a state of risk was suddenly sprung on the mass of supporters who came to the press conference and large public gathering which announced the sanctuary. The resister and soldier marched out, followed by a group of twenty-five to thirty Resistance people, and it was announced dramatically that this group has vowed to "stand with the two brothers, keeping sanctuary with them and risking possible arrest" and that everyone else who would join the community should come forward. My field notes show the turmoil I felt as I was faced with this public decision:

> As M. began the invitation, I felt fear in my throat. Fear, shame, guilt — both a desire to join the group that surged forward after M.'s invitation and a (stronger) reluctance, since I didn't feel I could risk arrest and realized that the pressures compelling me to go forward

were of a group rather than individually-thought-through kind. But that realization didn't seem to minimize the emotion. People began leaving their pews and going forward. Eventually there seemed to be only a few scattered people remaining in the pews. M. commented over the microphone, "There seem to be more up here than down there." I felt all eyes were upon me; I was sure my face was flushed; I found myself fingering my purse, almost in readiness to run up. But I didn't. It occurred to me that I was feeling the way people feel who can't bring themselves to turn in their draft cards, but who finally do it under crowd pressure.

The group — more like a community given its size and solidarity — stood in a solid bunch, spilling out over the sides of the front of the chapel, but clearly demarcated from those of us, scattered and far from constituting a group, who remained in the pews. The spatial arrangements dramatized the gap between the committed and the uncommitted.

As it turned out, the authorities arrested only the resister and the soldier, although there was a physical confrontation with the police when federal marshals forcibly removed the resister from the church. But I experienced that occasion as a moment of truth about the limits of my participation.[4]

I was drawn to the total involvement and adventuresome spirit of the Resistance. For example, my field notes detail one long, all-absorbing day that began at 5:30 A.M. with an early morning foray to a working-class draft board and animated talk and exchange of gossip with the little band that went; then going to the N.E.R. office, which was at a peak of activity in preparation for a large induction refusal demonstration. Someone there asked me to drive some resisters and an AWOL soldier who had decided to turn himself in at a nearby army base, and thus began another spirited adventure on enemy territory, with our hippy-looking band enjoying the stares and imagined dangers in the stark, bureaucratic environment of the base. We returned, full of stories to tell the eighty people crowded in the office basement for the weekly N.E.R. dinner. Since the newspaper was due at the printers, I joined in and we worked late into the night, going out for beer, laughing, and reaching a state of heady exhaustion. Finally I was so tired I took my leave and went home. The next morning when I woke up and realized I would spend the day typing field notes alone, I felt quite depressed and almost jumped into my car and headed for the printers, where the gang was.

Throughout my months with the Resistance, I sensed, sometimes guiltily,

---

[4] Other participant-observers have described similar moments of truth about boundaries between them and the group they were studying. Whyte (1943) describes helping his Cornertown friends cheat at the polls, and later regretting the action, partly because it violated his personal principles. In my case, taking part in the Resistance was in accord with my personal principles (although part of my hesitation at the sanctuary came from not having time to think through the action and its personal and political implications). My main discovery was that I was reluctant to take risks and give up a safe future — a reluctance I had psychologically and structurally tied up with my researcher's role.

that I could have my cake and eat it too. I could share in the excitement, the thrills of participating in events that seemed almost magnetic — and be spared the costs: the uncertainty of risk-taking, the possibility of jail.

The ethnographic literature suggests that this is a recurring phenomenon: sociologists and anthropologists venturing into exciting, taboo, dangerous, perhaps enticing social circumstances; getting the flavor of participation, living out moments of high drama; but in some ultimate way having a cop-out, a built-in escape, a point of outside leverage that full participants lack. The sociologist can have an adventure, but usually takes it in a controlled and managed way.

Conflicts Over the Interpretation of Experience

As an active and committed participant, I was pressed to allocate my daily time and effort in ways structured by the Resistance, and to join the movement's community of fate. But my other role — as a sociologist gathering data for a thesis — conflicted with the movement's prescriptions for activity, pointing to daily agendas geared more to the goals of observing than to being politically effective, and helping set limits to my willingness to take risks. I also experienced epistemological conflict: the movement's ways of defining and interpreting experience ran counter to the more detached and routinizing perspectives I maintained as a sociological observer.

The Resistance was a sect-like organization, emphasizing conformity of belief as well as external behavior. Movement participants would not have tolerated the intimate presence of an avowed neutral, but I discovered that partisanship and participation are both a question of degree. I believed (i.e., I opposed the war and the draft, shared the movement's analysis of their origins and injustices, and generally supported Resistance strategies of protest), but I also sought to assume psychological distance from the daily life and ideology of the Resistance, and to refer its happenings to an outside, comparative framework. I participated, but I also watched carefully and later recorded and reflected on what had occurred — for purposes that extended beyond the movement and its goals.

In general, at least in this society, people tend to feel uncomfortable if they know a participant in an encounter is also observing, analyzing, and recording the interaction for an outside purpose. But some situations have a stronger proscription against such detached and instrumental activity than others. For example, Riesman, Watson, and their colleagues (1964) experienced extensive difficulty in doing participant observation in parties and other gatherings of sociability, perhaps because such gatherings presume expressiveness, unseriousness, and a suspension of consequentiality, and these assumptions conflict with the more instrumental and consequential attitudes involved in doing sociological research. (In contrast, participant observers might experience less epistemological strain in studying a shopping mall or a bureaucracy — settings whose rules for experience are more various, and less distant from the detached and instrumental behavior, and marginal commitment of sociological observing.)

Some of the difficulties I experienced as an observer stemmed from the rules for experience and knowing which are basic to highly partisan social movements: demand for complete involvement based on a totalizing world view; a sense of crisis and apocalypse; and emphasis on collectivity and control by the group. I discovered the contours and strength of some of these basic assumptions by trying to mix participation in the movement with the detached, routinizing, and comparative outlook, and the instrumental purposes, involved in doing sociological research for a dissertation.

The temporal rhythm of the Resistance was very different from the tempo of observation and research. The movement was infused with a sense of crisis and apocalypse; the present often overshadowed awareness of either past or future. Although demonstrations, sanctuaries, and confrontations were located by calendar time, these occasions, which were central to Resistance life, had their own temporal qualities, well described by Schechner's (1969:74) phrase, "event time." Some events, like the massive response to the assassination of Martin Luther King, Jr. (which came right after the April 3rd draft card turn-in) emerged quickly and unexpectedly, and had no visible end. On April 11th one resister remarked, "The last week seems like one long day." The sense of being engulfed by the present and uncertain about the future was expressed in leaflets distributed at the opening of the Arlington Street Church sanctuary. "Liberation-Renaissance," one leaflet read, and outlined a long list of political and cultural activities scheduled "to last for the duration." The event was contingent on government response; its timing was uncertain; the experience was sharpened and "heated" (Goffman 1967:261) by the presence of risk. People spoke of being "in sanctuary," a phrase which described the sense of total involvement, of living *inside* an event, bracketed from both past and future.

This atmosphere of shared crisis (fed by risk-taking, intense activity, irregular schedules, and going without sleep) separated the movement from the outside world of business-as-usual and reinforced individual commitment and a sense of shared fate. During the most intense periods of crisis, the Resistance had the flavor of a millenarian movement. The movement chose the omega as its symbol partly because of its apocalyptic reference, and the word "apocalypse" was sometimes mentioned around Resistance circles, often in jest, but capturing a mood which was in the air.

As an active member, I often got caught up in this sense of crisis and apocalypse. I cried with many others as hundreds came forth to turn in their draft cards during the April 3rd demonstration; when we learned of pending government indictments of draft resisters, I shared the movement mood of anguish and uncertainty about the future. But as a sociologist, I made a continual effort to routinize the sense of crisis through the daily rhythm (often sustained with great difficulty, and occasionally neglected altogether) of recording happenings and sociological reflections in my field notes. As I moved back and forth between these two perspectives — getting caught up in movement events and emotions, and later recording and analyzing them in a more detached and objectifying way — I experienced inner conflict.

From the movement's perspective, "doing sociology" on its activities constituted a sort of epistemological betrayal. There was general hostility to proclaimed neutrals and observers, and social scientists were seen as part of this camp; if the apocalypse is at hand, one should not be watching and taking notes. During an extended discussion of tactics at a gathering during one of the sanctuaries for an AWOL soldier, a fellow stood up and prefaced his comments with, "I'm only here as a witness . . ." He was cut off with a vehement reply: "There have been enough witnesses! There were witnesses at Auschwitz and Dachau — it's time for everyone to stand and act!"

Individuals and groups in a state of crisis may resist not only detached observation, but also the comparative attitude which is basic to theoretical understanding of social life (Hughes 1971; Becker 1964). In comparing the Resistance with other social movements, I implied (and one part of me always believed) that the situation was not unique and final, that it was just another millenarian movement, rather than the millennium itself.

The conflicts I experienced between being a committed participant and an observing sociologist often took the form of great pangs of guilt, and a sense that I was betraying the movement. The issue of betrayal was thrust upon me in a direct and painful way when I eventually realized that some movement members had come to regard me with great suspicion, wondering if I was a "Fed."

Fieldworker as Fed

A common ritual around backstage Resistance gatherings was to play a sort of guessing game: Who's the Fed? It was generally suspected that there were infiltrators from the F.B.I., military intelligence, or the local police; the N.E.R. phone was often answered, "New England Resistance, this line is tapped." Insiders and outsiders said that Resistance people were "paranoid," but it is interesting to note that there is no ready phrase in English for chronic fear which may turn out to be justified ("paranoid" suggests fear with no factual basis). The Resistance anxiety looked and felt like paranoia, since it had no *certain* basis, but the facts just were not known. Although, to my knowledge, specific surveillance of the Boston groups has not come to light, there have been sufficient revelations about government infiltration of other radical and antiwar groups of the 1960s to make it now seem likely.[5]

There were people around the Resistance who claimed they had a sixth sense for spotting Feds; one spoke of a sort of bell that went off in his head when he encountered an infiltrating spy. Descriptions were offered about typical Fed behavior, and I listened closely, trying to figure out the mores of this invisible, yet possibly present hostile tribe. I was told that Feds could be spotted by "the kinds of questions they ask" and by biographies that did not check out.

There were other types of infiltrators around the Resistance: members of other leftist sects (who did not always reveal their outside allegiance, and who were often present to recruit from the Resistance membership and to steer it to a given political line), and media reporters, who usually made themselves known, but sometimes disguised their purpose. It was discovered that a reporter from the local newspaper most hostile to radical activities had come for draft counseling posing as a law student and had tried to push the counselor into telling him to resist.

This feeling of being spied upon, of having many unfriendly outside groups trying to siphon off information which could well be used to send people to jail, kept the Resistance in a constant state of nerves. The fear of Feds increased the sense of crisis and apocalypse that underscored even mundane activities. One learned to be careful while talking on the phone, to be cautious in draft counseling and in talking about the plans and workings of the Resistance to strangers around the office or outside.

Although the draft resistance movement began in a spirit of openness, with a strategy of turning in draft cards and breaking the law in a public, visible, almost proud way, it was hard to sustain an attitude which seemed almost suicidal, especially as the Resistance began working with AWOL soldiers, and as the possibility of conspiracy indictments (in addition to the charge of breaking the Selective Service law) became real. The New England Resistance, which operated in the sphere of risk more than the B.D.R.G., became more and more secretive, especially when it began planning sanctuaries, which required secrecy in the planning stages to prevent a bust before the event surfaced.

In that atmosphere of uncertainty and suspicion, with a lack of firm factual grounding, my private anxiety and guilt about being an observer took root and flourished. In the late spring of 1968 I began to sense the

[5] Gary Marx (1974) observes that as government surveillance of radical movements proliferates, as it has in recent times, the movements themselves are changed in important ways. This subject warrants more empirical research, although it is a slippery phenomenon, since surveillance is usually uncovered — if at all — only after the fact. Glazer (1972) adds other issues for social scientists to consider in an era of widespread and secret surveillance: Will research be used and treated as surveillance work, to the detriment of the subjects? How can we reconcile our research probing with the general dangers of increased invasion of privacy?

people in the N.E.R. regarded me as a likely candidate for Fed. When I went to the office, I often received a cold shoulder from people who had previously been warm and friendly. I watched the way they treated other Fed-candidates, and found the same cold reception, an attempt to squeeze the suspected person out of the collectivity. Although several of my trusted friends (and their trust seemed increasingly precious) commented that there was a lot of Fed-guessing going on, I found that the game was not often played in my presence. I learned of it second-hand and realized that being included in the guessing ritual of Who's-the-Fed was a proof of trust. Exclusion meant that one was suspect.

I found this attitude of mistrust painful. I also did not know what to do about it because the implicit accusation was hard to shake. If directly asked, "Are you a Fed?" (as Resistance people often did to one another under the guise of humor but also as a vocalization of generalized doubt), what could one reply? Too loud or soft a protestation would be equally telling.

But the fact remained that my loyalty was *not* pure, that I was *not* giving total allegiance to the Resistance. I not only held out from casting my future with the movement and joining the community of risk; I also was myself doing a kind of spywork not unlike what I imagined a Fed would do. I was systematically observing; I kept my ear out for a range of information and detail that exceeded what was necessary in performing my tasks of being a regular member of the group. I asked the kinds of questions a Fed would also want to know: "When did you turn in your draft card?"; "What led up to that decision?"; "What organizations had you been in?" And I listened attentively, committing the responses to mind for later recording. At demonstrations, in order to get a range of perspectives, I sometimes left the Resistance ranks and walked to the side to stand with spectators or even reporters (later, when I came to realize the strong symbolic import of space in expressing partisanship, I did less of such wandering). My efforts to straddle all the groups in the Resistance orbit made me doubly suspicious (one B.D.R.G. activist exclaimed one day, "Since you jump so much from group to group, all you need is a final tie-up with the C.I.A." A thrifty kind of Fed, getting double the information).

Although at the time I felt scapegoated in being regarded as a Fed, from a later vantage-point the accusation has a certain plausibility. Although I believed in the goals and basic ideology of the Resistance, and acted as a sincere participant, my loyalty was qualified by four undeniable facts: I had an outside allegiance and tie; I was keeping records (which, in spite of my efforts to keep them confidential and my intention to burn them if they were subpoenaed, could be stolen and used against the Resistance); the records, which were not under the movement's control, would go into a report on the Resistance made available to outside audiences; and I expected to receive external rewards (a Ph.D. and publications) from my participation in the movement. Some movement members realized that I would receive

Establishment rewards for activities which in their lives meant giving up safe futures; "I wish I could get a Ph.D. for all this," a woman activist once said to me with an edge of resentment.

Although I always had a strong intention not to let my study damage the movement or its members, I could not be sure in what ways the information might be used. My dissertation would be available to an audience outside the Resistance, and would not be under the direct control of the movement.[6]

Conclusion

When, near the end of my involvement in the Resistance, I became an active and nonresearching member of the feminist movement, I felt great relief. Now and then in a feminist meeting or discussion, I remembered how I felt in Resistance gatherings, and, in contrast, experienced great comfort based on unity of self and purpose. To be fully trusted as a movement activist, and to feel I warranted that trust, was a warming experience which sharpened my memories of what it was like to live with constant ambivalence and anxiety during my days with the Resistance.

Within the women's movement I continued to think and speak in a sociological way and to slip in and out of an attitude of detachment and observation. I kept a diary, which, although briefer, resembled the field notes I recorded during the Resistance. But my sociological insight took place and evolved within a movement context; I didn't intend to refine and use this knowledge primarily within the academic world or to further my own career.

Comparing my experiences in the Resistance and in the feminist movement, I realized that the sociological imagination — the insight that can come from detachment, comparison, and systematic analysis — should be distinguished from other components of the research role. Sociological understanding and information can be organized in various ways, including as part of movements for social change. For example, I believe my contributions to discussions of strategies and tactics in the Resistance (e.g., in our long debates about the efficacy of draft card turn-ins and draft counseling) were strengthened by my ability to think sociologically, and by the systematic observations I had made of the movement over time. However, putting these insights into a dissertation and journal articles, geared for a different audience, was less useful for the movement.

One issue, therefore, has to do with the location and distribution of sociological knowledge and understanding. Hymes (1969) has aptly focused some of these concerns: ethnographers deal with knowledge of others, and

---

[6] These specific worries have lessened with time. The movement had dispersed by the time I finished my dissertation and long before I published anything from the study, although I am still troubled by the possibility that my research may be put to future use by those seeking to suppress other radical movements.

that involves special political and ethical responsibilities, especially since social science knowledge is generally more accessible to elites and to those protecting the status quo, than to the powerless or to those working for social change. When the group studied is especially vulnerable to political control, as the Resistance was, these problems become all the more pressing. I emerged from the antiwar movement more keenly aware of the need to create political and social locations for knowledge which will further social change, rather than perpetuating existing structures of domination.

This experience also taught me about the limits of sociological knowledge. Detached gathering and analysis of information, and theoretical reflection, can help inform political action, but such action always involves stepping into the unknown, beyond the boundaries of the predictable. I still think back to the Arlington Street Church sanctuary, and the way I held back from the risk, the plunge into the uncertain, that radical political acts require. Some of this hesitation was because I was not sure that particular action was politically wise, but I also had to confront my personal reluctance to take the sort of risks I believed might be necessary to end the war and bring about social justice.

Others in the movement, e.g., as they anguished over whether or not to turn in their draft cards or refuse induction as gestures against the war, also felt the dilemmas bound up in political action. But my conflicts had a special twist: my research role became a retreat, a justification I used to myself for avoiding risks when activism felt threatening. As I made such retreats, I came to see that strong political commitment and action necessarily involves other outlooks and ways of experiencing the world. I also discovered ways in which academic careers tend to encourage investment in the status quo, and to foster individualism instead of collectivism — they run counter to the commitments and actions basic to radical politics. These issues remain live ones for me; participant observation in the draft resistance movement taught me as much about sociology as about political activism.

Postscript (1983)

In keeping with the tradition of separating the research report from reflections on experiences in the field, I initially drafted this paper as an appendix to my dissertation (Thorne, 1971). In fact, the appendix was the very first thing that I wrote. Sitting down to write the dissertation, I felt deep emotional conflicts about my relationship to the Resistance. Writing about these conflicts and feelings — they came out in a rush — helped me work them through, and thus settle into the process of analyzing the movement and "them" rather than me. What I have come to see, over a decade later, is that there is a deep logic to this way of writing, that these personal experiences were neither confessions, minor preliminaries, nor mere "how it was done" appendages to the main study, but were closely tied to, and even generative of, the study and its substantive findings. In this postscript I want to reflect on some of the ways in which these personal and emotional experiences in the field were central to processes of discovery, and hence raise deep methodological issues.

From the very start I was highly involved in and committed to the Resistance as a political movement. This sort of involvement had a number of important effects. Some were conventionally methodological. For example, as an insider I had more access to the backstage of the movement than did less active participants, especially as the Resistance became self-protective and sought to keep away the noncommitted. On a deeper level, I was open to the emotional contours of the Resistance and *felt* its trajectory in ways a classically detached observer would not. I developed an inside understanding of the dilemmas of politics-in-action which strengthened my analysis of the movement. For example, my discussion of movement conflicts over strategies and tactics (Thorne 1971; 1975b) was anchored in my having been in the thick of the debates. At the time, I didn't suspend my emotions, as a detached observer might have done. I cared about the practical and political consequences, for example, of draft counseling, compared with the turning in of draft cards. Having myself argued the pros and cons, I gained better understanding of the strong feelings which accompanied these movement schisms.

My involvement and commitment (which, although conflicted, was certainly there), also transformed *me* in very basic ways. Being in the Resistance and the antiwar movement made me into a highly political person, eventually both a feminist and a socialist. Had I been the classic detached observer, participating in limited ways and privately thinking that the beliefs of those I studied were odd or curious, I would not have undergone this sort of transformation. (Indeed, in part because I sought such personal change, I had deliberately avoided doing fieldwork in a movement whose beliefs I abhorred or found weird.)

But while I was an active participant in the movement, I remained something of an outsider simply because I continued to be a sociologist. I felt the consequences of "doing sociology" both for my actions and for my consciousness. In retrospect, I can see more clearly the ways in which I confused the role of researcher with my own personal and political ambivalence about being fully committed to the Resistance. It was not the demands of continuing fieldwork which finally held me back from joining the risk-takers at the Arlington Street Church; rather, and more personally, I was unsure about the politics of the strategy, felt manipulated by the surprise invitation to risk such heavy jeopardy, and above all, I was afraid of going to prison. Instead of fully acknowledging these personal limits to total involvement, I told myself — in a kind of bad faith — that plunging into such risks was not in keeping with doing fieldwork. I now believe that doing fieldwork sets no intrinsic limits to the taking of risks. I could have joined the sanctuary and even gone to prison, and continued to observe as well as to participate, as did Laud Humphreys, also a sociologist and antiwar activist, who continued to take field notes when he was sent to jail for burning draft files.

I now believe that the intrinsic limits to a fieldworker's being a full member of a setting lie not primarily in actions, but in consciousness. To do fieldwork entails a double consciousness. One learns to experience and even act within the everyday reality of members (something I did in a fuller way than has been customary in social research), but by virtue of doing sociology, one *also* experiences analytically and with detachment — recording, comparing, theorizing about the things one sees. While members often theorize about their daily worlds, the sociologist theorizes toward a different end: the development of more abstract, comparative knowledge. And the sociologist theorizes with outside audiences in mind.

The role segregation that some fieldwork accounts depict, between being committed "in the field" and detached at the desk, is oversimplified. One shifts back and forth at the time of doing fieldwork, sometimes with ambiguity and anguish. But the fact of doing sociology inevitably draws one apart from holding the full perspective of an insider (see the paper by Bittner, this volume).

Being a fieldworker in this particular setting entailed especially sharp conflicts of consciousness. The detached, comparative perspective of fieldwork was at great odds with the emotional urgency, sense of apocalypse, and demands for partisanship and collectivity which were central to daily life in the movement. The conflicts had implications that were neither "merely personal," and hence ignorable or "appendix-able," *nor,* more seriously, "defects" or "bias," as if there were some transcendent way of getting access to the Resistance. The conflicts of consciousness which I felt while doing fieldwork in the Resistance provided me with insight into the movement world of meanings, as well as into the contrasting ways of knowing and feeling which are bound up in social research.

Looking back on my study, I can see that the way in which I participated influenced my overall angle of vision. For example, during most of my fieldwork I tended to think of the Resistance as characterized by its most activist central core. In my dissertation I analyzed varied levels of membership in both movement groups, but the charismatic, inner core of activists, whose charisma tugged at me as a person at its edges, felt the most "real." This perspective shaped many of the analytic issues I pursued, for example, processes of risk-taking, and the "event-time" experienced by the most active draft resisters.

My position in the Resistance, and hence the vantage-points of my study, were also shaped by my gender. This compounded my marginality, especially in the New England Resistance, where the imagery of full membership was male: a club or "brotherhood" of draft resisters. Women, who couldn't be drafted but were nonetheless active in the movement, had derivative status, e.g., as "resister-sisters." Over time, the women in the Resistance came to question our marginal and subordinate position, a collective process in which I was actively involved and which led to my becoming a feminist. By the time I wrote my dissertation, I was keenly aware of issues of gender, and the first article I published was about the changing position of women in the draft resistance movement (Thorne 1975a). My own transformation as a participant eventually altered my understanding of the movement. I became critical of my earlier assumption that the visible group of male leaders was the core of the Resistance, and I became more aware of hierarchies internal to the movement. I came to understand that social movements, like institutions, depend upon the devalued, almost invisible daily labor of subordinates, who are usually disproportionately women. Movements look quite different when viewed from the perspective of subordinates rather than those at the top. When I concluded my study, I had shifted perspectives in a way closely tied to my personal change of consciousness as a participant in the movement. Such personal changes are not just private realities, publicly confessed; they lie behind, and help shape, the directions of research.

The Dynamics of Inclusion and Distance in Fieldwork Relations

Melvin Pollner
Robert M. Emerson

Introduction

On many levels, the actual conduct of field research reveals a chronic tension between the demands of involvement and withdrawal, of participation and detachment. Conceptually, the fieldworker wants to achieve an empathic understanding of the meanings and concerns of the researched, yet he or she will inevitably employ a distanced, detached sociological framework in analyzing what has been so apprehended. Practically, the fieldworker wants both to get close to those studied — to become immersed in their daily rounds of life — and to move freely among them, with the latter goal requiring a certain limit on commitment to the local scene.

Discussions of fieldwork methods devote much attention to the processes of getting close, but little attention to the processes of becoming or staying detached.[1] It should not be surprising that processes of becoming an insider have tended to preoccupy fieldworkers, as this concern mirrors the ordinary sequence of tasks in most fieldwork. The researcher must, after all, get in the door and become welcomed before he or she can begin to observe and analyze in earnest. Distance, especially at the start of the project, is something to be overcome, and later, even when desired, appears easily achieved. In this paper, however, we not only want to examine specific processes of distance and detachment in fieldwork, but also to call attention to the ways in which distance and detachment are problematic in fieldwork interactions, both analytically and in practice. We will do so by analyzing some features of perhaps the prototypical fieldwork activity involving distance — observation.

Any act of observation involves and creates distance; the very term "ob-

---

Used by permission of the authors. Copyright © 1983 by Melvin Pollner and Robert M. Emerson.

[1] Interactional processes and strategies for achieving involvement — ways of making entree, "establishing rapport," and creating "trust" — have been closely examined in a number of accounts (e.g., Berk and Adams 1970; Johnson 1975). Where distance and detachment are discussed, they are tied to two standard issues. First, the literature is replete with warnings against "overrapport" (Miller 1952), against too intimate or sympathetic identification with those studied (Douglas 1976). Second, fieldwork accounts frequently recommend a pattern of sequenced immersion and withdrawal, the latter to take place after the more active phases of fieldwork have been concluded (e.g., Schwartz and Schwartz 1955).

server" connotes someone who stands back from the ongoing rush of events in order to look at what is taking place.[2] In fieldwork, however, the researcher cannot stand back and watch social interaction in the way an observer behind a one-way mirror can. For the fieldworker is inevitably present *in* the interactions that are the focus of observation, whereas the laboratory observer is not interactionally present in this way.

At times the necessary distance may be achieved conceptually. The researcher may bifurcate into levels of awareness or consciousness, one of which is immersed in the activity at hand, the other sustaining a more detached, observational standpoint. In other circumstances, however, the researcher will seek distance in a more palpable way and strive to preclude, avoid, or evade attempts to draw him into deeper social involvements. In these instances, observation is neither a subjective attitude nor a passive stance but an interactionally managed position.

As interactional achievement, observation can often be very precarious, as its continued achievement depends not only on what the researcher says and does, but also upon the willingness of the observed to sustain the presence of such a marginal member in their midst. Moreover, the major threat to observation is often not that the observer will be expelled by the observed, although this is of course an everpresent possibility. Rather, the major threat to observation derives from pressures that dissolve the stance of "mere observer" by according the researcher some more consequential presence in the ongoing scene. This occurs when fieldworkers become incorporated, for a variety of reasons, into the ongoing social life in some central and consequential way.

In this sense, the role of the observer is a collaborative interactional achievement. "Observing" is a continuously accomplished or negotiated arrangement in which observer and observed organize so as to allow the researcher to witness with only minimal consequence and involvement. It is not a position given or obtained once and for all but rather one which is continuously reproduced, threatened, and preserved through the particulars of interaction. And as an interactional achievement, "observing" requires the coordination of two forms of interactional work. There is first the work of the observed, which by and large consists of acts of circumspection, inhibition, and restraint through which the researcher is allowed to maintain

---

[2] To the extent that one is actively involved in these very events, "observation" in a strict sense is not possible; or better, observation becomes a form of *self-reflection*. Observation in this distanced sense will play a greater or lesser role in fieldwork depending upon the particular balance of involvement and detachment developed by the fieldworker. In practice no fieldworker can effectively act as the "complete observer" (Gold 1958), but short of completely "going native" even the most participatory fieldworkers will want to forego direct involvement at some moments, in some situations, in order to observe events and actions which they have no direct part in creating.

a seemingly detached or uninvolved position in relation to local activities. Second, there is the work of the observer, work which consists of social wariness and interactional agility whereby the researcher seeks to stay physically present to witness but seeks also to avoid any direct role in shaping or playing out those events.

In the following pages we will first consider the nature of the inducements and overtures to deeper involvement and the ways in which a researcher may experience, to paraphrase Lemert (1962), *the dynamics of inclusion*. In so doing we indirectly explore the nature of the suppressions and restraints through which the boundary between observer and observed is possible. We will then examine directly some of the common practices used by the observer to sustain this boundary. Such practices for "doing observing" are often reactive in nature, anticipating the moments and conditions in which the setting may expand its frame and acting to preclude, deflect, defer or sidestep the more aggressive overtures. Alas, owing to the emphasis on rapport — even in reflexive ethnography — there are precious few descriptions of researchers' exercise of the arts of distance. Our discussion of the concerted achievement of "observer" is thus intended less as a systematic analysis than as a venture aimed at exploring the hitherto little examined work whereby ethnography is accomplished.

The Dynamics of Inclusion

As suggested previously, every transaction (and indeed every absence of transaction) between observer and observed is a threat to or reaffirmation of the stance of "mere observer." In unperturbed talk and action, without apparent reference or orientation to the observer, the fieldworker is implicitly established as a kind of non-person — and in fact may come to feel that he is witnessing a reality impervious to his presence. Alternatively there are moments when the seemingly Archimedian perch is threatened as group members find they cannot or do not want to disregard the fieldworker's presence. In a variety of ways fieldworkers may be of potential use and significance to group members, and may find themselves drawn or invited to the center to participate in the very activities they came to observe.

While these pressures toward inclusion and involvement may assume forms as varied as the possible uses groups can imagine for someone constantly present in their affairs, fieldwork accounts suggest that three types of overtures arise with particular frequency: First, efforts may be made to induct the observer as a worker and situational resource in dealing with various instrumental tasks; second, groups often try to induce fieldworkers into full membership, regarding them as potential recruits; and finally, those studied may seek to establish greater intimacy than a strictly research relationship would entail.

Fieldworker as Worker and Resource

Fieldwork is often conducted in occupational settings where pressure to get the work done may be brought to bear on the fieldworker. In some settings, there is strategic or symbolic value in having the researcher appear to be a worker. Not only may it preclude having to give what are felt to be awkward or untimely explanations, but "real" workers may feel it contributes directly to the efficient management of the work at hand. Thus, workers may actively facilitate misidentification of the researcher in order to create a strategically useful aura.

> One detective team regularly identified the researcher to citizens as a researcher from the University of Toronto, except when the encounter involved a suspect who might prove troublesome. In these circumstances — e.g., during a search and attendant interrogation at a suspect's residence — the detectives would remain silent about the researcher's identity, at least until after they had obtained the evidence they desired. Similarly, when the citizen was in the role of informant, detectives led him to believe that the researcher was a detective, even when the citizen directly asked about the researcher's identity. (Ericson 1981:37)

Relatedly, the fact that the researcher's identity is unknown to client populations may make him or her immensely useful as whatever kind of person a member happens to need to organize or control circumstances. Researchers may be identified not simply as another worker but as a special kind of worker — usually a superior, authority, or expert who is called upon to support the members in dealing with dubious or recalcitrant clients. Gussow (1964:236), for example, describes several incidents in which teachers used fieldworker entry into the classroom to chide classes for their unruly behavior.

The researched may not only portray observers as work colleagues, but may also seek to have them actually perform as such. Under certain circumstances the researcher may acquire a competence over the course of research, indeed by virtue of the research, and become progressively more attractive to workers as a possible partner or, in the most extreme instance, as a substitute for workers. In our research on psychiatric emergency teams (see Emerson and Pollner 1976), for example, some team members felt that a second team member was not necessary because one of the researchers could serve as a back-up. At one point it was uncertain, owing to a worker's other responsibilities, whether a PET team could be fielded and it was half-jokingly suggested that, given our experience, we, the two fieldworkers, would comprise the team.

Aside from any competence the researcher may have in terms of the direct instrumental concerns of the group, he or she may have skills or resources generally valued or needed by the group. While the researcher may be initially forthcoming as part of *quid pro quo* relations, the asset may be of such great value that the demand is incessant and overwhelming. McCurdy (1976), for example, entered the field with a modest supply of pharmaceuticals and he was transformed into a medicine man of such repute that he almost lost control of his research efforts:

> If I had had any thoughts about extricating myself from paramedical practice, they were dashed by the success of aureomycin, penicillin, sulfa, and the wonderfully fragile local bacteria that had never encountered antibiotics before. These medicines worked too well; village resentment over their denial would have driven me from Ratokote. Instead I continued medical activities, to run what really amounted to a clinic. Villagers marveled at the power of "Sāb's medicine." They bragged about it to their friends and relatives in other communities, and made it and me a status symbol for Ratokote. I found myself sought out by more and more people, strangers, from neighboring villages. One man even walked all the way to Ratokote from Udaipur because someone had told him that, "Sāb cures better than the hospital." . . .
> Treating patients used up valuable time, and the more patients there were the more time treatment took. Even worse, patients interrupted research activity. They arrived at their own convenience, at any time during the day or night that suited them. They would catch me as I hurried to meet an informant for an interview, interrupt as I tried to type field notes, or pull me away from the observation of an interesting religious event. (McCurdy 1976:14)

It is not necessarily the researcher's uncommon skills that are valued or needed by the group. Indeed, the fact that the researcher is a more or less competent adult may make him eligible to do many mundane tasks. Johnson, for example, reports that over the course of his investigations of a social welfare office he served as driver, reader, luggage porter, babysitter, money lender, ticket taker, note taker, phone answerer, book reader, book lender, adviser on automobile purchases, party arranger, bodyguard, letter writer, messenger, and other things (1975:107). As this range of tasks suggests the fieldworker qua resource may be an amorphous presence — an organizational Rorschach blot — whose particular significance is defined by developing situational needs and the artfulness of members in construing the uses to which he or she may be put. While the upsurge of the setting does not necessarily preclude distance, at times the use of fieldworkers as situated resources may implicate them in the scenes they would much prefer to observe.

Observer as Prospective Members

Perhaps the greatest difficulties in maintaining a nonconsequential presence occur in groups which by their very nature are ceaselessly striving to proselytize and induct members. From a researcher's point of view the proselytizing propensity is a mixed blessing: on the one hand such groups may be easily approached, inquired about, "observed"; on the other hand, the group may eventually come to ask a high price — the researcher's total commitment and participation. In such contexts, despite wishes and protests, the observer may come to be regarded as a prospective recruit. While many political and religious groups share this nature, the assimilative propensity is dramatically visible in small, intense proselytizing groups whose members possess a truth which the world must be made aware of. Often the truth may be regarded as apodictic, as self-evident with the consequence that even though the researcher initially believes he or she is being allowed simply to observe, group members are continuously monitoring the researcher's actions for signs of commitment:

> It seemed that there was an implicit contest going on among group members to see who could convert one of us first. As stated, for the first few years of our research, nearly every interview was a contest of wills (and patience — on both sides). We regularly heard our names mentioned in prayers in their public gatherings, and some members made continual efforts to "win us to Christ." The importance of this issue to the group members was graphically illustrated when rumors of the impending conversion of a member of the June 1972 interview team swept the camp. There was much premature rejoicing among group members, who plainly assumed that the only "real purpose" of our being there was to "get converted." Apparently what had happened was that an interviewer had expressed to a respondent an interest in finding out more about the group ideas, and he had started to read the Bible during his spare time. Just the sight of him reading the Bible seemed to be enough to set the rumor mill in motion. In some of our later visits, people still asked about the interviewer, desiring to know if he finally decided to convert. (Richardson, Stewart, and Simmonds 1978:15)

Of course, religious cults are not the only groups which seek out new members. A range of secular groups may also see the researcher not simply or even as an observer but as a lively addition to a declining or decrepit membership (see, for example, Chrisman 1976:140–141).

Observer as Intimate

As we have noted, the observer role is almost invariably included within a more encompassing relation which is often of greater salience to the observed — indeed, on occasion the condition of having an observer in the first place. Frequently, the strongest and most salient bond to the researcher is established along a personal dimension in which congeniality and personal attractiveness are paramount attributes. As many have noted, people are often most intensely concerned with whether the researcher is a "nice," "regular," or otherwise acceptable person. The personal dimension of the relation may be intensified by the deepening access of the researcher to more intimate, sensitive, or backstage areas of group and subjects' social world. Insofar as the researcher is able to modulate the friendship so as not to move it to levels that he or she would like to exempt from consideration, then a balance between personal and professional relations may be maintained. But the direction and intensity of a relation are not unilaterally determined and researchers may find that, having taken a step in the level of intimacy, their subjects demand, expect, or hope that they will take more.

By virtue of the observer's access to intimate or "inside" aspects of the observed's life, the subjects may feel threatened by the researcher's presence. Despite professions of "neutrality" and confidentiality the observed may feel that they are nevertheless being evaluated or judged and that embarrassing or discrediting details may be used in a humiliating fashion. These fears may, of course, be the grounds for denying the researcher access, but alternatively they may animate efforts to secure his or her friendship, sympathy, or support. Berk and Berheide (1977), for example, noted that informants in their study of housework moved to an intimate level of discourse with extraordinary dispatch:

> In particular, we were often treated as new friends in whom subjects seemed prepared to invest substantial affect. While this process was difficult to document when access was initially being negotiated, once we entered people's homes we were offered coffee, engaged in conventional ice-breaking topics of conversation, and soon questioned in a friendly manner about our personal lives (e.g., Where in town do you live? Do you have any children?). Often it was not long before we were told about difficult personal experiences (e.g., medical problems) and various life complaints ... What was most striking about these conversations was the speed with which they unfolded. Perhaps subjects wanted to remove the ambiguous elements of our role as soon as possible; the uncertainty was extremely uncomfortable. Alternatively, there was something about the behavior we were going to observe which demanded rapid movement to a more intimate level of interaction. (Berke and Berheide 1977:36, 37).

Persons may strive not only for personal but for sexual intimacy as well. Given ethnographers' renowned tendency to describe only the "second worst" thing that happened in the field, the nature of sexual overtures and relations and their impact on research activity are virtually unknown. There is, however, sufficient indication that researchers and subjects are not exempt from the human condition and that subjects may regard sexual availability as the paramount dimension despite researcher's desires and expectations. In some situations the time collaboratively spent in research activities may be viewed by persons as time spent in the cultivation of a potential sexual relation.

Treatment of the researcher as an intimate may be particularly evident as the researcher terminates the field relation. Insofar as the people studied had already terminated the research relation by interpreting it as friendship, "leaving the field" may prove difficult. In her study of marriage and family relations among the Western-educated elite of Sierra Leone, Barbara

Harrell-Bond (1976) established cordial relations with fourteen families
but found that while she might leave as researcher, she did not — perhaps
could not — leave as intimate. Having established close personal ties with
these families, she had assumed a set of relational obligations that pursued
her on her return from the field:

> On several occasions I was asked to take a child back to England with
> my own family for education. Some people still assume that there will
> always be room for one of their relatives to live in my home while he
> is studying in Britain. (1976:117)

As Harrell-Bond concluded, "In similar ways I am continually faced with
the realization that there is no way to 'bow out' of such relationships" (118).

The Dynamics of Distance

On his or her side, the fieldworker may from the very start disclaim any
intention of becoming a central, consequential force in the setting under
study, often taking up the stance, "I'm just here to watch; go on about your
business as if I weren't here." Of course, just what those studied will make
of this claim is another matter entirely, and exactly what "just observing"
amounts to will await members' emerging reactions to the fieldworker. In
addition, the fieldworker is rarely only an observer, as he or she must develop coherent relations with participants to ensure access to the scenes to
be witnessed or to ask about their understanding of the meaning and import of witnessed events. Processes of distancing, of remaining marginal
and non-consequential, are handled against the background of these already
existing relations with those studied. For the fieldworker, the problem is
rarely setting up a detached, limited field relation from the start, but rather,
trying to maintain the degree of distance already esablished in an ongoing
relationship. In this respect, effective observation is not threatened so much
by participation *per se* as by invitations (or inclinations) to move beyond
the level of participation that has come to prevail up to this point. Thus,
it is not that the researcher does not want to be an intimate, but not this intimate; not that she doesn't want to be instrumentally involved, but not this
involved; not this much of a help, and not this much of an ally. In effect
the researcher's problem is not how to reach a transcendental or Archi-
medean vantage point to non-consequentially observe on-going activity but
rather how to manage an already developed relation so as to prevent it from
expanding its claim on his identity and commitments.

Particularly when we turn to practices for distancing, we confront the
fundamentally indexical character of social interaction. The ways in which
fieldworkers can become drawn into deeper involvements, and the corresponding ways in which they can avoid, decline or hedge such overtures,
are probably inexhaustible in number and form. In what follows we will
not even attempt a systematic identification of these forms, but will limit

ourselves to four major processes: essentially preemptive moves aimed at precluding overtures to deeper involvement; a variety of responses to explicit overtures that directly decline or otherwise reject greater inclusion; a further variety of responses that indirectly deflect, hedge, or evade such overtures; and finally, responses that involve full participation on the behavioral level but withdrawal and distance on the subjective level. In all cases, we will devote particular attention to the possibility that these practices may not be understood by the researched in quite the way they were intended by the would-be observer.

Preclusions

Overtures are elicited by virtue of the situated attractiveness, usefulness, or accessibility of the researcher. Insofar as these are manipulable or alterable qualities, or insofar as the fieldworker happens to be "naturally" unattractive or useless in terms of group needs and interests, overtures may be nipped in the bud. Indeed, from the point of view of efforts to sustain distance, qualities and styles often viewed as obstacles to rapport and trust can provide useful resources in precluding unwanted overtures before they even begin. Many common field relations have this character: a white European among black or brown third world peoples, women among men, a young graduate student among older, experienced workers, are effectively preempted from certain forms of engulfment.

The role of novice, initiate, or learner, and perhaps ignorance in general, may also serve to preclude certain kinds of inclusionary moves, and some fieldworkers will work long and hard to hold on to their apparent ignorance of local ways exactly in order to enjoy this exemption. The problem, of course, is that this exemption is never total and absolute, and also tends to wear out over time.

The preclusion of overtures may also assume a much more dynamic interactional expression in which the fieldworker exploits his or her developing sense of the setting to anticipate overtures and to evade them before they occur. Decisions regarding physical positioning provide one such area. The available options in any particular setting may furnish opportunities to minimize the likelihood of unwanted overtures. Almost by definition, the periphery or background of whatever focused engagements comprise a setting's main involvement (Goffman 1963b) are attractive niches for observing. Fieldworkers may acquire an agility in moving to the outer edge as the fore- and background regions of a setting form and shift. In some circumstances, members may collaborate with the fieldworker's backgrounding ploys. Johnson (1975:102), for example, after being frequently drawn into the center of client home visits on being mistaken for a welfare worker, adopted the following strategy with the social workers he accompanied into client homes:

I would tell them that it appeared that the physical location of the furniture in nearly all the homes included at the minimum a couch and an adjacent chair. From earlier experiences, it seemed interaction would not focus on the researcher if he was positioned at either end of the couch-chair combination. So the social workers were instructed to "manage" me to one end or the other, out of the direct line of fire, to reduce the chances that my presence in the setting would disturb the ongoing interactions.

A position on the periphery, however, is inherently unstable: a shift in concerns, a glance, a turn of the head, may reconstitute the rim as the center. At such moments, or just before they occur, the observer may strategically manage facial expression, eye movements, body direction, and public demeanor to minimize accessibility. In this way, fieldworkers will often employ a "looking at no one in particular" gaze to avoid engulfing engagements or become immersed in an engrossing side-involvement (taking notes provides a convenient one) to preclude an imminent overture.[3] Here also, however, fieldworker intent may not be what members come to perceive and react to, showing once again both the collaborative interactional work that underlies observation and the fieldworker's common presumptuousness in assuming that he or she has been a "mere observer." Consider the significance found in the fieldworker's silent, watchful presence in the following field note involving a psychiatric emergency team call:

> I (RME) accompanied a PET team composed of two women, a psychiatric social worker and a public health nurse, to the home of a 21 year old black ex-mental patient named Albert Roy. The young man's mother had initiated the visit, claiming his behavior was extremely disoriented and something had to be done. After introductions and some preliminary talk about Albert's recent problems, I seated myself in an easy chair slightly removed from but with a good view of the couch where the workers and Albert sat talking. I assiduously observed and took notes on all that was said about Albert's mental condition, efforts to get a job, problems with medication, etc. At various points Albert became somewhat "agitated," at one point getting up and standing two feet away from one of the PET workers, shaking his fist in her face and yelling that he can take care of himself. At this point, his mother, standing in the kitchen area watching all this, pointed toward me (I had said absolutely nothing) and warned her son: "Sit down Albert! Or that man over there will get you. That's what he's here for!"

Insofar as preclusion succeeds, overtures are preempted or prevented: subjects feel no need or desire to incorporate the observer. Once an overture has been made, however, the fieldworker's options change dramatically; any response is now monitored for what it may signify about the fieldworker's character, commitments, and relation to the group. Under these circum-

---

[3] See Strickland and Schlesinger's (1969) discussion of the technique of "lurking," where the researcher maintains a distracted, preoccupied, disinterested or engrossed demeanor in order to unobtrusively monitor public transactions.

stances, the fieldworker's distancing options involve either making a direct refusal or an indirect evasion. These practices are treated in the following two sections.

Declarations

At some point, as members make inclusive demands and requests, the fieldworker may feel compelled to respond with open refusals in order to sustain some sort of non-consequential presence. Often this is achieved through some comparatively explicit declaration either reasserting field-worker identity as a researcher or observer, or stating his or her unwilling-ness to participate in the way or to the extent proposed by the overture. Where such an overture or request is made explicitly, the fieldworker will often have to respond with a direct "no," drawing a line which establishes that some action entails a level or degree of involvement that is fundamen-tally incompatible with the fieldworker's identity as a researcher.[4] In other situations, inclusive overtures may be more implicit or latent, with the re-sult that the fieldworker's declaration of research priorities and identity may be advanced in a more roundabout way. Briggs's (1970:25) tensions in resolving the conflict between the demands of her research and the expecta-tions of the Eskimo family with whom she lived provide a case in point:

> I found it hard sometimes to be simultaneously a docile and helpful daughter and a conscientious anthropologist. Though Allaq appeared to accept my domestic clumsiness as inevitable, she may have felt less tolerant on the occasions when it was not lack of skill that prevented me from helping her but anxiety over the pocketful of trouser-smudged, disorganized field notes that cried out to be typed. A number of times, when I could have helped to gut fish or to carry in snow to repair the sleeping platform or floor or could have offered to fetch water or make tea, I sat and wrote instead or sorted vocabulary — tiny slips of paper spread precariously over my sleeping bag and lap.

However, the sense and significance of even an explicit declaration de-pend upon contextual interpretation. Consequently what may appear to be direct or unequivocal declinations from one point of view may be under-stood in an entirely different way by members. Golde (1970:84–87) noted, for example, that when her refusals of amorous propositions were filtered through indigenous cultural understandings their meaning and implications

---

[4] It is our impression that such outright denials are relatively hard to find in the fieldwork literature, a fact which may well reflect members' sensitivities in what they will ask of fieldworkers, and fieldworkers' reluctance to make an outright refusal, perhaps thereby risking rapport and access. Supporting this possibility are a number of reports in which fieldworkers failed to say no when, in members' eyes or in their own retrospective evaluations, they should have; Whyte's (1955:312ff) regret for having voted under others' names provides one example. Fieldworkers do report making direct declarations of refusal when asked to report on their observations to outsiders or superordinates, but such refusals, of course, reaffirm ties to those studied by denying any obligation to these other parties.

were transformed. "The difficulty was that it was expected of the female always to appear unwilling initially," Golde writes, "so that my lack of interest and my refusals were not always taken at face value but were interpreted as typical female behavior" (1970:86).

In some circumstances the capacity to go beyond "face value" may be so comprehensive or systematic that the researcher is virtually bereft of any direct means of declaring distance: try as he or she might to voice them, the declarations are treated as signifying the need for greater involvement. Snow's (1980) efforts to terminate his fieldwork in the Nichiren Shoshu Buddhist movement provide a case in point. Committed members of this group responded to those showing signs of disaffection or withdrawal with renewed contact and involvement. In the following field note Snow reports the following reaction to initial declaration to leave the group (1980:110):

> No sooner had I finished (telling my group leader about my growing disillusionment) than he congratulated me, indicating that (such feelings) were good signs. He went on to suggest that ... something is really happening in my life ... Rather than getting discouraged and giving up, I was told to chant and participate even more. He also suggested that I should go to the Community Center at 10:00 this evening to get further guidance from the senior leaders ... Later in the evening my group leader stopped by the apartment at 10:00 — unannounced — to pick me up and rush me to the Community Center to make sure that I received "guidance."
>
> While I was thus trying to curtail my involvement and offer what seemed to be legitimate reasons for dropping out, I was yet being drawn back at the same time.

Even where such declarations do succeed in terminating unwanted overtures, they may lead members to review their relation with the fieldworker until that point and to examine what ought to be done about such a recalcitrant presence.[5] Such review and reexamination may have drastic consequences for the fieldworker, and may also make explicit for the first time on just what terms members had been suffering the presence of an "observer." Lofland's experiences with what proved to be the beginning of the Unification Church are exemplary (1966:274):

> Through all these months, there *appeared* to be a shared understanding of my interest in the DP [Divine Precepts]: I was personally sympathetic to, and accepting of, them and desired to understand their endeavors, but I was not likely to be a convert. There were understandable and kidding suggestions that I should "witness" and convert, but

---

[5] Briggs (1970:40) provides a case in point, noting how her recalcitrance and refusals to enter fully the family member role constructed for her resulted in her coming to be treated as a non-person:

> Though my physical needs for warmth, food, and protection from danger were still taken care of, socially I was simply "not there." There was one other person in the community similarly ostracized: a woman of about my age, who appeared to be of subnormal intelligence. (41)

the ostensible reason for my presence was to study the movement.

Then, in January, 1963, Lee told me that she was tired of playing the "studying the movement" game. She made it clear that she was very concerned that, after all these months and all that the members had told me, I had not become a convert. I responded that my interest was necessarily professional. Lee expressed regret: "If I had known from the beginning that you only looked at our Precepts as a scientist — why should I have bothered?"

It seems, in fact, that for eleven months I had unwittingly and systematically misled the DP's with the standard participant observer's open, permissive, sympathetic stance. While I was trying to appear non-committal, although very interested, the DP's were reading this as existential concern.

Evasions

Given the potential costs of direct refusal, it is not surprising to find fieldworkers adept in the arts of vagueness, ambiguity, and situational diplomacy whereby overtures are evaded or avoided without direct confrontation. Fieldworkers may respond to requests for involvement with a variety of hedges and excuses. Members' efforts to get the fieldworker to express his or her own opinion about an event that has just transpired may be met with a therapist-like counter question, e.g., "What did *you* think about that?" [6] Attempts by one side to draw the fieldworker into local factional disputes may be dodged by refusing commitment, or met by a response carefully measured to maintain a balanced, "neutral" position.

In some situations the fieldworker is fortunate enough to have the inclusive overture framed so indirectly that it can be responded to in kind without either party feeling publicly embarrassed or humiliated. Golde (1970:86) found, for example, that when a man actually advanced an amorous invitation in the Mexican village she studied, "it was often presented so tentatively, so indirectly, that I could pretend I didn't understand and he could pretend he hadn't really said anything, and both our feelings were saved." In other circumstances overtures may be framed very explicitly and responses closely scrutinized. For example, just as anthropologists often speak of "my tribe," tribes and particularly divisions therein may come to think of the researcher as their friend and ally — over and against other divisions. The researcher may find her wit and diplomacy tested when she is publicly asked to commit herself to one or another "side" (skills clearly revealed in Rosalie Wax's practices for continuing fieldwork in the face of constant crises in the highly factionalized environment of the Japanese relocation camp [1970:59–174]).

---

[6] The practices through which fieldworkers manage overtures resemble the practices of other professionals who strive to simultaneously establish both relation and distance. It would be of particular interest to compare therapist strategies for managing transference with those described here.

In certain respects evasions are a consummate test of the researcher's ethnographic grasp of indigenous structures of interpretation. Not only must the evasive fieldworker respond but he must do so in such a way that members do not press for further involvement, are not offended, and do not treat the researcher as evading. Because of the compounded indexicality of evasions it is not unusual that responses intended as hedges fail in one or another of these respects. Thus, for example, responses intended to be "neutral" and non-committal may be transformed into patently partial statements. The following excerpt from *When Prophecy Fails* provides a dramatic case in point:

> At the end of the December 3–4 meeting, Bertha sat for "private consultations" between the individual members and "the Creator" who spoke through her. All the observers dutifully asked a question or two of the Creator and accepted the answers passively, quitting the situation as soon as they politely could. The last observer to go through this ritual was not allowed to be merely passive and nondirective, however. The voice of the medium droned on for a few minutes and then said: "I am the Creator." Next the voice asked our observer: "What do you see when I say 'I am the Creator'?" To this the observer replied, "Nothing," whereupon the medium's voice explained: "That's not nothing; that's the void." The medium then pressed further: "Do you see a light in the void?" Our observer struggled with this impasse by answering, "A light in the void?" and got, as a reply, a fuller explanation of the "light that expands and covers the void" together with an increasing flood of elaboration that terminated when the medium called other members into the room and asserted that the observer had just been "allowed to witness Creation"! The medium further stated that this "event" was validation of her speaking with the Creator's voice since, every time her voice said "I am the Creator" our observer saw the vision of Creation! (Festinger, Riecken, and Schachter 1964: 242–243)

As these fieldworkers lamented: "Against this sort of runaway invention even the most polished technique of nondirective response is powerless" (243).

Even successful use of these practices involving evasion (and those using preclusion as well), however, gives the fieldworker a straining, if not strange, presence in the local setting. For as observer, or while observing, the fieldworker limits involvement in and commitment to the social activities underway. The fieldworker does not give him or herself up to the immediate interaction to the same degree and in the same way that members do, but remains at least partially aloof from its claims and responsibilities. Despite having spent a great deal of time in the midst of the group, and despite seeming to support its goals and projects, the fieldworker will, at critical moments, fail to come forth with the desired expressions of commitment. Asked to act to further members' collective purposes, the fieldworker will often back off or out; pressed for a personal opinion about a matter of deep concern to a member, the fieldworker will frequently venture only an evasive, non-committal response. While many fieldworkers find that the notion of "the stranger" resonates with the ambiguous and elusive practices for turning, ducking, and holding back, perhaps the concept of the alienated participant in social interaction developed by Goffman (1967: 113–136) strikes closer to home. And as is the case with any interactionally alienated person, those who have to make up for the lack of expected involvement may become resentful and put off. In particular, members may feel that they have exposed themselves to the fieldworker to an extraordinary degree, but have not received such intimacies in turn. As feelings about the lack of reciprocity fester, members may come to feel that they have been shamed or betrayed and come to view fieldworker responses as mere gambits to evade higher or deeper responsibilities. In this light, the angry, betrayed reaction of a member of a fundamentalist religious group to a non-committal observer expressed in the following field note may be unusual only in its open vehemence:

> And we're rapping about the situation at God's Love (commune) and where her head's at, etc., and then, just as an afterthought, she says, "Are you a Christian?" And I went into my stereotyped song and dance about "This is a study and I can't talk about," etc., and she got furious. She was very angry, and she went on about how she considered me to be a friend, and she had told me intimate things about herself and I had acted friendly and then all of a sudden I had copped out on a friendship whenever she asked a personal question of me. She also said something about how I was trying to cop out of being a Christian by doing a "scientific trip" (taped field note). (Robbins, Anthony, and Curtis 1973:266)

The strain and the alienation are clear; as the authors ask, "How could the researcher refuse to discuss his personal feelings when subjects had openly discussed with him their intimate spiritual experiences?" (Robbins, Anthony, and Curtis 1973:266)

These reactions to the researcher's best efforts to manage overtures can generate considerable psychological pressure. The researcher may feel compelled to abandon attempts to ward off overtures and resign him or herself to a level of immersion deeper than he or she would have otherwise preferred. No longer sustaining their distance interactionally with others, researchers who for one reason or another dive deeply into the life worlds of those they study may find they must sustain their position as "observer" through interaction with themselves.

Reminding

In a range of situations fieldworkers will be unwilling or unable to preclude, avoid, or evade overtures; rather, they commit themselves to deep involvement. At these moments the individual may find that the sole link to their identity as "researcher" or "observer" is through their ability to recollect and remind — indeed to re-collect and re-mind — themselves of their original project. Particularly for anthropologists who are more apt than sociologists to be totally surrounded by if not immersed in the worlds they study, the ability to perceive themselves as "researcher" may grow progressively more tenuous as they find their very ways of thinking engulfed. The venerable Evans-Pritchard gives an indication of the depth of psychological engulfment to which the researcher may be subject, even in dealing with cultural beliefs so alien as witchcraft:

> Azande were talking about witchcraft daily, both among themselves and to me; any communication was well-nigh impossible unless one took witchcraft for granted. You cannot have a remunerative, even intelligent, conversation with people about something they take as self-evident if you give them the impression that you regard their belief as an illusion or a delusion. Mutual understanding, and with it sympathy, would soon be ended, if it ever got started. Anyhow, I had to act as though I trusted the Zande oracles and therefore to give assent to their dogma of witchcraft, whatever reservations I might have. If I wanted to go hunting or on a journey, for instance, no one would willingly accompany me unless I was able to produce a verdict of the poison oracle that all would be well, that witchcraft did not threaten our project; and if one goes on arranging one's affairs, organizing one's life in harmony with the lives of one's hosts, whose companionship one seeks and without which one would sink into disoriented craziness, one must eventually give way, or at any rate partially give way. If one must act as though one believed, one ends in believing, or half-believing as one acts. (1976:244)

Even fieldworkers who participate to a lesser extent are subject to psychological engulfment. The fieldworker's stance as an observer may be threatened not because of explicit overtures from the group but because the researcher is so affected by what she observes that she is drawn to ever deeper levels of involvement. Barrie Thorne has suggested that ethnography affords the researcher "controlled adventure" into exciting, tabooed, dangerous, enticing circumstances, while retaining the ability to control the time, extent, and costs of participation. It is important to consider, in addition, the possibility that sights and circumstances offered by ethnography may metaphorically or otherwise seduce the researcher. In a variety of ways the ethnographic experience may provide opportunities to construct selves and have experiences not always available in other circumstances. PET work, for example, had a certain adventurous aspect to it and from time to time provided opportunities for fieldworkers to become "situational heroes" insofar as they could provide solutions to managing clients. In effect, we found that while we occasionally received overtures to become workers, we also experienced the situationally attractive possibilities of becoming a worker. At moments like these, one fends off or manages not the overtures of others but the impulses from oneself.

The psycho-symbolic controls which fieldworkers exercise upon themselves, the ways in which they define and bound themselves as "observers" to themselves, may very well have interactional and structural dimensions.

At the very least it is worth reviewing the arrangements of fieldwork for the way in which they may anchor an individual in his or her role as researcher. From this point of view, daily note-taking, letters to and from the field, chairs of dissertation committees and the like comprise the apparatus through which the researcher is re-minded of his commitments. Indeed, there are even instances in which the researched not only refrain from overtures but warn the researcher about the dissolution of his own identity. Whyte (1955:304) provides a revealing illustration:

> At first I concentrated upon fitting into Cornerville, but a little later I had to face the question of how far I was to immerse myself in the life of the district. I bumped into that problem one evening as I was walking down the street with the Nortons. Trying to enter into the spirit of the small talk, I cut loose with a string of obscenities and profanity. The walk came to a momentary halt as they all stopped to look at me in surprise. Doc shook his head and said: "Bill, you're not supposed to talk like that. That doesn't sound like you."

Conclusion

The epistemology of the social sciences demands the distinction between researchers and researched, observer and observed, and, at the most abstract level, between subject and object.[7] Indeed, the very notion of a science is possible only to the extent that these distinctions can be sustained. Insofar as one cannot suppose a determinate reality standing independent of the efforts to observe it, the fundamental grounds of a science are threatened with dissolution.

The workaday practices of the human sciences vary in the extent to which the distinction between observer and observed is a problematic or taken-for-granted structure of inquiry. At one extreme are the studies of dead sociality in which historical residues — documents, records, bones — comprise the "observed." In their docility, residues allow the researcher to examine them as he will without fear of rebuff or rejection.[8] In a literal sense

[7] Investigation presupposes one or another variant of the subject-object duality. Insofar as the duality cannot be sustained at some level of awareness the entire idiom which it founds and which includes the very idea and possibility of "inquiry" (as well as "truth") dissolves. Thus, even researchers who strive to overcome the subject-object duality in order to become completely immersed in the world of those they study often reconstruct the duality at a meta-level as they distance themselves from their experiences in order to describe them. The inability or unwillingness of the researcher to reestablish the duality is a central process of "going native."

[8] The docility of objects — their inability to respond to, resist, or for that matter, accept inquiry — is relative. There are a variety of ways in which the physical world reacts to observation: the Heisenberg Uncertainty Principle suggests that aspects of the universe are a good deal more sensitive to observation than supposed by classical physics. Generally speaking, however, the physical world passively reacts rather than actively responds to observation: objects do not object.

The autonomy of humans of course is also relative. Thus, some ethnographers (see Nash and Wintrob 1972) have noted the ways in which the presence of colonial powers provided the foundation of comparatively nonproblematic access, observation, and description of subjugated peoples.

the documents and bones are *objects* comparatively indifferent to investigation though, of course, their keepers and owners may not be as stoic or accepting. However, as autonomous, active agents come to comprise the focus of study the primordial epistemological conditions of research become more problematic. Insofar as the "object" of concern can resist or refuse the inquirer's efforts to examine and explore, the subject-object dichotomy is transformed from an abstract philosophical scheme presupposed by the researcher to a relation which must be continually and collaboratively produced. Thus, even the survey researcher, though he or she will ultimately render interviews into docile records, must invite or cajole the respondent into being an object (and giving an interview).

The problematics of achieving an appropriate epistemological relation are most intensely encountered by ethnographers, that is, researchers who choose to be with and among those they study for relatively long periods of time. As with the survey interviewer there is the everpresent possibility of rebuff and rejection. And, indeed, the difficulties of access and rapport are dominant methodological issues. Ethnographers, however, are confronted with yet another order of problem, one which does not often appear in transactions with docile objects and only in truncated form in transactions with survey respondents and laboratory subjects: it is the problem of engulfment.

If rejection destroys the grounds of research by "exploding" as it were the relation between observer and observed, the grounds may also be dissolved by a "fusion" of observer and observed. The ethnographer may be drawn so deeply or entangled so complexly in the world and affairs of members that in the extreme he or she can no longer regain the epistemological distance or stance of an "observer." To be sure, involvement may be actively elicited and strategically useful in affording the researcher a perch from which to observe activities occurring at either side or as part of a reciprocal relation in which labors given in one domain are exchanged for access to another. At times however the involvement may be so comprehensive, preemptive or entangling that the researcher's capacity to observe is undermined or threatened. Instead of being *at* a scene, the observer finds she is *in* the scene: the boundaries between observer and observed have dissolved. Given the everpresent possibility of engulfment, the ethnographer must create the epistemological conditions of her research. In an interesting sense an ethnographer is a *practicing* epistemologist. Whereas researchers in other disciplines may be assured of or can take for granted the basic epistemological conditions of their endeavors, the ethnographer must recreate them in each and every encounter.

IV

Ethical and Political Issues in Field Research

Introduction

John Van Maanen
The Moral Fix: On the Ethics of Fieldwork

Murray L. Wax
On Fieldworkers and Those Exposed to Fieldwork:
Federal Regulations and Moral Issues

John F. Galliher
Social Scientists' Ethical
Responsibilities to Superordinates:
Looking Upward Meekly

Introduction

In carrying out any field study researchers inevitably run up against a variety of confusing ethical dilemmas and thorny political issues. Ethical problems arise in a number of different forms. While some such problems are endemic to social life generally, others are tied specifically to fieldwork as a research enterprise involving participation in a long-term and often intimate way in the daily lives of people who have their own distinctive interests and moral beliefs. Fieldwork under these conditions almost inevitably produces ethical issues of several different sorts: First, such fieldwork leads to moments of dissemblance and even outright deceit. Second, such fieldwork affects the lives and circumstances of those studied in ways that may be difficult to assess and which may well entail harmful consequences. In the following pages I will explore the ethical issues arising both from the use of dissemblance and deceit, and from the effects and possible harms caused by the fieldworker's actions.

Fieldworkers face political as well as ethical dilemmas. While the distinction between the ethical and the political is often not clearcut, the latter characteristically involves collective (rather than individual) conflicts over legitimacy and power. Fieldwork takes on political implications as the fieldworker becomes involved and enmeshed — however minimally — in the day-to-day and long-term affairs of a collectivity. The politics of collectivities — social movements, institutions, organizations, communities — can, as Becker (1967:240–241) has emphasized, assume different forms. In some settings political issues are latent rather than overt; Becker talks about these settings as "apolitical," indicating by that term not that struggles and conflicts over power and legitimacy are absent, but that they have been submerged.[1] Other settings may be politicized from the very start, as different factions and their interests are well organized and articulated. In situations marked by conflicts and factions, no matter how latent, the presence and actions of the fieldworker can become very consequential. As a result the

[1] "No situation is necessarily political or apolitical. An apolitical situation can be transformed into a political one by the open rebellion of subordinate ranks, and a political situation can subside into one in which an accommodation has been reached and a new hierarchy been accepted by the participants" (Becker 1967:241).

fieldworker will often face situations and decisions with significant political implications, where a stance of "neutrality" can be achieved only tenuously if at all. I will return to political issues in the final section of this introduction.

Deception and Dissembling in Fieldwork

Fieldwork is often carried out with deceit and dissemblance. Some fieldworkers conduct disguised research in which they deliberately assume false identities in order to gain entree into an otherwise closed social situation. Others, while they may overtly identify themselves as fieldworkers, engage in less blatant forms of deception, recurrently misinforming and misdirecting those studied in a number of ways. As Gans has noted of the fieldworker in this role (1968:314):

> He pretends to participate emotionally when he does not; he observes even when he does not appear to be doing so, and . . . he asks questions with covert purposes of which his respondents are likely to be unaware.

Despite the fact that they substantially overlap and share a number of common moral implications, it is worthwhile to separately examine deceit in covert research and dissembling in openly identified research situations.

False Identities and Covert Research

Over the years fieldwork conducted through covert means has generated substantial controversy, particularly where the fieldworker has assumed a disguised identity. The most notable of these writings include: Caudill et al. (1952); Festinger, Riecken, and Schachter (1956); Sullivan, Queen, and Patrick (1958); Lofland and Lejeune (1960); Humphreys (1975); and more recently in Britain, Homan (1978). The elaborateness of the deceptions has varied greatly: At one extreme, an elaborately documented false identity was created in order to allow an officer to pass as an enlisted man (Sullivan, Queen, and Patrick). At the other, Humphreys simply assumed the role of "watch queen"/voyeur in order to observe sexual activities taking place in public toilets (tearooms).

Erikson's critiques of such disguised observation are the most pointed and eloquent put forth to date, and it is worthwhile to outline his arguments in detail. While the use of disguised participant observation occurs relatively rarely in sociological research, Erikson (1967:367) has argued that "the practice of using masks in social research compromises both the people who wear them and the people for whom they are worn." With regard to the latter, disguised observation not only "constitutes an ugly invasion of privacy and is, on that ground alone, objectionable," but it also can bring injury, harm, and pain to those studied in ways that the researcher cannot anticipate. Among the possible harms are the violation of trust and the exposure of personal worlds. As Erikson emphasizes (1967:368):

> Nor does it matter very much how sympathetic the observer is toward
> the persons whose lives he is studying; the fact of the matter is that
> he does not *know* which of his actions are apt to hurt other people,
> and it is highly presumptuous of him to act as if he does — particu-
> larly when, as is ordinarily the case, he has elected to wear a disguise
> exactly because he is entering a social sphere so far from his own
> experience.

Erikson recognizes that all field research in fact involves some amount
and degree of disguise, that the deliberate misrepresentation of identity
falls somewhere along a continuum of secrets and less than full disclosure
about research and its general purposes. Yet he feels that disguised observation is sufficiently extreme to be singled out from other forms of misrepresentation. He proposes this principle (1967:373): "It is unethical for a
sociologist to *deliberately misrepresent* his identity for the purpose of entering a private domain to which he is not otherwise eligible."

Other field researchers, however, defend the use of disguised observation.
Some claim that covert methods provide the only way to gain access to important research settings and issues; openly identified fieldworkers are apt
to be denied access to centers of political power or illegal activity, for example. In light of such efforts to hide the dirty laundry of social and political life, Douglas (1976) has argued that "infiltration" is an essential
tactic in field research. The major defense of covert methods, however,
usually centers on the argument that the pursuit of scientific knowledge and
truth justifies whatever deceptive means are used. The covert researcher,
after all, has no selfish or overtly political axe to grind, and he or she may
provide knowledge about a particular group that is important for society
generally. Denzin (1968:502) provided one of the more forceful statements
of this position:

> ... the sociologist has the right to make observations on anyone in any
> setting to the extent he does so with scientific interests and purposes in
> mind ... The only qualification is that the method employed not
> in any deliberate fashion damage the credibility or reputation of the
> subject.

Those who advocate this position often also insist that the deceptiveness
of covert methods tends to be exaggerated by those who criticize them on
ethical grounds. For example, Denzin (1968:502) argued that the line
between public and private behavior in our society is shifting and highly
situational, making it difficult to specify a priori exactly what would count
as an invasion of privacy. Similarly, he suggested (503) that the distinction
between "true participants" and those wearing disguises is a difficult one to
make in light of Goffmanesque notions of the presentation of self and the
varieties of everyday deceits even the most sincere engage in.

Finally, many defenders of covert methods argue that those so studied
have never in fact been directly harmed in any significant way (Douglas

1976). Critics insist, however, that there are several less direct negative consequences from disguised research. First, they assert that disguised research damages sociology in general in the public eye, a trend which in the long run will create deep public suspicion and distrust of sociology and make future fieldwork more difficult to conduct. Second, critics suggest that the researcher's moral sensibilities (and research sensitivities) are blunted by the deceit. Cassell (1980:35) has advanced this argument with the framework of a Kantian ethic that "persons be treated at all times as ends in themselves, never merely as means." Covert research not only violates the autonomy of those researched in this sense, but also harms the researched, since "in deceptive research the investigator presents an inauthentic self, making the research interaction inauthentic."

Problems confront the effort to make the "good faith" of the fieldworker's assumption of a particular identity the central ethical issue rather than more overt harm. Roth (1962:284), for example, has asked:

> Does the manner in which one comes to be a secret observer affect the morality of the situation? Is it moral if one gets a job in a factory to earn tuition and then takes advantage of the opportunity to carry out a sociological study, but immoral to deliberately plant oneself in the factory for the express purpose of observing one's fellow workers? If the outcome is the same — e.g., if the manner in which the observations are used is the same — I, for one, see no moral difference in these two situations . . .

Similarly, on grounds of the researcher's "good faith," it would be ethical for a sociologist to study his hospital experience when he has suffered a "real" mental breakdown and been hospitalized for depression (Killian and Bloomberg 1975), but unethical to have himself admitted to a mental hospital to conduct a study when he was not "really mentally ill" (Caudill et al. 1952). Or what about those who undertake their research in "good faith" but conclude in retrospect that they at least in part misled themselves? Thorne, for example, became a good-faith member of the Draft Resistance movement, but ultimately she learned that such good faith did not entail the same sort of total commitment to the movement that activists without research concerns manifested. Or what about those who undergo some fairly arduous training in order to become fully qualified to enter otherwise inaccessible settings? Goffman, for example, learned to be a dealer to study "gambling action" in Las Vegas; Van Maanen underwent police academy and field training in order to carry out his observation of police work on the streets. In such instances notions of disguised and misrepresented identity, not to mention those of means and ends, become blurred. Even if those studied remain uninformed of the research purposes, the fieldworker has become immersed fully in the situation, makes a long-term, arduous, and continuing commitment, and confronts on a level of parity all the risks and dangers facing those "naturally" in the setting. To *become* a patrolman or a casino dealer in this sense thus raises ethical issues of a different order than, for example, attending an AA meeting.

Dissemblance in Explaining the Research

Assuming a false identity for research purposes is only the tip of the iceberg of fieldwork ethics. On many levels, there are no clear distinctions between overt and covert research (Dingwall 1980:876), but only differences in emphasis, situation, and degree. The basic criticism leveled against covert methods — that those subject to research efforts remain uninformed of these attentions and hence cannot be on guard to protect themselves from any harm the research or researcher might do them — applies in a lesser degree to most "overt" fieldwork as well. For as Roth (1962:283) has so graphically put it: "All research is secret in some ways and to some degree — we never tell the subjects 'everything.' "

In ordinary fieldwork practice, even where the sociologist is overtly identified as a researcher, deceptions and secrets frequently enter into dealings with those being studied. Such secrets begin with negotiations for access: Even in openly negotiating entree as a researcher, the fieldworker rarely reveals fully what he or she is all about. Thorne (1980:287), for example, observes that in seeking access fieldworkers provide self-introductions that often represent "partial truths," especially "vague and even misleading initial statements of identity and purpose." Gans (1962:344) provided a not atypical example:

> Although I did tell people that I was in the West End to make a study, I described my research mainly as a survey of organizations, institutions, and the redevelopment process. I mentioned but did not stress my interest in studying the everyday life of West Enders, and did not mention at all that I attended social gatherings in the dual role of guest and observer.

Another problem with self-introductions goes less to their content than to the extent to which they are offered. In many situations, for example, fieldworkers tell the immediate "host" of the research more or less what the fieldwork is about, but they are less likely to provide such information to those they observe less frequently and more episodically during the course of the research. Hospital staff, for example, may know who the fieldworker is, but many times patients do not, and it may be difficult and highly intrusive to inform them.[2]

---

[2] Similarly, institutional superordinates, acting as "gatekeepers" (M. Wax 1980: 279–280), may learn more about the research than the subordinate populations ultimately studied.

Even if fieldworkers reveal the specific focus of the research, often a near necessity simply in order to obtain access to the kinds of events they wish to observe, they may withhold from those studied their basic analytic concerns and commitments. These, as Thorne suggests (1980:288), may have fundamental relevance for those studied. In studying psychiatric settings, for example, we often fail to tell the staff that we are theoretically committed to looking at events from the perspective of the patients, an analytic commitment that has deep implications for how the overall setting will be depicted (Bloor, this volume pages 166–168, encountered problems on just this score).

In addition, fieldworkers may gloss over the specific methods of the research and its implications, although the practical problems of negotiating the exact sort of access they desire may mitigate against this approach. Thus, Thorne has noted (1980:289): "People aware of a fieldworker's general purpose and presence do not realize what the methodology entails: making daily and detailed written records of ongoing behavior."

Finally, fieldworkers may engage in a variety of tactical presentations of self that involve deceits and secrets. Fieldworkers frequently seek to come across as uninformed novices in order to be able to get those under study to talk about issues and assumptions that would be taken for granted by the knowledgeable. Parts of the self may be suppressed in order to appear ignorant and harmless in these ways.

There are, of course, a number of good reasons for using such deceptions. Fieldworkers may not know what they are studying in specific terms when they start out, but only discover what it is all about as they go along, or even after the fieldwork is completed. They may not want to tell those studied exactly what they are interested in for fear that knowledge will affect them in some significant way. Fieldworkers may want to avoid the more obvious kinds of reactive effects, for example. To tell those studied the specific research topic may intimidate or make them self-conscious: The humor of those who have been told that a field researcher is studying their humor will of necessity be something very different than that of those who do not know of this research interest. Finally, there are secrets born of misunderstanding and miscommunication: At an extreme, how useful is it to children to be told the nature and purpose of research?

Few fieldworkers, then, would advocate complete avoidance of deception in each and every situation, even if this were possible. The question is rather, as Roth (1962:284) has suggested, "How much secrecy shall there be with which people in which circumstances? . . . Posing the question in this manner puts us in the same boat with physicians, social workers, prostitutes, policemen, and others who must deal with information which is sometimes delicate, threatening, and highly confidential." Secrecy neither can nor should be avoided; "It is rather a problem to be faced as an integral part of one's work" (Roth 1962:284).

Effects and Harm in and to the Field

Implicit in the evaluations of covert research is the recognition that, independent of the social and psychological consequences of deception, fieldwork can have very direct if sometimes subtle effects on those studied, effects which the fieldworker will be unable to anticipate and which are as likely to be harmful as neutral or beneficial.

In many instances, the fieldworker's mere presence in a setting may have major consequences which may be harmful for at least some of those involved. Goldkind's (1966, 1970) return to the Yucatan village Chan Kom studied earlier by Redfield and others provides an extreme but revealing example. Relying on a different set of informants than Redfield and his co-workers, Goldkind concluded that the rise to prominence and uncontested political hegemony of the "progressive" leader, Don Eustaguio Cime, was made possible by the support of Redfield and other Americans. Briefly, Don Eus managed to monopolize local contacts with Redfield's anthropological expedition (as he had done also with earlier archaeological expeditions) and to gain control of the important resources (jobs and money) these groups brought to the village. In addition, Eus parlayed Redfield's political support and published statements into financial and other support from the Mexican government. The presence of the anthropologist was thus highly consequential in ways that were not appreciated initially.

Clearly, such local consequences derived from the fieldworker's *power,* including material resources, political connections, and social prestige. Cassell (1980) has in fact argued that close consideration of the distribution of power between fieldworker and hosts is necessary for evaluating ethical issues in fieldwork. She suggests that fieldwork can vary on a number of dimensions, notably the researcher's power as perceived by those studied, and his or her control over the immediate setting and wider context of research. In many situations fieldworkers may be protected from significant effects by their relative powerlessness, but even this status is subject to wide variation from situation to situation. As carriers of Western culture and potential contacts with colonial or other administrators, anthropologists may face these sorts of problems much more routinely than sociologists who stay in their own culture. Ploeg (in Appell 1978:47–48) noted, for example, that the Papuan settlers that he studied in New Guinea credited him (mistakenly) with getting the government to change certain detested local land policies: "They believed that I had thus succeeded in shaming the administration and compelling it to take action."

Research inquiries themselves may affect events in the field, sometimes in harmful ways. Briggs (in Appell 1978:92) provided an indirect report of an extreme instance:

> One of the administrators I met warned me to be very circumspect in my study of shamanism among the Eskimo. He said that the Eskimo

are aware that whites frown on the practice, and he related to me the consequences of one investigation into shamanism. The anthropologist had been working in a highly missionized Eskimo community and had finally persuaded some Eskimo to sing shamanistic songs for him. Shortly thereafter, one man who had recently converted to Christianity committed suicide as a result of his guilt over participating in an activity which was an important part of the native religion.

Even the "neutral" presence of a fieldworker during a psychiatric interview, to give an example, may be read by the interviewer as a sort of validation of his or her procedures and emerging decision, even when the observer's opinion is not directly sought. In short, the fieldworker's presence is rarely neutral, but has effects in the setting. The fieldworker may anticipate some effects and even try to avoid them, but inevitably others will be unanticipated and even undetected.

Up to this point I have considered the effects of commission. But since the fieldworker is usually involved in fairly intimate and trusted ways with those studied, possible harm can also arise from the fieldworker's failure to perform in ways that those studied had expected from their readings of the commitments implied by this relation. In his article that follows Van Maanen discusses some of the possible harmful consequences of omission which emerged on police patrols where he was counted on to back up the officers he rode with in the face of danger. As he emphasizes, the moral choices confronting the fieldworker in this sort of situation are not only complex, deeply troubling, and not amenable to formulated solution — especially since to do what one is counted on to do often injures the interests of another party — but must be resolved on the spot. As Dingwall noted (1980:885), "Ethical problems in fieldwork often require an immediate resolution," and cannot be taken in for consultations.

In contrast to these sorts of effects and possible harms, further harms may result from publication (or dissemination) of research reports. The publication of field observations could have harmful consequences for individuals involved. Typically fieldworkers try to anticipate this problem by disguising individual identities in written reports. In some cases it is difficult to effectively disguise identities from insiders, and if such people recognize themselves and others, interpersonal relations can be negatively affected (Becker 1964:267). Published or written reports may also have important effects on collectivities (Warren 1980). Becker (1964) has pointed out the potential harm that publication might bring to stigmatized groups whose habits or even existence may not have been known by the public at large. Similarly, Warren (1980:294) noted that the public defender office she studied in fieldwork on involuntary mental hospitalization proceedings felt betrayed and harmed by her depiction of them as "nonadversarial." [3]

[3] Warren adds here (1980:295): "And how did the court know I was writing about it, given our discipline's pledge of anonymity? As I discovered about six

Professional and Governmental Ethical Regulations

There have been two attempts at formal response to and regulation of these sorts of ethical issues in field research. One response has been the effort to develop professional codes of ethics (see the following readings by Wax and Galliher for a review and evaluation of these attempts). The other has been the development and extension to field research of a variety of federal regulations seeking to protect human subjects in scientific research (DHEW 1974, 1978). These regulations require the "informed consent" of "subjects at risk" ("risk" broadly defined as "the possibility of physical, psychological, or social injury"), ordinarily by means of signed forms, for their participation in field research. Fieldworkers have been sharply critical of these regulations (M. Wax, this volume, 1980; Cassell 1978, 1980; Thorne 1980) on two major counts.

(a) The Risk-Benefit Calculus. The federal regulations require a utilitarian calculation of risks to subjects in relation to possible benefits of the research. Yet the harms and benefits of fieldwork are "less immediate, measurable, and serious" than those associated with other forms of research (Cassell 1980). And since both risks/harms and benefits derive primarily from publication of findings and not directly from the conduct of research, this sort of risk-benefit calculus is difficult to apply to fieldwork, particularly in advance of the actual study. As a result, "weighing potential harms against benefits before research is carried out becomes an exercise in creativity, with little relevance to the ethical dilemmas and problems that may emerge during the research" (Cassell 1980:32).[4] Klockars (1977:225) similarly argued that applying a cost-benefit equation to his study of a professional fence would have provided his informant with less than adequate protection; the process would have offered no substantively workable criteria for deciding "whether a researcher should risk injury to his subjects or should be judged guilty of this abuse."

(b) Informed Consent Procedures. Fieldworkers have sharply criticized federal informed consent requirements, noting that these procedures, generally designed for biomedical and experimental research, embody assumptions that are not compatible with standard fieldwork methods (see M. Wax,

---

months after the article's publication, the usual geographical clues were not the only ones. In writing of 'one Metropolitan mental health court,' I did not realize that the court in question is the only mental health court in the nation."

[4] In addition, this sort of weighing remains difficult even after the completion and publication of field research. Thus, in response to Warwick's (1973) cost-benefit critique of his tearoom study, Humphreys responded that his study "is increasingly cited by attorneys seeking acquittal for clients arrested in public restrooms" (1975:232).

this volume page 289). Thus, informed consent procedures envision research as a short-term, essentially contractual encounter between strangers possessing grossly different amounts of power and knowledge, whereas consent in fieldwork relations is emergent, negotiable, long-term, and usually marked by some degree of equality. As opposed to one-time consent given in advance to fixed procedures, fieldwork methods are intrinsically flexible, "sequential and conditional so that consent is a continual process, dependent upon mutual learning and development" (M. Wax 1980:275). Furthermore, in most field situations, the researcher neither possesses great power, as perceived by those studied, nor exercises (unilateral) control over the setting, conduct, or interactional contours of the research encounter (Cassell 1980). Rather, most fieldwork is carried out through a process of negotiation and reciprocity that is belied by the power differential assumed by the informed consent model.

The informed consent model assumes that the researcher confronts a series of *individual* subjects. Yet most fieldworkers do not recruit individual subjects, and few or no "formal choice points" arise for participation in the study. In short, "the contours of the natural groups and settings of field research run against the individual model of informed consent" (Thorne 1980:293). Similarly, the informed consent model assumes that the researcher relates to those studied within a narrow, researcher-subject role relation. In fact, fieldwork involves multiple roles rather than a single role, as Klockars (1977:218) emphasized in discussing his relations with his informant: "Vincent was not only my subject but also my teacher, student, fence, friend, and guide. Likewise, to Vincent I was not only researcher, but biographer, confidant, customer, friend, and student." Each of these role relations entailed "multiple obligations and responsibilities and expectations," many at odds with those involved in a research-subject relation, and hence inadequately protected by informed consent requirements.

Finally, many fieldworkers have expressed grave doubts about both the advisability and feasibility of governmental and professional regulation of research ethic. They fear not only that such regulatory efforts will subject fieldwork to rigid and formal bureaucratic controls, but also that in their current form these regulations will favor the politically entrenched and powerful. Later in this section Galliher notes that current professional codes of ethics provide no right to study those in publicly accountable positions. Moreover, current federal regulations would require obtaining their informed consent as a condition for undertaking such research. M. Wax (1980:279–280) has cited a number of instances in which protection of human subjects regulations were invoked by "gatekeepers" controlling access to hospitals, schools, and prisons to exclude fieldworkers wanting to study the institutionalized populations they controlled. Galliher explores a variety of issues that arise in trying to develop an ethical stance that accords different needs and degrees of protection to the more and the less powerful.

Others question the very possibility of developing meaningful codes of ethics in the first place. Dingwall (1980:883), for example, suggests that "It is not possible to write an unambiguous set of rules for ethical behavior," and he anticipates that the result of codes that will be established will be the enforcement of conventional morality.

Political Issues in Field Research

Those involved in fieldwork have become increasingly conscious of the political dimensions of their research. In both anthropology and sociology, fieldwork is increasingly conducted in more openly politicized settings which frequently call into question the conduct and implications of the research.

In colonial circumstances the political dimensions of anthropological fieldwork remained latent and implicit. On the one hand, the fieldworker, while allied with and supported by the political power of the colonial administration, could remain outside of or above local political concerns. As Barnes suggested (1967:198):

> Behind the ethnographer was the support of the colonial administration, so that it was difficult or dangerous for the chief to resist the ethnographer openly. Appropriate gifts could smooth the way, for in the main the ethnographer's activities, if incomprehensible to the chief, did not threaten his position in any way. Though the ethnographer might not approve of, say, the arbitrary power wielded by a chief, or of the tribal subjection of women, or of the moral code and religious ideas of the people, he did not try to alter what he saw. Instead, he tried to understand and explain without passing moral judgments of his own.

On the other hand, these political arrangements created both the space within which fieldwork could be conducted, and the terms on which it would be carried out:

> The colonial power structure made the object of anthropological study accessible and safe — because of it sustained physical proximity between the observing European and the living non-European became a practical possibility. (Asad 1973:17)

With challenges to colonialism, these conditions have been radically transformed, and the political underpinnings of fieldwork are now explicit and unavoidable. Access is not automatically granted, but has to be negotiated with both the independent government and local authorities, as well as with the particular group to be studied. Local groups may no longer allow the detached presence and basic asymmetry once characteristic of anthropological field relations.[5] The researcher may not be allowed to set

[5] Asad (1973:17) located one indicator of this asymmetry in the following observation: "It is worth noting that virtually no European anthropologist has been won over personally to the subordinated culture he has studied; although countless non-Europeans, having come to the West to study its culture, have been captured by its values and assumptions, and also contributed to an understanding of it."

the research focus without considering the issues that administrators want studied. And both the administration and those studied can no longer be assumed to be uninterested in the fieldworker's findings and conclusions. In sum, anthropological fieldwork has become politicized; or, more accurately, the political system within which such fieldwork is carried out and upon which it relied has been transformed so that its political underpinnings are visible and unavoidable.

Similar tendencies, although perhaps weaker in force, also seem apparent in sociological fieldwork. On the one hand, governmental and other political agencies have an increasing interest in what gets studied and in what ways. As one example, to the extent that fieldwork deals with disadvantaged or hidden groups that have become of interest to governmental agencies, its findings assume more direct political and social implications in bureaucratic society. As a result, fieldworkers tend to become more sensitive and aware of the outside and official uses of their findings. Particularly with the possibility of blatantly exploitative research funding (Horowitz 1967), it is difficult to present fieldwork as nonpolitical and of only intellectual relevance.

In addition, many of the relatively powerless and subordinate groups traditionally studied by fieldworkers have become politicized, and hence have gained greater awareness of and control over research. As Thorne notes (1980:284): "Groups of Blacks, Native Americans, and other minorities, and members of protest movements have begun to claim the right to review research proposals and to negotiate conditions; sometimes they have refused to be studied at all." Self-consciousness may be promoted by these sorts of pressures for cooperation with or at least accountability to research groups.[6]

As fieldworkers have become more sensitive to the political uses and implications of their research, the decision as to who gets studied has emerged as a significant issue. In characterizing fieldwork in the United States in 1969, Laura Nader remarked that "we find a relatively abundant literature on the poor, the ethnic groups, the disadvantaged; there is comparatively little field research on the middle class and very little first-hand work on the upper classes" (1969:289). She recommended "studying up," a reorientation of fieldwork toward "the colonizers rather than the colonized, the culture of power rather than the culture of the powerless, the culture of affluence rather than the culture of poverty" (see also Galliher, this volume page 300).

[6] Perhaps activism in subordinate groups can politicize the whole social environment: not only do the activities and concerns of such groups come to concern the government, but also these groups increasingly seek to influence governmental policy and decisions. The environment in which fieldwork is conducted thus tends to be doubly politicized: The subjects have rebelled and are concerned with the political and social implications of fieldwork, just as the state has an increased interest in these groups.

Sociological fieldwork on deviance has been specifically criticized for its "voyeuristic" attraction toward studying the strange and the exotic; in this way Liazos (1972) decried the focus of much fieldwork on the marginal and subordinate in American society: on "nuts, sluts, and perverts." Some field researchers have suggested that ethnographic study of the lives and worlds of the marginal may have a number of harmful consequences, for example, publishing accounts that "break the protective secrecy in which a subjugated population wraps itself" (Nicholaus 1968). Warren (1980:292) provided a concrete example raised by gay men in response to her study of the gay community:

> In my own research on the gay world several respondents expressed the fear that if I published a "true" account of the gay world as one in which effeminacy stereotypes do *not* prevail, then noneffeminate homosexuals might suffer by being suspected . . . While my gay respondents did not argue that it was not "true" that most gay males are not effeminate, they did argue that it would be preferable for them — they would suffer less adverse effects — if the "false" stereotypes continued to prevail.

Yet the intent of most of those who do field studies of deviant and marginal groups is to present *their* meanings, perspectives, and justifications in a relatively sympathetic way. Becker, in his manifesto for underdog sociology, "Whose Side Are We On?" (1967), argued that sociologists have a responsibility to represent the concerns and points of view of such subordinate groups who are routinely unrepresented within the larger society. Along these lines, Humphreys (1975) has defended his tearoom trade study not only on the grounds that it did not harm anyone specifically, but also that it was of political and legal use to some in the gay community.

Where fieldwork involves studying groups involved in open conflict with dominant governmental institutions, however, even the best of intentions on the part of the researcher may prove inadequate to represent their interests and concerns. Sagarin (1973:62) has argued that for U.S. Army deserters living in Sweden during the Vietnam war:

> Any self-knowledge or politically useful information that a sympathetic or objective researcher may unearth for [their] benefit . . . will be essentially useless to them because of their political impotence and their inability to implement meaningful programs.

Under such conditions, Sagarin contended, "knowledge for the sake of knowledge" does not provide adequate justification for studying such politically vulnerable groups.

Even with regard to less overtly political situations, "the quest for knowledge is a political question, rather than a taken-for-granted value as so many scientists have always assumed" (Warren 1980:292). No description is entirely neutral, and this result is not only a product of the ends to which such descriptions can be put by others, but also of their implications for those studied. For there is often a deep tension between even ethnographic accounts of a scene or collectivity and the perspectives that members hold. As Becker has noted (1964:273):

> Everett Hughes has often pointed out that the sociological view of the world — abstract, relativistic, generalizing — necessarily deflates people's view of themselves and their organizations. Sociological analysis has this effect whether it consists of a detailed description of informal behavior or an abstract discussion of theoretical categories.

Descriptive accounts, then, may not accord with members' views, whether the public, professed ones, or their private views; in this sense the accounts have political implications. For example, when the field researcher treats as problematic what members take for granted or view as sacred, those versions may have real implications for those studied.

These problems are particularly apt to arise, as Becker (1967) has emphasized, in studies of institutions and settings marked by the dominance of a subordinate group or category by a superordinate group. To present the view of the former is to challenge part of the political domination of the latter, to counter its established "hierarchy of credibility" with the perspectives and concerns of the less credible group. And since hierarchies and factions characterize the life of almost any group, one of the most fundamental, politically laden decisions the fieldworker makes is how to move through these factions, and, ultimately, how to represent each with its distinctive concerns. Any particular description may reflect and hence in some fashion overrepresent the distinctive concerns of one side and underrepresent those of the other.

Such overrepresentation may infuse description and analysis in subtle yet significant ways. As Thorne observed in her postscript (this volume, pages 233–234), for example, to direct her attention and analysis to the charismatic leadership and risk-taking process in the draft resistance movement implicitly oriented her account to the activities and concerns of the male movement leaders, and neglected the more routine, "supportive" activities of women movement participants. Or, Rochford's (1982) study of the Hare Krishna movement, an account that is sympathetic to the participation and contributions of marginal members and ex-members, is by that very fact antithetical to the perceptions of the central leadership, which demanded total commitment from members and deemed ex-members ("bloops") to be both unrepresentative and peripheral to the real force of the group.

The Moral Fix: On the Ethics of Fieldwork

Background

While a graduate student at the University of California, Irvine, in September, 1969, I began contacting police officials across the country seeking permission to conduct a one-man field study inside a large, metropolitan law-enforcement agency. I wished to study the kinds of cultural understandings necessary to operate in the occupational world of patrolmen by witnessing at firsthand the way in which young men went about learning the ropes of city policing. Although I encountered some initial difficulties in locating a department willing to tolerate my planned foray into its organizational spheres, eventually I managed to gain access to one police organization largely through the sponsorship of a man I met almost by happenstance, a university professor who had several rather close and well-placed friends in the police department. After a short, almost *pro forma* period of negotiations with the ranking officials in this agency (herein referred to under the pseudonym Union City Police Department), I entered a regular recruit training class in April 1970 with a reserve police commission. I had tentative approval for a period of observation in the patrol division (subject to my graduation from the police academy) and, perhaps most importantly, something of an administrative commitment from the Chief of Police to see my research carried out.[1]

Reprinted with permission from *Social Science Methods, Vol. 1: Qualitative Social Research*, pp. 115–139. Copyright 1982, Ballinger Publishing Company.

Many people have helped me with this paper. Conceptually, Peter K. Manning provided a most illuminating critique of an earlier draft, a critique that forced me to attempt to spell out many more of the assumptions that governed my actions in the field than would otherwise have been the case. Operationally the conclusion of the story presented here might well have been different were it not for the aid and comfort provided me by James D. Carroll, the director of an important study conducted at Syracuse University on the "Confidentiality of Research Sources and Data" (Russell Sage Foundation, 1976). Professor Carroll provided some knowledgeable assistance to the attorneys struggling to build some sort of case to defend the stance I had taken in the legal matters discussed in this paper. Finally, my faculty colleagues as well as the administration at M.I.T. never backed away from my case and supported my position both financially and, with few exceptions, morally.

[1] My method and the problems I encountered in carrying it out are detailed elsewhere (Van Maanen, 1978b). . . . Several reviews of the field methods employed in studying the police are available; see Manning (1972, 1976b), McCall (1978: chapter 3), and Fox and Lundman (1974). The best description I have read on the use of observational techniques to study the police is located in the appendix of Buckner's (1967) unpublished doctoral dissertation.

Throughout the study I worked in the fashion of a traditional ethnographer or participant observer, made no attempt to disguise my scholarly aims or identity, and met with little overt hostility from the men whose everyday affairs were the explicit subject of my investigation. In most respects I felt my mode of inquiry approximated both the substance and spirit of Evans-Pritchard's classic formulation of the ethnographic technique: "to get to know well the persons involved and to see and hear what they do and say" (quoted in Barnes, 1967:202). To this end I completed the thirteen-week police academy course in Union City and then spent a little over five months as an observer riding patrol with both rookie and veteran police officers in several selected districts of the city — in particular, the skid row district. After an absence of over two years I returned to Union City for several months in early 1973 and again spent considerable time viewing police actions from the vantage point of patrol cars. Since that period I have been back to Union City on several occasions both to renew friendships and to check out certain findings.

The writings that have emerged from this lengthy but interrupted period of fieldwork have focused primarily upon patrolmen and their work. Specifically, I have been concerned with such topics as police socialization (Van Maanen, 1973, 1975), work rules (Van Maanen, 1974), and police labeling practices (Van Maanen, 1978a). More general publications have also relied substantially, although less exclusively, upon my police experiences (Van Maanen, 1977; Van Maanen and Schein, 1977). In all of these writings, I have made much use of the field notes I compiled during and following my various stays in Union City. These notes selectively detail the diverse sights and sounds, facts and fictions, conversations and actions, thoughts and feelings that I experienced while embedded within, and preoccupied with, the police scene.

Critically, my methodological goal during the study was to become an accepted part of the Union City policeman's day-to-day work world. That is to say, I wanted my presence in the training class, in the patrol car, on the street, in the courtroom, in the city jail, in a saloon, or wherever certain policemen might be at a given time to be taken as more or less natural. From the outset of the study I wanted to work (some may say worm) my way into a research position wherein my presence would not alarm or otherwise disturb those policemen with whom I was to share a portion of my life. While I was not welcomed with obvious glee, I believe that over time I was able by and large to approach this position, a position somewhat akin to a state of grace. But there was both a personal and social price to be paid for such a success. It is to certain troublesome and altogether chilling implications of this success that the remainder of my remarks in this paper are directed.

A Case in Point

In October of 1974, while teaching in Cambridge, Massachusetts, many miles from Union City, I was served with two subpoenas ordering me to appear at a deposition hearing to give oral testimony and to surrender certain research materials concerned with matters stemming from a libel action brought by several Union City police officers against a major Union City newspaper. One subpoena read in part: "You are further required to bring with you all your notes and other file materials covering the periods commencing July, 1970 and ending March, 1973." The other subpoena was somewhat more specific, asking for "notes, tapes, and other file materials made pertaining to the arrest of Chester A. Blazier" (all names used here are, of course, disguised). The deposition hearing and the occurrences that led up to it and followed it provide a convenient and concrete frame of reference through which some inescapable and perhaps insoluble ethical dilemmas of fieldwork can be examined. The story itself is complicated, but it illustrates several crucial moral issues at stake when one undertakes firsthand observation.[2] I will first tell the story and then attempt to draw out several rather vexing ethical problems that penetrate to the very core of the tale.

Chester Blazier was arrested on a slow Sunday night in February, 1973. He was also beaten severely that night in the back of a patrol car summoned to transport him to the city jail. He wound up lying in the intensive-care unit of a Union City hospital with three broken ribs, a punctured lung, lacerations to the head and body, temporarily blinded in one eye. He was charged with several criminal offenses, all resulting from actions that took place after he had been arrested on "suspicion of public drunkenness." The events leading up to this exercise in what I have elsewhere called "street justice" (Van Maanen, 1974) can best be recounted by the field notes I wrote some five or six hours after the incident itself (and only several weeks after I had returned to Union City following a long absence). This excerpted (and slightly edited) account begins about an hour into the 7 P.M.-3 A.M. shift I was working with Officers Barns and McGee.[3]

[2] In general, discussions concerned solely with the ethical and moral issues involved in fieldwork (or for that matter in all social research) are few and far between. There are some notable exceptions, however. See in particular Myrdal (1944: Appendix 2) and Sjoberg (ed.) (1967).

[3] All quotes appearing here are only as accurate as my memory and ear allow. During the observational sequences of the Union City study I did not employ a recording device and took very few notes while on the street with my police informants. However, excluding those instances when weariness got the better of me, I typed out as extensively as I could my recollections of the "day's" events, talks, hunches, and so forth immediately upon returning to the relative sanctuary of my home.

... While parked under the elevated highway drinking coffee and chatting, a slow moving freight train rumbles by and both men play idly with the squad car spotlights trying to see if any tramps are freeloading on the flatbeds or rails. As always, McGee is quiet, almost taciturn, and Barns, ever talkative, seems to run the show. Over the radio comes a familiar call to investigate a disturbance complaint lodged by the owner of a tavern well known to the skid row cops as a "fag joint."

... arriving at the Tavern, the owner tells us simply that this middle aged black man sitting calmly at the end of the bar is "causing a commotion and refuses to leave." The Tavern at that moment has three other patrons sitting in a booth quietly sipping their drinks and watching us. Barns then walks briskly over to the man and asks for some identification. McGee, following Barns, jerks a half-full bottle of whiskey from the man's back pocket and hands it to me. The man pulls out his wallet, removes his driver's license from its plastic container (indicating to the officers that perhaps they are dealing with a "cop wise" character who has had previous dealings with the police), hands it to Barns, who, after looking at the license, then pulls the wallet from the man's hands and rummages through its contents revealing among other things, an unemployment check, a naval shipyard identification badge, and a soiled picture of a woman and two children. "This your wife?" asks Barns. "Yeah," says the man now believed to be Chester A. Blazier. McGee chimes in with the remark, "You know this is a fag joint, don't you? You like gay people?" Blazier, to his undoing, replies smartly, "Yeah, don't you?" The following exchange then took place:

McGee: "Get the fuck outta here now."
Blazier: "Come on man, I ain't doing no harm, just minding my own business."
McGee: "Listen you cocksucker, this lady here called and said you threatened her and are causing a disturbance in this 'fine' establishment. Now get going."
Blazier: "Sure, sure, I'm going. Gimme back my stuff. ... You got my check."
Barns: "Here you are, 'sir.' Now shag your black ass down that road 'cause if we see you around here again tonight, you're going in. Got it?"

We walk the "troublemaker" out to the street. McGee takes the man's whiskey bottle from me and smashes it against the curb, gives Blazier a light shove to get moving, and we walk back to the patrol car parked across the street. Both men comment on what a "jerkoff" Blazier was and how they have to deal with "his kind" all the time. They also wonder whether or not they've seen him before in their district. They can't decide. We then drive around the block and return to the vicinity of the bar. Rounding the corner, Barns notes that Blazier has changed his direction from the time we last saw him and now appears to be heading back toward the Tavern. Enraged, Barns flips on the lights and siren, says, "That's it, let's take him, the sonofabitch." McGee calls the station asking for the "wagon" (the police van used to take prisoners to the city jail). Blazier, having noticed the sudden police reappearance, quickly picks up his pace and walks right past the tavern. Both Barns and McGee yell at him to stop: "Hold it, asshole, you're going in." Blazier halts in his tracks and the two officers, jumping from the prowl car, grab him, perform a hasty but rough body search, set him down on the curb and then stand a few feet away to await the arrival of the wagon.

... When the wagon arrives, Blazier is readied for his short ride to the city jail, there to be booked as a "stand-up drunk" (suspicion of public drunkenness). As they attempt to push him into the wagon, Blazier balks by stretching both arms across the backdoor entrance to the van. It was as if a signal had been provided to both Barns and McGee, for all hell breaks loose. McGee kicks Blazier at the knees and Blazier falls to the ground and begins to rather half-heartedly kick back (a serious mistake). Barns and McGee, both kicking and swinging, finally succeed in getting Blazier into the wagon. Both of them now follow Blazier into the van and Barns has his personal "nigger-knocker" [nightstick] out. From outside the wagon I can hear the very distinct smack of wood meeting flesh and bone. After perhaps a half a minute or so, Blazier, thoroughly dazed and maybe unconscious, is pulled from the wagon, bounced to the pavement, handcuffed and tossed back into the van.

McGee then told the reserve officer driving the police van to take Blazier to the emergency room at Hillside Hospital. The reservist, however, did not know how to get there, so Barns led a two vehicle procession to Hillside. On the drive over, Barns remarked: "What a place to try and put somebody out. It's so fucking cramped and dark in that van you don't know what's going on. I kept hitting something with my stick but didn't know what it was until I heard that creep's glasses shatter. Then I kept hitting that same spot until I felt it get kind of squishy."

When we reached the hospital, Barns called the squad sergeant on the phone, explained briefly what had happened, and asked him to come over to the hospital. The reserve officers went back to the street and Barns, McGee, and I went to the employee's cafeteria at the hospital to begin doing some of the paperwork associated with the arrest. Barns suggested a number of possible charges to be brought against Blazier: resisting arrest, assaulting a policeman, disturbing the peace, disorderly conduct, carrying a concealed weapon (a "church key"—sharp-edged bottle opener), using abusive language, and so forth. ...
The initial draft of the major arrest report was, however, received by the squad sergeant in the following manner: "I don't like the way it sounds. You've gotta remember that IID (the Internal Investigation Division of the Union City Police Department) won't talk to you first, they'll just read this report and ask themselves why didn't you guys just shove him in the wagon and forget it."

... returning to the station house, Barns filled out the many reports associated in the incident and passed each of them to the sergeant for approval. The sergeant carefully read each report and then returned the "paper" to Barns saying that he better claim he was kicked in the face *before* he entered the patrol wagon or Barns would get a heavy brutality complaint for sure. He also told Barns ... heavier charges (against Blazier) were necessary to protect Barns from IID. Finally, after some discussion and two rewrites, Barns finished a report which the sergeant said "covered their asses." (February, 1973)

The sergeant was apparently wise to the ways in which such affairs unfold, for the next day Blazier filed a formal complaint charging the arresting officers with the use of unnecessary force. Two Internal Investigation Division (IID) officers were assigned to investigate the affair, an investigation that resulted in five interviews — Blazier, the four officers on the scene of the arrest (Barns, McGee and the two reserve officers handling the wagon), and myself. Two days after the arrest occurred, I gave my account to IID in testimony that was both under oath and tape recorded. In that testimony I recounted the incident as accurately as I could from memory (not including the report-writing encounter with the squad sergeant). I did not bring my notes of the incident to the IID interview nor did I make reference to their existence. Almost five weeks later the officers were exonerated by IID, and the complaint itself was ruled "unfounded." Blazier, then out of the hospital and out on bail, threatened through his attorney to file a civil suit against the city, charging economic and physical impairment as a result of the police beating. Several days before his scheduled trial on the felony counts, the district attorney's office agreed to drop all charges against Blazier if he in turn would sign a waiver absolving the city from all responsibility in the matter. He signed.

The story, which is a common one in police circles, would have ended there had it not been for a relationship I developed with a police reporter in Union City. I had been introduced to this reporter by, oddly enough, Officer Barns at a squad party several weeks after the Blazier arrest, and we became rather good friends over the course of the following year. We visited with one another, exchanged many letters, and in general talked a good deal about police work. We had both spent considerable time in the skid row district of Union City and had observed the particularly active and aggressive patrol tactics used in that part of town. Since we both knew Barns rather well, the Blazier incident arose in a few of our conversations. Indeed, while I was still in Union City, the reporter, Barns, and I had once talked rather candidly and argumentatively about the events (and our various interpretations of them) that surrounded the beating of Chester Blazier.

In early 1974, almost a year after we had met, my reporter friend wrote a series of articles on "Skid Row Cops." Each article was constructed as something of a profile on the working style of a particular patrolman. The articles all dealt with patrolmen I had known well, although I had nothing directly or knowingly to do with the production of the articles themselves. Appended to the profile on Officer Barns was a story about the Blazier incident entitled "A Citizen Fights for His Rights — Was He Wrong?" In this story, the reporter recounted interviews he had held with Blazier, Barns, and McGee sometime well after the incident had been disposed of by the courts; he also quoted from the arrest report filed the night Blazier was arrested. No mention was made in any of the articles of my presence on the scene in Union City, nor could I detect the use of any private information I conceivably might have slipped to this reporter about the Blazier incident during our numerous conversations. Moreover, I felt then (and now) that taken as a whole the stories were, if anything, biased toward the police view of the world, romantic in their depiction of the "harsh, bitter, and dangerous tasks performed by the men in blue," and downright evasive when it came to describing the circumstances through which Blazier almost lost his life.

Nonetheless, the patrolmen who were featured in the stories — in particular, Barns — were agitated and angered by what they took to be a rude violation of their privacy and with what they also took to be the antipolice stance taken by the paper. Within a month after the articles appeared, two separate civil suits were filed by the Union City Patrolmen's Association on behalf of two of the profiled officers (including Barns), charging the newspaper with libel and slander.[4] The newspaper then subpoenaed my testimony and records, apparently on the reporter's request, in order to support what they must have felt to be the essential truthfulness of the stories.

I was in a moral fix. I could obey the subpoena, turn over my notes, and perhaps assist in making the newspaper's case. Or I could refuse to comply, risk possible sanction, but in the process protect what I took to be the best interests of the patrolmen I had known in Union City. I chose the latter on multiple grounds. First, the terms of the subpoenas were so broad and inclusive that many other officers (across the ranks) would unavoidably be made vulnerable to departmental or legal sanction for actions having nothing whatsoever to do with the Blazier incident. Buried within my notes were numerous raw details about questionable, irregular, and illegal police actions with the names of those involved (or said to be involved)

---

[4] To be more complete, I should note that in the background of the two police suits against the newspaper stand several other pertinent details. Among most of the policemen I knew in Union City ran some intense and hostile feelings toward the paper. It was seen as "a liberal rag," "out to get the police," "distorting the news," and more generally quite unsympathetic to the men of the police department. Furthermore the paper had also kept a recent police scandal in the daily headlines, whereas the other major paper in the community appeared to play down the story, relegating the emerging specifics of the corruption disclosures to the inside pages. Needless to say most policemen did not take kindly to the one paper's screaming display of embarrassing matters. Finally, the Patrolman's Benevolent Association (the organization sponsoring the libel actions) also had an ax to grind since its president was at times mocked and treated quite unseriously on the editorial pages of the paper. All of these factors probably played a part in the officers' decision to sue the paper. More details were no doubt also pertinent, but, since I was some distance from Union City during the time of legal maneuvering, the face-to-face social relations necessary to learn some of these details were unavailable to me. I should note too that because of this distance my own anxieties in the matter were heightened, since I could not really understand what exactly was going on beneath the public surface in Union City at that time. Only later did I learn some of the factors that apparently prompted the police suit, factors which I have summarized in a most incomplete and dross fashion here. See Harris (1973:50–52) for a similar view of how the police view the press.

necessarily attached. For instance, I had materials bearing on possible police burglaries, drug dealings, payoffs, planting of evidence, and so on. Many of these incidents were, to be sure, merely conjecture on my part or unverified (and perhaps unverifiable) stories I had heard told by patrolmen in Union City (usually about other patrolmen). But a few of these tales had been confirmed by my own observations.

Needless to say, however, I wished to keep information gathered in confidence confidential, and although I had no doubt betrayed this principle through some of my all-too-casual conversations with the police reporter, I was not about to compound this error with another patently more serious and extensive betrayal. Second, I had previously given sworn testimony on the Blazier incident, and a tape of my interview was presumably available from the police department. This tape was eventually turned over to the newspaper, although it took a court order to pry it out of a most reluctant department. Finally, the attorney representing the newspaper in the case had also been a key public figure, a special federal prosecutor in a police scandal that had erupted in Union City several years before, and hence would have probably been a poor choice indeed to handle sensitive materials. At the deposition hearing itself I appeared and brought with me the subpoenaed materials but refused to turn them over to either the court or the newspaper. On the advice of my lawyers I based my claims for privilege on the elegant, prestigious, but thoroughly nonexistent grounds of "research confidentiality."

The legal staff representing the newspaper then began preparing a case for a district court in Massachusetts in which they would ask the court to find me in criminal contempt for not having complied with the terms of the subpoena. They would argue that the public's right to know (in this case, the newspaper's right to know) clearly outweighed my ambiguous claims for research confidentiality. Before I went to trial, however, a Union City judge in a preliminary hearing on one of the police libel and slander suits dismissed the case on the grounds that the officers had failed to show damage as a result of the newspaper articles. The other suit was soon dropped by the Patrolmen's Association, and my case then became moot. This was most fortunate, for I had been advised by a number of attorneys and scholars that I had a very poor case and would most likely lose in the district court. Hypothetically, at least, I was at the time prepared to go to jail if necessary, believing it unlikely (but untested) that I would be kept there for more than a few days. Yet in cases of this variety there are precious few precedents to go by.[5]

---

[5] Despite some claims to the contrary I must emphasize the point that *there is absolutely no legal protection guaranteed to the social scientist on the grounds of research confidentiality.* Perhaps the leading legal works on the confidentiality of sources and data in social research are Ruebhausen and Brim (1965) and Nejelski and Lerman (1971). However, both of these articles were written before the U.S.

Fieldwork Ethics

It would be easy to oversimplify the ethical issues raised by this case. My dilemma was not simply deciding post hoc whether or not to turn over what I took to be confidential materials to the court or the newspaper. Rather, as the case partially illustrates, I was making ethical choices (some good, some not so good) every day during the study. Merely my presence among the skid row squad of patrolmen may have served symbolically as a signal to the press that perhaps something unusual or interesting was occurring there, something that had potential for "good copy." Nor was my dilemma confined simply to deciding post hoc what material to publish. Very clearly, moral choices are made day in and day out in the field when deciding what data to go after, how to get them, who to talk to, how and where to record and store data, and so forth.[6] Too often, discussions of ethical materials in the social sciences turn only on either the decisions concerning the disclosure of research intent to those who are studied, or on the problems posed by the publication of sensitive materials, so that the privacy, reputation, and good will of the studied are protected. These are important matters, of course, but they fail to touch directly on the sorts of immediate, personal, and excruciating decisions made by a researcher working out practical solutions to the multitude of problems faced in the field.[7]

Supreme Court's decision in the Branzburg v. Hayes (33L. Ed. 2d 626) case, in which the court ruled that the First Amendment does not provide a newsman (and perhaps, by implication, a researcher) any constitutional testimonial privileges against answering court-directed questions as to either the identity of particular research subjects or information received in confidence. However, the only occasion I know of in which a social scientist was actually jailed for refusing to divulge information was the Samuel Popkin case in Massachusetts. In 1972 Popkin served seven days for refusing to provide a grand jury certain information regarding the activities of Daniel Ellsberg at the Rand Corporation. Popkin was interviewing Rand personnel (including Ellsberg) during the period in which the Pentagon Papers were released, and the grand jury was interested in what he might know about the circumstances under which the secret papers were made public (see Carroll, 1973, for a full discussion of this case). For a broader perspective on some of these legal issues see Yablonski (1965, 1968); Vidich, Bensman, and Stein (eds.) (1964); and a special issue of *Social Problems*, 14, 2, 1967.

[6] Further complications in these matters have been introduced of late with the advent of university committees and rules on what is often called the "experimental use of human subjects." If this trend continues, it may make certain kinds of research increasingly difficult to pursue, since, to receive approval for a particular project, the researcher may have to produce some stringent documentation as to the "importance" of the planned study as well as the "care" that has been taken beforehand to protect the subjects of the investigation from potential harm or embarrassment.

[7] Aside from the writing around the issue of a fieldworker's use of either open or disguised observational techniques, little is available in the literature that bears upon the everyday decision making engaged in by the researcher while in the field. The implication is consequently that the fieldworker need not worry much about ethical matters until deciding what material to publish and how to present it ("do whatever you want in the field, but be careful when writing it up"). Perhaps the problem lies in the relatively few detailed descriptions of what it is that fieldworkers do.

From this standpoint virtually every aspect of my study in Union City represents the personal resolution of various ethical dilemmas. There are no easy or a priori moral stances to be taken by the researcher in fieldwork situations. Certainly, fieldworkers cannot know what they are "getting into" until they "get into" it. As Becker (1964) has observed, there may be some very broad guidelines available, such as not violating confidences or bringing harm to subjects, but in practice these guidelines are elusive and mean different things to different people. Seldom has there been even a modest attempt to provide a detailed interpretation of the behavioral or contextual implications of guidelines as protecting one's informants. Indeed, there is something of a general consensus — at least among sociologists — that rejects the idea of producing concrete, specified rules for the "ethical conduct" of field research.[8] Some reject the idea primarily as inadvisable and impractical, since such rules would likely preclude the gathering of certain kinds of data (Douglas, 1976; Roth, 1962). Others reject it as reprehensible, if not repugnant, since such rules would in effect place the fieldworker in a debatable but morally superior position vis-à-vis others, including those who are studied (Klockars, 1974; Rainwater and Pittman, 1967). Still others reject it as theoretically impossible, given the inherently incomplete and evolutionary character of all rules (Mehan and Wood, 1975; Becker and Friedson, 1964). Nonetheless, ethical decisions do get made and accounted for by fieldworkers. Below I will briefly review what I consider to be the most ethically troublesome areas raised by the in situ observation of the police. I hasten to add, however, the following discussion merely illustrates rather than resolves the moral fix a fieldworker may encounter when working in law-enforcement settings. In short, there is no suitable solution that will fit the peculiar and always particular issues that are raised in field studies. Ultimately, the choice about when and where to draw a moral and ethical line must rest on an individual, not a collective, conscience.

Participation

How far does a participant observer go in assisting the police with their daily tasks? Had Blazier actually been fighting the officers, for instance, I have few doubts that I would have entered the fray on the side of the police.

---

[8] Take for example Rule 5 of the American Sociological Association's Code of Ethics, which reads in part: "Confidential information provided by a research subject must be treated as such by a sociologist. Even though research information is not a privileged communication under the law, the sociologist must *as far as possible* protect subjects and informants. *Any promises* made to such persons must be honored ..." (italics mine). On the basis of this professional edict certain questions can be raised not only about the meaning of the phrase "as far as possible," but also about the meaning of "promises." Since subjects may deceive themselves as to what the research is about, interpreting what constitutes a "promise" may well be difficult. As I have suggested elsewhere, the research bargains that are struck in the field always have a fluid character (Van Maanen, 1978b).

This is a sort of "member test" for ethical decision making. If one joins with the police in order to study them, one is under considerable obligation to help them when needed. The height of moral duplicity would be for an observer to pose as a friend and supporter of the police (and there is unlikely to be any way around this if one is to develop a sustained and intimate research relationship with them) and then refuse to abide by this pose when aid is required. I know from my own experience that on occasion patrolmen entered certain situations without additional police support solely because of the additional safety they felt my presence provided them. Of course, this does not imply that the researcher need go along on all matters that do not endanger the safety of the observed, nor does it necessarily mean that one go along blindly on all matters that do. But the fieldworker does have the obligation to inform those who are studied just where the line will be drawn or perhaps just when that line is being approached. As I have suggested elsewhere, I drew few lines (Van Maanen, 1978b).

It is important to note also that many if not most of the agreements between the researcher and researched in field situations are tacit. That is, research understandings about who will do what, when, and where arise recursively over time as a result of, for example, previous silences maintained by the researcher about potentially incriminating and embarrassing matters. These understandings may also come about as a consequence of specific cooperative or collusive arrangements that emerge from particular incidents. I once was privy to a conversation in which a veteran police officer constructed a cover story with the able assistance of several other officers concerning the sloughing off of a knife on an unwary suspect arrested for a relatively minor offense (Van Maanen, 1973). Shortly thereafter, since I had not reported the incident, I too was embraced in the verbal conspiracy that surrounded the affair and was therefore as vulnerable to sanction as were all the officers involved in developing the story line. I suspect any researcher who spends more than a superficial amount of time with the police is party to much information of a discrediting (and probably illegal) nature. Thus, those who remain are likely to have entered, however inadvertently, into a silent bond of mutual protection — a bond supported by what Westley (1970) called the "no-rat rule." Yet, if one wishes to be where the action takes place in police organizations, a certain moral relativism is required. As Buckner (1967) suggests, firsthand observation may well require the suspension of single-minded (perhaps simpleminded) standards for judging the behavior of others. At least in police organizations, fieldwork demands of the researcher an ability to allow to pass without accusatory comment certain actions that may well be viewed as morally repugnant. The hope, of course, is that in the end the truth, when it is depicted fully, will help us all out.

Nonetheless, the observer in police settings is subject normally to the same restrictions, both legal and departmental, that presumably regulate the conduct of those who live everyday in the setting. The fieldworker is not beyond the law in this respect. The Blazier affair makes this point quite well. I felt I was under an obligation to report what I had witnessed to IID when ordered to do so. And, if called upon, I would have been willing to testify in court upon this matter, but *only* upon this particular matter. I was under no illusions that the cloak of science could or should protect me from legal complications. In refusing to testify to broader matters, I exercised a moral freedom, not a legal one. The point here is simply what I see to be the ethical necessity facing researchers to share the same risks as those they observe. This is the "dirty hands test." The researcher whose hands are dirty must run the same risks as anyone else in the situation. Fieldworkers may refuse to give information on a specific incident, but they cannot expect special compensation for so doing simply because they were also doing something called research. It is not a cost/benefit ratio that will decide the just and proper ethics of the fieldworker's response to a certain situation. Indeed, there is no way the vague program called "advancing knowledge" can ever be balanced on the same scale against legal and human considerations.

Being forced into the fire, as it were, makes immediate and practical the ethical choices made by researchers in police situations. They may choose to observe illegal acts, but they do so with the knowledge that they are as culpable as those performing such acts. Of course, researchers may voice their objections to what they observe, thus forcing the police to contend with yet another influence on their actions, but these choices will be made in context, not on the basis of decree. The real dilemma for persons doing police studies comes after some illegal activity has been observed. Then the researcher must decide what shall be done, if anything, with or about such observations.[9]

Guilty Knowledge and the Protection of Individuals

As the documentary films of Frederick Wiseman graphically demonstrate, people will engage in sometimes incredibly stark and incriminating actions while in front of klieg lights and cameras. Those who have studied the police firsthand report much the same thing (e.g., Skolnick, 1966; Reiss, 1971; Rubinstein, 1973; Manning, 1977). Perhaps police departments, like all organizations, are characterized as much by patterned evasion of some norms as they are by strict adherence to other norms. If one wishes to observe these evasions repeatedly, it is obvious that the only tool available is

[9] Ironically, the best discussions on these matters are to be found in the literature on observing criminals. Polsky (1967:109–143) is both succinct and blunt when he argues: "If one is effectively to study adult criminals in their natural settings, he must make the moral decision that in some ways he will break the law himself. He need not be a 'participant' observer and commit the criminal acts under study, yet he has to witness such acts or be taken into confidence about them and not blow the whistle" (133). See also Becker (1970b:30–45).

a verbal and behavioral commitment to protect the confidentiality of sources who reveal and sometimes demonstrate such evasions. This means in effect that the researcher must violate the law in order to understand something of its implementations. There is no way around this; if fieldworkers were to reveal their personal sources of information (as the law technically demands), it would not be long before they had no personal sources of information left.

Maintaining the confidentiality of individual informants is then intended not only to protect the individual from harm, but also to protect the research enterprise itself. Fieldwork proceeds more or less successfully depending upon the degree to which those with the data trust those who want the data to protect them from personal, social, or organizational injury. Thus, there are expedient, self-serving, and moral reasons for guarding the trust of informants. Perhaps with information gathered covertly some moral strings are cut, but even here the researcher must place considerable reliance on the data resulting from human ties the covert observer has established within the organization — ties that *would not exist* were it not for the fact that research is being done. Only the "unobserved observer," who works entirely but surreptitiously with data gathered unobtrusively from public, archival, or other indirect sources, would seem to be free of this moral constraint binding researchers to those whom they observe. In studies where any disclosure of purpose is made, the rule of thumb would appear to be that the closer one is to an informant and the more explicit the promise of confidentiality, the greater the researcher's obligation becomes to protect the informant.

This rule of thumb is hardly absolute, however. How far would I have gone to protect my police acquaintances had Blazier been killed by the police that January evening? There must always be the possibility that the researcher's personal morality will force him to violate implicit or explicit research agreements or perhaps even to abandon the study itself. To suggest the contrary would be to make a machine of the researcher and to dehumanize fieldwork.

Who Is to Be Harmed?

Becker (1967) has argued with considerable justification that the principal ethical problem in publishing the results of field studies lies in deciding who is to be harmed, not whether or not harm will result. Paraphrasing Becker, any study that is done well will no doubt please some people and anger others. Thus, the choice boils down to who will be angered. This problem arises precisely because the social scientist, of necessity, often reports on matters that some would prefer to keep quiet. When fieldworkers write up a research report, they will inevitably betray the trust and confidence some informants have placed in them. To wit, throughout my study

I attempted continually to convey the impression to police administrators that my work was harmless to them. Eventually, however, I knew I was bound to violate whatever misplaced trust I might have created, since the tone and thrust of what I wrote would undoubtedly indicate that things were not as the administrators said they were and, furthermore, that little or nothing was being done about it.

For the general readership individuals are relatively easy to disguise in field reports. Particular administrations and organizations are less easy to disguise, although it is common practice to try. This latter problem I find less morally bothersome than the former, since administrations and organizations have far greater resources to defend themselves or to strike back than do individuals, particularly those at the lower levels, who are relatively helpless. Yet, even in disguise damage may result to those inside an organization, where it may be reasonably easy to determine who's who in the fieldworker's report. For example, I have little doubt that several of the individuals involved in certain anecdotes I have published are, at best, thinly disguised and hence recognizable to intimates within the Union City Police Department. The problem, of course, lies in forecasting the likely consequences of any given report, a near impossible task.

To take the Blazier case again as an illustration, when I appeared at the deposition hearing, the attorney representing the Union City newspaper read for the record a section of one of my published papers that dealt with the incident in detail and used the fictive names of Barns and McGee to identify the officers involved. I was then asked the true identities of not only Barns and McGee but of the sergeant, the reserve officers, and other policemen on or around the scene that night. I refused to answer publicly, again on the feeble grounds of "research confidentiality." Privately I refused to answer because of the general research bargain that had unfolded between myself and the police in Union City, because of my close personal ties with the particular officers, and because of the potential complications that my answering one question might have on the other more general questions that were being asked. Further, the Blazier case was over, I could do nothing to erase what had already happened nor was I at all interested in seeing the officers reprimanded for an act all too familiar to police observers (Chevigny, 1968, 1972; Reiss, 1971; Westley, 1970). To disclose my notes and memories of the incident beyond that which I had done for the IID investigators would very clearly have injured the officers involved. Yet, there was also a related factor in this decision, a factor I now discuss with some trepidation.

Overrapport

Before beginning my studies, I felt, in the abstract, that if and when I penetrated the patrol division in Union City, I could carve out a rather non-participatory research role. For a vast number of reasons discussed elsewhere this did not turn out to be the case (Van Maanen, 1978b). Indeed, after the police academy I wished to be treated as any other rookie might be treated and wanted to see the "real" nature of police work. By and large this occurred, but I also believe that I created the conditions under which a rather tragic charade was acted out for my benefit partially as a result of my initial and rather full acceptance into the police world.

I had just returned to Union City after an absence of over two years when Chester Blazier was arrested. The men I spoke with during my return stay were apparently quite happy to see me again and, of critical importance here, were seemingly very willing to display what they had learned occupationally since we had parted. This prideful situation was not obvious to me at the time, but it was some six weeks later. I began to develop an inkling about what might be occurring as I watched my former classmates work rather hard — in comparison to what I had observed to be the routines several years before — at certain aspects of their job. Indeed, several men remarked that they wanted to show me what it was like now that they "really knew" what they were doing on the street. On patrol we always ate in the better restaurants at a reduced or nonexistent price. This so-called policeman's discount or freebie was on several occasions enforced openly and argumentatively by my police hosts on patrol. I watched some of my former colleagues as they sought out, pushed around, and goaded several of their informants apparently only to demonstrate to me the fact that they now had their own intelligence networks — though to a man they thought their informants to be "scum." I once witnessed a bizarre encounter in which a boy, perhaps ten or eleven years old, was verbally assaulted and then thrown to the pavement because he had aimed a ceremonially upright third finger in the direction of the patrol unit as it passed by — a gesture from a child that would have been routinely ignored (or returned) in my previous experiences. These and other similar events forced me eventually to reckon with the possibility that perhaps my police friends were literally showing off for my benefit. They were occasionally taking action on my account as a part of documenting their acquired competence. In short, they were demonstrating for my benefit (though perhaps for their own as well) that they had learned the police game thoroughly. They were now in command and therefore, as many said in both word and deed, "did not have to take any shit on the street." I cannot unequivocally prove that the Blazier incident was a direct result of my presence on the scene, though I believe this to be the case.[10]

[10] Obviously, other interpretations are also possible. Perhaps the patrolmen I knew had really learned to be *continually* brutish, nasty, and downright vicious on the street. Perhaps too the fact that the night was slow or that Blazier had "mouthed off" to the officers had much to do with the incident. Maybe the trigger for the beating was Blazier's race, social status as a "welfare case," or apparent sexual preference.

Skolnick (1966:36) has remarked ". . . if an observer's presence does alter police behavior, I believe it can be assumed that it does so only in one direction. I can see no reason why police would, for example, behave more harshly to a prisoner in the presence of an observer than in his absence." I think perhaps I have stumbled sadly upon one such reason. The police, like all of us, take considerable pride in some of the work they do. And when the occasion presents itself, they will exhibit the special skills they believe they possess, particularly for what they take to be an appreciative audience. The participant observer who has gained their trust and who seems therefore to exhibit a good deal of existential concern for their welfare is no doubt representative of an unusually appreciative audience. After all, the observer claims to guarantee anonymity, often provides assistance on mundane and not-so-mundane matters, is empathic to an extreme, is nonevaluative in the field, and in general acts out the part of a knowledgeable "police buff." The paradox is that this is the way I believe the researcher must behave if he is to penetrate the rings of individual and collective secrecy enclosing police actions.[11]

Miller (1952:98) coined the apt but bulky term *overrapport* to express "the idea that the researcher may be so closely related to the observed that his investigations are impeded." He used this term to refer to those field situations in which the researcher cannot question closely the basic attitudes of the observed because such questioning might destroy the "all-accepting friendships" that have been carved out in the setting. He also used the term to refer to those situations in which the observer becomes so closely attached to the feelings and sentiments of the studied group that the detachment necessary to carry out the ethnographic craft is lost (i.e., "to go native"). To these very real dangers of fieldwork I would add a third: Overrapport can be said to exist in those situations where the observed consistently behave in a fashion designed to increase or maximize their

---

Whatever alternatives exist, they are all beyond my reach to thoroughly overrule, though personally I find these reasons unconvincing in light of my own experiences in the police world. It is probable that all of the above accounts provide something of the necessary or enabling conditions for the event's occurrence; however, I believe that it was my presence that represented the sufficient or clinching condition.

[11] I must note that these "tactics" were hardly conscious or sharply motivated ploys I developed to further the study itself. At the time, unfortunate as it may be, I thought about them little more than I thought, about when to draw a breath. In retrospect, the tendency is to make my methods appear considerably more rational and sly than in fact they were. I wished only to get as close to the "action" as I could, and I felt the best way to do so would be to develop personal friendships in the field. Once these friendships were struck, however, they took on a momentum of their own. Furthermore, both the Blazier affair and the concrete fear of being jailed forced me to consider far more closely my methods than perhaps I would have done otherwise. Although my field notes do allow me to trace many of the specific details of what at the time seemed to be a most inchoate set of complex and shifting beliefs about my emerging fieldwork methodology, I am in agreement with Burke (1961:446) that "the situation remembers, not the man."

status and worth in the eyes of a peculiar kind of intimate, the fieldworker. I choose these words carefully for I am talking of matters that go well beyond the conventional experimenter effects described in the behavioral science literature (Rosenthal, 1976). Indeed, as the term itself implies, I am referring only to those situations in which a warm and trusting relationship has already been created and the researcher is known by the researched to have some knowledge of the everyday activities that take place in the setting. It is therefore not so much merely a Goffmanesque matter of impression management per se as it is a matter of the particular impression that is to be managed. The phenomenon I am describing is something akin to youngsters considering whether or not to dive from the highest springboard at the public plunge. They will spend their courage, as it were, only during those periods when their familiar and respected acquaintances are both present and watching. Overrapport, in the sense that I append to it here, implied that it is the close personal regard between the observer and the observed that is crucial to the matter, not the simple presence of the observer. . . .

Given that there is likely to be no "best" way to conduct field studies and that each study depends upon the situational and biographical particulars of who is observing whom for what purpose, what strategic options does the fieldworker have available to choose from in order to counter the potential trap of overrapport? Taking the so-called neutral stance is perhaps one tactical option. Yet, at least in the police world neutrality is unlikely to get the researcher very far. Indeed, the game of work played by most policemen pits various teams, cliques, cabals, or other vertically and horizontally partitioned players within the organization against one another (Manning, 1976a; Rubinstein, 1973; Van Maanen, 1973). Hence, an observer who wants to gain any appreciable knowledge about the players on any given team must at least appear to stand with them at least for a while. Furthermore, patrolmen in general must be assured that the fieldworker understands their orientation and position on certain matters. Yet, to demonstrate such an understanding implies an ability to take the side of the observed by using their language, demonstrating a concern for their problems, and displaying the ability to evaluate their actions as they do. Over many occasions such a stance is unlikely to be interpreted as neutral. The bromide of "neutrality" is therefore both unstable and replete with the possibility of entrapment for the researcher. . . .

In the final analysis establishing the proper amount of rapport with the observed is something of an intangible creation, and even if it can be achieved, it is certain to decay. It represents at best a passing or transitional stage in the long-range temporal history of a research relationship. Whether or not such a relationship will eventually move toward under- or over-rapport is a matter over which the fieldworker has some control, though probably less control than desired (or perhaps believed).

I do not think overrapport is common in police studies. In my case it arose out of a lengthy and intense period of participation during the observed's initiation period into the occupation. In this period camaraderie and identification with one another were both natural and unavoidable. Furthermore, many of my most difficult moral problems arose primarily because of a long absence in which a warm welcome back should have been (but was not) expected. The overly aggressive patrol tactics I witnessed upon my return more or less disappeared once I had reestablished a routine observational post in the patrol division. Indeed, the convincing bit of evidence I draw on in this regard comes from those officers with whom I spent three or more shifts upon my return. By the third shift together things had begun to settle down into a rather normal tour of patrol duty. Such tours again began to be filled by long breaks, much conversation about non-police matters, and a working style governed by the calls dispatched from headquarters over the police radio. Yet even here there was a certain pretense about the police activities I observed that told me that at least some patrolmen were apparently trying harder to be "good cops" than they normally would. A few in private said as much. Consider the following, in part congratulatory, yet nonetheless chilling remark made to me by a young patrolman I had once worked closely with on the street:

> You know John, I miss you a lot out there. You really got me to thinking about some shit I don't usually think about. . . . It was fun working with you 'cause you're not like most of the other bulls around here who don't really want to do very much at all. *When you were along, we always seemed to find some real police work to do.*

The choice of what the researcher should do under these circumstances still remains unanswered. And, as I have tried to show in this paper, this choice will always be difficult for there are no magical formulas to offer which can alleviate the very real moral dilemmas of fieldwork and yet allow the work to proceed unchanged. In my own case, I have continued my work in Union City, avoiding whenever and wherever possible those officers whom I felt were most likely to become carried away with their police performance as a result of my presence on the scene.[12] However, it is

[12] Unlike the issues of participation, privacy, and who is to be harmed, the fieldworker has few moral or strategic options available to him other than avoidance when it becomes clear that certain others are continually reacting more to his affable presence on the scene than to the more ordinary matters at hand. In such situations, he has become a part of what he originally wished to understand and has ruptured the necessary link between sustained observation and minimal disruption of social world under investigation. The researcher may not have "gone native" in the sense of adopting the ways and perspectives of the observed, but his observations are likely to be as misleading, if not more so, than if he had. Based upon my own experience, I suspect such troubling situations are far more common in police field studies than one would gather from reading the carefully assembled research reports that have appeared. Indeed, it is often difficult simply to detect the presence of the person who stands behind the research report. See Van Maanen (1978b) for a further discussion of this issue.

certainly the case that other fieldworkers might have left the scene entirely. Others might have become far more actively engaged in the social drama than I. Unfortunately, even with the luxury of considerable hindsight, I can not conclusively or with total conviction say that the moral choice I made was a good one. To be sure, I can defend it but it is up to others to decide whether or not to accept my defense.

On Fieldworkers and Those Exposed to Fieldwork: Federal Regulations and Moral Issues

Murray L. Wax

While much has been written about the dangers of research for the participants, both in medical and social science research, there is almost no attention paid to the effects of different "control systems" on the creation of science. Participants will not be harmed if no research is conducted, but then there will be no empirically based scientific knowledge. If the creation of scientific knowledge is brought to a standstill by procedures designed to protect the subjects, is the problem solved? (Reynolds 1972:706)

Federal Regulations and Social Research

Universities and their researchers have suddenly been affected by a set of federal laws and regulations which are novel in scope and sanctions. These rules require a multiplication of administrative procedures, an expansion of university bureaucracy, and a large expenditure of faculty energies. Their precise effects on the conduct of research are (as yet) unknown, but even casual observation yields the impression that some types of valuable research are being discontinued and others radically redesigned, while overall the pace is slowed and the flexibility curtailed by procedural constraints. In short, the traditional and hard-won rights of academic freedom, including the freedoms of research and scholarship, are being threatened from a novel direction and with unusual rationalizations.

Despite the considerable impact upon social research, these laws and regulations were brought into being without prior consultation with professional associations and without regard to social-scientific reviews of the moral questions and dilemmas of their researches. While it cannot be claimed that social scientists are more moral than others, they have been highly conscious of the moral effects and political implications of their research activities, and they have generated a significant body of literature, as well as pertinent action. Thus, the Society for Applied Anthropology reviewed the issues of their professional work at numerous meetings and produced a Statement on Professional and Ethical Responsibilities (1974). The American Anthropological Association maintains a functioning Committee on Ethics, which has dealt with both real and hypothetical cases.

Reproduced by permission of the Society for Applied Anthropology from *Human Organization* 36(3):321–328, 1977.

The American Sociological Association appointed a committee which framed an elaborate code of ethics that triggered a good deal of discussion, but which failed of adoption, mainly (I should guess) because most sociologists were professionally sceptical about the protections afforded "clients" by such organizational codes.

In each generation of social scientists, a few cases have become prototypical of the ethical problems generated by research activities: Springdale (Becker 1964; Vidich and Bensman 1964), "T-Rooms" (Horowitz and Rainwater 1970; von Hoffman 1970), Camelot (Horowitz 1965; Sjoberg 1967), counterinsurgency and anthropological fieldwork, etc. Yet, so far as is apparent, the body of federal regulations noted above were imposed and instituted in disregard of the rich and complex professional discussions of these troublesome cases.

The Human Subjects' Protective System

In the course of biomedical researches, several experiments were performed which placed subjects, unwittingly, in substantial jeopardy. As these experiments became known, they became the subject of public discussion and condemnation. Even more notorious were certain psychological experiments which were simple and colorful and which imposed upon innocent subjects some risks that may have been psychically significant (although there is no reliable judgment on these risks). In the climate of the 1970s these incidents precipitated the federal formulation and imposition of regulations designed to protect the human subjects of biomedical and behavioral researches, notably DHEW regulations on "Protection of Human Subjects" (Federal Register 1975) as mandated by the National Research Act (Public Law 93-348).

Underlying this regulative system is an imagery of the research act as a contractarian transaction between two strangers: on the one hand, the knowledgeable and powerful experimenter (e.g., physician), and, on the other hand, the ignorant and powerless subject (e.g., clinic patient). The image assumes that the researcher has influence and authority such as to intimidate the subject and that the latter unwittingly allows his person to be used for the performance of dangerous clinical tests. The regulations then attempt to redress the balance of power by insisting that the experimenter provide information to the potential subject, making it clear that the latter is free to withhold consent from participating. Thus, the physician-experimenter may wish to compare the efficacies of two different drugs in a clinical trial. The regulations are supposed to protect the potential subject by insuring that the nature of the experiment and of its possible consequences are explained to him and that he is then offered alternatives.

These regulations were universalistic in that they were applied, not merely to the kinds of biomedical and psychological researches wherein had occurred the original disreputable incidents, but throughout the range of university (and institutional) activities that deal with human beings who might be denominated as "the subjects" of research.

Fieldwork and Human Subjects Protective Systems

Historical

During the past two centuries, the social sciences have made great advances, consequent in large measure upon an enlarged and deepened knowledge of the peoples and social systems of the world. For obtaining that knowledge one of the principal methodologies has been personal intensive fieldwork. Often known as "participant observation," the methodology underwent its primary development with the investigations of Bronislaw Malinowski in the Trobriand Islands and with his subsequent series of publications (Wax 1972). However, prior to Malinowski, the methodology was employed to some extent by natural historians, ethnographers, explorers, and missionaries (e.g., Göhre 1895; Doughty 1936), who helped to generate the data that stimulated the theoretical work of Karl Marx, Emile Durkheim, Sigmund Freud, Edward B. Tylor, and others.

Malinowski conducted his own fieldwork among an exotic, nonliterate folk who had been incorporated into an imperialistic system. But the impetus of his work was such that even among the first generation of his students there were scholars, such as Powdermaker (1966), who applied the methodology to the investigation of race relations in a southern U.S. town (1939), to the cinema industry of Hollywood, and to mining towns of Rhodesia. Others, such as William Foote Whyte (1955), applied it during the late 1930s to study urban neighborhood groups; and, in time, still others, to mental asylums, schools, factories, and taverns (Adams and Preiss 1960; Denzin 1970; Filstead 1970; Hammond 1967; Vidich, Bensman, and Stein 1964).

Power, Dependency, and Interdependency

I propose now to examine some of the realities of fieldwork in order to contrast them with the model of research which is implicit in the regulations of the Human Subjects Protective System. Because fieldwork can involve such different researchers in an incredible variety of situations, it is not easy to generalize; moreover, the literature is not as ample nor as frank as one should prefer. For simplicity and brevity, I will tend to draw on the model of community studies. Critical readers can extend or modify this presentation in relationship to other varieties of fieldwork.

In contrast to biomedical research, where the physician confronts the hapless patient, most fieldwork places the investigator in a position of social inferiority and moral dependency with regard to the people he (or she) hopes to study. In the most extreme case of ethnographic research among an exotic people, the researcher is ignorant of their language and customs, yet desirous of learning them, so that socially his position (in this respect) is akin to that of a child. In addition, he is often dependent upon these people for the resources basic to existence, shelter, food, and water. While he may have some resources (trade goods, cash, survival rations), he is in a position of economic dependency which requires that he enlist the assistance of the local folk in order to survive and maintain himself over time.

Even in situations within a civilized society, where the group to be studied seems to be politically subordinate, as, for example, a prison population, or inhabitants of an urban minority ghetto, the fieldworker finds that he has minimal resources of power. Thus, if he strives to live in ghetto housing, he may not be able to achieve this safely without the protective hospitality of local residents (Stringfellow 1966).

The relationship or interdependency between fieldworker and people studied has been well analyzed and illustrated by Rosalie H. Wax (1971). In successful fieldwork, the two parties manage to develop a relationship of social parity in which each party may be of assistance to the other. The fieldworker teaches or trains "natives" to be respondents and informants about the workings of their culture or group; they in turn train him how to be helpful and useful, in accomplishing goals important to themselves. In many cases, the fieldworker can be the source of distinctive kinds of wealth; sometimes he brings knowledge of the operations of institutions important to the local folk; in the past, and still today in some cases, he might be a medical resource for exotic peoples. In such fashion, an interdependency is constructed.

While it is often true that to the people studied the fieldworker represents agencies or a nation of power and wealth, it does not follow that he will be granted the assistance necessary to the achievement of his research. In many areas of the contemporary world, being identified as American (or even European) is more likely to result in political condemnation than in respectful assistance. Likewise, within the U.S., a person identified with powerful institutions may find this more of a handicap (or a mixed blessing) than an asset. Even when the fieldworker is identified as being associated with power and wealth, this does not translate into an ability to coerce people into assisting his field research.

Flexibility and Prior Consent

In the formal experimental designs of biomedical and psychological researchers, the experimenter can describe nearly exactly what manipulations he proposes to perform with what population of subjects. In contrast, the fieldworker can only partially predict. In her anthropological autobiography, Powdermaker (1966) describes a range of such difficulties: on her first field trip she prepared to work in highland New Guinea (and had studied the relevant grammar), but she ended in a coastal village of New Ireland (in a different linguistic environment); on a later field trip she prepared to work in Uganda (and had studied Swahili), but she ended in Rhodesia (again in a different linguistic environment). Even where the fieldworker can work with the people he had planned to study, he may find that the powers-that-be will not permit him to reside among them or may attach onerous conditions to his enterprise, so that his original research design becomes meaningless (as happened to Wax and Wax among the "Six Friendly Tribes"; cf. Wax 1971). Under these circumstances, many, if not most, fieldworkers find it difficult to conduct research in strict accord with their initial and prior conceptualizations, and they cannot reliably request approval for a project which may not prove to be the one actually conducted.

Again, once located in the field in a durable situation, the fieldworker may discover phenomena of far greater interest than those which initially he thought to study (e.g., the local folk may be in the throes of social or political transformation; or their economic situation may be drastically different). Or, having left the field, the investigator may find in analyzing his notes the materials for a discussion quite different than he had thought would be the focus of his researches.

Abstract Projects and Personal Realities

Few of the peoples of the world understand the goals and ideals of social science; of those who might comprehend, fewer still feel any involvement in their realization. Under those circumstances, it is meaningless or difficult for the fieldworker to provide an initial *exact* picture of what he intends to achieve, in order that he might thereby gain the permission and consent of the group or its leaders. Most of these people will judge the fieldworker as a fellow human being and by the pragmatic standards of how, or whether, they might derive some benefit from his presence. Conversely, in some politicized contexts, local leaders may hope to secure advantage by attacking a fieldworker as a representative of an alien or undesirable power, and in these situations, abstract oral explanations stressing disciplinary competencies or virtues are of no avail. In general, most fieldworkers find it necessary to describe themselves and characterize their activities in terms of the roles that are locally familiar or intelligible.

In general, I would hold with Erikson (1967) and others that the fieldworker should identify himself as a researcher and describe to local folk what he plans or hopes to accomplish. Not only is such a narration morally proper; but, usually and in the long run it also facilitates the research, because the fieldworker has identified himself as a person who will be inquiring and seeking to observe and generally wishing to learn and understand these alien ways. Yet, here again, it is important to recall that relationships are constructed over time, and it may often happen that the explanation which makes but little initial sense can at the close of fieldwork be much better comprehended, so that the fieldworker's accounting of himself may therefore vary during the course of his research. An especially interesting case of the problems of describing oneself and one's study came with Galliher's restudy of Plainville (1964).

Even greater complexity derives from the tendency of the fieldworker to conduct his craft where he may be. As Roth (1962) has commented: "Most of us, in fact, never cease observing the social sphere about us and are continually interpreting the behavior of people about us. Some of these observations are systematically organized into a 'research project,' but most of the observations and interpretations are casual and never recorded. . . ."

The Secret and the Public

All peoples have activities which they wish to protect as private or secret from some other set of people. Given the ignorance and relative subordination of the fieldworker, those under study have at their disposal many instrumentalities for guarding the secrecy of an activity. Indeed, it is one of the classic chapters in accounts of prolonged personal ethnography, for the investigator to narrate how — after months of diligence and frustration — some aspect of communal life became exposed that previously had lain concealed; this illumination signalizes the growth in his understanding and maturity as well as his being granted a more regular or adult status in the community to the point where he can be trusted (to a degree) with more significant information. Thus, Wax (1971) narrates how, after months of poor communication between herself and the Japanese-Americans, she was gradually allowed to learn of the intense but covert political conflicts. As she demonstrated that she understood and could be trusted, more information was exposed to her gaze, because the participants wanted her to know. Some wanted her to record their deeds of heroism and patriotism; others wanted her to relay discreet aspects of their activities to third parties; still others hoped that she could assist in other fashions.

In a different type of situation, Berreman (1962) found that it was extremely difficult for him to conduct his ethnographic researches. With patience, determination, and consequent luck, he learned that the villagers were trying to screen their conduct from what they presumed to be the critical vision of high-caste Hindus, who would derogate them because they violated Brahminical standards.

These and other cases indicate that secrecy (and privacy) are not absolutes, but correlatives depending upon the relationship of actor to audiences. During the course of his research, the fieldworker may shift in people's vision from being identified with one audience to another and so may be allowed to acquire more or different kinds of information.

Nuisance and Risk; Cost and Benefit

Recent nationalistic literature by some North American Indian writers has ridiculed the anthropological fieldworker with comments such as, "The typical Navajo family consists of a woman, her children and relatives in the female line, plus in-married males, and an anthropologist." Actually, such statements indicate that the worst that can be attributed to most fieldworkers is nuisance value, for in the main, Navajo are hardheaded realists, and when a family chooses to admit an anthropologist into their circle, they must thereby be deriving some compensation. This may consist of having about a willing and foolish stooge, or a naive but avid listener, or a boarder who pays proportionately more than his own way, or an agent who will cope with governmental bureaucracies.

Summary

The notion that adult human beings have to be "protected" from the observations and inquiries of fieldworkers (or kindred social scientists) is patronizing. The imagery is of ignorant, powerless, innocent "subjects" who become the victims of the sly maneuvers of crafty professors. Let us counterpose to that romantic imagery, the realities of a conventional college professor trying to secure information from a Black ghetto hustler, or of a student anthropologist interviewing a nationalist American Indian leader (who has verbally fenced with television interviewers, FBI agents, Department of Justice attorneys, and newspaper journalists) or of a fieldworker trying to locate in a small southern town. Admittedly, these counterexamples are also extreme, but the truth is that even by adolescence, most people are well able to protect themselves — their privacy and their interests — from outsiders, and that professional social scientists have little on their side but patience and determination.

In order to relate to, and learn from, real (not fictitious) persons, and to lead them to relax their normal defensive strategies for dealing with strangers, the social researcher has to be patient and flexible. He cannot proceed as does the representative of a regulatory or legal system with definite procedures, rigid contractual relationships; nor can he proceed as does the stereotyped social scientist with identical questions, unvarying methods. Instead he must be inventive, compassionate, empathic, and above all flexible.

Of course, the truth is that no social scientist can successfully operate with the rigidity that bureaucratic norms seem to require. As has many times been asserted, to know the exact questions to study and the precise procedures for studying is in fact to know most of the answers. The good scientist must have the capacity to be surprised; and the well-conceived project has to have corresponding flexibility. Yet, the imagery of the HSPS is of a contractual relationship with limited freedom for the researcher.

Issues in the Regulatory Process

In the course of a particular investigation, consent to continue the fieldwork — or to deepen or redirect it — must continually be renegotiated. Within any human relation, interaction is always changing, so that even simple continuation is never assured. In fieldwork, the interactions are even more delicate and labile. Some consent — of some kind and by some parties — is necessary for the investigatory activities, but the process cannot be formalized. For example, within a community study, the researcher will usually encounter pronounced factionalism, such that the more closely he becomes attached to one faction, the more distantly he will be regarded by the other. At any moment, some persons will be enthusiastic about his presence, while others will be reserved, critical, or even hostile. Moreover, as he continues to reside in the community, the perceptions of who he is, how it is that he is living there, and what might be gained (or lost) from associating with him are in flux. As a different example, the social object under study may have a formal structure of authority, as in the case of a business organization; the fieldworker may then have difficulties in gaining approval for his researches from all of the various persons and parties concerned; the cliques within management, the factions within the union, the groups on the assembly line, etc. Often the fieldworker will find his sympathies lie with those less powerful, but yet those in authority are the ones who have the power to exclude him physically from the social region. Not infrequently, the fieldworker begins with the consent and endorsement of the authority, but the antagonistic and fearful suspicion of the ruled; then, after a few months, he may gain an increasing welcome from the latter, only to find himself regarded with increasing hostility by the authorities, who may order him to depart, just when a majority of all concerned wish that he might remain.

In contrast to the foregoing complexities, the federal·system for the protection of human subjects is framed about a contractarian model in which the actors are conceived as free and unattached individuals who meet for a specific and temporary purpose. The model assumes that the researcher has influence, power, and knowledge such as to intimidate the subject, and a major purpose of the regulations is to compensate for the imbalance of power by requiring that the subject be provided with more information both as to the activity that is planned and as to the alternative courses of action which are then open to him. Typically, the rules require formal explanation and the gaining of consent before any investigatory work is undertaken, but in fieldwork, where the activity is emergent and developing, this requirement serves as an obstacle to initiating a human relationship.

The Impact of the Fieldworker

No claim is here advanced that fieldworkers are more moral — more sensitive ethically — than other human beings. As opportunities present themselves, fieldworkers doubtless are tempted, fall into error, and harm their associates or the persons whom they are studying. If fieldworkers did not suffer human frailties, they would be likely to be unable to comprehend the ongoing human lives of those they wish to study. Moreover, even with the best of intentions, a fieldworker may disrupt normal events, because he is a stranger and ignorant of local custom.

Yet the facts are that living is full of risks and troubles, and in any human interaction, those involved may comport themselves more or less strictly and with more or less regard for the others. What we don't know in any detail is how much benefit and how much harm accrues to a people because they were studied by a fieldworker. Nor, assuming (for argument) that there may have been net harm, do we know how to balance this against whatever gains in social knowledge may have resulted from the work.

Take, for example, the case of Bronislaw Malinowski (Wax 1972), who worked among the Trobriand Islanders during World War I. We know that the islands were under British hegemony and that the natives were used and abused by the plantation owners. We know that Malinowski compensated the natives with modest gifts of tobacco in order to live among them, inquire as to their customs, and have the benefit of domestic service. His posthumous diaries reveal contempt for both his fellow Europeans, whom he scorned as uncultured, and the natives, some of whom he termed "niggers." Yet there is no real evidence that this frail hypochondriac harmed any native, or that his presence was of significance and weight compared to the crushing impact of the imperial and commercial British presence. While, on the contrary, we do know that the volumes generated from this research served to revolutionize not merely the social sciences but general sociopolitical thought about "savage peoples." Although Malinowski himself utilized the label "savages," nevertheless, the Trobrianders emerge in his writings as being as fully human as Europeans — equally as rational and irrational, as moral and immoral.

As another example, Powdermaker conducted fieldwork during the 1930s in "Indianola," a small biracial town in Mississippi. The white authorities were suspicious of this outsider and, despite a letter of introduction from the state superintendent of education, she could not even locate a place to stay: "The leading citizens of Indianola were completely unconvinced by Mr. Green's oration or by my few words. They were suspicious of a Yankee and did not want their 'niggers' studied by anyone" (Powdermaker 1966:139). Only the personal intervention of Will Percy, who was of the local "aristocracy," saved her from expulsion and secured her a room in a boarding house. Powdermaker concealed her Jewish identity and, passing as a Methodist, attended the Negro churches and asked for the assistance of the parishioners.

In retrospect, we do not know what changes she may have helped to initiate in Indianola: what harm she may have done or benefits she may have provided, nor to whom, specifically. Her account reveals that she violated some of the taboos connected with interracial association, e.g., addressing blacks with titles of gentility (Mr., Mrs.), and that she often feared that she would get herself into trouble by this courtesy. Yet, she was also concerned to protect the blacks from being harmed by whites; although she was not concerned to assist the whites in maintaining the system of racial caste. In all, it would be fair to estimate that, compared to the risks of daily living, her presence may have brought some slight benefit to the blacks. Of most impact was the publication of her book, *After Freedom* (1939), which helped to deepen the knowledge of the larger world about black and white existence in the Deep South.

As a final classic example, Whyte (1955) conducted fieldwork during the late 1930s in an Italian slum neighborhood that he called "Cornerville." His efforts to enter the community proved fruitless, until a social worker in the local settlement house introduced him to "Doc," an intelligent and talented young man, who heard out Whyte's explanation of his interests, and then agreed to help him. After much other discussion, Doc asked, "You want to write something about this?"

"Yes, eventually."

"Do you want to change things?"

"Well — yes. I don't see how anybody could come down here where it is so crowded, people haven't got any money or any work to do and not want to have some things changed . . ."

"I think you can change things that way. Mostly that is the way things are changed, by writing about them." (1955:292–293).

Whether, or to what extent, *Street Corner Society* affected the policies that then changed Cornerville is hard to say. Certainly the book helped to transform the thinking of social scientists and other educated persons about the nature of ethnic slums.

During the course of his study, Whyte became abundantly familiar with the illicit operations that took place about Cornerville, and himself participated in some. Possibly, the most criminal of his actions was to engage in multiple illicit voting, although, as he acknowledged with hindsight, there was no real necessity for him to have done so. Otherwise, and in addition, Whyte tried to make himself useful to the "corner boys" during his research, and, even after the project was over, he tried to assist some of them, and was in fact occasionally successful.

While the cases of Malinowski, Powdermaker, and Whyte may not wholly be typical of all fieldworkers, they do represent common patterns, and, to the extent that this is so, it is evident that during the course of the investigation, the fieldworker usually has only a modest impact compared to that of the larger world on the peoples in question, and, moreover, that modest impact is usually more positive or neutral than negative. True, our selection of cases may be biased (because these three were unusually gifted persons); but, even if this is so, the burden of proof is on the accuser to show the contrary that, during the course of fieldwork, the typical fieldworker has a serious negative effect on the peoples studied.

Proposal Concerning Consent

In the light of the foregoing discussions, it is here proposed that what should be required of fieldworkers is *not* prior written and informed consent from those about to be studied. Rather, the appropriate procedure would be ex post facto. At some interval, say six months, during the course of the fieldwork, and at the close of the fieldwork period, the investigator shall submit a detailed accounting: which peoples he studied, where he lived, and how he proceeded; with whom did he discuss and explain his research, and what did he say about it; from whom and under what circumstances did he gain consent to remain and conduct his researches. During the fieldwork, what effects or impacts were consequent upon his presences? Were there persons or groups who disapproved of his presence; how is it that they felt that way; and how did he handle their objections?

In many cases, this full and frank report would have to be treated as private and confidential, since it would reveal much about the peoples studied which otherwise the fieldworker should prefer (on grounds of privacy) not to have disclosed. Nevertheless, it would be salutary to require the writing of such a report and to have it read by a critical jury of one's academic and professional peers.

The review committee should have the authority to require the investigator to appear for personal discussion and questioning, or to furnish further information. They would also have the responsibility of recommending censure of the investigator (or possibly even the denial of further external funding for research).

Final Commentary

The writing of this essay was stimulated by the application of HSPS to fieldwork research. Given the diversity of field investigations and the changes in research approaches consequent upon recent political, as well as social and military, transformations, I could in this brief essay only touch upon some of the ethical problems of fieldwork. In particular, I am conscious that I have dealt neither with the issues surrounding publication of findings, nor with those associated with projects such as "Camelot" and "counterinsurgency." Rather, my intent was to focus on the HSPS and to initiate discussion and action among those affected, rather than to deal globally with problems of anthropological ethics. Even so limited, my analysis suffers from lack of specificity because the federal regulations become operative via a system of internal institutional review: depending on how the local staff have interpreted the federal rulings, and on how the local review committees are composed, fieldworkers will experience different constraints — some beneficial, others not.

Perhaps our wisest course is to refine our analysis of the ethical problems of fieldwork, then to formulate our own system of review and regulation, and finally to challenge the HSPS and other systems which have been formulated in ignorance of our needs and problems.

Social Scientists' Ethical Responsibilities to Superordinates: Looking Upward Meekly

John F. Galliher

Social scientists have recently been exhorted to study superordinate people and groups. The anthropologist Laura Nader (1969:289–301) observes that "scientific adequacy," or complete description, requires that social scientists "study up" as well as down. She argues that social scientists already know a good deal about the poor, so that the time has come to "study up" in the stratification system. Nader continues by arguing that "democratic relevance" also requires studying up since "citizens need to know something about the major institutions, government or otherwise, that affect their lives."

Sociologists Rainwater and Pittman (1967:365–366) have challenged others in their own and related disciplines to increase the accountability of elites in business and government. They have concluded that:

> Sociologists have the right (and perhaps also the obligation) to study publicly accountable behavior. By publicly accountable behavior we do not simply mean the behavior of public officials (though there the case is clearest) but also the behavior of any individual as he goes about performing public or secondary roles for which he is socially accountable — this would include businessmen, college teachers, physicians, etc.; in short, all people as they carry out jobs for which they are in some sense publicly accountable. One of the functions of our discipline, along with those of political science, history, economics, journalism, and intellectual pursuits generally, is to further public accountability in a society whose complexity makes it easier for people to avoid their responsibilities. (1967:365–366)

Considering anthropologists, Nader resolves the question as follows:

> For the most part, anthropologists working in the United States can be said to have worked on the "private" sphere: we study families, small groups, those aspects of communities which are more private than public. We should not necessarily apply the same ethics developed for studying the private, and even ethics developed for studying in foreign cultures (where we are guests), to the study of institutions, organizations, bureaucracies that have a broad public impact. (1969:304–305)

Reprinted with the permission of the Society for the Study of Social Problems and the author from *Social Problems*, V. 27, no. 3, 1980, pp. 298–308. Copyright © 1980 by the Society for the Study of Social Problems.

Thanks are due Richard Hessler and James McCartney for help in exploring the obligations we all have to each other.

And more specifically, she concludes:

> Furthermore, it could be argued that access to bureaucratic organizations (such as governmental agencies) frequented by the wealthy and powerful should be open to social scientists by virtue of laws which protect public access to information affecting the public interest. (1969:302–303)

Considering psychological research, Ruebhausen and Brim argue:

> ... privacy is in conflict with other valued social interests, such as informed and effective government, law enforcement and free dissemination of the news. ... public figures, particularly those who appeal to the public for elective office, have impliedly consented to the yielding up of some areas of private personality. (1966:424–431)

And several years ago I (Galliher 1973) suggested that the American Sociological Association so alter its Code of Ethics as to support the right of sociologists to conduct research on the behavior of those in public positions where they are accountable to all citizens. Such calls for accountability do not necessarily assume that public officials are inherently evil but merely that their high position gives them power which can be abused. Publicly, social scientists have not objected to the general idea of such research, but simply ignored it. ...

A hint as to why this avoidance takes place is in the controversy found in the report of the American Sociological Association Committee on Professional Ethics. In drafting the Association's Code of Ethics the Committee recognized some areas of "unfinished business" which were "impossible to resolve":

> To what extent can public figures claim the same rights of privacy as ordinary citizens? To what extent does the injunction about the confidentiality of research sites prevent legitimate criticism of organizations that have cooperated in the research? ... Clearly, much more thought and analysis must be devoted to such questions, and others as well (American Sociologist 1968:316)

The Committee could not resolve these issues so it dropped them. Agreement on a general level about the role of social science research in the accountability of public officials did not lead to agreement on specifics. ...

Sociology, anthropology, psychology and political science developed new codes of ethics in the 1960s and 1970s (*American Sociologist* 1968; American Anthropological Association 1970; *American Psychologist* 1963; *P.S.* 1968), and at least in the case of sociology this was a clear consequence of the threat of federal controls (Galliher 1975). None of these codes nor the AAUP Statement on Academic Freedom make any provisions for public accountability, although the latter does state: "The teacher is entitled to full freedom in research and in the publication of the results, . . ." (Academic Freedom 1940:49). It goes on to say: "A university or college may not place any restraint upon the teacher's freedom in investigation" (1940: 52). Yet over the past decade there has been a steady increase in federal controls on university researchers' activities through efforts to *protect human subjects.* These new controls on research "limit both research and consequent criticism of local officials" (Galliher 1978:251), for there is no allowance in these federal controls for public accountability (Code of Federal Regulations 1977). The attitude implied by both the federal guidelines and professional codes of ethics is that public accountability can best be left to the mass media, but surely the First Amendment guarantee of freedom of the press does not necessarily exclude social scientists and their journals, such as the *American Anthropologist,* the *American Sociological Review* or the *American Political Science Review.*

Definitional Problems

If research subjects' rights of privacy must be protected, it must first be determined who qualifies as a research subject. Are groups as well as individuals defined as subjects? If groups have rights that must be protected, as Shils (1973) claims was true according to the Department of Health, Education and Welfare-approved guidelines at Berkeley, then research on the powerful seems impossible, for people often become powerful through their groups, as in the case of Pentagon generals and General Motors presidents. Yet Shils reports that DHEW-approved guidelines prohibited the study of any group, explicitly including churches, universities and prisons, without their informed consent, when the research risks placing "the reputation or status of a social group or an institution in jeopardy" (1973:292). Such restrictions will necessarily constrain social science research, focused as it is on the understanding of groups and organizations. There is also the knotty problem of who can speak for the group? If one relies on the traditional practice of allowing organization leaders to give or withhold research entry, then public accountability of such leaders is impossible. Moreover, if others are asked about these superordinate persons, who are the research subjects: the elites or the respondents themselves? For example, an opinion survey question might have asked respondents if they felt former President Nixon knew about the Watergate burglary before it occurred. The subject of the research in this example is clearly Richard Nixon, but the research subjects are the citizens chosen in a sample.

There are other definitional problems. If it is not always clear how we shall define research subjects, it is equally unclear who qualifies as a superordinate or an elite who should be held accountable for a public performance. Rainwater and Pittman explicitly include business executives, college professors, and physicians. But Black and Reiss (1970:65), by snooping on the behavior of police officers, seem to extend the definition.

Clearly, Henry Ford II is an elite and is superordinate to almost all Americans. It is equally clear that the chronically unemployed, lower-class ghetto dwellers are not elites and are superordinate to few other citizens, if any. Between those two extremes the definition of superordinate becomes problematic. For example, the beat patrolman is superordinate to some citizens but is only a marginally middle-class wage earner who does not set governmental policy (Galliher 1971). The question is, should police officers lose their rights of privacy when performing their public role? If we agree with Rainwater and Pittman that physicians are superordinates who should be publicly accountable, is the same true of registered nurses? And if nurses are to be held publicly accountable, how about ambulance drivers and hospital orderlies? If professors can be held publicly accountable (and I feel they should be), how about graduate teaching assistants? If business or government executives can be held publicly accountable, is this true of all people in business and government? In fact, does this mandate of Rainwater and Pittman extend to a large proportion of all citizens and include anyone who serves the public, not just obvious targets such as physicians and corporation heads, but also waitresses and cooks, cab and bus drivers, and garbage collectors? We have then a ready-made justification for holding almost anyone accountable to the social scientist. This seems somewhat absurd on the face of it, but if we choose not to hold nurses, cops, and assembly line foremen accountable, we may be closing off avenues for learning about the abuses of power of physicians, police chiefs, and industry heads, for it is often only through these lower-level superordinates that we can learn about the abuses of power of high-level policy makers.

Tempest in a Teapot: Debate About Methods

Whether it is useful and necessary to conduct research on elites, however defined, has not been the main bone of contention. Rather, attention has focused on the appropriateness of the methods for collecting the data, usually without a similar concern with the political, theoretical, and philosophical significance of such methodologies. By alleging that certain methodologies are simply not scientific, one can ostensibly disallow the researches on professional and intellectual grounds, rather than admitting to political reasons.

It has become popular for social scientists to condemn Humphreys (1970) for disguised observation of gay men in homosexual encounters and Douglas (1977) for his research on a nude beach. Unfortunately, both Humphreys and Douglas have not studied the powerful but have trivialized clandestine observation and thereby made it easy prey for opponents. In a *Psychology Today* article, Warwick (1975:105) asserts, "It is highly doubtful that any study involving deception ultimately promotes human welfare." And, he continues, "The dangers in bracketing the civil liberties of some citizens seem too obvious to deserve comment" — but he does. He continues in this and another statement (Warwick 1974) that approval of clandestine research (such as I have advocated, 1973) uses the same ends-justifying-the-means reasoning used by former President Richard Nixon and his White House friends. However, the means-ends distinction seems to obscure rather than clarify this issue because those who claim that methods involving deception are never justified have elevated the means of the research to an end. . . .

Warwick (1974:158) was quite right in observing that I ignored the body of information available on important people "mainly because there are more people watching them," as shown in the work of Arthur Schlesinger, Jr. He also correctly observes that one can use existing records of congressional hearings as did I. F. Stone. There are, however, limits to the value of these latter public documents, for their use often presumes that the truth is spoken on the House and Senate floor and in hearing rooms. Moreover, it is noteworthy that in his rebuttal Warwick relies on the examples of Schlesinger, a historian, and Stone, a journalist, and he admits: "The fact of the matter is that sociologists, with few exceptions, have not made use of often very revealing public material" (1974:159). The practices of historians and journalists are really beside the point when considering sociologists. Most sociologists do not consider the study of existing records, as practiced by Schlesinger or Stone, to be fully professional, and their judgment is based on technical rather than ethical considerations. Sociology, more than history and perhaps some other social sciences, has been drowning in a sea of arcane statistical techniques (McCartney 1970; Brown and Gilmartin 1969). These statistics usually require a search for large numbers which must be easily gathered or observed. Sociologists seldom get around to discussing the ethical consequences of research as conducted by Stone or Schlesinger because it does not meet their technical requirements.

However, I was a little melodramatic in discussing clandestine methods; and, without overemphasizing my influence, some of the heat of the debate which ensued (also see Lundman and McFarlane 1976; Christie 1976) is probably my responsibility and a product of my distrust of government after the late 1960s and early 1970s. It is not just that government should be monitored, but I implied that it is the people's enemy:

> While all people may be worthy of the same respect as human beings, it does not necessarily follow that their activities merit the same degree of protection and respect. As indicated earlier, Lofland questioned possible prohibitions on the undercover study of fascist groups. It is questionable whether the files of the American Nazi Party are deserving of the same respect as any other data source; must one secure the active cooperation of the Ku Klux Klan, or for that matter of the Pentagon, before conducting research in their organizations or with their personnel? While doing research in South Africa, van den Berghe concluded: "From the outset, I decided that I should have no

> scruples in deceiving the government. . . ." The question is, how much
> honor is proper for the sociologist in studying the membership and
> organization of what he considers an essentially dishonorable, morally
> outrageous, and destructive enterprise? Is not the failure of sociology
> to uncover corrupt, illegitimate, covert practices of government or in-
> dustry because of the supposed prohibitions of professional ethics
> tantamount to supporting such practices? (Galliher 1973:96; internal
> citations omitted)

I suggested the use of key informants and confidential records, scandals,
and court subpoenas, and clandestine participant observation — all except
the last used in the Watergate investigation. Countering what some may see
as my verbal swashbuckling is the work of Frederick Wiseman (see Friedenberg 1971), who has made muckraking films about a high school, a mental
hospital, a police department, and a military boot camp. He has found that
people in official positions will sometimes volunteer damning information
because they are so sure that theirs is the only reasonable position.

Obviously, the high-ranking do not always volunteer damning information, and it is especially unlikely when their behavior involves criminal activity. There are, moreover, "obstacles and objections" (Nader 1969:301–
302) to research on elites. "The powerful are out of reach on a number of
different planes: they don't want to be studied; it is dangerous to study the
powerful; they are busy people. . . ." Similarly, Gans (Woodward 1974:78)
comments about economic as opposed to political leaders: "Since the rich
don't let themselves be studied, and it's pretty hard to get into a fancy club
on your own, sociologists go where they have easier access." For example,
Domhoff (1975) relied heavily on key informants in his research on private ruling-class retreats. High-ranking people do not want social scientists
around, in part merely because the latter are lower-ranking. Even with
limited resources, a researcher can spend a summer in Harlem; but few, if
any, social scientists have the money or prestige to be welcome as participant observers in prestigious eastern clubs or in a General Motors board
meeting. Nader recognizes that scholars cannot use participant observation
when studying up, but recommends the use of personal documents, mem-
oirs, and interviews. The composite picture then from looking at the work
of Nader, Wiseman, and Warwick is that even eschewing more aggressive
and clandestine techniques, social scientists could do a lot more with established methods to learn about the powerful.

Actual Research on Superordinates

Because social scientists have been bogged down in disputes about methodology, they do not usually get past the talking stage and into actual research. According to Nader (1969:303), anthropologists have not had an
intense interest in social reforms in their research because of their usual
cultural relativism and commitment to being value free, and perhaps also

due to their thinking that sociologists are doing this type of research. But we typically are not. The point of ignorance of the powerful is forcefully emphasized by Green (1971) in citing the lack of any independent academic study of an organization such as Standard Oil of New Jersey, a mammoth corporation with vast national and international influence.

Oddly, until called on to prepare this essay, I had not reflected on my own field research experiences among powerful Americans during the past decade, to test my ideas about research ethics and methods. In interviewing state government officials, civil servants and business leaders in Nebraska (Galliher et al. 1974), Utah (Galliher and Basilick 1979) and most recently in Nevada, I have found few refusals and little hostility in studies of the origins of criminal laws, even when the details of such interviews are discrediting to respondents. In beginning each study, I was quite willing — and even eager — to use duplicity, but it never was necessary. There was never any information that was not freely available. In Nebraska, for example, I found a blatant case of special interests being served by a criminal law. A Nebraska prosecuting attorney active in Republican party politics freely told me that, to protect his son, a reduced penalty for marihuana possession was passed into law and made retroactive to the date of his son's arrest. My research experiences with governors, state senators, and other state officials, as well as with corporation heads lead me to believe that Wiseman is correct. Powerful people seem so convinced of their own righteousness and so sure of their power that they usually talk freely.

In my research, however, I have been careful to try to present myself as someone as much like my respondents as possible. I have gotten a haircut and shaved my beard and worn a business suit and necktie. While I was in Utah, I wore only white shirts, in keeping with the usual Mormon garb. My success as a researcher was manifest in a zero rate of refusal from Mormons and several invitations to dinner, as well as invitations to join their church. Stone (1962) observes that in our manner of dress we create a presentation of self, and by wearing suits and white shirts, I feel I was less than completely honest. My tactics in this regard go beyond the usual practice of dressing so as not to distract or annoy respondents. Another possible dilemma is that even without naming the individual involved, it is sometimes impossible to describe events and attitudes without indicating the source as, for example, in discussing a governor's timing and rationale for a veto or a Senate finance committee chairman's techniques and reasons for pushing a bill through his committee. Clearly the information itself can only come from one source. Surely governors, senators, and presidents must realize this and recognize that this lack of privacy necessarily comes from a public role.

Yet in some studies of elites or superordinates, greater stealth (than merely shaving) may be necessary in collecting information. The Watergate story would probably have been impossible to write if all information had to pass White House censors or federal guidelines for the protection of human subjects. Duster et al. report on clandestine research sponsored by the Department of Housing and Urban Development (HUD) to determine the extent of racial discrimination by realtors. Black and white couples answered newspaper advertisements and blacks experienced "documentable discrimination by rental agents three out of four times" (Duster et al. 1979: 136). Obviously informed consent is not possible in such research. Further, the study of organized crime by most social scientists is laughable because such research usually relies on government reports (Galliher and Cain 1974). In his actual field research into organized crime, Chambliss (1978) relied heavily on key informants to learn about the behavior of powerful people (this tactic was also true in the Watergate story). Yet in spite of journalists' success in the Watergate story, the field of public accountability should not be left to the press, in part because the free press in the United States is not really *free*. A handful of giant corporations own a larger and larger percentage of newspapers and television stations, and fewer and fewer American cities have competing daily newspapers. These patterns suggest a growing monopoly ownership of the American mass media. Moreover, at its best, social science offers a unique type of interpretation of events not usually found in the more individualistically oriented American journalism.

Conclusion

In conclusion, both technical problems and moral considerations are associated with the practice of fieldwork with superordinates. Technical problems involve the search for complete description, and without more adequate description social science theories will be hopelessly miscast. The moral consideration is whether public officials are deemed to have the same rights of privacy as other citizens; if the answer is affirmative, then it seems unclear what part social scientists or any other group can play in the task of holding public officials accountable, or in examining and fully understanding their social world.

The Code of Ethics of the American Sociological Association is, for example, a moral mandate that contains a claim of what sociology as a discipline is, can be, and should be. The Code also reflects an implicit theory of the workings of society, or description of social order, which is bereft of any hint of stratification, whether racial, sexual, or economic. Since the Code makes no mention of social stratification, one can assume that sociologists feel social stratification is irrelevant to the ethical concerns of social scientists. Looking only at the rights of individual research subjects implies an overly technical, individualistic, and nonsociological definition of rights, ignoring as it does the structural environment in which the research takes place. . . .

Having established that ethical issues in the protection of human subjects are seldom related to social stratification, what is the consequence of making such a linkage? Attempting to associate what social scientists know about the nature of the effects of social stratification with protection of human subjects would lead one to conclude that not all actors are equally free to make informed choices about research participation and therefore not all actors require the same protection. Presumably, those who are least free require the most protection. Does anyone really believe that corporation presidents or United States presidents need the same warnings and protection from social scientists as do undergraduates or ghetto dwellers? Must Jimmy Carter or Henry Ford II really be told that his participation in a study is voluntary? Indeed to give such equal warnings may help maintain unequal protection of human subjects.

For social scientists, moral considerations or dilemmas include not only obligations to the individual studied and to one's government, but also to all the citizens in one's society and those of other societies. If we are to deal fairly with peoples of other cultures and with American economic and racial minorities, unequal treatment of some others may be required. As reasoned in Affirmative Action Programs, powerless and deprived groups must be given special consideration to help rectify the effects of past discrimination which have put them at a great disadvantage. Specifically in social science research, if all research subjects are told the same thing about the research, some poor people may still feel coerced in ways that the more affluent are not. Anthropologists and sociologists undoubtedly look a great deal like social workers or police detectives who routinely disrupt the lives of the poor (Coser 1978). Therefore, special efforts may be necessary to give the poor the same freedom of choice the more affluent have always had. According to this reasoning, superordinates are not necessarily due the same degree and type of consideration by researchers as are other more deprived and powerless individuals.

Even more basic to such issues, if one makes ethical judgments about social stratification, one may conclude that not all actors merit the same degree of respect. In racist societies such as South Africa or the United States, do social scientists have any ethical obligation to attempt to redress these wrongs through their research? If the answer is yes, then in such societies perhaps social science cannot operate ethically by always avoiding harm to *all* subjects. Perhaps those executives of corporations owning slum dwellings should be embarrassed, harassed, and ultimately discredited by social science research. The same is true of others who profit from, and contribute directly to, racism and economic exploitation (e.g., the Duster et al. case involving realtors who refuse to rent to minorities). If we agree that social stratification and its consequences are relevant ethical concerns of social science, then to remain silent implicitly endorses this stratification.

Few social scientists would be likely to claim that stratification is irrelevant to their science. . . .

Perhaps a reason for the lack of clarity regarding the specifics of professional ethics is that we have not usually addressed the underlying issue of the general ethical goals of social science. Usually such general considerations are eschewed in favor of analyses of specific ethical problems encountered in research. Such general questions might include: What is the use of social science? Are the products of social science to be equally available to the very rich and to the very poor and to all nations equally, including South Africa? Do social scientists have a vision of a just or ethical social ordering toward which they strive in their research? Is it possible, even if we assume that all individuals have rights as research subjects, that some rights are in conflict with and prior to others? The report on the confrontation of demonstrators and police in Chicago during the National Democratic Convention of 1968 is, in fact, entitled *Rights in Conflict* and refers to the conflict between the "right to dissent and a community's right to protect its citizens and property" (Walker 1968:vi). During epidemics, for example, conflict exists between the right of the general public to safety and the rights of individuals who on religious grounds refuse immunization. In the case of social science research, it may be that many people's rights to physical survival could depend in part on a social scientist overriding another person's rights as a research subject. The social scientist might agree to do so, unless the choice of the research method is elevated to an end in itself. Such a case might involve the analysis and publication of the illegal practices of a slum landlord or a realtor who refuses to rent to minorities. Duster et al. conclude:

> . . . the blanket application of these [federal] rules obscures conflicts of interest . . . are the subjects to be protected the thousands of Americans who consume or the business people who work the system? . . . In some situations "informed consent" may in fact impede the protection of some human subjects, for example, when the question before the researchers — and the public — involves possible unethical behavior, like fraud and discrimination. . . . To mechanically apply to powerful institutions a bureaucratic rule originally meant to protect the powerless forgets the reason behind the reform. (1979:140–141)

In regard to such a case, Bennett observes that many of those who invoke the right of privacy are "the people who do have something to hide, from outright crime to malevolence. . . . Their secrets impinge on the welfare of others and the moral imperative may demand their exposure" (1967:375). Attempting to achieve the greatest good or well-being for the greatest number of people is one rule of thumb for placing priorities on rights which are in conflict. Certainly one's right to free speech is overridden by the personal safety of others and prohibits one from falsely yelling "fire" in a crowded theatre. However, such considerations fall short of a complete answer because as Vaughan and Sjoberg (1978) observe, such an orientation may not adequately draw attention to the concerns of numerical minorities. This discussion merely suggests that ethics are based on a sense of social justice and cannot be created bereft of such considerations.

Cassell (1978) repeats a question often raised in judging the ethical merits of research. These judgments are often made by weighing the risks to human subjects against the potential benefit of the research. Cassell focuses the question more precisely:

> In cases involving deception, there is a conflict between the potential harm of the invasion of privacy, and the emerging value of the public's "right to know." There is no clear solution to this conflict through abstract analysis, nor is there a clear formula for the risk-benefit calculus. (1978:137)

And Cassell asks doubtfully, "When one person or group benefits from the risks of another, can risk and benefit be weighed against each other?" (1978: 139) Only by considering the public's right to know about the activities of those in positions of public trust is the analysis of otherwise private details generally considered acceptable and even necessary in democratic states.

There may seem to be an irony about asking for greater freedom for social scientists while at the same time asking that professors be held publicly accountable. Social scientists are at present held publicly accountable by the federal government for their research with human subjects, but exercise very little professional freedom. Public accountability is only appropriate in those roles where occupants are free to exercise some professional discretion. Public accountability without the exercise of professional discretion lends itself to political coercion and harassment.

Finally, is there *ever* a justification for a social scientist deceiving *any* research subject? The easiest and of course the conventional answer to this question is to assert that deception is never tolerable because, if deception is sometimes held to be tolerable, one must then specify under what conditions this holds true. But if one contends that deception by social scientists is never tolerable, is it (a) because deception of research subjects at all times is wrong when done by anyone including journalists, or (b) because of the unique nature of social science? If one chooses (b) as the grounds for opposition to clandestine techniques, one must then specify in what ways social science is unique.

If clandestine research is never tolerable in the United States, is it justifiable in South Africa or in Nazi Germany? Most social scientists possibly would agree that in these latter two examples some deception is justified, for in these settings social research is likely to be possible only with deception. More importantly, the variation in judgments regarding the appropriateness of deception in investigations shows how research ethics imply a specific political climate. If only the extreme circumstances of South Africa and Nazi Germany are believed to justify covert research, then the myriad of American professional codes of ethics and government regulations which prohibit deception indicate that — in spite of United States' traditions of genocide of Native Americans, racism, sexism and grinding poverty — the largely middle-class, Caucasian members of professional associations and government regulatory agencies do not feel that circumstances in America are extreme enough to warrant deceptive research practices.

References

Academic Freedom and Tenure Committee. 1940. "Statement of Principles." *Bulletin of the American Association of University Professors* 26:49–54.

Adams, Richard N., and Jack J. Preiss, eds. 1960. *Human Organization Research: Field Relations and Techniques.* Homewood, Ill.: Dorsey.

Agar, Michael H. 1973. *Ripping and Running: A Formal Ethnography of Urban Heroin Addicts.* New York: Seminar Press.

Agar, Michael H. 1980. *The Professional Stranger: An Informal Introduction to Ethnography.* New York: Academic Press.

Agar, Michael H. 1982. "Whatever Happened to Cognitive Anthropology: A Partial Review." *Human Organization* 41:82–86.

American Anthropological Association. 1970. "Principles of Professional Responsibility." *Newsletter of the American Anthropological Association* 11 (November):14–16. (Adopted May 1971.)

American Psychologist. 1963. "Ethical Standards of Psychologists." 18:56–60.

American Sociologist. 1968. "Toward a Code of Ethics for Sociologists." 3:316–318.

Anderson, Nels. (1923) 1961. *The Hobo: The Sociology of the Homeless Man.* Chicago: University of Chicago Press.

Appell, George. 1978. *Ethical Dilemmas in Anthropological Inquiry: A Case Book.* Waltham, Mass.: Crossroads.

Asad, Talal, ed. 1973. *Anthropology and the Colonial Encounter.* London: Ithaca Press.

Baldamus, W. 1972. "The Role of Discoveries in Social Science." In *The Rules of the Game: Cross-Disciplinary Essays on Models in Scholarly Thought,* ed. Teodor Shanin. London: Tavistock, pp. 276–302.

Barker, Roger G., and Herbert F. Wright. 1954. *Midwest and Its Children: The Psychological Ecology of an American Town.* Evanston: Row, Peterson.

Barnes, J. A. 1967. "Some Ethical Problems in Modern Field Work." In *Anthropologists in the Field,* eds. D. C. Jongmans and P. Gutkind. Assen, The Netherlands: Van Gorcum, pp. 193–213.

Becker, Howard S. 1953. "Becoming a Marihuana User." *American Journal of Sociology* 59:235–242.

Becker, Howard S. 1958. "Problems of Inference and Proof in Participant-Observation." *American Sociological Review* 23:652–660.

Becker, Howard S. 1964. "Problems in the Publication of Field Studies." In

Reflections on Community Studies, eds. Arthur J. Vidich, Joseph Bensman, and Maurice R. Stein. New York: Wiley, pp. 267–284.

Becker, Howard S. 1967. "Whose Side Are We On?" *Social Problems* 14:239–248.

Becker, Howard S. 1970a. *Sociological Work: Method and Substance.* Chicago: Aldine.

Becker, Howard S. 1970b. "Practitioners of Vice and Crime." In *Pathways to Data,* ed. Robert W. Habenstein. Chicago: Aldine.

Becker, Howard S., Blanche Geer, Everett C. Hughes, and Anselm L. Strauss. 1961. *Boys in White: Student Culture in Medical School.* Chicago: University of Chicago Press.

Becker, Howard S., and Eliot Freidson. 1964. "Against the Code of Ethics." *American Sociological Review* 29:409–410.

Bennett, Chester C. 1967. "What Price Privacy?" *American Psychologist* 22:371–376.

Bennett, John W. 1946. "The Interpretation of Pueblo Culture: A Question of Values." *Southwestern Journal of Anthropology* 2:361–374.

Berk, Richard A., and Joseph Adams. 1970. "Establishing Rapport with Deviant Groups." *Social Problems* 18:102–117.

Berk, Sarah Fenstermaker, and Catherine White Berheide. 1977. "Going Backstage: Gaining Access to Observe Household Work." *Sociology of Work and Occupations* 4:27–48.

Berreman, Gerald D. 1962. *Behind Many Masks.* Monograph No. 4, Chicago: Society for Applied Anthropology.

Berreman, Gerald D. 1966. "Anemic and Emetic Analysis in Social Anthropology." *American Anthropologist* 68:346–354.

Berreman, Gerald D. 1968. "Ethnography: Method and Product." In *Introduction to Cultural Anthropology: Essays in the Scope and Methods of the Science of Man,* ed. J. A. Clifton. Boston: Houghton Mifflin, pp. 337–373.

Biernacki, Patrick L. 1982. *The Natural Recovery from Opiate Addiction.* Forthcoming.

Bittner, Egon. 1964. "The Concept of Organization." *Social Research* 31:239–255.

Bittner, Egon. 1973. "Objectivity and Realism in Sociology." In *Phenomenological Sociology: Issues and Applications,* ed. George Psathas. New York: Wiley, pp. 109–125.

Black, Donald J., and Albert J. Reiss, Jr. 1970. "Police Control of Juveniles." *American Sociological Review* 35:63–77.

Blalock, Hubert M., Jr. 1968. "The Measurement Problem: A Gap Between the Language of Theory and Research." In *Methodology in Social Research,* eds. Hubert M. Blalock, Jr. and Ann B. Blalock. New York: McGraw-Hill, pp. 5–27.

Bloor, Michael J. 1976. "Bishop Berkeley and the Adeno-tonsillectomy Enigma: An Exploration of Variation in the Social Construction of Medical Disposals." *Sociology* 10:43–61.

Bloor, Michael J. 1978. "On the Analysis of Observational Data: A Discussion of the Worth and Uses of Inductive Techniques and Respondent Validation." *Sociology* 12:545–552.

Bloor, Michael J. 1980. *A Report on the Relationship between Informal Patient Interaction and the Formal Treatment Programme in a Day Hospital Using Therapeutic Community Methods.* Occasional Paper No. 4, Institute of Medical Sociology, University of Aberdeen.

Bloor, Michael J. 1981. "Therapeutic Paradox — the Patient Culture and the Formal Treatment Programme in a Therapeutic Community." *British Journal of Medical Psychology* 54:359–369.

Bloor, Michael J., and J. D. Fonkert. 1982. "Reality Construction, Reality Exploration, and Treatment in Two Therapeutic Communities." *Sociology of Health and Illness* 4:125–140.

Blumer, Herbert. 1939. *An Appraisal of Thomas and Znaniecki's The Polish Peasant in Europe and America.* New York: Social Science Research Council.

Blumer, Herbert. 1947. Introduction to *Opiate Addiction*, by Alfred Lindesmith. Bloomington, Ind.: Principia Press.

Blumer, Herbert. 1969. *Symbolic Interactionism: Perspective and Method.* Englewood Cliffs, N.J.: Prentice-Hall.

Boas, Franz. 1911. *Handbook of American Indian Languages.* Washington, D.C.: Bureau of American Ethnology, Bulletin 40.

Bodemann, Y. Michael. 1978. "A Problem of Sociological Praxis: The Case for Interventive Observation in Field Work." *Theory and Society* 5:387–420.

Bogdan, Robert, and Steven J. Taylor. 1975. *Introduction to Qualitative Research Methods: A Phenomenological Approach to the Social Sciences.* New York: Wiley.

Briggs, Jean L. 1970. *Never in Anger: Portrait of an Eskimo Family.* Cambridge: Harvard University Press.

Broadhead, Robert. *Professional Identity and Private Life.* New Brunswick, N.J.: Transaction Books.

Brown, Julia S., and Brian G. Gilmartin. 1969. "Sociology Today: Lacunae, Emphases, and Surfeits." *American Sociologist* 4:283–291.

Bruner, Jerome S., J. Goodnow, and G. Austin. 1956. *A Study of Thinking.* New York: Wiley.

Bruyn, Severyn T. 1966. *The Human Perspective in Sociology: The Methodology of Participant Observation.* Englewood Cliffs, N.J.: Prentice-Hall.

Bucher, Rue, and Leonard Schatzman. 1962. "The Logic of the State Hospital." *Social Problems* 9:337–349.

Buckner, H. Taylor. 1967. "The Police: The Culture of Social Control Agency." Unpublished Ph.D. Dissertation, University of California, Berkeley.

Bulmer, Martin. 1979. "Concepts in the Analysis of Qualitative Data: A Symposium." *Sociological Review* 27:651–677.

Burke, Kenneth. 1961. *Attitudes toward History* (2nd ed.). Boston: Beacon Press.

Calkins, Kathy. 1970. "Time: Perspective, Marking and Styles of Usage." *Social Problems* 17:487–501.

Camilleri, Santo F. 1962. "Theory, Probability, and Induction in Social Research." *American Sociological Review* 27:170–178.

Carroll, J. 1973. "Confidentiality of Social Science Research Sources and Data: The Popkin Case." *Political Science* 6:11–24.

Cassell, Joan. 1978. "Risk and Benefit to Subjects of Fieldwork." *American Sociologist* 13:134–143.

Cassell, Joan. 1980. "Ethical Principles for Conducting Fieldwork." *American Anthropologist* 82:28–41.

Cassell, Joan, and Murray Wax. 1980. "Ethical Problems of Fieldwork." *Social Problems* 27:259–264.

Caudill, William, Frederick C. Redlich, Helen Gilmore, and Eugene Brody. 1952. "Social Structure and Interaction Process on a Psychiatric Ward." *American Journal of Orthopsychiatry* 22:314–334.

Cavan, Sherri. 1966. *Liquor License: An Ethnography of Bar Behavior.* Chicago: Aldine.

Chafe, W. L. 1970. *Meaning and the Structure of Language.* Chicago: University of Chicago Press.

Chambliss, William J. 1978. *On the Take: From Petty Crooks to Presidents.* Bloomington: Indiana University Press.

Charmaz, Kathy. 1973. "Time and Identity: The Shaping of Selves of the Chronically Ill." Unpublished Ph.D. Dissertation, University of California, San Francisco.

Charmaz, Kathy. 1980. "The Social Construction of Self-Pity in the Chronically Ill." In *Studies in Symbolic Interaction,* ed. Norman L. Denzin. Greenwich, CT: JAI Press, pp. 123–145.

Charmaz, Kathy. 1980. *The Social Reality of Death.* Reading, Mass.: Addison-Wesley.

Charmaz, Kathy. 1982. "Chronic Illness and Single Women: An Exploration into Support and Betrayal." Paper presented at the combined meetings of the Society for the Study of Social Problems and Sociologists for Women in Society, San Francisco.

Charmaz, Kathy. "Loss of Self: A Fundamental Form of Suffering of the Chronically Ill." *Sociology of Health and Illness.* Forthcoming.

Chevigny, Paul. 1968. *Police Power: Police Abuses in New York City.* New York: Pantheon.

Chevigny, Paul. 1972. *Cops and Rebels.* New York: Pantheon.

Chrisman, Noel J. 1976. "Secret Societies and the Ethics of Urban Fieldwork." In *Ethics and Anthropology: Dilemmas in Fieldwork,* eds. Michael A. Rynkiewich and James P. Spradley. New York: Wiley.

Christie, Robert M. 1976. "Comment on Conflict Methodology: A Protagonist Position." *Sociological Quarterly* 17:513–519.

Cicourel, Aaron V. 1964. *Method and Measurement in Sociology.* New York: Free Press.

Cicourel, Aaron V. 1968. *The Social Organization of Juvenile Justice.* New York: Wiley.

Cicourel, Aaron V. 1974a. *Cognitive Sociology: Language and Meaning in Social Interaction.* New York: Free Press.

Cicourel, Aaron V. 1974b. "Interviewing and Memory." In *Pragmatic Aspects of Human Communications,* ed. Colin Cherry. Dordrecht, The Netherlands: D. Reidel.

Cicourel, Aaron V. 1978. "Field Research: The Need for Stronger Theory and

More Control Over the Data Base." Unpublished paper, University of California, San Diego.

Cicourel, Aaron V., Kenneth H. Jennings, Sybillyn H. M. Jennings, Kenneth C. W. Leiter, Robert MacKay, Hugh Mehan, and David R. Roth. 1974. *Language Use and School Performance.* New York: Academic Press.

Clarke, Michael. 1975. "Survival in the Field: Implications of Personal Experience in Field Work." *Theory and Society* 2:95–123.

Code of Federal Regulations. 1977. "Protection of Human Subjects." 45 Public Welfare CFR Part 46, Revised October 1. Washington, D.C.: GPO.

Conklin, Harold C. 1969. "Lexicographical Treatment of Folk Taxonomies." In *Cognitive Anthropology,* ed. Stephen A. Tyler. New York: Holt, Rinehart and Winston, pp. 41–59.

Coser, Ruth L. 1978. "Comment." *American Sociologist* 13:156–157.

Coulter, Jeff. 1971. "Decontextualized Meanings: Current Approaches to Verstehende Investigations." *Sociological Review* 19:301–323.

Cressey, Donald R. 1953. *Other People's Money: A Study in the Social Psychology of Embezzlement.* Glencoe, Ill.: Free Press.

Daniels, Arlene K. 1967. "The Low-Caste Stranger in Social Research." In *Ethics, Politics, and Social Research,* ed. G. Sjoberg. Cambridge, Mass.: Schenkman, pp. 267–296.

Davis, Fred. 1959. "The Cabdriver and His Fare: Facets of a Fleeting Relationship." *American Journal of Sociology* 65:158–165.

Dean, John P. 1954. "Participant Observation and Interviewing." In *Introduction to Social Research,* ed. John T. Doby. Harrisburg, Pa.: Stackpole, pp. 225–252.

Deegan, Mary Jo, and John S. Burger. 1978. "George Herbert Mead and Social Reform." *Journal of the History of the Behavioral Sciences* 14:362–372.

Deegan, Mary Jo, and John S. Burger. 1981. "W. I. Thomas and Social Reform: His Work and Writings." *Journal of the History of the Behavioral Sciences* 17:114–125.

den Hollander, A. N. J. 1967. "Social Description: The Problem of Reliability and Validity." In *Anthropologists in the Field,* eds. D. G. Jongmans and P. C. W. Gutkind. Assen: Van Gorcum, pp. 1–34.

Denzin, Norman K. 1968. "On the Ethics of Disguised Observation," *Social Problems* 15:502–504.

Denzin, Norman K. 1970. *The Research Act: A Theoretical Introduction to Sociological Methods.* Chicago: Aldine.

Denzin, Norman K. 1971. "The Logic of Naturalistic Inquiry." *Social Forces* 50:166–182.

Department of Health, Education and Welfare. 1974. "Protection of Human Subjects." Washington, D.C.: Federal Register, May 30, 1974 (39 FR 18914).

Department of Health, Education and Welfare. 1978. "Protection of Human Subjects: Institutional Review Boards." Washington, D.C.: Federal Register, November 30, 1978 (43 FR 56174).

Diesing, Paul. 1971. *Patterns of Discovery in the Social Sciences.* Chicago: Aldine-Atherton.

Dingwall, Robert. 1980. "Ethics and Ethnography." *Sociological Review* 28:871–891.

Domhoff, G. William. 1975. *The Bohemian Grove and Other Retreats*. New York: Harper & Row.

Doughty, Charles M. 1936. *Travels in Arabia Deserta*. New York: Random House.

Douglas, Jack D. 1976. *Investigative Social Research: Individual and Team Field Research*. Beverly Hills: Sage.

Douglas, Jack D., ed. 1970. *Observations of Deviance*. New York: Random House.

Douglas, Jack D., ed. 1972. *Research on Deviance*. New York: Random House.

Douglas, Jack D., Paul K. Rasmussen, and Carol Ann Flanagan. 1977. *The Nude Beach*. Beverly Hills: Sage.

Dumont, Robert V., Jr. 1971. "Learning English and How to Be Silent: Studies in American Indian Classrooms." In *Functions of Language in the Classroom*, eds. Vera P. Johns, Courtney B. Cazden, and Dell H. Hymes. New York: Columbia University, Teachers' College Press.

Duster, Troy, David Matza, and David Wellman. 1979. "Field Work and the Protection of Human Subjects." *American Sociologist* 14:136–142.

Easterday, Lois, Diana Papademas, Laura Schorr, and Catherine Valentine. 1977. "The Making of a Female Researcher: Role Problems in Field Work." *Urban Life* 6:333–348.

Emerson, Robert M. 1981. "Observational Field Work." *Annual Review of Sociology* 7:351–378.

Emerson, Robert M., and Melvin Pollner. 1976. "Dirty Work Designations: Their Features and Consequences in a Psychiatric Setting." *Social Problems* 23:243–255.

Emerson, Robert M., and Melvin Pollner. 1982. "Results and Insults: Taking Findings Back to the Field." Unpublished paper. University of California, Los Angeles.

Ericson, Richard V. 1981. *Making Crime: A Study of Detective Work*. Toronto: Butterworth.

Erikson, Kai T. 1967. "A Comment on Disguised Observation in Sociology." *Social Problems* 12:366–373.

Evans-Pritchard, E. E. 1964. *Social Anthropology and Other Essays*. New York: Free Press.

Evans-Pritchard, E. E. 1976. "Some Reminiscences and Reflections on Fieldwork." Appendix IV in *Witchcraft, Oracles and Magic among the Azande* (Abridged). Oxford: Clarendon Press.

Fahim, Hussein, and Katherine Helmer. 1980. "Indigenous Anthropology in Non-Western Countries: A Further Elaboration." *Current Anthropology* 21:644–663.

Federal Register. 1975. "Protection of Human Subjects." Washington, D.C.: Dept. of Health, Education and Welfare, 40:11854–11858.

Ferber, M., and S. Lynd. 1971. *The Resistance*. Boston: Beacon Press.

Festinger, Leon, Henry W. Riecken, and Stanley Schachter. 1956. *When Prophecy Fails*. New York: Harper & Row.

Feyerabend, Paul K. 1975. *Against Method: Outline of an Anarchistic Theory of Knowledge.* Atlantic Highlands, N.J.: Humanities Press.

Fichter, Joseph H., and William L. Kolb. 1953. "Ethical Limitations on Sociological Reporting." *American Sociological Review* 18:544–550.

Filstead, William J., ed. 1970. *Qualitative Methodology: Firsthand Involvement with the Social World.* Chicago: Markham.

Firth, Rosemary. 1972. "From Wife to Anthropologist." In *Crossing Cultural Boundaries,* eds. S. Kimball and J. Watson. San Francisco: Chandler.

Fox, J., and Richard Lundman. 1974. "Problems and Strategies in Gaining Access in Police Organizations." *Criminology* 12:52–69.

Frake, Charles O. 1961. "The Diagnosis of Disease among the Subanun of Mindanao." *American Anthropologist* 63:113–132.

Frake, Charles O. 1962a. "The Ethnographic Study of Cognitive Systems." In *Anthropology and Human Behavior,* eds. T. Gladwin and W. C. Sturtevant. Washington: Anthropological Society of Washington, pp. 72–85.

Frake, Charles O. 1962b. "Cultural Ecology and Ethnography." *American Anthropologist* 64:53–59.

Frake, Charles O. 1964a. "A Structural Description of Subanun 'Religious Behavior.'" In *Explorations in Cultural Anthropology,* ed. Ward H. Goodenough. New York: McGraw-Hill, pp. 111–129.

Frake, Charles O. 1964b. "Notes on Queries in Ethnography." *American Anthropologist* 66:132–145.

Frake, Charles O. 1964c. "How to Ask for a Drink in Subanun." *American Anthropologist* 66:127–132.

Frake, Charles O. 1969. "Struck by Speech: The Yakan Concept of Litigation." In *Law in Culture and Society,* ed. Laura Nader. Chicago: Aldine, pp. 147–167.

Frake, Charles O. 1975. "How to Enter a Yakan House." In *Sociocultural Dimensions of Language Use,* eds. Mary Sanches and Ben G. Blount. New York: Academic Press, pp. 25–40.

Frake, Charles O. 1977. "Plying Frames Can Be Dangerous: Some Reflections on Methodology in Cognitive Anthropology." *The Quarterly Newsletter of the Institute for Comparative Human Development,* 1:1–7.

Friedenberg, Edgar Z. 1971. "The Films of Frederick Wiseman." *The New York Review of Books* 17 (October 21):19–22.

Gallaher, Art, Jr. 1964. "Plainville: The Twice-Studied Town." In *Reflections on Community Studies,* eds. A. J. Vidich, J. Bensman, and M. R. Stein. New York: Wiley.

Galliher, John F. 1971. "Explanations of Police Behavior: A Critical Review and Analysis." *Sociological Quarterly* 12:308–318.

Galliher, John F. 1973. "The Protection of Human Subjects: A Reexamination of the Professional Code of Ethics." *American Sociologist* 8:93–100.

Galliher, John F. 1974. "Professor Galliher Replies." *American Sociologist* 9:159–160.

Galliher, John F. 1975. "The ASA Code of Ethics on the Protection of Human Beings: Are Students Human Too?" *American Sociologist* 10:113–117.

Galliher, John F. 1978. "The Life and Death of Liberal Criminology." *Contemporary Crises* 2:245–263.

Galliher, John F., and James A. Cain. 1974. "Citation Support for the Mafia Myth in Criminology Textbooks." *American Sociologist* 9:68–74.

Galliher, John F., James L. McCartney, and Barbara Baum. 1974. "Nebraska's Marijuana Law: A Case of Unexpected Legislative Innovation." *Law and Society Review* 8:441–455.

Galliher, John F., and Linda Basilick. 1979. "Utah's Liberal Drug Laws: Structural Foundations and Triggering Events." *Social Problems* 26:284–297.

Gans, Herbert J. 1962. *The Urban Villagers.* New York: Free Press.

Gans, Herbert J. 1968. "The Participant-Observer as a Human Being: Observations on the Personal Aspects of Field Work." In *Institutions and the Person,* eds. Howard S. Becker, Blanche Greer, David Riesman, and Robert S. Weiss. Chicago: Aldine, pp. 300–317.

Garfinkel, Harold. 1960. "The Rational Properties of Scientific and Common Sense Activities." *Behavioral Science* 5:72–83.

Garfinkel, Harold. 1967. *Studies in Ethnomethodology.* Englewood Cliffs, N.J.: Prentice-Hall.

Garfinkel, Harold, and Harvey Sacks. 1970. "The Formal Structure of Practical Actions." In *Theoretical Sociology: Perspectives and Developments,* eds. John C. McKinney and Edward A. Tiryakian. New York: Appleton-Century-Crofts.

Geertz, Clifford. 1976. "From the Native's Point of View: On the Nature of Anthropological Understanding." In *Meaning in Anthropology,* eds. K. H. Basso and H. A. Selby. Albuquerque: University of New Mexico Press, pp. 221–237.

Georges, Robert A., and Michael O. Jones. 1980. *People Studying People: The Human Element in Fieldwork.* Berkeley: University of California Press.

Glaser, Barney G. 1978. *Theoretical Sensitivity.* Mill Valley, Calif.: Sociology Press.

Glaser, Barney G., and Anselm L. Strauss. 1965. *Awareness of Dying.* Chicago: Aldine.

Glaser, Barney G., and Anselm L. Strauss. 1967. *The Discovery of Grounded Theory: Strategies for Qualitative Research.* Chicago: Aldine.

Glaser, Barney G., and Anselm L. Strauss. 1968. *Time for Dying.* Chicago: Aldine.

Glaser, Barney G., and Anselm L. Strauss. 1971. *Status Passage.* Chicago: Aldine.

Glazer, Myron. 1972. *The Research Adventure: Promise and Problems of Field Work.* New York: Random House.

Goffman, Erving. 1959. *The Presentation of Self in Everyday Life.* Garden City, N.Y.: Doubleday.

Goffman, Erving. 1961a. *Asylums: Essays on the Social Situation of Mental Patients and Other Inmates.* Garden City, N.Y.: Doubleday.

Goffman, Erving. 1961b. *Encounters.* Indianapolis: Bobbs-Merrill.

Goffman, Erving. 1963a. *Stigma: Notes on the Management of Spoiled Identity.* Englewood Cliffs, N.J.: Prentice-Hall.

Goffman, Erving. 1963b. *Behavior in Public Places: Notes on the Social Organization of Gatherings.* New York: Free Press.

Goffman, Erving. 1967. *Interaction Ritual: Essays on Face-to-Face Behavior.* Chicago: Aldine.

Göhre, Paul. 1895. *Three Months in a Workshop: A Practical Study.* Trans. A. B. Carr. London: Swan Sonnenschein.

Gold, Raymond L. 1958. "Roles in Sociological Field Observations." *Social Forces* 36:217–223.

Golde, Peggy, ed. 1970. *Women in the Field.* Chicago: Aldine.

Goldkind, Victor. 1966. "Class Conflict and Cacique in Chan Kom." *Southwestern Journal of Anthropology* 22:325–345.

Goldkind, Victor. 1970. "Anthropologists, Informants and the Achievement of Power in Chan Kom." *Sociologus* 20:17–41.

Goodenough, Ward H. 1957. "Cultural Anthropology and Linguistics." *Georgetown University Monograph Series on Language and Linguistics* 9:167–173.

Goodenough, Ward H. 1967. "Componential Analysis." *Science* 156:1203–1209.

Goodenough, Ward H. 1971. "Culture, Language, and Society." Reading, Mass.: Addison-Wesley Modular Publications.

Gould, Leroy, Andrew L. Walker, Lansing E. Crane, and Charles W. Lidz. 1974. *Connections: Notes from the Heroin World.* New Haven: Yale University Press.

Gray, Bradford H. 1975. *Human Subjects in Medical Experimentation.* New York: Wiley.

Green, Philip. 1971. "The Obligations of American Social Scientists." *The Annals of the American Academy of Political and Social Science* 394:13–27.

Gurwitsch, Aron. 1966. *Studies in Phenomenology and Psychology.* Evanston, Ill.: Northwestern University Press.

Gusfield, Joseph R. 1955. "Field Work Reciprocities in Studying a Social Movement." *Human Organization* 14:29–33.

Gussow, Zachary. 1964. "The Observer-Observed Relationship as Information about Structure in Small-Group Research: A Comparative Study of Urban Elementary School Classrooms." *Psychiatry* 27:230–247.

Haak, Ronald O. 1970. "Co-opting the Oppressors: The Case of the Japanese-Americans." *Transaction* 7(12):23–31.

Habenstein, Robert W., ed. 1970. *Pathways to Data: Field Methods for Studying Ongoing Social Organizations.* Chicago: Aldine.

Hall, Edward T. 1959. *The Silent Language.* New York: Doubleday.

Hammond, Phillip E., ed. 1967. *Sociologists at Work: The Craft of Social Research.* New York: Doubleday.

Hannerz, Ulf. 1980. *Exploring the City: Inquiries toward an Urban Anthropology.* New York: Columbia University Press.

Hanson, Norwood R. 1958. *Patterns of Discovery: An Inquiry into the Conceptual Foundations of Science.* Cambridge: Cambridge University Press.

Harrell-Bond, Barbara. 1976. "Studying Elites: Some Special Problems." In *Ethics and Anthropology: Dilemmas in Fieldwork,* eds. Michael A. Rynkiewich and James P. Spradley. New York: Wiley.

Harris, Richard. 1973. *The Police Academy: An Inside View.* New York: Wiley.

Hearnshaw, Leslie S. 1979. *Cyril Burt, Psychologist.* Ithaca: Cornell University Press.

Hollingshead, August B., and Frederick C. Redlich. 1958. *Social Class and Mental Illness: A Community Study.* New York: Wiley.

Homan, Roger. 1978. "Interpersonal Communication at Pentecostal Meetings." *The Sociological Review* 26:499–518.

Honigmann, John J. 1976. "The Personal Approach in Cultural Anthropological Research." *Current Anthropology* 17:243–251.

Horowitz, Irving L. 1965. "The Life and Death of Project Camelot." *Transaction* 3(7):44–47.

Horowitz, Irving L. 1967. *The Rise and Fall of Project Camelot.* Cambridge, Mass.: M.I.T. Press.

Horowitz, Irving L., and Lee Rainwater. 1970. "Journalistic Moralizers." *Transaction* 7(7):5–8.

Huber, Joan. 1973. "Symbolic Interaction as a Pragmatic Perspective: The Bias of Emergent Theory." *American Sociological Review* 38:274–284.

Hughes, Everett C. 1971. *The Sociological Eye: Selected Papers.* Chicago: Aldine.

Humphreys, Laud. 1970. *Tearoom Trade: Impersonal Sex in Public Places* (2nd ed., 1975). Chicago: Aldine.

Hyman, Herbert H., William J. Cobb, Jacob J. Feldman, Clyde W. Hart, and Charles Herbert Stember. 1954. *Interviewing in Social Research.* Chicago: University of Chicago Press.

Hymes, Dell H. 1962. "The Ethnology of Speaking." In *Anthropology and Human Behavior,* ed. Thomas Gladwin and William C. Sturtevant. Washington, D.C.: Anthropological Society of Washington.

Hymes, Dell H. 1964. "Introduction: Toward Ethnographies of Communication." *American Anthropologist* 66:1–34.

Hymes, Dell H. 1969. "The Use of Anthropology: Critical, Political, Personal." In *Reinventing Anthropology,* ed. Dell Hymes. New York: Pantheon, pp. 3–79.

James, William. 1970. *The Meaning of Truth: A Sequel to Pragmatism.* Ann Arbor: University of Michigan Press.

Janowitz, Morris. 1966. "Introduction" to *W. I. Thomas: On Social Organization and Social Personality.* Chicago: University of Chicago Press.

Johnson, John M. 1975. *Doing Field Research.* New York: Free Press.

Jongmans, D. G., and P. C. W. Gutkind, eds. 1967. *Anthropologists in the Field.* Assen, The Netherlands: Van Gorcum.

Jules-Rosette, Bennetta. 1975. *Vision and Realities: Aspects of Ritual and Conversion in an African Church.* Ithaca: Cornell University Press.

Kanter, Rosabeth Moss. 1977. "Some Effects of Proportions on Group Life: Skewed Sex Ratios and Responses to Token Women." *American Journal of Sociology* 82:965–990.

Karp, Ivan, and Martha B. Kendall. 1982. "Reflexivity in Field Work." In *Explaining Human Behavior: Consciousness, Human Action and Social Structure,* ed. Paul F. Secord. Beverly Hills: Sage.

Kay, Paul. 1966. "Comment on B. N. Colby, 'Ethnographic Semantics: A Preliminary Survey.'" *Current Anthropology* 7:20–23.

Kay, Paul. 1970. "Some Theoretical Implications of Ethnographic Semantics."

In *Current Directions in Anthropology*. Bulletins of the American Anthropological Association 3 (no. 3), part 2.

Keating, Peter, ed. 1976. *Into Unknown England, 1866–1913: Selections from the Social Explorers*. Manchester: Manchester University Press.

Killian, Lewis M., and Sanford Bloomberg. 1975. "Rebirth in a Therapeutic Community: A Case Study." *Psychiatry* 38:39–54.

Klockars, Carl B. 1974. *The Professional Fence*. New York: Free Press.

Klockars, Carl B. 1977. "Field Ethics for the Life History." In *Street Ethnography*, ed. Robert S. Weppner. Beverly Hills: Sage, pp. 201–226.

Klockars, Carl B., and Finbarr W. O'Connor, eds. 1979. *Deviance and Decency: The Ethics of Research with Human Subjects*. Beverly Hills: Sage.

Kluckhohn, Florence. 1940. "The Participant Observer Technique in Small Communities." *American Journal of Sociology* 46:331–343.

Lazarsfeld, Paul F. 1944. "The Controversy over Detailed Interviews — An Offer for Negotiation." *Public Opinion Quarterly* 8:38–60.

Leach, Edmund R. 1976. *Culture and Communication*. Cambridge: Cambridge University Press.

Lee, Dorothy. 1949. "Being and Value in a Primitive Culture." *Journal of Philosophy* 46:401–415. Reprinted in *Freedom and Culture*. Englewood Cliffs, N.J.: Prentice-Hall, 1959.

Lemert, Edwin M. 1962. "Paranoia and the Dynamics of Exclusion." *Sociometry* 25:2–25.

Levy, Charles J. 1968. *Voluntary Servitude: Whites in the Negro Movement*. New York: Appleton-Century-Crofts.

Lewis, Oscar. 1953. "Controls and Experiments in Field Work." In *Anthropology Today*, ed. A. L. Kroeber. Chicago: University of Chicago Press, pp. 452–475.

Liazos, Alexander. 1972. "The Poverty of the Sociology of Deviance: Nuts, Sluts, and Perverts." *Social Problems* 20:103–120.

Liebow, Elliot. 1967. *Tally's Corner: A Study of Negro Streetcorner Men*. Boston: Little, Brown.

Lindesmith, Alfred R. 1947. *Opiate Addiction*. Bloomington, Ind.: Principia Press.

Lindesmith, Alfred R. 1968. *Addiction and Opiates*. Chicago: Aldine.

Lindstrom, Walter. 1967. "The Problem of Objectivity in Kierkegaard." In *A Kierkegaard Critique*, eds. H. A. Johnson and N. Thulstrup. Chicago: Henry Regnery, pp. 228–243.

Lofland, John. 1966. *Doomsday Cult: A Study of Conversion, Proselytization, and Maintenance of Faith*. Englewood Cliffs, N.J.: Prentice-Hall.

Lofland, John. 1971. *Analyzing Social Settings: A Guide to Qualitative Observation and Analysis*. Belmont, Calif.: Wadsworth. Second edition, with Lyn H. Lofland, in press.

Lofland, John. 1976. *Doing Social Life: The Qualitative Study of Human Interaction in Natural Settings*. New York: Wiley.

Lofland, John F., and Robert A. Lejeune. 1960. "Initial Interaction of Newcomers in Alcoholics Anonymous: A Field Experiment in Class Symbols and Socialization." *Social Problems* 8:102–111.

Lohman, Joseph D. 1937. "Participant-Observation in Community Studies." *American Sociological Review* 6:890–898.

Lowie, Robert H. 1937. *The History of Ethnological Theory*. New York: Farrar and Rinehart.

Lundman, Richard J. 1974. "Routine Police Arrest Practices: A Commonweal Perspective." *Social Problems* 22:127–141.

Lundman, Richard J., and Paul T. McFarlane. 1976. "Conflict Methodology: An Introduction and Preliminary Assessment." *Sociological Quarterly* 17:503–512.

Malinowski, Bronislaw. 1922 (reprinted 1984). *Argonauts of the Western Pacific*. Prospect Heights, IL: Waveland Press, Inc.

Malinowski, Bronislaw. 1935. *Coral Gardens and Their Magic*. 2 vol. (Reprinted with "Introduction" by Edmund R. Leach). Bloomington: Indiana University Press, 1965.

Malinowski, Bronislaw. 1967. *A Diary in the Strict Sense of the Term*. New York: Harcourt, Brace and World.

Manning, Peter K. 1972. "Observing the Police: Deviants, Respectables and the Law." In *Research on Deviance*, ed. Jack Douglas. New York: Random House.

Manning, Peter K. 1976a. "Rules, Colleagues and Situationally Justified Actions." In *Colleagues in Organization*, ed. R. A. Blankenship. New York: Wiley.

Manning, Peter K. 1976b. "The Researcher: An Alien in the Police World." In *The Ambivalent Force* (2nd ed.), eds. A. Neiderhoffer and A. Blumberg. Chicago: Dryden Press.

Manning, Peter K. 1977. *Police Work*. Cambridge, Mass.: M.I.T. Press.

Manning, Peter K. 1978. "Analytic Induction." Unpublished paper, Michigan State University.

Manning, Peter K. 1979. "Metaphors of the Field: Varieties of Organizational Discourse." *Administrative Science Quarterly* 24:660–671.

Manning, Peter K., and Horatio Fabrega, Jr. 1976. "Fieldwork and the 'New Ethnography.'" *Man II*:39–52.

Maquet, Jacques. 1964. "Objectivity in Anthropology." *Current Anthropology* 5:47–55.

Marcus, George, and Richard Cushman. 1982. "Ethnographies as Texts." *Annual Review of Anthropology* 11:25–69.

Marriott, McKim. 1955. "Western Medicine in a Village of Northern India." In *Health, Culture, and Community*, ed. Benjamin D. Paul. New York: Russell Sage Foundation.

Martindale, Don. 1973. "The Mentality of the Crusader." In *Psychiatry and the Law*, eds. Don and Edith Martindale. St. Paul, Minn.: Windflower.

Marx, Gary T. 1974. "Thoughts on a Neglected Category of Social Movement Participation: The Agent Provocateur and the Informant." *American Journal of Sociology* 80:402–442.

Matza, David. 1969. *Becoming Deviant*. Englewood Cliffs, N.J.: Prentice-Hall.

Maybury-Lewis, David. 1965. *The Savage and the Innocent*. London: Evans.

McCall, George J. 1969. "Data Quality Control in Participant Observation." In

Issues in Participant Observation, eds. George J. McCall and J. L. Simmons. Reading, Mass.: Addison-Wesley, pp. 128–141.

McCall, George J. 1978. *Observing the Law: Field Methods in the Study of Crime and the Criminal Justice System.* New York: Free Press.

McCall, George J., and J. L. Simmons, eds. 1969. *Issues in Participant Observation: A Text and Reader.* Reading, Mass.: Addison-Wesley.

McCartney, James L. 1970. "On Being Scientific: Changing Styles of Presentation of Sociological Research." *American Sociologist* 5:30–35.

McCurdy, David W. 1976. "The Medicine Man." In *Ethics and Anthropology: Dilemmas in Fieldwork,* eds. Michael A. Rynkiewich and James P. Spradley. New York: Wiley.

McKeganey, N. P., and Michael J. Bloor. 1981. "On the Retrieval of Sociological Description: Respondent Validation and the Critical Case of Ethnomethodology." *International Journal of Sociology and Social Policy* 1:332–354.

McKinney, John C. 1966. *Constructive Typology and Social Theory.* New York: Appleton-Century-Crofts.

Mead, Margaret. 1949. *The Mountain Arapesh. V. The Record of Unabelin with Rorschach Analysis.* New York: Anthropological Papers of the American Museum of Natural History 41 (Part 3).

Mehan, Hugh, and Houston Wood. 1975. *The Reality of Ethnomethodology.* New York: Wiley.

Metzger, Duane, and G. E. Williams. 1963. "A Formal Ethnographic Analysis of Tenejappa Ladino Weddings." *American Anthropologist* 65:1076–1101.

Miller, G., E. Galanter, and K. Pribram. 1960. *Plans and the Structure of Human Behavior.* New York: Holt.

Miller, S. M. 1952. "The Participant Observer and 'Over-Rapport'." *American Sociological Review* 17:97–99.

Mishler, Elliot G. 1979. "Meaning in Context: Is There Any Other Kind?" *Harvard Educational Review* 49:1–19.

Moerman, Michael. 1969. "A Little Knowledge." In *Cognitive Anthropology,* ed. Stephen A. Tyler. New York: Holt, Rinehart and Winston, pp. 449–469.

Moore, Joan. 1978. *Homeboys: Gangs, Drugs, and Prison in the Barrios of Los Angeles.* Philadelphia: Temple University Press.

Moskos, Charles C. 1967. *The Sociology of Political Independence: A Study of Nationalist Attitudes among the West Indian Leaders.* Cambridge, Mass.: Schenkman.

Myers, Vincent. 1977. "Toward a Synthesis of Ethnographic and Survey Methods." *Human Organization* 36:244–251.

Myrdal, Gunnar. 1944. *An American Dilemma* (vol. 2). New York: Harper & Row.

Nader, Laura. 1969. "Up the Anthropologist — Perspectives Gained from Studying Up." In *Reinventing Anthropology,* ed. Dell Hymes. New York: Vintage, pp. 284–311.

Naroll, Raoul. 1967. "Native Concepts and Cross-Cultural Surveys." *American Anthropologist* 69:511–512.

Nash, Dennison, and R. Wintrob. 1972. "The Emergence of Self-Consciousness in Ethnography." *Current Anthropology* 13:527–542.

Nejelski, Paul, and Lindsey Miller Lerman. 1971. "A Researcher-Subject Testimonial Privilege: What to Do Before the Subpoena Arrives." *Wisconsin Law Review*: 1085–1148.

Newcomb, T. M. 1953. "An Approach to the Study of Communicative Acts." *Psychological Review* 60:393–404.

P.S., Newsletter of the American Political Science Association. 1968. "Ethical Problems of Academic Political Scientists." 1:3–28.

Park, Robert E. (1915) 1952. "The City: Suggestions for the Investigation of Human Behavior in the Urban Environment." In *Human Communities: The City and Human Ecology*. Glencoe, Illinois: Free Press.

Pask, G. 1970. "Cognitive Systems." In *Cognition: A Multiple View*, ed. Paul Garvin. New York: Spartan.

Paul, Benjamin D. 1953. "Interview Techniques and Field Relationships." In *Anthropology Today*, ed. A. L. Kroeber. Chicago: University of Chicago Press, pp. 430–451.

Pike, Kenneth L. (1954) 1967. *Language in Relation to a Unified Theory of the Structure of Human Behavior*, Part I. Second edition. The Hague: Mouton.

Platt, Jennifer. 1981. "On Interviewing One's Peers." *British Journal of Sociology* 32:75–91.

Platt, Jennifer. 1982. "The Origin Myth of 'Participant Observation'." Paper presented to the American Sociological Association meetings, San Francisco.

Pollner, Melvin. 1975. " 'The Very Coinage of Your Brain': The Anatomy of Reality Disjunctures." *Philosophy of the Social Sciences* 5:411–430.

Polsky, Ned. 1967. *Hustlers, Beats, and Others*. Chicago: Aldine.

Powdermaker, Hortense. 1939. *After Freedom: A Cultural Study in the Deep South*. New York: Viking Press.

Powdermaker, Hortense. 1966. *Stranger and Friend: The Way of an Anthropologist*. New York: Norton.

Rainwater, Lee, and David J. Pittman. 1967. "Ethical Problems in Studying a Politically Sensitive and Deviant Community." *Social Problems* 14:357–366.

Redfield, Robert. 1953. *The Primitive World and Its Transformations*. Chicago: University of Chicago Press.

Reinharz, Shulamit. 1979. *On Becoming a Social Scientist: From Survey Research and Participant Observation to Experiential Analysis*. San Francisco: Jossey-Bass.

Reiss, Albert J., Jr. 1968. "Police Brutality — Answers to Key Questions." *Transaction* 5:10–19.

Reiss, Albert J., Jr. 1971. *The Police and the Public*. New Haven: Yale University Press.

Reiss, Albert J., Jr. 1976. *Selected Issues in Informed Consent and Confidentiality with Special Reference to Behavioral/Social Science Research/Inquiry*. New Haven: Yale University.

Reynolds, Paul D. 1972. "On the Protection of Human Subjects and Social Science." *International Social Science Journal* 24:693–719.

Richardson, James T., Mary W. Stewart, and Robert B. Simmonds. 1978. "Researching a Fundamentalist Commune." In *Understanding the New Religions*, ed. Jacob Needleman and George Baker. New York: Seabury Press.

Riesman, David. 1976. "Some Questions about Discontinuities in American Society." In *The Uses of Controversy in Sociology,* ed. Lewis A. Coser. New York: Free Press, pp. 3–29.

Riesman, David, and Jeanne Watson. 1964. "The Sociability Project: A Chronicle of Frustration and Achievement." In *Sociologists at Work,* ed. Phillip E. Hammond. New York: Basic Books, pp. 235–321.

Robbins, Thomas, Dick Anthony, and Thomas E. Curtis. 1973. "The Limits of Symbolic Realism: Problems of Empathetic Field Observation in a Sectarian Context." *Journal for the Scientific Study of Religion* 12:259–271.

Rochford, E. Burke. 1982. *A Study of Recruitment and Transformation Processes in the Hare Krishna Movement.* Ph.D. dissertation, Department of Sociology, University of California, Los Angeles.

Rock, Paul. 1979. *The Making of Symbolic Interactionism.* Totawa, N.J.: Roman and Littlefield.

Rohner, Ronald P. 1966. "Franz Boas: Ethnographer on the Northwest Coast." In *Pioneers of American Anthropology,* ed. June Helm. Seattle: University of Washington Press.

Rosenthal, Robert. 1976. *Experimenter Effects in Behavioral Research.* New York: Irvington.

Rosett, Arthur I., and Donald R. Cressey. 1976. *Justice by Consent: Plea Bargains in the American Courthouse.* Philadelphia: Lippincott.

Roth, Julius A. 1962. "Comments on 'Secret Observation.'" *Social Problems* 9:282–284.

Roth, Julius A. 1966. "Hired Hand Research." *American Sociologist* 1:190–196.

Rubin, Lillian. 1979. *Women of a Certain Age.* New York: Harper & Row.

Rubinstein, Jonathan. 1973. *City Police.* New York: Farrar, Straus & Giroux.

Ruebhausen, Oscar M., and Orville G. Brim, Jr. 1965. "Privacy and Behavioral Research." *Columbia Law Review* 65:1184–1211.

Ruebhausen, Oscar M., and Orville G. Brim, Jr. 1966. "Privacy and Behavioral Research." *American Psychologist* 21:423–437.

Rynkiewich, Michael A., and James P. Spradley, eds. 1976. *Ethics and Anthropology: Dilemmas in Fieldwork.* New York: Wiley.

Sagarin, Edward. 1973. "The Research Setting and the Right Not to Be Researched." *Social Problems* 21:52–77.

Sanday, Peggy Reeves. 1979. "The Ethnographic Paradigm(s)." *Administrative Science Quarterly* 24:527–538.

Sanders, William B., ed. 1974. *The Sociologist as Detective: An Introduction to Research Methods.* New York: Praeger.

Schatzman, Leonard, and Anselm L. Strauss. 1973. *Field Research: Strategies for a Natural Sociology.* Englewood Cliffs, N.J.: Prentice-Hall.

Schechner, R. 1969. *Public Domain: Essays on the Theater.* New York: Bobbs-Merrill.

Schnaiberg, Allan, and Michael Armer. 1972. "Measurement Evaluation Obstacles in Sociological Surveys: A Grounded Reassessment." Paper presented at the American Sociological Association meetings, August 1972, New Orleans.

Schutz, Alfred. 1962. *Collected Papers, Vol. I: The Problem of Social Reality,* ed. M. Natanson. The Hague: Martinus Nijhoff.

Schutz, Alfred. 1964. *Collected Papers, Vol. II: Studies in Social Theory,* ed. M. Natanson. The Hague: Martinus Nijhoff.

Schutz, Alfred. 1967. *The Phenomenology of the Social World.* Evanston, Ill.: Northwestern University Press.

Schwartz, Gary, and Don Merten. 1971. "Participant Observation and the Discovery of Meaning." *Philosophy of the Social Sciences* 1:279–298.

Schwartz, Howard, and Jerry Jacobs. 1979. *Qualitative Sociology: A Method to the Madness.* New York: Free Press.

Schwartz, Morris S., and Charlotte Green Schwartz. 1955. "Problems in Participant Observation." *American Journal of Sociology* 60:343–354.

Scott, Marvin B. 1968. *The Racing Game.* Chicago: Aldine.

Scott, W. Richard. 1965. "Field Methods in the Study of Organizations." In *Handbook of Organizations,* ed. James G. March. Chicago: Rand McNally, pp. 261–304.

Seeley, John R. 1964. "Crestwood Heights: Intellectual and Libidinal Dimensions of Research." In *Reflections on Community Studies,* eds. Arthur J. Vidich, Joseph Bensman, and Maurice R. Stein. New York: Wiley.

Shaffir, William B., Robert A. Stebbins, and Allan Turowetz, eds. 1980. *Fieldwork Experience: Qualitative Approaches to Social Research.* New York: St. Martin's Press.

Shaw, Clifford R. 1931. *The Natural History of a Delinquent Career.* Chicago: University of Chicago Press.

Shils, Edward. 1973. "Muting the Social Sciences at Berkeley." *Minerva* 11: 290–295.

Sieber, Sam D. 1973. "The Integration of Fieldwork and Survey Methods." *American Journal of Sociology* 78:1335–1359.

Sjoberg, Gideon, ed. 1967. *Ethics, Politics, and Social Research.* Cambridge, Mass.: Schenkman.

Sjoberg, Gideon. 1967. "Project Camelot: Selected Reactions and Personal Reflections." In *Ethics, Politics and Social Research,* ed. G. Sjoberg. Cambridge, Mass.: Schenkman.

Skolnick, Jerome H. 1966. *Justice without Trial: Law Enforcement in Democratic Society.* New York: Wiley.

Snow, David A. 1980. "The Disengagement Process: A Neglected Problem in Participant Observation Research." *Qualitative Sociology* 3:100–122.

Spradley, James P. 1979. *The Ethnographic Interview.* New York: Holt, Rinehart and Winston.

Stone, Gregory P. 1962. "Appearance and the Self." In *Human Behavior and Social Processes: An Interactionist Approach,* ed. Arnold M. Rose. Boston: Houghton Mifflin.

Stouffer, Samuel A. 1962. *Social Research to Test Ideas.* New York: Free Press.

Strachan, Don. 1979. "In Search of Don Juan." *New West* (January 29):90–91.

Strauss, Anselm L. 1978. *Negotiations.* San Francisco: Jossey-Bass.

Stringfellow, William. 1966. *My People is the Enemy.* Garden City, N.Y.: Anchor Books.

Strickland, Donald A., and Lester E. Schlesinger. 1969. " 'Lurking' as a Research Method." *Human Organization* 28:248–250.

Sturtevant, William C. 1964. "Studies in Ethnoscience." *American Anthropologist* 66:99–131.

Sullivan, Mortimer, Stuart Queen, and Ralph Patrick, Jr. 1958. "Participant Observation as Employed in the Study of a Military Training Program." *American Sociological Review* 23:660–667.

Sykes, Gresham. 1958. *The Society of Captives*. Princeton, N.J.: Princeton University Press.

Thorne, Barrie. 1971. *Resisting the Draft: An Ethnography of the Draft Resistance Movement*. Unpublished Ph.D. Dissertation, Brandeis University.

Thorne, Barrie. 1975a. "Women in the Draft Resistance Movement: A Case Study of Sex Roles and Social Movements." *Sex Roles* 1:179–195.

Thorne, Barrie. 1975b. "Protest and the Problem of Credibility: Uses of Knowledge and Risk-taking in the Draft Resistance Movement of the 1960s." *Social Problems* 23:111–123.

Thorne, Barrie. 1979. "Political Activist as Participant Observer: Conflicts of Commitment in a Study of the Draft Resistance Movement of the 1960s." *Symbolic Interaction* 2:73–88.

Thorne, Barrie. 1980. " 'You Still Takin' Notes?' Fieldwork and Problems of Informed Consent." *Social Problems* 27:284–297.

Turnbull, Colin M. 1962. *The Forest People*. New York: Simon and Schuster.

Turner, Ralph H. 1953. "The Quest for Universals in Sociological Research." *American Sociological Review* 18:604–611.

Useem, Michael. 1973. *Conscription, Protest, and Social Conflict: The Life and Death of a Draft Resistance Movement*. New York: Wiley-Interscience.

van de Vate, Dwight. 1971. "The Problem of Robot Consciousness." *Philosophy and Phenomenological Research* 32.

Van Maanen, John. 1973. "Observations on the Making of Policemen." *Human Organization* 32:407–418.

Van Maanen, John. 1974. "Working the Streets: A Developmental View of Police Behavior." In *Reality and Reform: The Criminal Justice System,* ed. Herbert Jacobs. Beverly Hills: Sage.

Van Maanen, John. 1975. "Police Socialization." *Administrative Science Quarterly* 20:207–228.

Van Maanen, John. 1977. *Organizational Careers: Some New Perspectives*. New York: Wiley.

Van Maanen, John. 1978a. "The Asshole." In *Policing: A View From the Streets,* eds. Peter K. Manning and John Van Maanen. Pacific Palisades, Calif.: Goodyear.

Van Maanen, John. 1978b. "Watching the Watchers." In *Policing,* eds. Peter K. Manning and John Van Maanen. Pacific Palisades, Calif.: Goodyear.

Van Maanen, John. 1981. "Notes on the Production of Ethnographic Data in an American Police Agency." In *Law and Social Enquiry,* ed. Robin Luckham. Uppsala: Scandinavian Institute of African Studies.

Van Maanen, John, and Edgar Schein. 1977. "Career Development." In *Improving Life at Work,* eds. J. R. Hackman and J. L. Suttle. Pacific Palisades, Calif.: Goodyear.

Vaughan, Ted R., and Gideon Sjoberg. 1978. "Comment." *American Sociologist* 13:171–172.

Vidich, Arthur J. 1955. "Participant Observation and the Collection and Interpretation of Data." *American Sociological Review* 60:354–360.

Vidich, Arthur J., and Joseph Bensman. 1964. "The Springdale Case: Academic Bureaucrats and Sensitive Townspeople." In *Reflections on Community Studies,* eds. A. J. Vidich, J. Bensman, and M. R. Stein. New York: Wiley.

Vidich, Arthur J., Joseph Bensman, and Maurice R. Stein, eds. 1964. *Reflections on Community Studies.* New York: Wiley.

Von Hoffman, Nicholas. 1970. "Sociological Snoopers." *Transaction* 7(7):4–6.

Walker, Andrew L., and Charles W. Lidz. 1977. "Methodological Notes on the Employment of Indigenous Observers." In *Street Ethnography,* ed. Robert S. Weppner. Beverly Hills: Sage, pp. 103–123.

Walker, Daniel. 1968. *Rights in Conflict* (The Walker Report to the National Commission on the Causes and Prevention of Violence). New York: Bantam Books.

Wallace, Anthony F. C. 1962. "Culture and Cognition." *Science* 135:351–357.

Warren, Carol A. B. 1980. "Data Presentation and the Audience: Responses, Ethics, and Effects." *Urban Life* 9:282–308.

Warren, Carol A. B., and Paul K. Rasmussen. 1977. "Sex and Gender in Field Research." *Urban Life* 6:349–370.

Warwick, Donald P. 1973. "Tearoom Trade: Means and Ends in Social Research." *The Hastings Center Studies* 1:27–38.

Warwick, Donald P. 1974. "Who Deserves Protection?" *American Sociologist* 9:158–159.

Warwick, Donald P. 1975. "Social Scientists Ought to Stop Lying." *Psychology Today* 8 (February):38, 40, 105–106.

Wax, Murray L. 1967. "On Misunderstanding *Verstehen*: A Reply to Abel." *Sociology and Social Research.* 51:323–333.

Wax, Murray L. 1972. "Tenting with Malinowski." *American Sociological Review* 37:1–13.

Wax, Murray L. 1980. "Paradoxes of 'Consent' to the Practice of Fieldwork." *Social Problems* 27:272–283.

Wax, Murray L., Rosalie H. Wax, and Robert V. Dumont, Jr. 1964. *Formal Education in an American Indian Community.* Supplement to *Social Problems* 11:4.

Wax, Murray L., and Joan Cassell, eds. 1979. *Federal Regulations: Ethical Issues and Social Research.* Boulder: Westview.

Wax, Rosalie H. 1952. "Field Methods and Techniques: Reciprocity as a Field Technique." *Human Organization* 11:34–37.

Wax, Rosalie H. 1960. "Twelve Years Later: An Analysis of Field Experience." In *Human Organization Research,* eds. Richard N. Adams and Jack J. Preiss. Homewood, Ill.: Dorsey.

Wax, Rosalie H. 1971. *Doing Fieldwork: Warnings and Advice.* Chicago: University of Chicago Press.

Wax, Rosalie H. 1979. "Gender and Age in Fieldwork and Fieldwork Education: No Good Thing is Done by Any Man Alone." *Social Problems* 26:509–522.

Webb, Beatrice P. 1926. *My Apprenticeship.* New York: Longmans, Green.

Webb, Sydney, and Beatrice Webb. 1932. *Methods of Social Study*. New York: Longmans, Green, and Co.

Weber, Max. 1949. *The Methodology of the Social Sciences*. Glencoe, Ill.: The Free Press.

Westley, William A. 1970. *Violence and the Police: A Sociological Study of Law, Custom, and Morality*. Cambridge, Mass.: MIT Press.

Whyte, William F. 1955. *Street Corner Society*. Chicago: University of Chicago Press.

Whyte, William F. 1979. "On Making the Most of Participant Observation." *American Sociologist* 14:56–66.

Wieder, D. Lawrence. 1969. "The Convict Code: A Study of a Moral Order as a Persuasive Activity." Ph.D. Dissertation, University of California, Los Angeles.

Wieder, D. Lawrence. 1974. *Language and Social Reality: The Case of Telling the Convict Code*. The Hague: Mouton.

Wiener, Carolyn. 1981. *The Politics of Alcoholism: Building an Arena Around a Social Problem*. New Brunswick, N.J.: Transaction Books.

Wilson, Thomas P. 1970. "Conceptions of Interaction and Forms of Sociological Explanation." *American Sociological Review* 35:697–710.

Wiseman, Jacqueline P. 1970. *Stations of the Lost: The Treatment of Skid Row Alcoholics*. Englewood Cliffs, N.J.: Prentice-Hall.

Wolff, Kurt H. 1964. "Surrender and Community Study: The Study of Loma." In *Reflections on Community Studies*, eds. Arthur J. Vidich, Joseph Bensman, and Maurice R. Stein. New York: Wiley.

Wolff, Kurt H. 1974. *Trying Sociology*. New York: Wiley.

Wolff, Kurt H. 1976. *Surrender and Catch: Experience and Inquiry Today*. Dordrecht, Holland/Boston: Reidel.

Woodward, Kenneth L. 1974. "Secrets of the Very Rich." *Newsweek*, October 7:78.

Worsley, Peter. 1968. *The Trumpet Shall Sound: A Study of "Cargo" Cults in Melanesia* (2nd ed.). New York: Schocken.

Wright, Rolland H. 1966. "The Stranger and the Urban World." Manuscript. Detroit: Social Sciences Division, Monteith College, Wayne State University.

Yablonsky, Lewis. 1965. "Experiences with the Criminal Community." In *Applied Sociology*, eds. Alvin Gouldner and S. M. Miller. New York: Free Press.

Yablonsky, Lewis. 1968. "On Crime, Violence, LSD, and Legal Immunity for Social Scientists." *American Sociologist* 3:148–149.

Yancey, William L., and Lee Rainwater. 1970. "Problems in the Ethnography of the Urban Underclass." In *Pathways to Data: Field Methods for Studying Ongoing Social Organizations*, ed. Robert Habenstein. Chicago: Aldine, pp. 245–269.

Zelditch, Morris, Jr. 1962. "Some Methodological Problems of Field Studies." *American Journal of Sociology* 67:566–576.

Znaniecki, Florian. 1968. *The Method of Sociology*. New York: Octagon Books.

Zola, Irving K. 1982. *Missing Pieces: A Chronicle of Living with a Disability*. Philadelphia: Temple University Press.

Index

Active participation, 146n, 182, 183–
184, 194, 216–234, 249–250,
257–259, 269–270
Actors' perspectives (meanings), 1–2,
11, 14–15, 19, 22–24, 46–48,
96n, 105–107, 112, 113, 114–
115, 149–155, 183–184
seen as "freely chosen," 106, 153–
155
Analytic induction, 97–99, 130–137,
140n, 172
and grounded theory, 98–99, 129
negative cases, 97, 98, 130–132,
134–135, 141
Anderson, Nels, 11, 12
Antagonistic field research, 179–180,
257, 308–311

Boas, Franz, 2–3

Chicago school, 7–9, 11–13, 110
case study method, 8–9, 11–12
social survey method, 6–8
Cognitive anthropology (ethnoscience),
28–31, 43–45, 65–67, 68–77
Confidentiality, 230, 260, 262, 274–
276, 278n, 293–294
and illegal activities, 212–214, 280–
281
and public accountability, 300–303,
308–310
lack of legal guarantees for, 276–
277n
Convict code, 33, 78–90, 139, 165n
and interactional formulation of
meaning, 89–90

maxims of, 78
as used by residents, 79–83
as used by staff, 83–87

Description, 19–35. *See also* Ethnography; Thick Description
and behavioral events, 69–74
as consequential in the setting described, 32–34, 60, 87–90, 169–
170, 267–268
and members' categories, 22–25,
28–30, 39–45, 61, 74–77
"simple" ("literal"), 20–22
Disjunctures between the situations
and consciousness of member and
fieldworker, 105–107, 150, 151–
155, 157, 160–161, 162–163,
167–168, 171, 197, 220–227, 233
Distance (detachment), 12–13, 51n,
179, 215, 216, 222–227, 233,
235–237, 242–252
Documentary method of interpretation, 35

Emic/etic concepts, 24, 65, 70
Entree, problems of, 10–13, 78–83,
138–139, 176, 257, 259–260,
265–266
Ethical issues, 212–214, 255–265,
277–287, 288–299, 303–305,
307–311
deceit, 217, 256, 259–260, 292–293,
304–305
false identities (covert fieldwork),
177, 179–181, 183, 217, 256–259,
303–305, 310–311

333